LACAN:
TOPOLOGICALLY
SPEAKING

LACAN: TOPOLOGICALLY SPEAKING

EDITED BY

ELLIE RAGLAND

and

DRAGAN MILOVANOVIC

Other Press
New York

This book was set in 11 pt. Berkeley by Alpha Graphics of Pittsfield, NH.

10 9 8 7 6 5 4 3 2 1

Library of Congress Cataloging-in-Publication Data

Lacan : topologically speaking / [edited by] Ellie Ragland and Dragan Milovanovic.
    p. cm.
Includes bibliographical references and index.
ISBN 1-892746-76-X
    1. Lacan, Jacques, 1901– Contributions in topology.   2. Psychoanalysis.
    3. Topology. I. Ragland-Sullivan, Ellie, 1941– II. Milovanovic, Dragan, 1948 –
RC506 .L23 2003
616.89'17—dc21

2002029301

Contributors

Bruce A. Arrigo is Professor and Chair of the Department of Criminal Justice at the University of North Carolina-Charlotte, with Adjunct Professor appointments in the Public Policy Program and the Psychology Department, respectively. Formerly the Director of the Institute of Psychology, Law, and Public Policy at the California School of Professional Psychology-Fresno, Dr. Arrigo began his professional career as a community organizer and social activist for the homeless, the mentally ill, the working poor, the frail elderly, the decarcerated, and the chemically addicted. Dr. Arrigo received his Ph.D. from Pennsylvania State University, and he holds a master's degree in psychology and sociology. He is the author of more than 100 monographs, journal articles, academic book chapters, and scholarly essays exploring theoretical and applied topics in critical criminology, criminal justice and mental health, and socio-legal studies. He is the author, coauthor, or editor of eight books, including *Madness, Language, and the Law* (1993), *The Contours of Psychiatric Justice* (1996), *Social Justice/Criminal Justice* (1998), *The Dictionary of Critical Social Sciences* (with T. R. Young,

1999), *Introduction to Forensic Psychology* (2000), *Law, Psychology, and Justice* (with Christopher R. Williams, 2001), *The Power Serial Rapist* (with Dawn J. Graney, 2001), and *Punishing the Mentally Ill: A Clinical Analysis of Law and Psychiatry* (2002). Dr. Arrigo is the past Editor of *Humanity and Society* and founding and Acting Editor of the peer-reviewed quarterly, *Journal of Forensic Psychology Practice.* He was recently named the Critical Criminologist of the year (2000), sponsored by the Critical Criminology Division of the American Society of Criminology.

Philip Dravers is currently completing his doctoral thesis "Fiction and the Real in the Theory of Jacques Lacan" for the University of Oxford and teaches in the MA program in psychoanalysis at Middlesex University. He has translated many psychoanalytic articles from the French, including Lacan's paper "British Psychiatry and the War" and is also a member of the editorial committee of the journal in which it appeared, *Psychoanalytical Notebooks of the London Circle.* He has previously published articles on Lacan, Joyce, and Bentham in both English and French and is currently researching the implications of the final period of Lacan's teaching for issues of our contemporary scene, its subjectivity, and its clinic.

Jean-Paul Gilson is the author of *La Topologie de Lacan: Une articulation de la cure psychanalytique* (1994). He is currently Professor of Psychology at McGill University in Québec. Previously he attended Lacan's seminars and is an analyst in private practice. He is also the founder of the Ecole du Quotidien, a school for psychotic children in Brussels, Belgium.

Jeanne Lafont, after an educational formation in Latin and Greek (B.A./licence and M.A./maîtrise), turned toward psychology (B.A. and M.A.). After receiving her diplomas in both fields, she obtained a doctorate (DEA) in the Freudian Field at the University, Saint-Denis, ex-Vincennes in 1981. She was an associate member of the School of the Freudian Cause from 1981–1992, and today belongs to Dimensions of Psychoanalysis, to the Association for a training in psychoanalysis, to EFEPS, to a Freudian ethics in social practice, GERP "A," and to a group of study and psychoanalytic research on autism, AIPEC. Her published books include *Topologie ordinaire de Jacques Lacan*, in the editions of ERES, in the collection Point Hors Ligne (1985), *Lacanian topologie et clinique analytique* (1990), and *Les pratiques sociales, en dette de la psychanalyse* (1994), as well as *Les dessins des enfants qui commencent à parler, reflexion sur l'autisme et l' écriture*, at EFEdition, Paris. She has also published numerous articles in French psychoanalytic journals, such as *Littoral, Grapp, Transition, Analytica,* and *Revue de psychanalyse.*

David Metzger is an Associate Professor of Rhetoric and Coordinator of Jewish Studies at Old Dominion University, Norfolk, Virginia. A former student of Ellie Ragland's, he is the author of *The Lost Cause of Rhetoric: The Relation of Rhetoric and Geometry in Aristotle and Lacan* (1995), guest editor of *Lacan and the Question of Writing* (a special issue of the journal *Pre/Text* [1994]), and co-editor of *Proving Lacan* (forthcoming). His other publications include forty articles and book chapters, two coedited volumes (*Medievalism and Medieval Studies* and *Medievalism as an Integrated Study* [*Year's Work in Medievalism X*] [1999]), and an edited collection, *Medievalism and Cultural Studies* (2000).

Jacques-Alain Miller is Professor and Director of the Department of Psychoanalysis at the University of Paris VIII, Saint Denis, and the editor of Lacan's Seminars. He has given a Course every year since 1981 to an international audience. He is the Director of the European School of Psychoanalysis and the World Association of Psychoanalysis, as well as an analyst in private practice. He has written numerous publications in various languages.

Dragan Milovanovic is Professor in the Department of Criminal Justice, Northeastern Illinois University, Chicago, Illinois. He received his Ph.D. from the School of Criminal Justice, State University of New York at Albany. He has written numerous articles on postmodern criminology and law. He is the author or coauthor of

15 books. He is Editor-in-Chief of the *International Journal for the Semiotics of Law*. The focus of his research has been in psychoanalytic semiotics, chaos theory, catastrophe theory, edgework, and constitutive criminology/law. His forthcoming books are *Criminal Criminology at the Edge*, *Sociology of Law* (3rd edition) and a coauthored publication, *The French Connection*.

Juan-David Nasio, psychiatrist and psychoanalyst, is Director of Studies at the University of Paris VII (Sorbonne) and Director of the Séminaires Psychanalytiques de Paris, a major center for psychoanalytic training and the dissemination of psychoanalytic thought to nonspecialists. He is a former member of the École Freudienne of Jacques Lacan and worked closely with the renowned child analyst Françoise Dolto. He is the Editor of the Psychoanalysis Series at Éditions Payot. The author of eight books on psychoanalysis, Dr. Nasio has published numerous articles and interviews in leading publications and has participated extensively in French radio and television broadcasts. He lives in Paris, where he practices psychoanalysis with adults and children.

Ellie Ragland is Professor and former department Chair of English at the University of Missouri, Columbia. She received her Ph.D. in French and Comparative Literature from the University of Michigan and has taught at the University of Paris VIII, Saint Denis (1994–1995). Now Frederick A. Middlebush Chair, she is the author of *Rabelais and Panurge: A Psychological Approach to Literary Character* (1976), *Jacques Lacan and the Philosophy of Psychoanalysis* (1986), *Essays on the Pleasures of Death: From Freud to Lacan* (1995), and *The Logic of Sexuation: From Aristotle to Lacan* (2004). She coedited *Lacan and the Subject of Language* with Mark Bracher (1991) and edited *Critical Essays on Jacques Lacan* (1999). She is the Editor of the *Newsletter of the Freudian Field*, now *(Re)-Turn: A Journal of Lacanian Studies*, and author of over 100 essays on Lacan, psychoanalysis, literature, and gender theory. Her forthcoming books are *Proving Lacan: Psychoanalysis and the Force of Evidentiary Knowledge*, coedited with David Metzger, and *The Logic of Structure in Lacan*.

Pierre Skriabine is a psychoanalyst who is a member of the School of the Freudian Cause in Paris and presently is a part of its working Council. An engineer and architect by professional training, he underwent a psychoanalysis with Jacques Lacan. After the death of Dr. Lacan, he underwent a psychoanalysis with Eric Laurent. He has practiced psychoanalysis in Paris since 1986. Author of over 100 articles and lectures, bearing not only on logic and topology in Lacan's teaching but also on the clinic—for example, the clinic of depression or on psychoanalysis in Japan (he is the Secretary of the Franco-Japanese Group in the Freudian Field)—Pierre Skriabine is also coauthor of several collective works. He has been particularly interested in the topology that is at the foundation of the refinement that Lacan produced of his teaching in the last years of his Seminar.

Luke Thurston is a Research Fellow in Languages and Literature at Robinson College, Cambridge. He is the author of *Impossible Joyce: Psychoanalysis and Modernism* (forthcoming) and the editor of *Re-inventing the Symptom: Essays on the Final Lacan* (2002). He has translated works by Jean Laplanche, André Green, and Roberto Harari and is currently working on a study of Fernando Pessoa.

Jean-Michel Vappereau was invited by Lacan in 1988 to give a lecture on the Borromean knot. Since that time, he has constructed a modification of the canonical classical Logic, manifesting a new type of negation. His construction is a topology of the subject that permits him to situate Freud's Letter 52 to Fliess in relation to Lacan's schemas L and R. He has also started a movement that defines a new topological invariant, linking the work of Pierre Soury to that of Lacan. He teaches a course in topology, linking Paris to Buenos Aires. He has also edited a series of teaching works, *Tee* (1985), *Essaim* (1988), *Etoffes* (1997), and *Lu* (1998).

Véronique Voruz lectures in law and criminology at the University of Leicester (UK). She has been studying Lacanian psychoanalysis since 1996 and her doctoral thesis, "Psychoanalysis and the Law beyond the Oedipus," strives to map the continuity that binds the subject to the political from the perspective of contemporary psychoanalytic theory. Her previous publications include an engagement with the Seminar Lacan dedicated to the work of James Joyce ("Acephalic Litter as a Phallic Letter," in *Re-inventing the Symptom*, ed. L. Thurston, 2002) and an analysis of the relationship between linguistics and legal responsibility, which draws from the *Memoirs* of President Schreber, the source of Freud's paradigmatic case study of psychosis ("Psychosis and the Law: Legal Responsibility and Law of Symbolisation," in *International Journal for the Semiotics of Law*, 2000).

Zak Watson finished his M.A. degree in Comparative Literature at the University of Georgia, writing a thesis on Herman Broch's *The Death of Virgil*. He is currently in the Ph.D. program in the English department at the University of Missouri, Columbia. Also forthcoming is his essay, "The Foundation of the Subject in Relation to Knowledge" in *Proving Lacan*.

Contents

III
Topology of Knots

Introduction: *Topologically Speaking*

ELLIE RAGLAND AND DRAGAN MILOVANOVIC

In the last 10 years, a flurry of books and articles has appeared, applying the teaching and theories of Jacques Lacan, a psycho-analyst (1901–1981), to literature, clinical studies, cultural studies, gender studies, discourse theory, and the social sciences (law, criminology, and social justice). No book-length manuscript, however, has yet been published in English devoted to applying Lacan's topological approach. This aspect of his work runs throughout his entire official teaching (1951–1981). Whereas during the 1950s and 1960s he developed the topology of surfaces (torus, Möbius strip, Klein bottle, cross-cap), from 1972 on he was to develop the topology of knots (Borromean, *le sinthome*). Indeed, his use of certain topological[1] forms, and the logic that explains how they function, are inseparable from his theoretical development of two meaning systems: the one of representations and the other, of a *jouissance* system of libidinal meaning that materializes language by placing desire, fantasy, and the (partial) drives in it.

There have been occasional articles, and some references in books regarding this topological approach, but no systematic explanation of Lacan's move from typology to topology. *Lacan: Topologically Speaking* is the first systematic book in English devoted to this central part of Lacan's teaching. Work on Lacan's topology is well advanced in France, as well as in many other countries. This is manifested by the presses that publish the books on Lacanian topological theory and praxis and the many journals that work on Lacanian topology from different angles, from pure theory to the most concrete work in the logic and clinic of autism.

Lacanian topology has much to do with the use of spatial figures and their manipulation, as well as their distortions, to indicate the complexities caused by the functioning of (seemingly contradictory) paradoxes in human mental life. The relationship of the subject to discourse is one such example. Beyond his discourse theory, Lacan's topology demonstrates that there is another meaning system that is not grammatical, but that operates logically and cohesively within the grammatical confines of regular language. Lacan called this the system of *jouissance* (libido) that cements fundamental fantasies in memory in *fixions* (fictions/fixations). That is, *jouissance* battens down meaning that is radically repressed because it was first created in response to excessive excitations and traumas that attach themselves in unary traits of identification (verbal, imagistic, and affective) to words and images. The "order" of meaning that inscribes excitation and/or trauma is what Lacan called the real. Thus, within secondary-process conscious language, one finds the "symptom" (respelled as *sinthome* in medieval French to capture its particularity). Lacan named this fourth order of the knot (Σ) the "symptom" (*sinthome*) and showed how its typical social function is the ideological one of sublimating an esteemed "Father's Name" signifier through identification with some leader (be it of a country or a street gang).

The "symptom" is important topologically because it holds the subject together, knotting the Imaginary, Symbolic, and Real orders that constitute the basic associational unit of meaning and memory. The base unit of structure to which Lacan refers here is the Borromean triadic associative unit of the Imaginary (identi-ficatory), the Symbolic (language and social conventions), and the Real (effects whose cause is repressed excitation or trauma). In-deed, Lacan called this topological unit structure itself, not meta-phor. And this structure functions topologically insofar as it is knotted by a fourth order—the order of the knot that belongs to each of the other three and also holds them together (except in psychosis where a pseudo-imaginary knot disappears, creating a break between the Real and the Symbolic). This break we also find in schema I.

The Real of the symptom "speaks" the topological language of contradictory and paradoxical meanings that compose impasses or knots in the meaning of any person's life. As the fourth order—part of, yet extrinsic to, the Imaginary, the Symbolic, and the Real, the symptom can always be "read" in the way time is deployed in a given person's discourse. In other words, both time and space are component properties of language. They function in different ways depending on a subject's symptomatology (normative, neu-rotic, perverse, or psychotic—all logical structurations of desire and *jouissance*). Time is the lack that *is* desire. It brings lack into lan-guage as the Symbolic *aporia* of lack, the Real space of the void (which produces anxiety), and the Imaginary space of the gap be-tween the image and the word, made manifest in jokes, dreams, poetry, and so forth. Desire, in turn, is libidinized by the real of the partial drives that materialize language in oral, anal, invocatory, and scopic fields. By using topological forms that show how para-dox and contradiction are truth functional, Lacan formalized a means for studying time and space in language. They dwell as lack, loss, the void, the cut, the "nothing"—all positivized aspects of the negative that dwells within language around the object *a* that ini-tially causes desire (when it is lost, thus inciting a subject—infant or adult—to seek a trace of the object in a return of a lost experi-ential constellation); the phallic signifier, which is in and of itself a neutral and abstract effect that marks the sexual difference; and the lack-in-being by which Lacan denoted the subject of the un-conscious ($) as a concrete gap or hole in the conscious signifying chain of language. This is a radically different notion of space than the one that supposes a homogeneous space to which the (whole) subject is external.

The cut of the subject is perhaps most clearly presented in schema R, topologically modeled by the cross-cap. The "cut" on the cross-cap, following a figure eight circling the central hole, produces a Möbius strip representing the subject, and a disk representing the *objet a*. It is only with this cut that the subject appears. It is a moment of the appearance of what looks very much like a coherent, centered subject in control. It becomes the moment of possible insertion in various discursive subject positions within particular discourses as an I which can speak, both representing the subject in discourse, and alienating it as it fades from the scene, represented by this very signifier—in line with Lacan's point that a signifier represents the subject for another signifier. This represents suturing of the Symbolic with the Imaginary on the backdrop of the Real ($\$ \diamond a$). Illusory it may very well be, but an illusion necessary for a representative appearance in ongoing discursive constructions and interlocutions. We are always less than what we appear and more than what we would want to present.

Lacanian topology provides a logic beyond the positivisms of symbolic logic in the analysis of the subject. Yet, it is only recently that this approach, laying out a logic of the Real of structure, is being applied to a number of disciplines. In other words, Lacan's engagement with modern logic (figures such as Frege, Russell, Boole) took him beyond the impasses of the concept to a logic of the cut, which is itself, a Real function in meaning. Anyone who refers to Lacan's "new writing" as a "concept writing" has not measured his declaration in *Seminar XIII: The Object of Psychoanalysis* (1965–1966) that topology is not a metaphor. Rather, topology shows structure, the Real of structure, insofar as it cannot be said, but only shown. Lacanian topology is, in one sense, a tacit showing of structure— the structure of the place one occupies in the Other, where a person's desire is situated vis-à-vis the Other. The three "dimensions" of space—the Real, the Symbolic, and the Imaginary—define three spaces. The graphs inscribe places and correspond to

Symbolic space; the schemas figure *Imaginary* space in the planes of the image, the surface (of the body) prevailing here. As for *Real* space, its representation supposes that one promote, along with the graphs and the schemas, the notion of a picture which presents *sites* which one could define as pure Real places. A graph, then, is meant to be read while a schema is meant to be seen. A picture—has a graph side and a schema side, but—is that which always supposes a knotting of the three orders inasmuch as one accepts that a writing is susceptible of showing, for example, the blankness between the lines. The picture shows what can neither be said nor seen. It *monstrates*.

Topology does not represent the subject, then. It presents the structure of the subject, the site where the subject emerges as an effect, presenting as well the foundations of the subject's position—combining itself as that which is neither simply said in the Symbolic nor only seen in the Imaginary, but shows desire and *jouissance* in the Real.

The subject is not only a combinatory of varying significations, then, for it also has an objectal side—the absolute *jouissance(s)* created as unary traits in the moments of the cut (of separation) which introduce time into meaning as the structure of desire. Across the impasses of alienation into language and separation from the primordial object as a wholeness, the subject desires the return of the lost object: $\$ \diamond a$ (the formula for fantasy). Here we see that the inverse face of lack is want and, thus, desire has the paradoxical structure of lacking/wanting. Desire (the subject as $\$$) has the structuration of a Möbius strip, both wanting and lacking appearing at the surface of language, with the alienated lost parts hidden in the folds of the twist. Lacanian desire does not conjure up an inside/outside container metaphor of a subject characterized by phenomenological qualities or quantities that can fill up or fill in an Imaginary emptiness. The emptiness, Lacan taught, is Real and has the structure of a void place ($\emptyset$) that is created from the start of life as an infant makes meaning in moments of time by retrieving identificatory master signifiers (unary traits) of images, words, and affect "dropped" from the "objects" (the breast, the voice, the urinary flow, the [imaginary] phallus, the phoneme, the gaze, the feces, the nothing) that are lost in the comings and goings of everyday life. These objects are not the organs that seem to produce them, but the effects of the loss of oneness an infant experiences when joined to these objects via another person, usually the mother. It is not the organ itself, then, that gives a seeming substantivity to an (Imaginary) body, but the belief in the oneness experienced in union with these objects. When they are lost in the regular rhythms of everyday life, the loss is traumatic for an infant. Such losses begin to build up the "dimension" of the Real out of inscriptions of traits of objects-cause-of-desire and the holes created by the traits that perforate space to create a paradoxical hole and its binding traits which, in turn, return as the (Real) particular conditions of *jouissance* that define a subject as more than a subject of language.

The cut also introduces loss into the three "dimensions" of space around the central object-cause-of-desire insofar as the four partial drives (oral, anal, invocatory, and scopic) aim to get replacement objects in order to secure the satisfaction or *jouissance* of Oneness that occurs in the moments the void is filled by the objects of the world as they substitute for the eight primary ones Lacan called a non-specular, Real Ur-lining of the subject.

Our edited book includes chapters on topology theory developed by Lacan primarily during the 1960s, although he was already employing them during the 1950s. It will also cover the Borromean knots developed by Lacan from 1972–1978, and will especially highlight the meaning of his fourth order—the knot of the *sinthome*—to which he devoted his *Seminar* of 1975–1976, taking as a point of reference the language of James Joyce's *Finnegans Wake*. Lacan used topology to explain the way in which the subject—the being that speaks from unconscious primary-process unconscious material and conscious secondary-process conscious material—is constituted. Lacan's topology goes far beyond his discourse theory and, as such, portrays the functioning of the subject, the "speaking being," or "speaking" (*l'être parlant, or parlêtre*) in relation to discourse. The various authors—all scholars of Lacan, some of them formally trained as topologists before adding Lacan to their work—

will explain the topological constructions (rubber geometry) of surfaces (the torus, the Möbius strip, the Klein bottle, the cross-cap
and the schema R/schema I) as well as the theory of knots. In his
theory of the knot (or the *sinthome/symptom*), Lacan depicted the
subject in terms of the interlinking of three circles, each representing one of the three Orders or "dimensions" of space mentioned
above (the Imaginary, the Real, and the Symbolic). It is here where
we can locate *objet a*, sense, phallic *jouissance*, and the *jouissance*
of the body. We can also identify a possible fault in the knot, a break
in the interlocking rings that renders the psychic apparatus without constancy. *Le sinthome*, Lacan was to argue, is what repairs this
fault, re-establishing constancy for the psychic apparatus.

No extensive book in the English-speaking community has
appeared on this subject either. This book—*Lacan: Topologically
Speaking*—will familiarize the reader with how to map the subject
of desire within each of the three exigencies or orders, as well as in
terms of the fourth order of the knot. Once their logic has been
explained and demonstrated, the structures and formations of drive,
fantasy, desire, and so on, are readily visible within literary texts.
One sees, finally, that the scope of thought itself is reducible to the
body and that thought only thinks within the limit of the body's
space. The effect of topology, then, is to show, to "monstrate," the
Real of structure itself, structure with grammar peeled off it. Equally
as important is that these structurations of desire and drive—hidden as they are by the pretenses and idealizations of secondary-
process language—make sense of political problems that worry
cultural-studies theorists.

Not only is Lacan's topological theory viable in and of itself,
it is practical and applicable within many domains of study. *Lacan:
Topologically Speaking* will focus on the explication and application of Lacanian theory to three areas: clinical (i.e., psychosis), literature (i.e., James Joyce, Herman Broch, Edgar Allan Poe), and
the social sciences (law, criminology, social justice). It will thus
not only explain the mode of thinking that underlay Lacan's entire
psychoanalytic enterprise, from the beginning to the end, but will
show how his revisions of Freud have created a new field which is

both theoretically practical and applicable as an heuristic tool in several disciplines.

We have asked some of the most important theorists in the Western world on Lacan and topology to contribute to this book and most of them have agreed to write chapters for it. This is a remarkable achievement in and of itself.

TOPOLOGY AND LACAN

Topology theory is often called qualitative mathematics. Sometimes it is even called a "rubber math," a "rubber geometry." Much of the lineage of contemporary work can be traced to Stephen Smale and Henry Poincaré.[2] It deals with how different shapes can be stretched, pulled, twisted, bent, deformed, and distorted in space without, at the same time, changing their intrinsic nature. It is a study of continuous properties. Cutting operations produce particular results. Various topological operations are somewhat analogous to traditional, Euclidean mathematics in the operations of squaring, adding, subtracting, equivalence, and so forth. We sometimes find that in three-dimensional space, intersections (i.e., singularities) may develop; but in four-dimensional space they disappear. This is quite apparent, for example, in projective geometry and the cross-cap.

For Lacan, topology is not metaphor; it is the precise way we may understand the construction and appearance of the subject. Topology provides an intuitive understanding of transformations. It encourages intuitive leaps and alternative conceptualizations. Often, multidimensional spaces, outside of our normal three space dimensions, are employed. To show this, Lacan made use of several topological constructions: torus, Möbius strip, Klein bottle, cross-cap, Borromean knots.

In her biography, *Jacques Lacan* (1997)[3], Elisabeth Roudinesco traces the influence of topological mathematics on Lacan from as early as 1950. She tells us that Lacan had met the mathematician Georges Guilbaud and established a friendship that was to remain for thirty years. In 1951 Lacan joined a study group with Benveniste,

Guilbaud, and Lévi-Strauss where the connections between the social sciences and mathematics and topology were analyzed. Lacan
was to keep in constant contact with Guilbaud in attempting to
resolve the various mathematical problems he came across in the
study group. Apparently, "in private they indulged together in their
shared passion, forever tying knots in bits of string, inflating
children's swimming belts, braiding and cutting things out."[4] Lacan,
in his late work, was to have been influenced by mathematician
Pierre Soury and by the young philosopher Michel Thomé. This
was very apparent in the development of the Borromean knots. Jean-
Michel Vappereau, another mathematician, was to meet Lacan in
1970, and was to engage in both analysis and discussions about
topological mathematics, according to Roudinesco.

The turn to the use of mathemes and the Borromean knots
is traced by Roudinesco to Lacan's reading of Wittgenstein in
1971. A year later, Lacan was to begin to formally speak of the
Borromean knots, apparently influenced by a chance encounter
with mathematician Valerie Marchande who mentioned the display of the Milanes dynasty, the Borromeos, which consisted of
three overlapping circles. This was timed with Lacan's encounter with Pierre Soury and later other topologically oriented theorists. By 1977, Christian Leger joined Lacan's group of topologists,
particularly Soury and Thome, and they were often consulted by
Lacan to solve a topological problem. As Roudinesco tells it:
"Often, after spending hours drawing surfaces, twisting the inner
tubes that they had delivered in large quantities, or filling bas-
kets with bits of string and cutouts of colored paper, the others
would get a message from Lacan asking them for the solution of
a problem."[5]

Thus Lacan's development of topology theory in its relation
to the speaking being, the *parlêtre*, has a long history of involve-
ments with various theoreticians from a variety of disciplines. This
story has yet to be completely told. It is truly remarkable that one
person could do the incredibly complex integrations with the early
works of Freud, and arrive at the new profound synthesis of the
nature of subjectivity. Even though Lacan, in his passing moments,

was to say that he was always a Freudian, many of us who have struggled through his complex *oeuvre* argue, no, he is Lacan.

CHAPTER SUMMARIES: TOPOLOGICALLY SPEAKING[6]

There are three parts to this book. In Part I, "Topologically Thinking," three introductory chapters are included situating the importance of using topology theory in explaining the relationship of the subject to desire and discourse. They will also suggest various possible applications. In Part II, "Topology of Surfaces," we include seven chapters on the relationship of the topology of surfaces to desire, subjectivity, and its application to three areas: clinical, literature, and social sciences. Included will be a specific discussion and application of the torus, Möbius strip, Klein bottle, cross-cap, schema R, and schema 1. Part III, "Topology of Knots," will focus on Lacan's late work on the Borromean knots and the fourth order, *le sinthome*. These knots are topological constructions that indicate the very structure of the subject.

Our introduction indicates how topology theory has been an important component of Lacan's extensive writings. It has introduced us to some of the features of topology theory and of Lacan's usage of them. It also provides more extensive summaries of each chapter in the book, to which we now turn.

In Part I, three theorists provide a general exploration of topology theory in Lacan's orientation. In Chapter 1, Jeanne Lafont, in "Topology and Efficiency," explains the importance of Lacan's topological theory for the social sciences and cultural practices. She discusses the Möbius strip, Klein bottle, and schema R. Each represents different surfaces necessitating a particular topology. She discusses *jouissance*, desire, reality, fantasy, transference, speech, and writing. She notes, "Each social group, each culture, in which a subject is counted (or unable to be counted, or does not want to be), produces a discourse about happiness and madness. This discourse organizes a topology where transference happens. And there is no other therapeutic tool. So a psychoanalyst must go with this topology." In discussing transference, she indicates how *"points de contrôle,"* or control points, are established for linguists where agreement exists between word and thing. It is in the context of social actors interacting that the effects of discourse produce certain realities. Psychoanalysts, as well as social workers, often transcend these control points; they often choose one side of a story from a context. It is therefore social praxis in relation to fantasy and transference that is critical to understand. Schema R, for example, allows us to see how the Imaginary and Symbolic are sutured, how transference and the treatment must engage in their dynamics to be successful. It is here that the "cut," the "extraction" of the subject, the figure eight cut producing the Möbius strip and the disk, subject and *objet petit a*, are constitutive of subjectivity and reality construction. Thus, in the topology of surfaces a "frame" supported by an "extraction" is the momentary fantasy with which we work and with which reality is constructed. In sum, Lafont argues it is through Lacanian topological thinking that insight is provided to the working of the psychical apparatus.

Chapter 2, by Jacques-Alain Miller, entitled "Mathemes: Topology in the Teaching of Lacan," tells us that "topology cannot be extracted from the teaching of Lacan." And Miller, Lacan's son-in-law and official heir and editor of the *Seminars*, following Lacan, insists that topology is not metaphor. It represents a structure. This essay indicates that topology was already present in the "Rome Discourse" (1953). There, Lacan retheorized Heidegger and the existentialist/phenomenological project(s) of becoming/being-toward-death in terms of the torus and the "word."[7] Topology is comprised of two areas: first the four objects associated with surfaces, torus, Möbius strip, Klein bottle, and the cross-cap; and second, are the Borromean knots, based on a very different mathematics than surface topology. Desire, for Miller, following Lacan, is dependent on topology rather than on some other dynamic. Miller shows how the torus allowed the "relationship of internal exclusion to be sustained." The notion of "extimacy" (a neologism of a noun and adjective) continues this tradition. Lacan often invented mathemes to represent his various constructions. Not everything could sufficiently be represented by mathemes, but their use could bring to light otherwise "unsayables." Topology is seen as existing everywhere: "Every living body has a topology." It often consists of matrices and "signifying combinatives." It is in this space that signifiers can be seen in their various combinations, tensions, and antagonisms. Thus, understanding the gaze is based on a topology of the gaze which is its support. The various holes that Lacan speaks of are also organized around topology. The Möbius strip, inherent in the "inverted (inner) eight," and representing the "cut" of the subject in schema R, implicates how the interior and exterior are interconnected. For Miller, it was Lacan's way of coming to terms with the abstract ideas in Sartre's *Being and Nothingness*. Miller also stresses how Lacan's "The Agency of the Letter" is organized around a topological space. The movement of the signifier appears on a localized space. In fact, he continues, the signifier cannot be predicated on a linear construction, but on a space, a surface. Finally, Miller comments on the discussion among Jacobson, Lyotard, and Laplanche on double inscription, and about the interconnection between metaphor-metonymy and condensation-displacement and cites Lacan as suggesting that the Möbius strip resolves the differences. It is here where the inside and outside are constituted as one surface that we may speak of an "interpretive cut" of the subject.

Chapter 3 offers Ellie Ragland's "Lacan's Topological Unit and the Structure of Mind." This chapter explains the relationship between topology theory, algebraic logic, and the mapping of the dynamics of "mind." Lacan could not be called a postmodernist or a poststructuralist, as some have claimed, even though he has had an enormous influence on both. Ragland begins with the Lacanian idea that with any combination of two we have a structure. This structure includes the "cut," the poinçon, fantasy, desire, the slashed subject of desire, lack, and so forth. It includes also the various limits defining each. Having said that, Ragland then goes on to focus on the latter part of Lacan's theorizing (1974–1981). The signifier, rather than having a dualistic structure (acoustic image, concept), in Lacan's formulation is triadic. A signifier, Lacan continuously tells us, is that which represents a subject for another signifier. This introduces a new space within which to think the subject. Topology, therefore, is concerned with lines, holes, and spaces, how they are connected, how they function, be it in contradictory ways. She asks us to envision the interplay of surfaces, "empty" spaces, cuts, holes, gaps, and rims, with lack, desire, *jouissance*, subjectivity— the very primordial beginning points as to how inscriptions of the signifier are constituted. In Lacan's final period, it is the fourth term, *le sinthome*, the father's name that ties together the Imaginary, Real, and Symbolic. Each *sinthome* is unique; each provides constancy for the psychic apparatus, and each is the basis of further ideological construction. The *objet a*, for Lacan, is at the center of these various knottings, Borromean knots, "units that are knotted in thousands of inter-linkages in a signifying necklace Lacan defines as memory/mind." These in turn lead to a diverse way of being for each subject; each has her/his own unique primordial repressions, desire, privileged *objet petit a's*, and forms of *jouissance*. Even though there seems to be some inspiration drawn by Lacan from Peirce's notion of firstness, secondness, and thirdness, Ragland argues that Lacan's formulation has it that the third always has constituted within it the other two, be they in fragmented and even antagonistic form. Thus empirical, positive sciences overlook that within language itself there are mechanisms of their own undoing; in other words, inherently dialectical relationships exist which cannot be subsumed neatly under some nominalization project. Language, therefore, is inherently triadic and topological. It is the very cuts of surfaces that produce differential dimensionalities. There is also continuity between schema R and the Borromean knots. The seifert surface in particular sheds light on this transition. The activity of writing could be exemplary as to the various cuts at play; consider how a writer stops or continues a line into another, intersecting it, undermining, reinforcing, and putting into question the contents. This is the mark of perpetuating continuities and discontinuities, flows, and marks, as in *Finnegans Wake*. The torus, too, argues Ragland, captures this flow, this movement from inside to outside, presence and absence. As Ragland says: "The *objet a* fills the hole created between words, making sure that we do not encounter the lacks-in-being too often." Beware, however, if the fundamental fantasy is destroyed, for this leaves the subject naked in its confrontation with the Real. All this leads to the question of the truth of the subject. All rests with the signifier. The signifier constituted both speaks and is spoken by the subject, both represents and alienates the subject. Thus, again, at the center of being is a hole; topology indicates how a double turn around this hole is possible, materializing a signifier representing desire, but which is an illusory representation of a fantasy of completeness which may never be.

Part II, "Topology of Surfaces," focuses more on how intersecting surfaces and various cuts produce subject-effects. Seven chapters are devoted to this. There are also applications to the clinical, literary, and social sciences.

Chapter 4 is by Pierre Skriabine, entitled "Clinic and Topology: The Flaw in the Universe." He is the official topology scholar in the *Ecole de la Cause* in Paris. In this section, he focuses on the topology of surfaces. In Part III, chapter 11, he develops a topology of knots. Skriabine presents a clinical view of topology theory in terms of twelve "remarks." They focus on: structure, the fold, topology and science, the flaw in the universe, $\emptyset$, $\$$, the cut, "there is no metalanguage," logic and topology, "the unconscious is structured like a language," the object a, and identification, drive, fantasy, or the topology of the transference according to the interior eight. Structure and topology are inherently related. As he tells us, "there is no subject, then, who is not topological." This is apparent in the Möbius structure. The subject appears with the cut, the "interior eight." Here the subject of the signifier and its object momentarily appear. For Skriabine, a mode of organization of the hole is topology. It is, for example, a double turn around the hole that produces the Möbius strip. In other words, an interior eight cut performed on the torus produces the Möbius strip. Lacan's work in the 1960s, according to him, was strongly focused on the Other, particularly with the presentation of various surfaces—Möbius strip, torus, cross-cap, Klein bottle. It is the lack in the Other, $\emptyset$, to which Lacan turns in a more systematic way in the 1970s with the Borromean knots. The Möbius strip, in Lacan's earlier writings, is a key topological construction. It can be derived from a particular cut of the torus. If we add a disk to one edge, we have a projective plane, the cross-cap, the very support of schema R. In the other direction, a figure eight cut on the cross-cap produces the subject (Möbius strip) and its objects of desire (the disk). If we glue two Möbius strips along one common edge we have the Klein bottle. This is about structure, about topology, about how the hole can be organized in a structured way, with effects. If we cut the Möbius strip down the middle we no longer have a Möbius strip; it disappears in this new cut. It is only a particular cut that produces the subject and its objects of desire. It is in the Klein bottle that the subject disappears within its metonymical nuances, its interjections in the signifying chain where the subject is merely that which is spoken for; the master signifier comes to represent it even as it is unaware of its support. And it is here where the signifier once again represents the subject for another signifier. Thus transference in the clinical situation, as an important component to the end of treatment, must consider the various identifications that are constituted by the various cuts. It is with the client's ability to be able to "cross the plane of identification," in situating itself momentarily in the Other, at the place of little *a*, whereby a new drive is constituted, that treatment can progress toward a cure.

Chapter 5, "Objet *a* and the Cross-Cap," is authored by Juan-David Nasio. Nasio explains the construction of schema R on the cross-cap. He indicates how various figure eight (the "interior eight") cuts can be performed on the cross-cap, and how these "cuts" of the subject produce a Möbius strip and a disk. The former represents the subject, the latter *objet a*. The cross-cap is a unique topological structure of which Lacan makes use in describing the continuity of the "inside" and the "outside" of the psychic structure. It has no "edge." This figure can only be represented ("embedded") in four-dimensional (e.g., the "abstract cross-cap") space without intersection. Here it is a unilateral surface. In three-dimensional space (e.g., the "concrete cross-cap") a singularity (standing for the phallus) exists, representing an intersection. It also possesses a bilateral surface. The singularity is at the center of all "cuts" of the subject, representing the ubiquitous effects of the phallus. The totality of points of intersections in the concrete cross-cap, represented in a line, is the "self-intersecting line" that also represents suture. The interior eight also represents repetition of the signifier and the consequences on the subject. Thus, with the figure eight cut, words that materialize also imprint the real with an effect. With each repetition completing the full circling of the figure eight, a new subject is produced along with a residue, the disk, representing *objet a*. The singularity found in the concrete cross-cap, a point hole, represents the phallic signifier. It can be reduced, in other words, to a point. Schema R, usually portrayed flattened in two-dimensional space, contains the flattened Möbius strip representing each of the four corners marked as I, M, i, m.

Chapter 6, "Floating between Original and Semblance," is by Zak Watson. He applies topology theory to literature. Specifically, he analyzes Hermann Broch's *The Death of Virgil*. It is in the depiction of the last two days of Virgil's life that the issue of edges and holes is quite apparent. It is in the voids that hermeneutical meaning is topologically constituted. He speaks against the empirical approach, be it philology or psychology, for it is inextricably based on masculine sexuation. Thus it cannot tell us much about truth and being. It is therefore to the Other we look in unraveling truth about meaning and being. Broch's work, according to Watson, brings out the point that "there is a truth that goes beyond words but paradoxically, is in words in some manner, just as the point hole in the cross-cap seems to be an exclusion that is within, a void in the Other whose relation is extimate." The primordial lost objects of desire can find substitutes that can be invested with a *jouissance* value. But these are illusory, always there, tantalizing, but always absent once reached. Hermeneutical projects, even if they seemingly offer a coherent written account or text, always have gaps from which the *objet a* falls. A text, therefore, in Watson's account, must not be seen in its apparent two-dimensional layout, but in its singularities, in its one-dimensional moments, in its "dialectic of the edge and hole present in the text." Watson turns to *The Death of Virgil* to show how various signifying chains are traveled by Virgil. But it is precisely the search for going beyond language that is problematic. Thus, the author's repeated statement, "not quite here but yet at hand." Is it therefore to pure voice that one looks for potential fuller meaning alongside language? But is this the answer? Does one attain fuller meaning by voice than the written language? Watson thinks Broch wants to leave this world behind in pursuit of another medium. Thus Watson tells us "ultimately for Broch, this world and its creations are worth something because there is something of the real reality that cuts through, just as the signifiable is split into the signifier and the real latent reference of the impossible to signify." In Watson's view, Virgil continues down the path of stripping away the layers of signifiers in his search to get closer to "real reality" where distinctions in the signifier as the One and Other are obliterated. Is it a return to the womb? The voice that resonates through the protective fluid? Ultimately, notwithstanding the journey by Virgil, the book ends with a twist of the Möbius strip; the end of the book is now the beginning.

David Metzger is the author of Chapter 7, "Interpretation and Topological Structure." He offers the idea that Lacan's work, among all other things, is a "topology of language." He first reviews Freud's *Psychopathology of Everyday Life*, then shifts to a Lacanian topological analysis of language. Metzger reviews Freud's analysis of forgetting in the example of the painter Signorelli, where Botticelli and Boltraffio, as displacements, were used instead. The explanatory point is whether Freud's approach on displacement and "chains of association" is more efficacious than a more direct approach as in Timparno's critique whereby the very properties of language itself rather than the unconscious are efficacious. Thus, in Timparno's critique, he questions whether Freud can make a distinction between linguistic possibility and unconscious force; between the operations of language itself rather than the operation of the unconscious. This impasse, according to Metzger, can be overcome by looking at Lacan's notion of *lalangue*, and in particular how a topology of language employing the Möbius strip can bring out the

Other dimension of language. This leads Metzger to distinguish between bodies and language within a topology of language whereby the former precedes the latter. He provides the example of a baby's burp and the constructed meaning by others in language. By conceptualizing a burp, a slip of the tongue, a display of the teeth, as "null-language markers" ("places where one could speak if one could"), as prior to signifier, we could then look at a topology of language. We could then envision, Metzger tells us, the null-language markers as *objet a*. Then, we could situate this analysis within the distinction of Lacan's *lalangue* and *langue. Lalangue* shows us where any metalanguage of grammar falls short of adequate explanation. This is due to the very holes in language itself. Finally, Metzger posits that Lacan's matheme, $S(A)[S(\emptyset)]$, supports a reading of language as being fundamentally topological. As he tells us, this matheme indicates "where language might make do without the Other and its discourse (the unconscious) by becoming the Other, the point where language might function as a pseudo-discourse, where language serves as the promise of a picture without a gaze, language as a-structural but nevertheless not without structure." The final point by Metzger provides a topological construction that indicates how signifiers are therefore connected. The Möbius strip in its relation to the torus demonstrates this. He concludes with seven steps by which Lacan's mathemes specify the relationship between the Möbius strip and a torus. And this, Metzger states, is the inherent topology of language.

In Chapter 8, "The Inside Out of the Dangerous Mentally Ill: Topological Application to Law and Social Justice," Bruce Arrigo employs the Klein bottle and Möbius strip in explaining the construction of legal identities in the medicolegal arena. More specifically, he looks at a recent U.S. appeals court decision-making on the mentally ill and dangerous homeless. The court decision had to do with a homeless woman who was civilly (involuntarily) committed to a mental hospital by a mobile mental health outreach program. Arrigo's analysis suggests that the Möbius strip is suggestive of how the return of the message in inverted form is indicative of how ideological constructions anchor speech in dealings with mental states, reasonableness, culpability, dangerousness, volition, and so forth. He shows how the Lacanian notion of metaphor is topologically modeled by the Möbius strip where medicolegal signifiers (i.e., "mentally ill," "dangerous") come to stand for the uniqueness of the subject. The Klein bottle, too, indicates topologically how psycholegal discourse invades all spoken signifiers within the psychiatric decision-making in law. He then goes on to show how particularly these two topological constructions were operative in the appellate court decision, *In the Matter of Billie Boggs* (1987). For example, Arrigo shows how the incarcerated woman's troubling action of tearing up money was interpreted metaphorically. But the uniqueness of the person was repressed "below the bar" and the substituted signifiers were medicolegal signifiers. In the process one meaning—the ideologically crafted medicolegal—was substituted for the subject. Thereafter, a "signifier [the medicolegal one] represented the subject [the incarcerated woman] for another signifier." One's ability to speak, in other words, is limited to the possible narrative constructions in medicolegal language. An utterance, for example, by the incarcerated woman would return in inverted form; in other words, the Möbius strip indicated how the uniqueness of the person was replaced with medical-based. legal terminology (signifiers). An example for the application of the Klein bottle is also provided. Consistency, for example, in medical-based legal discourse, is maintained insofar as any discourse being uttered in the legal arena is continuously infused with official, medicolegal signifiers. The "neck" of the Klein bottle coming back into itself suggests this. From "inside" (the medical-based legal edifice), constant infusion of master signifiers into ongoing legal dialogues assures that legal construction predominates over other forms of discourse. It works effectively to silence the unique subject of desire (here, the psychiatrically constituted citizen).

Chapter 9, Dragan Milovanovic's "Psychoanalytic Semiotics, Chaos, and Rebellious Lawyering," makes use of Lacan's schema R in developing an alternative form of legal discourse, a replacement discourse, in the encounter between client and lawyer. He applies

Lacan's topological constructions (primarily schema R, but also the Borromean knots) to Lopez's book *Rebellious Lawyering: One Chicano's Vision of Progressive Law Practice* (1992). This book introduced Paulo Freire's dialogical pedagogy in the construction of an alternative form of dialogical encounters ("dialogical problem solving") between client and lawyer, which challenges the conventional forms of lawyering (e.g., the "regnant form"). More specifically, Milovanovic integrates chaos theory, Lacanian psychoanalytic semiotics—particularly the use of Lacan's four discourses—with Paulo Freire's dialogical pedagogy, in suggesting how a new discourse could emerge. That is, he is concerned with how new master signifiers could replace dysfunctional, nonrepresentative ones, and thus contribute to an alternative construction of the "what happened," the point of controversy. First, Milovanovic develops three possible interacting factors within the client's and lawyer's narrative constructions. These three axes represent Lacan's three Orders. Here, one may have various identifications with particular discursive subject positions (i.e., juridic, oppositional, revolutionary), master signifiers, and discourse (abstract vs. language of the body). Second, he shows how chaos's notion of the "bifurcation" diagram can incorporate the dynamic of Lacan's four discourses. Third, he indicates how the "problem-solving form" of interaction can be integrated with Lacan's discourse of the analyst in indicating how new master signifiers may emerge. Fourth, he argues that these various stages on the bifurcation diagram can be conceived as constitutive of the various "cuts" of the subject found in schema R. Finally, in his fifth point, he indicates how there will be a tendency toward the *conscientization* of the subject in which a relatively stabilized replacement discourse will emerge supported by alternative master signifiers. Applying *le sinthome*, Milovanovic also indicates how an alternative anchoring of the subject can develop where desires are given more complete expressive form in discourse.

Philip Dravers's analysis in Chapter 10, "To Poe, Logically Speaking: From 'The Purloined Letter' to the *Sinthome*," provides a transitional chapter to the topology of knots. He focuses on the circuitry of the signifier in Lacan's analysis of "The Purloined Letter." Dravers's reading, following Lacan, has it that topology can reveal how networks of signifiers, bound with *jouissance*, remain in structured movement with effects. He reviews Lacan's classic analysis of the signifier (the letter) in structured movement in Poe's short story, "The Purloined Letter." He then shows how a close reading indicates the work of repetition and how a hole introduced in the Real by the letter is to have effects in various meaning constructions of the interlocutors. Schema R is particularly implicated in showing how fantasy acts as a support for the relations between the subject and Other and how internally it is of the form of the Möbius strip. He also shows how Lacan's late works on the Borromean knots and its focus on the symptom indicate various relations with *jouissance*. It is here, Dravers argues, that an alternative mode of writing is being delineated. The two he specifically explains is a writing indexed on the split subject and that indexed on *objet petit a*. This, in turn, sheds light on writing that is indexed on the signifier, and writing that is indexed on *jouissance*. In Poe's short story, it is the letter which carries a potential *jouissance*, a *jouissance* available for whoever makes use of the letter. In Lacan's "*La Troisième*," *objet a* is placed at the very center of the intersecting circles (registers: Imaginary, Symbolic, Real) of the Borromean knots. Thus *objet a* is where a particular *jouissance* situated in one of the registers is interrupted by the intersection of the other two.

In Part III, "Topology of Knots," we find six chapters on the use of the Borromean knots and/or the fourth order, *le sinthome*. In Lacan, we find a remarkable consistency in the transition from a topology of surfaces to the topology of knots.

Chapter 11 by Pierre Skriabine, entitled "The Clinic of the Borromean Knot," introduces the reader to the last period of Lacan's teachings on the Borromean knots and *le sinthome*. Skriabine specifically applies his chapter to the clinical realm. He summarizes Lacan as follows: The speaking being is supported by three registers—the Real, Symbolic, and Imaginary. Within these articulations we find *jouissance*. In Freud, these three registers remain independent of each other. It is "psychical reality" which acts as "the fourth," the Oedipus complex, that provides a knot and hence constancy for the psychic apparatus. This binding in four is already implicit in Lacan's interlinked three rings, according to Skriabine. Unknotted we have "foreclosure." It is in need of a fourth, "supplementation." In Lacan, it is the "name-of-the-father" which functions to name; nomination. But there are three distinct nominations, three "names-of-the-father," one for each register. Inhibition is connected with the Imaginary, anxiety with the Real, and symptom with the Symbolic. It is an issue, then, of the various possible failings, faults, in the fundamental Borromean knot that produce distinct clinical results. In other words, R, S, and I can be arranged in various ways, leading, for example, on one extreme to madness, on the other, to the paranoic and the neurotic. The fourth ring, *le sinthome*, is what is capable of repairing the fundamental fault in the Borromean knot. This was extensively explained by Lacan in his analysis of James Joyce's writings in "Joyce *le Sinthome*." An analyst, according to Skriabine, then, attempts to do various forms of interpretation or "grafting." Lacan's interpretation of James Joyce's writings is that they are enigmatic precisely because *le sinthome* of Joyce is his ego, a correction of the fundamental fault. It produces an undoing and redoing of language, a unique form of writing according to Skriabine's summary of Lacan. And even as it does, it retains a trace of the original fault: thus the idiosyncratic epiphanies in Joyce's writings.

Chapter 12 by Jean-Paul Gilson, "The Square of the Subject," shows the continuity of Lacan's topology from the mirror-stage to the end of his work on knot theory. In stressing the dimension of Writing, Gilson places it as an act on which one will act as he or she must. Writing is based on four anchoring points: the thread of continuity of one's life, sex, pleasure, and reality. But Writing is not limited to a simple representivity of thought. There are layers of Writing: differential, planary, nodal, virtual, and ternary. Gilson isolates a double movement of thought: "The mark of a trace erased in order to deceive the Other is regained by the subject under the form of knowledge." It is an unspeakable ditch. Lacan's topology is a Writing, "mark of an erased trace . . . of the subject which fades away when the jouissance of the living makes a break in the heart of Symbolic repetition, as well as in the virtuality of the Imaginary, or in the inertia of the Real." Lacan's own trajectory was nodal, a rewriting of Freud: condensed in a quadrature of circles, Gilson writes that the sexual principle of desire interfaces with pleasure, and need interfaces with reality. To explain this double Writing, Gilson gives an example from the Chinese banking world in which "good faith finds itself founded on the single regluing together of the separated pieces of the piece [of a newspaper] initially broken in two." The word always takes itself for the object of its own aiming. The signified of this self-reference is Writing. This is a Writing-knowledge-means-of-*jouissance*.

Chapter 13 by Véronique Voruz, entitled "The Topology of the Subject of Law: The Nullibiquity of the Fictional Fifth," sets out to indicate how the topology of the knots is continuous with Lacan's earlier work and to point out some practical usages including some for formal law. She cites Lacan: "I have invented what can be written as the Real. [. . .] I have written this Real in the form of the Borromean knot." Thus the Borromean knots are a form of writing itself. Discourse is topologically constructed. It is the heterogeneous registers, articulated in particular form, that infuse spoken language with embodiment of desire and particular form. Voruz continues, following an explication of Lacan, that the "fourth" is usually the name-of-the-father, which in actuality could be any signifier. She then takes us through an explication of the difference between the Freudian father and the Lacanian symptom and the logic of exception in Lacan's "Tables of Sexuation" from *Seminar XX*. She summarizes the various possibilities, including the notion of *pas-toute*, not all. Assuming the position of the male in a predominantly phallocentric symbolic order provides access to phallic *jouissance*; assuming the female position negates this, but provides access to the *jouissance* of the body. As she tells us, "she is 'not-all' because she is not subjected to her belief in the truth of the Other: indeed, *she is the truth of the Other*." This brings Voruz to her point on formal law. This is the "locus *par excellence* of the encounter with the Other of exception . . ." On the side of the juridical, there must be failure, for enunciation is "taken up in the circuits of the subject's interpretation of what he or she is for the Other." Thus law has a tall order: it needs to provide alternative senses of being. It functions, then, according to Voruz, "*to keep its subjects at its door.*" So law effaces the subject's truth as possibly being connected, in being read, in the Other. Hence, Voruz indicates that law is incapable of providing a "universal supplementation." In its practice, in law's reduction of uniqueness of the human being to management exercises, it renders an understanding of the human being a disservice—"an utter disrespect for human particularity." Law, for Voruz, "serves a purely regulating function in the service of those in power, and . . . it does so with a view to perpetuating an entrenched status quo and to defusing the particular dangers potentially posed by 'social deviants.'"

Chapter 14, "Specious Aristmystic: Joycean Topology," by Luke Thurston, deals with Lacan's final period on the *le sinthome*. Thurston comments on Lacan's analysis of James Joyce's writings. In response to a question about the knots and topology, Lacan had said: "It does not constitute a model in the sense that it entails something before which the imagination is insufficient. I mean that, properly speaking, the imagination as such resists imagining the knot. And the mathematical approach to it in topology is also not enough." The knot, in Thurston's reading, "is not of this world," it escapes human imagining, remains independent of any formal signification. It merely "ex-sists." For Joyce, it was with the failure of the name-of-the-father that an alternative nomination was necessitated, and it was the fourth term, *le sinthome*, that made the knot hold. It was a form of naming; here, Joyce *le sinthome*. Absent the name, R, S, and I are untangled and the topological constancy, the coherence, of the subject is undermined. Thurston then juxtaposes a schema from Joycean topology, the Wakean figure, onto the knot anchored by *le sinthome*. Thurston first argues that the topology of the knot was a mutation from the Freudian-based Oedipus complex, anchored by the name-of-the-father; constancy, for Lacan, could now find a new basis in *le sinthome*. In comparison with Joyce's Wakean figure, which Thurston likens to a topology encouraging "endless semantic transformation and multiplication," Lacan's knots speak more to "a silent monstration of something irreducible to the *dit-mension* of the speaking subject." Ironically, perhaps, but with its intent apparent, Joyce's figure, although placed within a modernist inscription, encourages polysemy, whose "secret scripture" transcends the boundaries of modernist inscriptions and restrictions. Thus, the commonality with Lacan's *sinthome*, according to Thurston, that resides with both is the very existence of the impossible at the center of the figures, a locus constituted by an inescapable instability and an incapability of being localized with precision. Ironically, for both, this is also the very principle for the respective relative cohesion in each's model.

Chapter 15 is by Jean-Michel Vappereau, entitled "Making Rings: The Hole of the *Sinthome* in the Embedding of the Topology of the Subject." This chapter travels full circle from the topology of surfaces back to knots. Thus it is an ending, and a beginning. It traces the very early work by Freud in 1895, struggling to provide a topology of the subject, to the knots of Lacan. Vappereau traces the development from Freud's earlier *Project for a Scientific Psychology* (1895), a somewhat linear construction, to the more refined topology appearing in *The Interpretation of Dreams* five years later, to the work of Lacan's topology found in schemas L and R. Vappereau develops a schema F from Lacan's schema L and imposes it on schema R. This is a unique contribution in reconceptualization of schema R. Vappereau also provides commentary on the Borromean knots and the fourth order. His chapter engages in a discussion comparing Freud's work with Lacan (i.e., the phallic function, the status of the unconscious, the lessons of Spinoza, the underlying neuron structure in the psychic apparatus, the signifying drive, optical geometry, the structure of language, the status of the subject, and finally, the topology of knots, and *le sinthome*). His chapter must be read as a weave covering the time periods from 1895 to the late 1970s, indicating some prominent topological developments.

Our final chapter, Chapter 16, by Dragan Milovanovic, entitled "Borromean Knots, *Le Sinthome*, and Sense Production in Law," integrates Lacan's late work on the Borromean knots and *le sinthome* with critical legal theory in illustrating how Lacan's work provides an important statement about the subject of law. The subject of law only appears in the guise of an abstraction, the juridic subject. Lacan's work shows how subjectivity finds only a circumscribed construction in the legal arena. *Jouissance* takes on the phallic form. *Le sinthome* is a politically determined construction that acts to repair the knot, providing constancy for the psychic apparatus. Disenfranchised voices are excluded in this articulation. They remain *pas-toute*. Constitutive theorizing in law, as opposed to the more instrumental Marxist and most structural Marxist forms, argues that law, ideology, and subjectivity are interconnected in a holistic manner. There is no abstracting the subject, for example, from outside of the context of political economy. Thus, constitutive theorizing argues that the desiring subject finds herself/himself in an ideological system, a phallocentric Symbolic order, where only restricted narrative constructions can take place. Milovanovic concludes by suggesting that a combined discourse of the hysteric and analyst may provide one direction for reconceptualizing subjectivity in the direction of developing the revolutionary subject. In Chapter 9 of this book there is some further analysis on how this might take place in legal service delivery. In both chapters, Milovanovic argues for the desirability of developing a replacement discourse, one in which desire finds more complete embodiment.

CONCLUSION

Reading Lacan's topological theory is a continuous journey, a continuous re-reading, an ongoing source of revelation, but also of despair on occasion where the reader has found the abstractions and verbal explanations sometimes perplexing, as in his late work on the knots and *le sinthome*. This book provides the thoughts of key thinkers who have worked through the many complex topological constructions of Lacan and who have found his work a source of ongoing surprise as to its consistency from the 1950s to the latter 1970s and exhilarating as to the potential insights that still remain within his work.

ENDNOTES

1. For an excellent introduction to topology theory, see D. Abbot, *Flatland* (1992). New York: Dover; T. Banchoff, *Beyond the Third Dimension* (1990). New York: Scientific American Library; S. Barr, *Experiments in Topology* (1989). New York: Dover Publications; J. S. Carter, *How Surfaces Intersect in Space* (1995). New Jersey: World Scientific Publishers; P.A. Firby and C.F. Gardiner, *Surface Topology* (1982). New York: Ellis Horwood; L. Henderson, *The Fourth Dimension and Non-Euclidean Geometry in Modern Art* (1983). Princeton, NJ: Princeton University Press; D. Hilbert and S. Cohn-Vossen, *Geometry and the Imagination* (1952). New York: Chelsea; C. Pickover, *Surfing Through Hyperspace* (1992). New York: Oxford University Press; R. Rucker, *The Fourth Dimension* (1984). Boston: Houghton Mifflin; F. Russell, *Foundations of Geometry* (1956). New York: Dover; J. Weeks, *The Shapes of Space* (1985). New York: Marcel Dekker.

See also the article "La topologie en clinique," in *Le Trimestre Psychanalytique*, No. 2, 1992; "Abords topologique," *Revue de Psychanalyse*, no. 5, June, 1982; specifically, on the construction of the cross-cap, see "Freud Lacan: Quelle articulation," *Revue de Psychanalyse*, no. 14, November 1984.

For a comprehensive mathematics of the knots, see C. Adams, *The Knot Book: An Elementary Introduction to the Mathematics of Knots* (1994). New York: W.H. Freeman and Company; R. Haddad and J. Trentelivres, *Plastique des Noeds Rares* (1992). Paris: Lysimaque.

2. There are several examples of non-Lacanian applications of the Möbius strip. In literature, see the collection of short stories by C. Fadiman, *Fantasia Mathematica* (1987). New York: Copernicus Books. Springer-Verlag; E. Ionesco, *The Bald Soprano* (1982). New York: Grove Press; V. Nabokov, *The Gift* (1991). New York: Vintage. In history and philosophy, see D. Haufsteder, *Goedel, Escher, and Bach* (1979). New York: Basic Books. In music, see the application of a Möbius strip by Bach and Schoenberg in the use of the "crab cannon," by which a score can be read normally from the beginning to end, and then flipped in reverse and played.

3. E. Roudinesco, *Jacques Lacan* (1997). New York: Columbia University Press.

4. *Ibid.*, p. 363.

5. *Ibid.*, p. 367.

6. We have elected to do more extensive summaries than normally appear in introductions of edited books for the purpose of providing the readers, particularly those less initiated in Lacan's discourse, some support for readings that follow.

7. J. Lacan, *Ecrits* (1977). New York: Norton, Sheridan, tr., p. 105.

I

Topologically Thinking

1

Topology and Efficiency*

JEANNE LAFONT

Topology is a part of mathematics, which formalizes places and shifts without measurement, but for psychoanalysis it is a writing of structure. Topology continues the project of structuralism. From Lévi-Strauss's work onwards, this trend was defined, in the sixties, by a symbolic dimension, beyond the levels of the imaginary and the real. "The components of a structure have neither name, nor signification. What remains? As Lévi-Strauss rigorously states: they have nothing but a direction (*sens*), a way, or meaning (*sens*) which is necessarily and uniquely one of position in a set."[1]

This is why we will begin by providing an overview of the set; then we will go on to specify a reflection about *jouissance* and speech that will lead us to consider the importance of surface for writing. This precise point concerns the Möbius strip. Third, we will define how differences and similarities occur between psychoanalytic treatment and social practices (*pratiques sociales*) such as social

---

*Translated by Jeanne Lafont and coedited by Ellie Ragland and Philip Dravers.

work. The efficiency of topology in these extended parts of psychoanalytic works will be the best way to prove the importance of the Lacanian use of topology.

OVERVIEW

Topology is a part of mathematics, but the use made of this knowledge by Jacques Lacan is sub(-)versive.[2] Already, to use the same word to name the three different periods of Lacan's topology—the graphs, surfaces, and knots,[3]—is to provide a summary that is not founded on mathematical distinction, or a historical one, but on the progress of psychoanalytic thought. *A contrario*, graphs are mathematical supports of the link with Freud. The very term *"seelisher Apparat,"* as Freud uses it in the *Entwurf* and in the schematic drawings of the apparatus in chapter 7 of *The Interpretation of Dreams*, provides a powerful argument for the use of topology[4] in formalizing his hypothesis.

The Q letter in the *Entwurf* designates an energetic quantity, but its only quality is to shift. Such shifts account for psychical life, for its anxieties and its unconscious. It has been taken up by Lacan through the signifier. In the Freudian text, in fact, the letter Q never operates as energy. Rather than resembling anything like physical "energy," a word that signs the ignorance of the being, in the Freudian text the letter Q, in fact never operates as energy. It concerns nothing but the functioning. With the signifier, Lacan keeps the shift. The translation of this letter as affect drives towards the content of this affect, and this is a mistranslation for the Freudian idea. Again, the only quality of affect is to shift. The psychic apparatus is explained by a complication of Q inscriptions, flaky, stretched, covered, concealed, shifts overlapped by others. Freud divides this functioning by attributing each particular function to a constitutive part of the apparatus.[5]

Moreover, the different psychic agencies are described as places, scenes, loci, in an order, in the sense of an ordinal succession with return, flash back, and so on. The succession does not go at random, but is determined. Already it is topology. Topology formalizes the rules of these shifts according to their order. The unconscious is a function of writing and of inscribing psychical events; the conscious is another way of bringing the same traces of work. Lacan's *"Seminar* on *'The Purloined Poe,'"* at the beginning of the French *Ecrits*, takes up the same letters to show how a writing, and a writing of a writing, a code and a codified code of this first code, arrange dimensions operating over each which prove the symbolic efficiency, only through this code: brackets and brackets within brackets [*parenthèse et parenthèse des parenthèses*]. It is not a material thing, a being, or a concept, but only a dimension, and thus topology. The computer does not surprise Lacan. This dimension is only based on language, as a specific topology, and provides a reference point for Lacan throughout his teaching.

With the Möbius strip, Lacan finds a figure which formalizes the topology of language. Then other topological objects, such as the torus, cross-cap and Klein bottle, are used to tackle problems of *jouissance*. For mathematics, these objects are monsters. It so happens that Möbius discovered his strip during a demonstration concerning the orientation of triangles, collections of triangles, and the law for joining them and maintaining the orientation. This is how the Möbius strip was born, as a collection of triangles which cannot be oriented. Subsequently, this paradoxical object allowed him to construct non-oriented objects and to say what the characteristics of these objects are:

- Unilateral (the strip has only one edge, one face) as opposed to bilateral (two edges, two faces as back and front).
- Unilateral objects are non-orientable, and bilateral objects are orientable.

These two characteristics allowed for the conception of objects which have no edge, such as the sphere and torus. These two objects are easy to make, but the cross-cap and Klein bottle cannot be made in our environment. It is possible to think them, but not to make them, give to them a physical and material being. Despite this impracticality, Lacan used the very fact that these objects can be thought, but not made in the real of everyday experience, in order to describe psychical events which only occur within the pure dimension of representation. Language is so made that it cannot signify an object except by a quasi-joke, which our everyday life, then experimental knowledge, proposes to us as evidence, or not.

Lacanian topology questions this evidence, in order to build mediums or ways towards madness, and the very dimension of psychical pain. There, *jouissance* leans upon (*s'appuit*) these particular surfaces. *Jouissance* is defined in articulation between language and these particular surfaces. Drawing on references, it is true that, for Lacanian topology, the unconscious is the back which always continues the front (*envers-endroit*). The unconscious is not separated from the conscious except by the time it takes to go there. The Möbius strip is a paradoxical, unilateral object which organizes the connection between the subject and language, and, to specific ends, the strange object, the object *a*. If a subject is ever present in spoken words, these words are spoken in a topology, in a set not entirely present in the moment of enunciation. Before the well-known Lacanian sentence, "That one speaks remains forgotten behind what is said in what is heard/understood" ("*Qu'on dise reste oublié derrière ce qui se dit dans ce qui s'entend*"), Lacan had already said, in "*Kant avec Sade*" in 1963: "it is thus the Other as free, the liberty of the Other, that the discourse of the right of jouissance puts forth as the subject of enunciation."[6] It is the same for psychic pain, and it is not a discovery. Everybody knows these moments where the spoken words do not present the things suffered. Topology explains these things, neither by affect, nor by hidden secret, nor by sentimental dimension, but by the set itself.

This set is a paradoxical set. It is represented by mathematics and rendered operative by psychoanalysis. Be careful; they are not the same. We may use mathematical concepts, but they cannot follow our use. The "subject" exists in our psychoanalytic formalization as a place of freedom, a place of desire, a place of activity, a place where a word is born inside the model, but not for mathematics. We must not lose this efficiency. Freud said "unconscious" is a formation to be translated in the dream-rebus,[7] inscribed on the body, in the fold of the symptom, as a letter. Lacan repeats "unconscious," of course, but he also specifies the organization of *jouissance*, the place from where the subject may speak and desire and live in written memory traces because the set is the dimension where psychical pains can be explained.

After this surface period, Lacan makes a second turn. After having specified *jouissance*, speech, and writing, in their incommensurable difference, incomparable beings, and also their happy or unhappy organization, he overcomes this difference by naming the knot between the three. The Borromean knot shows the dimension of articulation. If it is possible to write something from a particular transference with a present human being, the knot writes the general data of a psychological knowledge. Of each of the three elements, or four, if the knot itself, the "knotledge," is counted, none is better than the others. In the knot, beyond their differences, each element is the same as the other. How can we put it better than by saying "it is the set" which is pertinent, the way the set is constituted.

With *jouissance*, speech, and writing, "three" is operative for the topology of the set. In the knot, writing as Real is strictly equivalent to *jouissance*, in the very moment they confront speech as a Symbolic dimension. But, this equivalence, in itself, implies that writing could be Symbolic, if the *jouissance* in question were Real, and so with speech, the Imaginary, and so on . . . for all the arrangements you want. No human being's organization is the same as another one. Here the psychoanalyst has to learn from everybody, transference is just the way to be inside an organization, as a set, and he must always interpret from the place he has in this specified set. This place moves. The differences among the three are thrown back according to the specification of each knot's ring and the moment of transference.

The relevance of such a theory in contemporary reflection, for psychoanalysis, as much for the clinic as for the number of theories which explain madness, is that Lacan proposes a second level of reading [*lecture*]. In a theory, it may so happen that each element, in regard to their sense and contents, is completely wrong, but if the articulation between each is correct, the theory may prevail in being successful for many human beings. So it is possible to think about the fascination of sets. In psychoanalysis, there is a first level which concerns characteristics of *jouissance*, of speech, and writing (*scripture*), and the way they fix, or unfix, the distance between them for one symptom or another to play a role. Then, there is a second level in which each has a function for the set, and the set itself may be more important in its function than the symptom and its history, even if the therapeutic is not possible without the first level, or the second. A symptom is produced by an unconscious articulation, which organizes the relation between forgotten words; the body, or muscles, as an inspiration surface; and pleasure, or *jouissance*. But this symptom also has a function that holds the Imaginary to the Symbolic, or, for that matter, any other articulation. Everything can occur.

Finally, what matters is not that one gives either content or sense as theory, but rather that one offers only a grid for a reading (*lecture*). Every analyst is in charge of his way of reading. This manner will be also be joined to the actual moment in transference. Do not forget Freud's sentence: "One cannot treat without learning something new."(*"On ne pouvait pas traiter sans apprendre quelque chose de nouveau."*)[8] In Lacanian terms, this means that there is no fixed knowledge in psychoanalysis. Indeed, contrary to the scientific way, what is important in psychoanalysis is that one does not give an any-which-way objectivity. There is no material objectivity in the psychic apparatus, but this does not mean that it does not exist, but that the materiality comes as a function of the topological set. In a delusion, for instance, some words are like things as a function which holds the Real to the Symbolic or Imaginary. But in an obsession, some thoughts come and come again as things one cannot throw away, because they are not things, but rather have this function which operates between the Imaginary and the Real.

The singer Leonard Cohen tells us, in a public summary of the way he composed the song "So Long, Marianne"; it was a written in a period when it could take him one or two hours to decide whether or not he wanted to go out with his hat. The obsessional symptom is easy to read for an analyst, but indeed, to speak about it without the dimension of pain, just as the spring for a world-successful song, shows how this symptom has a function, and how this function makes pain disappear in a therapeutic manner. Leonard Cohen admits much in this story, but he does not say anything about the elements of his pain, just the retro-way to do things—a song!—and the success of that song is the consequence. Everybody in the world receives the pain, not as a particular organization, but as a general duty to do with time, death, and love . . .

Topology, as Lacan uses it, allows us to formalize a rigorous theory of the psychic apparatus, without any way or anywhere fixing an objective "way" for the human subject.

From this overall view, how can we explain something about surfaces and their difference, while remembering that the surface is also joined to *jouissance*, speech, and writing? The three terms are present by retrogression.[9] This makes an argument possible. Is a social practice possible as an operative praxis, using psychoanalytic concepts? How can we formalize difference and similitude between a psychoanalytic treatment and the social support provided by our occidental cultures? If we work in a typological way with questions concerning transference, reality, and fantasy, and if we dare to depart from a notion of "treatment" *stricto sensu*, we will be able to draw some precision from the elements of our inquiry, while aiming our reflection at a social praxis.

In this text for the American public, the formalization of social praxis is essential, insofar as, for a French woman, the arrangement of analytic treatment in the USA seems not to be a treatment *stricto sensu*. Sorry for the violence! But through the very fact that medical science dominates the entire therapeutic endeavor in the American way of life, psychoanalysis has become a "social praxis." The treatment does not base itself on the pact of speech, as Lacan defined it, as it occurs in Paris, where there is no diploma for therapists, no medical guarantee, and no public money. It is forbidden for the analyst to base the propositions for a treatment on any social surface. So the signifiers of transference will be particular to each analyst. This organization also has disadvantages. Certainly I am not up to everything. But, a long time ago I claimed that a social praxis can rightly follow Lacan's order as well as the Freudian order of therapeutic transference.

Topology makes it possible to think these praxes which are connected by the place psychoanalysis has in different countries, or in different periods. Each social group, each culture, in which a subject is counted (or unable to be counted, or does not want to be) produces a discourse about happiness and madness. This discourse organizes a topology where transference happens. And there is no other therapeutic tool. So a psychoanalyst must go with this topology. Sects clearly demonstrate how the therapeutic plan may be perverted by group discourse. Even this purpose is an element of that topology where a transference occurs. Nobody lives on a desert island. We can even say that no psychoanalytic treatment exists outside of the social discourse, outside of this topology, as extra-territorial, enjoying indemnity, not guilty, unharmed from the effects of social discourse, pure! Every therapeutic relation is immersed in discourse. The topological mathematical word is a plunging (*plongement*). Perhaps thinking the opposite is just the very retro Imaginary of a purity for which Europeans have paid the great price. Indeed, this implies, the very return of a signifier, the main word between social discourse and the place left to a subject, that is to psychoanalysis.

But, if this "purity" is so essential for European analysts, there is no reason to be shocked if this word is not a part of U.S. topology, strictly, unless the term "new world," means the US would not be guilty of European mistakes. To tell the truth, American readers, it would be best for you if you believe this is so. I only want to show this topology, that is, this set where every reflection on psychoanalysis has to be placed. In this topology, there is the Real of History connected to politics, *stricto sensu*.

It is true that a psychoanalytic treatment is not necessarily beneficial, but to leave it only under the medical power, as a guarantee of this "good," is not without an effect of the treatment. Purpose, aim, against, under. There are so many words which show the main importance in this topology of the orientation. Not orientable or not oriented is not the same. There are surfaces, which are not oriented before somebody, something makes it so.[10] Thus, the importance of transference. The theory, the topological set, does not necessarily give an orientation, but only the presence of a transfer, that is, the act of a psychoanalyst for a patient, in the very present moment, each one after another . . .

Indeed, there is no guarantee that one psychoanalyst might be beneficial for one patient and not for another one. It may even happen that, in a treatment, a psychoanalyst begins by being beneficial, becomes neutral, and then maleficent at an other time, and it occurs sometimes that the wrong way may be necessary for a better way after . . . Indeed, as Freud says with the term "*Todestriebe*," patients show a real will to stay in the wrong way of their symptoms. Unluckily, the true transmission of psychoanalysis must risk it.

A psychoanalysis is not true, in itself, according to an ontology of truth. Logical, mathematical, and philosophical work make it more rigorous, and these efforts are important inside psychoanalysis.

The psychoanalytic treatment is a frame (*cadre*) in which definitions of language, transference, and *jouissance* have been provided, a topology is born, and social praxis can use it. So, *a contrario*, an argument is founded *nachträglich* (after the fact) for the topological theory of psychoanalysis. The English word of "deferred action" does not include the "turn over" of the demonstration, the orientation with two directions, and perhaps many others.

We are staying inside the topology of surfaces with two directions.

THE TOPOLOGY OF SURFACES

Jouissance, speech, and writing, for the first turn; transference, reality and, fantasy, for the second; such is the perspective from which I view the topology of psychoanalysis. Of course, as in topology, I should begin the other way round, contrariwise, or otherwise.

Topology organizes a set. Now we use "space" to differentiate it from set theory, which is a theory of one to one elements. These two words sign the presence of structuralism in mathematics. Whether born in linguistics with Saussure's teaching, or in ethnology with that of Lévi-Strauss, a structuralism comes into psychoanalysis.

What is important is to define the link that exists for any element, between the whole and its parts, even if there are different elements; or how they are separated from each other. There are many "wholes" possible. The elements of any one space have no quality by themselves, but only through the connections between them. In this space, how does shift or revolution operate? In this space, how is an element changed by the shift, or not, and in which conditions? What are the constants, of the objects in a space, or of the space, and which operations are possible?

The main hypothesis of a Lacanian topology is to think the psychical apparatus as a topological space. Although this space is a space of language, it is not only that. This hypothesis also leads us to construct, in the first moment, a particular topology where it is necessary to think immaterial elements, such as words, in the same time as the material objects of life, such as a table for instance, or bodies, and "my body" and, above all, other human beings with whom we share a common language. Already a paradoxical space appears which is only defined by topology. Humans learn language. Language is a space where anybody can enter, and nobody can leave. Those human beings that we call "autistic," however, show no sign of entry into language. What kind of space is a space that has an entrance that is not also an exit? The Klein bottle, unilateral, without an edge surface, is a model for this aporia.

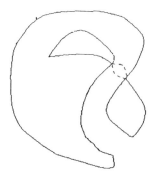

Figure 1–1.

So this language dimension is characterized by something with no consistence, no existence, no hole.[11] Signifiers are not beings in an ontological theory. This is how Lacan defines the signifier in 1964: "A signifier represents a subject for another signifier."[12] Already, the paradoxical link appears between signifiers, so many and different, and the subject as one. It is a topology, unlike the space of our ordinary life. Every signifier is just not the same as another. And this forcefully poses the question of the connection with raw material. This question is not so far from quantitative physics. What are bodies and the objects of the world? It is not obvious, and Lacan answers, in part, with the concept of *jouissance* and the mathematical concept of "covering" (*recouvrement*).

For his definition Lacan used three words taken from mathematical reflection. Continuity (from Cantor) is the opposite of discretion (from set theory). A set is composed of discrete elements, separated from each other, not continuous like water. What matters is to recover the first by the second, or inversely. The Möbius strip is the solution of how to constitute a compact object at the end of the Möbien process, with what is left of the subject as a writing effect of *jouissance* as a continuity, thus always slipping out the link between words, while providing the material of the link, of the necessary link of each word representing "one" for another word—endlessly (but not infinitely!)—all the while affixing a trait to an other human being. *Jouissance*, as continuous, knows neither pleasure nor pain; either it is mine or yours, or theirs; either it is past or present . . . you have to speak to know that, and when you speak *jouissance* slips out. Lacan says: "Jouissance is forbidden to he who speaks."[13] Concepts of Lacanian psychoanalysis may be characterized by the point of view in relation to this *recouvrement* or covering. When you speak to define something at the level of *jouissance*, there is a term, but if you speak from language there is another one. So desire is the term for the urge, which drives anyone to speak again, and again, towards what it is impossible to catch of *jouissance*. In order to explain this shift, Lacan uses Zeno's paradox of Achilles and the tortoise.[14] Topology is used too.

The endless substitutions of language only grasp discrete objects, through the process of the Möbius strip. One draws, one shift, one edge, but the material of the strip consists. For a local moment, a surface is born between two edges, which are the same from a global point of view.

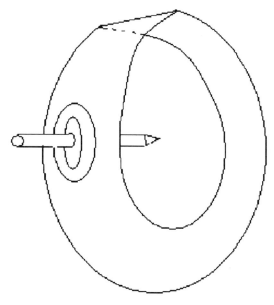

Figure 1–2.

So there is a determinate opposition between the local [surface] where objects are always in a frame,[15] and the global surface where objects are not. The global is always forgotten, when a word is pronounced, but it is the global surface which carries itself, between the words themselves, the pain, the joy, the pleasure, the love . . . desire and symptoms . . . madness or harmony . . . and so forth, generally the psychic dimension of life.

For instance, a teenage patient speaks about her anorexia, which had stopped for a while. During her treatment the anorexia is repeated, and she says her mother's words, from a long time ago: "Later you will regret having ruined today the woman you would have been able to become." This first time is spoken all over again and fixes the symptom and the way *jouissance* appears. What is important is the global wish of this mother, rather than the affect. As Lacanian psychoanalysts say, there is no hole, no lack for the patient and her desire. This sentence encloses the whole time in its space. And it is the mother's space, not the patient's. Just by interpreting the global way, putting together the present, past, and future, the patient cries a lot about the mother's wish, so near to herself, "and laughs again, and cries"[16] and anorexia never reappears, beyond the fact of her having no great appetite. This mother was not guilty, she just wants something good for her daughter, but the sentence is too enclosed, that's all. Never mind! The instance is too simple, of course. I will just show how a Möbien organization may be reduced to few words.

This organization is not marked in space, or in time, but by the structural necessity of the time to speak, following a one way time in which, if I want somebody else to listen and understand, one word is pronounced after another. There is a torsion, ever present in each word, as a global set, which encloses my sentence in a dimension I ignore, but from which possibility itself hangs. Lacan says that a "passion for ignorance" poses the most difficult obstacle to transference. I cannot see the torsion, but perceive it, recognize it, if I read the traces left by this torsion: in this instance, the anorexia itself. If I read, there are letters. And so "writing" is the third term of this presentation of Lacanian topology. The unconscious is to be read, to be listened to, of course, because reading these traces, like the process of association between words, hides the letters left behind by the forbidden *jouissance* inside the Möbien shift of speech. This is why it is inscribed, as a letter (secret, deformed), as over-under in the drawing of the Möbien torsion, allowing the torsion itself to appear in the transference, in the whole relation with a therapist. And in this torsion lies the possibility of bringing back the inscription as the fixed letter of a symptom. When an interpretation effects a cut, it means that some words come, at the right time, at the right place, for a global point of view, at this present moment, to push away the fixation of that torsion.

Moreover, the psychoanalyst has to know that the pain comes from fixed letters, but "no fixation" is painful in itself. Here is the place of fantasy.

Figure 1–3.

The projective plan, a surface without edge, on the Möbius strip itself is necessary for fantasy, and the articulation between a subject, his or her desire, and the object in the world to which his or her subjective life gives such great importance. This surface "plays in some sense the same role of complement in relation to the initial eight (Möbius strip or interior eight) as a sphere in relation to a circle. A sphere would close what the circle would already offer itself as ready to contain."[17]

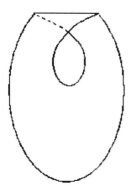 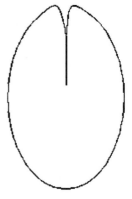

Figure 1–4.

The whole set is there between the Möbien process and the continuity of *jouissance*. Anyway, this last drawing is a little too complicated to describe, or to speak about simply. It is the limit of that topology. In the following topology, Lacan passes on towards knots.

A set's harmony is not set forever, in fact never, nor madness either. Transference is the way anybody, if he or she accepts to speak and speak again, may discover a set of connections that will enable him or her to be happy. But it is not the purpose of the psychoanalyst himself, for the simple reason that desire constituted in such a way that it is as if it is the psychoanalyst's desire, cannot be that of the patient! (in a global point of view). The psychoanalyst comes inside too, near the articulation between *jouissance* and speech. It is the way he is therapeutic, so he cannot be anything else . . . never, nothing must be added, rigorously, not even your supervisor.[18] Whatever now orients social praxis, it claims to work for the happiness of the clients.

To summarize, the Möbius strip allows us to experiment with a model to explain three dichotomies at once: signifier versus signified, enunciation versus the statement, and sense versus signification. I propose the same plan that Pierre Soury uses:[19]

signifiant (signifier)	signifié (signified)
sens (meaning)	signification (meaning)
énonciation (enunciation)	énoncé (enunciated)

Figure 1–5.

- "Signifier versus Signified" is founded in this local space, always in fact named by way of an object and in a frame. This is the space of scientific works. In this view, the things (under) are separated from words that name them (top), unless you prefer the things to be on top and the words to be underneath . . . What matters is that they are separated.
- "Sense versus signification" stands as the very space of the cut and of the interpretation. Every interpretation moves the surface's material (*ensemble tissu ou chose*) from unilateral to bilateral, so it turns into a signification (affect and word, past and present, unconscious and conscious, idea and picture . . .), the sense of an element, for example, the double sense, the superposed meanings of a symptom . . . In this cut the one hole of the whole set appears, for example, the Phallus, as the compacification of that nothing.[20] Therefore, sexuality is the very origin of the symptom, as Sigmund Freud asserts, from 1900.
- "Enunciation versus statement" is the nearest to the question of transmission, to other fields of knowledge and praxis. Here the lie and truth sit, when we speak about a "false-self" or authentic subjective desire, or project. It is not scientific exactitude. Anyway, this dimension is the place of the relations between psychoanalysis and social praxis. When every psychoanalyst is also a doctor, there are no words pronounced by the analyst which are not under this signifier, as the place of enunciation. What happens there is that, whatever you want, the whole set supposes you want the good for your patient, and you have to do so. It is a compact place at the very structure's place that needs a hole. In transference, truth imposes itself to make a hole, to organize a place of nothing. It is the place of lies. It is possible and the modern movies show this many times.

The best instance for the discourse in this text appears in the 1998 winner of the Grand Prix du Jury at the Cannes Film Festival, *Life Is Beautiful* by Roberto Benigni. The whole of this movie is built to produce these following statements. In the last quarter of the story:

> —They're going to make buttons out of us, said Giosué, the son.
> —Giosué, what are you saying, asks his father.
> —They're going to put us in the oven.
> —But who told you that?
> —A man began to cry and he said they're going to make buttons and soap with us.
> Guido burst out laughing . . .
> —Giosué! You've let yourself be abused once more. And I thought you were an alert and clever little boy!

A scene follows for five minutes where Guido takes one of his buttons, and says, "Giorgio fell out of my hands" or "I am washing myself with Bartholomeo" . . . at the end, "*Un beau jour, on va finir par te dire qu'avec nous, il feront des abats jour, des presse-papiers, et toi tu prends au sérieux, demain matin j'ai une course de sacs avec les méchants.*" (One fine day, they're going to end up telling you that they'll make lamp shades and paper presses, and you're going to take that seriously. Let us take some things seriously. Tomorrow morning I have to run an errand with some bags with the bad guys.)[21]

Only, the spectator knows that Guido's sentences are a lie, or nearly so. Only in the enunciation does the truth shine, unsaid, and the third person is the only one able to bear the truth. This structure always works in social praxis. And this operation is formalized in the topology not as a cut, not really, but as a cut and its repair (iligature).[22] The operation digs the two edges to lead the third person—and not the son, one edge, or the father, the other edge—to bear the fact that: these "two" are not two, but only one: I bear the truth as an evanescent subject and know what it is in reality, in the end. The whole set is constructed for this "only one," namely for the very specific unity of a human being.

This sort of game between the statement and the enunciation is the point through which transmission may occur, because, in psychoanalysis it does not matter what the object of material transmission is, nor the psychic something you can say with words, but the very whole of a situation, with words, objects, reality, love (from the father towards the son, from the son towards the father) and with the essential possibility of psychic freedom (as creative) before things. . . . Indeed, saying "hole" or "nothing" is not what matters because it is not negation in itself, even if negation is the very term needed to speak about "that" in language. What matters is certainly not really saying it, because of the necessary closure inside a signification. It is the moment where language finds its limits.

I think you will accept that we can say "hole," even if we are not talking about a sphere's hole as a tissue's tear, or a torus's hole, inside and intimate outside, (*extime*)[23]—though they are not without connection here—but the Möbius strip's hole. This last hole is always present; it does not merely hang on its edge, but on the torsion of its edge, and it is visible only in its under-over inversion, thus through an inscribed point, a sort of global letter. I will say that this is the point of enunciation, the moment where the "said" turns over into the "unsaid," the point where it may forever be just a subject who bears having an unconscious, in the ignorance of what it is, in the actual present, and who disappears in the same act.

Now that the topology of language in its connections with *jouissance* and writing has been demonstrated, we can use it to distinguish social praxis from psychoanalytic treatment by defining the transference as being the same for each, but not the frame. For, if reality is the frame of social praxis, it is not the frame of the treatment and so the psychoanalyst's act will be different.

SOCIAL PRAXIS

In the first place, there is the similarity: transference. Let us remember that Freud said: "It is not a fact that transference emerges with greater intensity and lack of restraint during psycho-analysis than outside it. In institutions in which nerve patients are treated non-analytically, we can observe transference occurring with the greatest intensity and in the most unworthy forms, extending to nothing less than mental bondage" (Freud, "The Dynamics of Transference" [1912] *SE* 12:95–108, p. 101).[24]

Somebody offers the transfer to somebody else. The function of such transference is to propose a frame in which everything (words, lacks, or exaltations . . .) will count as an element of the situation. The effects of the intimate relation, in the moment of speaking out of *jouissance*, are not created by psychoanalysis. The transference is the whole Möbius strip's topology in action. The psychoanalyst and his patient are connected together by affects arising from one edge or the other, which, for the unique set of the situation, are the same in the turning of language. It is based on forbidden (indeed sexual) *jouissance*, of course, because language is, for the whole set, opposed to *jouissance*. Here, pleasure is the measure according to which somebody can accept *jouissance* into the flux of words. The drive is the term for the flux, before, or in the moment where this continuity connects with the body, and the body's holes. Everyone is different in this regard, and may change to a greater or lesser extent. There is a story, a subjective story. Transference is the way to produce speech about something which has not yet been caught by words, and this requirement writes a new moment of the subjective story. There will be a new past, a new construction of the past, indeed, and for the whole set a new future, and a present that will necessarily be different.

I cannot see why the effectuation of the whole set in a frame would be reserved for a psychoanalytic frame *stricto sensu*. Demand for the standard scenario, three times a week, with payment for each session, at the same intimate place, with no direct eye contact, is a solution, but it is not the only one. And many exist. What is important is that one incorporate the whole set and its characteristics within the analysis. This was done in a 1997 movie about treatment (*Good Will Hunting*) with Robin Williams: The conflict is in the same institution between a therapist and his colleague. It occurs when one begins to pay the other and this is shown as an essential moment in the set for understanding the transference and the story of the patient. This conflict does not lie outside the possibility of treatment, which is nothing really new for this side of the Atlantic! The way to make a transference therapy is to globalize, but not through the frame itself. The frame is the limit towards the outside. The frame is the function that requires a local limit and it is allowed inside a global-relation. The topology of the Möbius strip allows this. The part is, in essence, not smaller than the whole set.

So social therapies work within the same transference, but with a different frame. There is no difference between them on that point. Social therapies use a social frame. And what is it? It is a reality larger than the regular appointments in a psychoanalytic room. But this is why reality itself, for Freud and Lacan, is a construction of discourse. And we have to argue for that if we want to use transference here.

For the linguist there is the *"point de contrôle,"* the control point, like a table or book, where everybody agrees that the reality is the same between a word and a thing. In speech these control points name some certainty in which communication is able to be guaranteed by the materiality of things. But materiality is not objectivity and quantitative physics shows us this. Never mind! As soon as reality concerns words and stories between humans, everything becomes complicated.[25]

The reality of a given situation, about which different actors would agree for the most part, is therefore an effect of discourse, which means that reality is built by the set of actors. The social worker is called in when such agreement is missing because of the reality, indeed, inside the reality. No successful agreement has been built into a necessary common share around some objective and material control points that are possible to see, to perceive, with respect to the different versions of each actor.

A contrario, a psychoanalyst chooses to listen to only one of several actors of a situation. He excludes listening to the husband and the wife, the mother and the child, . . . and so on. In such a frame there is no control point. The doctor has the objective signs of his auscultation, the teacher has the exercise notes, the judge has the investigations of the police . . . and the testimony of the witness. What has the social worker got? In the same way, every one of these professions may consider also, beyond the dimension of the control points, the whole set of the transfer relation. Never mind! Is the psychoanalyst the only one to remain in the sole dimension of transference? What about the social worker? Like the psychoanalyst, the social worker has no control points either. He has no auscultation, he has no investigation, and he has no notes. So, can somebody answer a little for each one?

I claim that the social worker also has to work within the sole dimension of transference and recognize in the demands made to the social, an effect of the plunging (*plongement*) of speech into a group. The loneliness of the psychoanalyst's room is a lure. A social worker, and he or she may be a psychoanalyst, has the social mission of allowing a reality to be constructed between each individual's version and the partial agreement of the group as a whole. The reality is not a concept, not an objective thing, unless under the form of a conquest, forever to be performed all over again.

This is how it is given by Lacan in schema R, which flattens a cross-cap, or simply a Möbius strip.[26]

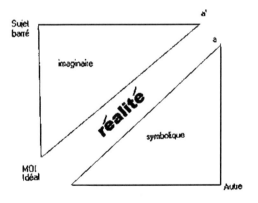

Figure 1–6.

In this schema, the reality is limited to one edge by the Imaginary and on the other by the Symbolic. The transference goes through it, from the "Other" place towards the "subject," which has to be supposed by the unconscious. The process of treatment is the whole of this diagonal, and the social worker has to do the same work in a nearer area. And in a torsion frequently found in structuralism, this means that the social worker has a larger point of view. His or her act is not the same; he or she does not work with the fantasy.

So schema R is in fact closed as a projective plane. Once this closure has been achieved, it is possible to show the fantasy as Lacan formalizes it: "It is as the representative of the representation in fantasy; therefore, that is to say as the originally repressed subject that $, the barred S of desire, here supports the field of reality, and this field is sustained only by the extraction of the object a, which, however, gives it its frame" (*Ecrits: A Selection*, p. 223).

Thus in topology, surface topology, there is a frame supported by an extraction, for example, an exclusion operating towards a point of view which is, however, necessary to the point of departure. This diagonal of reality appears simple as a rectangular bilateral, but when the whole of the set is turned over, as a Möbius strip,[27] through the function of time, it reveals itself as the cut of fantasy.

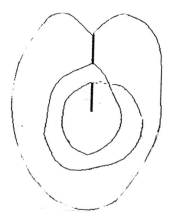 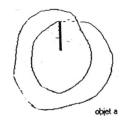

Figure 1–7.

The fantasy is an organization of letters which form a psychical apparatus out of which the subject, armed only with language, makes an instrument to be adapted to the world. The subject is born in language and this experience forms a sort of screen that takes every outside perception inside itself. Psychoanalysis teaches us that without a fantasy, the subject cannot see the world, and, at best, the subject enters into a delusion. Delusion is an attempt to take over from the absent fantasy, which issues from the Oedipus constellation. This aspect of psychoanalysis is well known and I will not discuss it further here.

The Möbien model, as a cutting of a projective plane, shows that the continuity of *jouissance* is delimited by language as a Möbien topology: So, in this limitation itself, from the global point of view of this cutting, a subject and an object—cause of desire, Lacan's object *a*, as a strange disk, that a body and its holes (ear, eyes, mouth, anus, or sexual parts)—are separated and made consistent through the imposition of a material edge. It is the object particular to a psychoanalytic treatment and certainly not the object of a social praxis, which knows more about this object than a few traces. Because social praxis concerns all the objects of a social life, like happiness, money, school, and so on, there is no place for the object *a* in itself. But fantasy is not to be changed. In the structure, what is changeable is only the social objects which translate the object *a* in a world. Translation according to fantasy is the act of social praxis and it is the effectuation of nothing but a showing of a hole, like the father's lies in *Life Is Beautiful*.

I hope you have been able to obtain, through these many words, a view of Lacanian topology as a way of thinking about the psychical apparatus. There are many other ways and it is the matter of this topology to leave each one bearing the words he says in front of a figure, which is not one of words, but a writing. Nobody can subtract another from this attempt. It is not a matter of comprehension, but a matter of your act, dear reader, when you use it. For psychoanalysis there is nothing anywhere else.

ENDNOTES

1. The citation in French is: *"Les éléments d'une structure n'ont ni désignation extrinsèque, ni signification intrinsèque, que reste-t-il? Comme Lévi-Strauss le rappelle avec rigueur, ils n'ont rien d'autre qu'un sens: un sens qui est nécessairement et uniquement de 'position'"* ("The elements of a structure have neither extrinsic nor intrinsic meaning; what remains? As Lévi-Strauss recalls with rigor, they have nothing other than a sense, a sense which is necessarily and uniquely of 'position.'"). Gilles Deleuze, *Le structuralisme* in *La philosophie au XXème siècle*, Marabout, 1979, Paris, p. 298.

2. There it is! the first example; the English word is "subversive." It is the same word as *subversif* in the French. CQFD (*ce qu'il fallait démontrer* = what was to be proved).

3. It is a question here of the essential findings from J.-P. Gilson's work, thesis of 1992, L'université catholique de Louvain, published under the title, *Topologie du sujet*. Montréal, Canada, 1994.

4. Sigmund Freud, *G.W.* II–III, 541.

5. Jacques Lacan, in *Ecrits*, *Kant avec Sade*, p. 771.

6. *Ibid.*

7. Rebus: a game where pictures represent the syllables of words.

8. Sigmund Freud, in *Analyse profane*, Folio p. 151. I owe to François Pouppez the idea that this possibilty is, in fact, an ethic.

9. René Lew: French term for *nachträglich*: *Freud ou l'autre rationnalité* in *Psychanalyse et reforme de l'entendement*, Lysimaque, Paris, 1997, p. 261. Lysimaque@wanadoo.fr.

10. Richard Abibon has offered this difference between an orientable disk, but not oriented, or not nonorientable, but also not oriented, which does not know it, in his work on *L'autisme*, (*tome* 1, p. 138, EF Edition, Paris, 1999). And the ensemble of *tome* 2 appeared in 2000.

11. These three words, consistency (Imaginary), existence (Real), and the hole (Symbolic), are the terms that Lacan uses and defines the whole year long in *Le séminaire RSI*, in 1975.

12. Here is the French formula: *"Un signifiant représente un sujet pour un autre signifiant."* ("A signifier represents a subject for another signifier.") "Every" is a Latin-originated word. They are the same as in French. CQFD.

13. Jacques Lacan, *Ecrits*, in *Subversion du sujet et dialectique du désir*, Paris 1966, p. 821: *"Ce à quoi il faut se tenir c'est que la jouissance est interdite à qui parle comme tel."* ("What you have to hold onto is that jouissance is forbidden to him who speaks as such.")

14. Marc Darmon, *Essai de topologie lacanienne*, Editions de l'Association Freudienne, Paris 1990, chapter 311 seqq.

15. The theory of chaos shows that the measures of objects, such as the coast of Bretagne, depend on the framework.

16. From the text of the song by Leonard Cohen.

17. Jacques Lacan, *Le séminaire* XI, 1964, published at Seuil, Paris, 1973, p. 143.

18. Just a little point, for the problem of the transmission of psychoanalysis. At this place, the patient would necessarily want to remain with his or her analyst, and necessarily, the psychoanalyst must get rid of him or her. It can only be done in the suffering of "unbeing" (*désêtre*), a term invented in French by Lacan for this necessary separation which holds uniquely to a global point of view, always, nonexistent, however, unpronounceable, non-objectifiable, the place of the ethic.

19. Pierre Soury, second part, *text* 100, edited by Michel Thomé and Christian Leger, Paris, Nov. 1988. He was my main teacher in topology, and I thank him.

20. Lacan's most consistent text on the subject is in *Encore, Le séminaire* XX, 1972, appeared at Seuil, Paris, 1975, p. 14 seqq.

21. The *text* has been published in the collection *Folio*, p. 212, *Folio*, Paris, 2000.

22. It is a future work that I am producing with Yves Baumstiller, Professor at l'Université de Paris VII.

23. "*Extime*" is a word forged by J.-A. Miller for the central hole of the torus. It is constructed on the contraction between "*intime*" and the preposition "*ex.*"

24. Sigmund Freud, *La technique psychanalytique*, Paris PUF, 1977, p. 53.

25. *Pratiques sociales en dette de la psychanalyse*; in this book I have given an example, commented on at length, of reality as an agreement of discourse among several persons. Point hors ligne, Eres, Paris, 1994.

26. *Ecrits*, in *Traitement possible de la psychose*, 1955, Seuil, Paris, 1966, p. 553 seqq, and the note added in 1966.

27. Topologically, a long series of designs is necessary to show it, and I have done this work in an article published by *Littoral* no 3, Eres, Toulouse, February 1982.

2

Mathemes: Topology in the Teaching of Lacan*

JACQUES-ALAIN MILLER

The conference organizers have suggested that I speak on topology in the teaching of Lacan, on the reasoning and importance of such a reference, on the reason why Lacan uses it. This seems to me to be a proper theme. Lacan regards topology as important, this is a fact. But, why?

Let's begin with the easy part—I won't draw any figures on the blackboard, except maybe something very basic—I will try to define the place of, and justify the importance of topology in the whole of the teaching of Lacan.

I am a reader of Lacan and I never fail to bring along his *Ecrits*. This style might perhaps seem more appropriate to a seminar than to a conference, but I think its usefulness rests in the fact that it shows that we aren't here to pore over texts day and night, but rather

*Translated by Mahlon Stoutz, from *Matemas*, Vol. 1, ed. by Diana Rabinovich (in Spanish), Buenos Aires, Argentina: Manantial Press, 1986; ed. by Ellie Ragland (in English).

to try to decipher Lacan, and I think we will be doing that for a long, long time.

Topology cannot be extracted from the teaching of Lacan. This proposition may be taken two ways. In the first place, one cannot cut off the teaching of Lacan from its topological part, on the assumption that it would then be arid, uninteresting and with no relationship to analytic experience. Lacan's topology is present in a discrete way from the time of the *Rome Discourse*, since 1953, where finally, while referring to the primordial function of death, he made his mark in eminent fashion.

Why primordial? In his vocabulary of the time, certainly a much more dramatic one, Lacan posits from the very beginning that death is linked to the emergence of the Symbolic order. He says so in a Hegelian manner, a fact important in itself: the symbol manifests itself first as the death of the thing. The symbol does not adhere to the thing, between the two there is no natural sympathy or accommodation; on the contrary, there is antipathy and a need for doing away with the notion that thanks to the symbol the thing becomes manifest. The symbol eternalizes the thing, it allows it to persist beyond its existence and, for example, it allows the human subject to be the object of reference beyond the limits of its existence. This analyst is quite Hegelian inasmuch as the Symbolic is not a correlate to the whole world, but instead functions as a release for the substance and materiality of this world. The materiality of the symbol is a supplementary one, an extra.

Nevertheless, it conditions death and Freudian desire, desire as eternal, desire that, unlike necessity, is not connected to this or that object in particular. Lacan recalls that the subject prior to speech is unreachable, except with regard to its death, to its significant mortification. The speaking subject, having been displaced by the symbol, immediately suffers mortification that will then make of it, for Lacan, a subject mortified by the signifier, $.

How do we situate death as it pertains to the symbol, co-substantial with it—even though the word "substance" is problematic—with regard to the function of the speech of the subject? We can simply say that death is what comes after life, it is something totally external to the speaking subject while the subject is sustained in the living being. If we admit, however, that in the speaking subject, mortified by the signifier, that death is not merely something beyond life, but that it is a function installed in the very nucleus of the experience of speech, we must then differentiate it from the death experience of the human qua animal. For the human animal, Lacan says, death is affected by the passage from the unconsciousness of life to death. On the other hand, death present in the subject of the symbolic occupies a central place in speech. From it, everything concerned with the existence of the subject acquires meaning. This arises especially in the neurotic question directed toward the existence of the subject. This mortal sense is, at the same time, external to language and central to the exercise of speech.

At this point Lacan introduces topology into his writings for the first time: *"To say that this mortal sense reveals in speech a center external to language is more than a metaphor and reveals a structure."*[1]

All the problems associated with Lacan's topology are present in this first phase. That one is dealing with a structure is obviated by the fact that a center with a conduit to speech has come into play: this is the paradox, a point at the same time central and external. This is the leap that Lacan makes. Many philosophers have approached this paradox; the thing about Lacan is that he wasn't satisfied just with the metaphor but, instead, had to find the structure that this spatial disposition implies.

In *The Atolondradicho*[2] [*L'étourdit*], and still farther along, we find this same movement dealing with spatialization: a rejection of metaphor and the implication of structure, until finally reaching the point where the problematic statute of the "real" is proposed. This movement is constant in Lacan. Where once only metaphor could be found, he once again institutes the structure that sustains it and, a third point, proposes that these same structures are related to the very Real that is in play. Let us again take up Lacan's paragraph: *"This structure is different from the spatialization of the circumference of the sphere in which some people like to schematize the limits of the living being and his milieu: it actually corresponds more closely to that relational grouping that symbolic logic designates topologically as a torus (annulus).*"[3]

So what are we talking about? If we delimit a space, we can situate an external point in it. The problem, linked to analytic experience and Lacan's own construction of the relationship between death and the Symbolic (order), is that we must again seek this exterior area in the interior. This death, perhaps too dramatic a term, is not merely peripheral, it is central as well. This is, simply put, the position of "internal exclusion" we encounter repeatedly at all levels of the analytic experience and of the investigation of said phenomenon which Lacan pursued throughout the periods of his teaching.

Thus, the thing Lacan hoped to introduce is justified. That which he would only develop many years later, a representation, a topological form: "*If one wanted to give an intuitive representation, it seems that more than the superficiality of an area, it is to the tri-dimensional form of a torus, that one should have recourse, by virtue of the fact that its peripheral exteriority and its central exteriority do not constitute more than a single space.*"[4] Precisely, the torus is introduced as a figure that allows the fundamental relationship of internal exclusion to be sustained.

There is much still to be said about this very first introduction of topology regarding its connection to death. We will see, shortly, how the construction of desire in Lacan is the logical consequence of it. The object of desire was first placed somewhat beyond the vector of desire, as if it were the thing towards which desire was being directed, and because it is metonymic, this object is fundamentally unattainable. A crucial movement in the teaching of Lacan came about when the object that causes desire was distinguished from the object of desire; the former, in fact, is nearer than the vector, which makes sense because the progression of desire can never recover the object that caused it in the first place. Again we have a relationship that makes us think of internal exclusion.

At this point, the biological human animal and its inconsistent march towards death should be compared to that which Lacan still calls the human being, capable of desiring death. It was not by blind chance that the example offered up by Lacan's pen, as topology first emerged, dealt with being destined for death: Empedocles throwing himself into Mount Etna and becoming, through this act, the very symbol of one destined to die. Nor was it blind chance when Lacan again used the example of Empedocles and his desire to die in another articulation of his topology, in the construction found in *The Position of the Unconscious*,[5] where alienation and separation are formulated. The connection between topology and death in Lacan is no accident; perhaps this gives us some indication as to the theme of his seminar *Topology and Time*.

We will again encounter this structure of internal exclusion when Lacan attempts to construct his topology of *jouissance*, going so far as to invent a term with more impact than internal exclusion, the term *extimacy*, which replaces the initial prefix of intimacy with the prefix -*ex*. He thereby resolves, in a single word, the difficult conjunction of a noun and an adjective that is fundamentally its opposite. This structure can also be useful in understanding repression, inasmuch as neurotic repression is linked to the return of that which is repressed in psychoanalytic theory. It's not enough to propose an external limit in the case of repression; one must also keep in mind the modalities of its return on what would be the internal surface.

When dealing with foreclosure, a different logic and different combinatory principles are required. Foreclosure is exclusion towards the exterior. When the term foreclosure is used, it becomes a correlate to a return in another dimension of the excluded element; in other words, that which is foreclosed in the Symbolic order returns in the Real.

Starting with a certain number of structures from the Lacanian clinic, the term extimacy allows us to form a series. There is in Lacan a continuous effort to reabsorb that which is pathematic in that which is mathematic, an effort which does not culminate in a complete reabsorption, an effort *The Atolondradicho* regards as the "conquest of psychoanalysis." Thus, for example, we have the fascination with the "much"; the name for this experience in Lacan is mysticism; psychoanalysis produces a matheme where the mystic finds an object of fascination. Obviously, not everything in psychoanalytic experience can be expressed with mathemes, but the thing that constitutes the stunning advance of Lacan's teaching is the constant effort to obtain mathemes of that experience that, in effect, it is impossible to express everything with a matheme. When one gives up on this effort, analytic practice tends to be an autonomous one and may be limited to nothing more than a fascination with the unsayable. Lacan's topology, of course, participates electively in this effort at mathematization, that is to say, in the effort to release the relationships that come into play among the terms present in the analytic experience. The sphere and the plane are not enough to represent these relationships as both are utilized in the case of animals.

This is a constant reference in Lacan, taken from the classic ethologists of the latter part of the nineteenth and early part of the twentieth centuries. This type of schematism is good enough in the case of animals. We could say that animals are in a position concentric to their environment, a position that adjusts itself precisely to that environment. There is accommodation between the animal and the *Umwelt*, between the environment and the *Innenwelt* which is the animal itself. Now, the first discovery of the analytic experience was that in the case of the subject of the word that's not the way it works. We cannot represent the relationship between the subject and desire in this way. It cannot demonstrate what it is that causes this harmony to be out of tune in the subject. One need only to ponder this paradox which Freud formulated as the death drive.

In the second place, this topology cannot be extracted from the teaching of Lacan with the intention of making it an independent discipline. This topology is useful only when embedded in the teaching of Lacan; it is not a discipline sui generis. Specialists in Lacanian topology shouldn't regard it as the whole of their teaching, as is the case with the *Innenwelt* and the *Umwelt* for example. We may take what happened to the idea that Freud practiced applied psychoanalysis as a reference point. It was thought that there was, on the one hand, the psychoanalytic experience, and on the other, the many areas understood by the university community, such as ethnology, folklore, history of art, and so forth. Whenever Freud referred to art history or ethnology, the thing that concerned him was always a question that had arisen in the analytic experience, and he would resort to these references in order to answer the question. *Totem and Taboo* is not an anthropological work: it was Freud's approach to the question of the father in analysis that forced him, for structural reasons, to resort to a mythical elaboration. In the case of Lacan, there is no way to imagine that the areas in which psychoanalysis is applied can be made autonomous.

In any case, there is no need to make Lacan's scientific references an autonomous pursuit, nor to create specialists in Lacanian topology, Lacan's theory of games, and so forth. If such a tendency were to develop, the result would be as empty as that of applied psychoanalysis, a fact that is especially true in the case of Lacan's topology, which can hardly be transformed into a discipline sui generis. So, what comprises this topology? First of all, there are three objects, and no more, with a very simple mechanism: we find them nowadays in game books, crossword-puzzle books, and so forth. This topology is on the same plane as analytical geometry and the three surfaces of this discipline which are referred to classically as *analisis situs*. These three objects are the Möbius strip, the Klein bottle, and the cross-cap, a somewhat more complex figure introduced by Lacan at a given moment in his seminar on identification. Second are the knots, precisely the Borromean knot, introduced in *Seminar XX, Encore*, which was transformed into the seminar *R.S.I.*, in a much more complex and more recent chapter on the teaching of Lacan, based on a mathematics that is itself unfinished, different from the former. Lacan's topology, then, is comprised by these two quite heterogeneous chapters (although they do share some points in common) and nothing else. Each one responds to questions on analytic theory that are not exactly the same.

Lacan's theory with regard to these schema is this: "*They aren't a metaphor.*" He had already said so in 1953 and is still saying so. He criticizes, and in fact makes fun of, the fact that Freud's schemas did not pretend to be the same kind of thing, because Freud always considered them to be illustrations. Lacan is especially critical of the schema of the second topic in the Caracas Seminar, where he opposes it to the Borromean knot. Topology, Lacan says, is not metaphor, it represents a structure, going so far as to propose that in some way the Real itself comes to bear on experience. It is necessary to qualify this assignation of the Real with regard to both structure and topology. This knot, composed of "metaphor, structure and Real," is a critical point for those especially interested in Lacan's topology. We represent this topology, we manipulate it spatially; sometimes Lacan enhances its value to the point of showing an enjambment of knots and saying: "*This is the thing itself.*" For many, this seemed excessive.

Topology consists of a series of matrices, of signifying combinatives. Only in a secondary sense, due to the birth of the thing, do we consider a space to be involved. Fundamentally, Lacan's topology (and he himself insisted on this point) may be integrally reduced to a set. This makes up part of the chapter concerning the topic of the signifier. The elemental graph, the Z schema, the one with the letters alpha and beta, the bi-level graph, all these are part of the same series, and we must not forget the combinative of the four discourses. All of these exercises may then be subsumed under a single term: the combinative. This term allows one to perceive that topology cannot be isolated in the teaching of Lacan. Topology is introduced with the signifier; wherever there is no signifier; wherever there is no "capture" on the part of the Symbolic, topology is unnecessary; in such cases, the topology of the sphere and the plane will suffice.

We may retain these ideas with a correction made by Lacan himself: every living body has a topology and therefore cannot be reduced to a simple extension, to a Cartesian *partes extra partes*. This explains how Lacan was able to launch into configurations of the living, human body, as torii, and so forth. These are inspirations more or less equivalent to "limits" in the same sense that we can find topological forms in nature, such as those found in cerebral membranes. Nevertheless, it is necessary to put a stop to such types of commentary as they otherwise turn into a philosophy of nature. We see then, with the correction that was just made, that topology is founded on the signifier. From this angle, what do combinatives, topology, even set theory, and theory of classes have in common? What do they have in common with something represented as a net, an axiom, and so forth? What all these things have in common is the key to understanding topology's place in Lacanian teaching: their common point is that they only need two dimensions to function. The place of the other in the Lacanian sense (which is the unconscious and the discourse) has no profundity. At this point, the style and the experience of the analysis directed by Lacan is opposed to everyone's experience: the unconscious is a superficial entity, not one of profundity. The unconscious is not something one has inside oneself. It is very difficult to think, maintain, or get used to the fact that the unconscious has no profundity; that it is not an internal thing. On the contrary, it is fundamentally external to the subject, to the point that the Symbolic order—a new concept and point of departure for Lacan's rethinking of Freud—is also the common discourse, all of which is tradition, that which speaks before the subject arises. The Other is just that, not simply the other in lowercase. In the greater range of its uppercase, the Other is our exteriority, the exteriority of every subject. If one reads *Seminar XI*, it is possible to appreciate the fact that the unconscious is not in the subject and the analyst is not there to make him spit it out; rather, the unconscious is exterior with regard to both of them and both ask for the opening of something that is still a space. In other words, the topology of the surface should lead us along a path where there is nothing intuitive about the unconscious.

I should revise a bit what I just said about topology being introduced with the signifier. This is exactly right, but it would be a mistake to conclude that the whole field of psychoanalysis might be reduced to whatever the signifier is, that all of analysis could be reduced to what Lacan highlighted in his text "The Agency of the Letter."[6] The agency of the letter exists, but it must be articulated with drive theory. In *Seminar XI, The Four Fundamental Concepts of Psychoanalysis*, Lacan did not include desire amongst them, he included drive. Of the four concepts, the most important thing is choice. For example, transference has traditionally been reduced to repetition; there was no distinguishing the two things and it is precisely their distinction that conditions the invention of the subject supposed to know. The subject supposed to know may be the motivation of the transference to the condition of having eliminated repetition as motivation. Desire, says Lacan in *The Place of the Unconscious*, depends on a topology rather than a dynamics. In any case, any dynamics depends on the signifier, because they depend on a number of signifying apparatuses in the world. We should recall the example Lacan cited frequently: Where is the energy in a waterfall? We must begin by providing it with energy (a dynamics), which assumes the introduction of a signifier so that the dynamics might make some sense. Lacan did not leave us with much information on the topology of the drive. But he did give us enough information if we retrace our steps to where reference is made to Stokes' theorems in *The Place of the Unconscious*,[7] and if we look particularly at vectorial analysis, all of this appearing, by the way, in an unexplored chapter of the greatest importance for understanding Lacan's topology.

Let us take the first inclination of topology, prior to *R.S.I.* On the one hand it is a topology of the subject and, correlatively, that of the object *a* and drive as well; the topology of the object *a* connects the two axes. What, then, does topology allow us to do with regard to these two points? Without topology, Lacan would have been unable to develop the insubstantial subject required by analysis. We use s.s.s. to say subject supposed to know (*sujet-supposé-savoir*); the same initials could designate insubstantial subject (*sujet-sans-substance*). The insubstantial subject is also the Cartesian subject Lacan proposes as the very subject of psychoanalysis, the subject that is nothing more than punctual once all of its properties and representations have been removed. In analysis, the subject has generally been treated as a substantial one, a subject that resists, an instinctual subject. Sustaining a discourse that induces a disjunction of subject and substance implies a supremely complex construct. This disjunction is already present in Aristotle's categories; there is no doubling between subject and substance, both terms have their own particular functions. For Lacan the insubstantial subject is sustained in topology and logic. We will again encounter the subject mortified by the signifier under the heading of insubstantial subject, which may be written with the help of what Lacan calls the general sign in the Möbius strip, the inverted eight; like that which, in the formulas of sexuation, serves only the purpose of being a variable of the phallic function.

I tried to find a reference to what it might be like to try to elaborate an insubstantial subject without recourse to mathemes. Descartes's subject is insubstantial in a very fleeting way; it is found in the fifth paragraph of the *Second Meditation*, but it immediately recovers its substance. Someone, based on Descartes, once tried to elaborate an insubstantial subject, someone who had a good deal of influence on Lacan, who was trying to reject the promotion of psychoanalysis of the *I* in the analytic experience carried on by the Anglo-Saxons. I am talking about Sartre, who is one of Lacan's references at the beginning of *Seminar II*,[8] who contributes to the achievement of an extreme statute of the subject, a statute of total desubstantiation, one of Sartre's intuitions. An opposition arises. On the one hand there is the self, the being as that which it is, a definition Lacan gives us in *Seminar III* when he talks of psychosis and suggests that here the Real is treated as that which it is, just like Sartre's insubstantial subject. Sartre attempts to isolate it through the magic of style; thus in *Being and Nothingness* he says: "The being of consciousness cannot be reconciled with itself in a preliminary acceptation."[9] The onset of identity is still regarded as a synthesis, or a unification; but when dealing with this being who is starting to crack, there is neither self identity nor coincidence. The bar that strikes the blows is the same one that distances the subject from the pure and simple onset of identity. Sartre perceived the consequences correctly: the subject is subject to identifying itself. Because there is a loss at the level of onset of identity, the individual in question is identified. There is an immediate relationship at the level of onset of identity and the tendency towards identification, something that Sartre analyzed quite well at the level of the Imaginary. I believe you know the famous example of the young man in a café who believes himself to be a young man in a café, an example of identification with the Imaginary sustained by a subject with a loss of identity.

Some formulas: "resemble your own coincidence," "escape your identity," "the subject is separated from himself and what separates him from himself is nothing," "the self (*para-site*) exists in the form of another side with regard to itself," "a being that is affected constantly by the inconsistency of being." Sartre then speaks of a lack of being, a defect of the individual. We have here a series of successful metaphors; they have the term lack, the connection between desire and lack. Sartre suggested that human reality must be lack in itself because it causes lack to arise and, whereby, the existence of desire as a human fact should be enough to prove it. Desire is not a psychic state; it is an escape from itself, a lack of being. I have only mentioned what I thought necessary to be able to perceive the lineage of the kind of being Lacan tried to depict in the case of the subject. The greatest difference is that the subject's loss of identity is never thought of with regard to the opaque self, and which is not situated at any time with regard to language.

When dealing with an insubstantial subject, Lacan would utilize the matheme, distinguishing, first of all, the conjectural aspects. He discovered a way, in the theory of games, of sets, and in a broader sense in topology's combinative, to assure the subsistence of the subject with no substance whatsoever, by proposing—a proposal not found in Sartre—the place of the Other as a space of combinatives, the condition for proposing the insubstantial subject, in which all the substance of the analytic experience resides. Lacan evokes a single substance as the substance of analysis: *jouissance*.

A space of combinatives, a symbolic space where the signifiers are articulated, where their chains are extended, a space that has nothing in common with any intuitive space or an aesthetic one in the Kantian sense. This can already be seen in the mirror stage, the first entry of an element foreign to the field of analysis, because the mirror stage is not a psychoanalytical experience, but, rather, one of observation. At the mirror stage the body is present essentially as an Imaginary body. We will have to develop all of the teaching of Lacan in order for us to formulate that the Imaginary is the body. This is very close to what he had already said regarding that which nurtures the fantasmatic life, as to how the Imaginary formations borrow from the fragmentation of the body. The Imaginary arises entirely from the body parts of the human being. The beginning of the mirror stage is the excision between the mirror body and the real body, that is to say, the state of maturation of the body. We must admit, however, that this is an experienced body; it is the body assumed to have gotten experience from the subject, facing us then as two types of stasis. It would be excessive to say that only the mirror body existed, but, in any case, there are two bodies; one is seen and the other experienced; in this sense, both of them concern stasis.

If this topology is necessary to sustain the insubstantial subject, it is also necessary with regard to Lacan's invention of the object *a*. Among these objects, Freud found only two: the oral and the anal. Lacan, it turns out—and we might ask thanks to what—added two more: the gaze and the voice, which *après-coup* have become commonplace in clinical analysis. Before Lacan the existence of voyeurism and exhibitionism were known, and it was known that psychotics hear voices. Once Lacan had elevated these two terms to the status of objects, they were never again questioned. How is it, then, that Freud did not discover them, when it is obvious that he organized his clinical texts around them? I believe it was due to a substantialist illusion; the two objects give us the sense of being material and, besides, they depend on demand; the breast is the object of demand to the Other, and the feces remit us to the demand of the other. Finally, the Other of demand is always the one that is pursued; this is the one in question. The gaze is something that is completely evanescent. It is quite difficult to admit that the eye is an object, one, even, with which a novelist might write a story. The obstacle standing in the way of acceptance of the gaze as an object resided in the fact that a substantial object was desired. The same thing happens with the light materiality of the voice; let us be content in this regard by remembering mental automatism. Lacan doesn't situate these two objects in the function of demand, but rather in that of desire. Nevertheless, the clinic makes them objects of the drive. The restitution of these last two objects passes through his topology, a fact that, in any case, is evident for the gaze. Without the topology of the gaze, it could not be validated as an authentic object; a support is needed for this insubstantial being, and only topology affords us an adequate support. This determines the great paradox in the field of the drive (*escópica*): that the object is inherent to the drive. Lacan achieved a subtle topological articulation to capture it and, without it, this object would be impossible to sustain. In general, topology is essential to any elaboration of analysis, (. . .) once we have become aware of it, just as Lacan approached it beginning with the Symbolic, that is to say, by emptying it, by erasing all that before had shaped the complete text of analysis, which is to say, the Imaginary formations, when he considered none of them to be determinate but rather that the significant transformations are what really count, and that no compilation of Imaginary formations affords us anything determinate about the subject; as a result of this extraordinary emptying of analysis, only a vacuum remains. Here, in fact, is the thing, for many analysts, that cannot be sustained in Lacan's practice: that he could have been able, through analysis, to arrive at the cut, an insubstantial being par excellence, that he could have first invented the cut as a function of the interception, like scansion, and that he could have progressively reduced the experience itself within a certain mode of knowledge. According to the aggressive variety of thought, which has arisen in recent years, all of this ends with: "But Lacan hadn't been doing [undergoing] psychoanalysis for ten years," in other words, a rather summary conception of the void. This is precisely the consequence of the symbol as death of the thing. It means either that the scope of the world lacks references or the references are missing from the language, that it is illusory to speak of references, and that no matter what extreme twists we manage to inflict on language, it still means something, but to clarify it is another matter.

The matheme's privilege resides in the fact that it is fundamentally the zero of the reference. What does Lacan call discourse?

How can there be discourse without references? This is true for every discourse. Lacan reduces analysis to this, to making the experience out of lack of references; it is an un-sustainable experiment in emptying the experience. And it is un-sustainable for those who should be the agents of this experience, who should put themselves at the level where the lack of references was proven. This is not at all the same thing one observes in the analysis mentioned initially, which was presented as the relationships of personalities typical, for example, of the Oedipus complex. In the end, what animates this movement is the experience of the lack of references, not some simple being. There are many types of holes; the hole is not a simple concept like the one, for example, that Sartre tried to capture at the level of the gaze as simple being. The hole is complex and topology allows us to construct holes while taking their diversity into account, which allows us to subtly explain how the reference is lacking according to the clinical structures.

Obviously it is difficult to maintain a level where signifiers, situations, and references are contradictory. This means that the only reference is signifying. Lacan called it "signification of the phallus," the phallus is the name of the signification inasmuch as this is the only reference that can be reached in analysis. Lacan didn't choose the German term *Bedeutung* gratuitously, the translation of which is always difficult as it might be translated alternatively as reference and signifier.

You are already familiar with the truly elemental topology of the inner eight. It is the bare essential for separating from the circle or the sphere, especially the circle, when reduced to a single point by homotopia. What Lacan demonstrates in his analysis is that the structure of the subject cannot be reduced to the sphere, the circle, or the point; he shows that there is no homotopia of the subject. The ad hoc object invented to mark this irreducibility, this lack of homotopia of the subject, is the object *a*. This is important on several levels. First, because it may be apprehended at the level of discordance between desire and demand. Desire is the effect of the impossible satisfaction of demand, the effect of the impossibility

of the Other to respond to demand, and it is along these lines that
Lacan will come to propose the object *a* as the cause of desire.

Next, this is perceived at the level of word analysis as it is
interpreted in the analysis. The fact that the analytical device might
be an interpretational one requires that the subject be thought out
in two areas that are topologically defined. This is what Lacan explains in his seminar on identification. There is a duplicity of the
subjective condition, reflected, on the other hand, in the two levels
of his diagram. The subject cannot be placed in a single place, a
matter Lacan will return to in *The Place of the Unconscious*, and each
time in a more refined and precise way. When the subject appears
in some place in a given form, it must disappear from someplace
else. There is always a subjective duplicity exactly opposite subjective unity. The subject, forced to constantly flee from itself, is
nothing more than an escape, being the simplest representation of
this duplicity of the inner eight. So we see, in short-circuit, the
relation between logic and topology. Do you know Russell's paradox? In it two terms are connected and one can see that the two
are not compatible in a single space; they are co-related and contradictory at the same time. This is the type of thing that perturbs
spatial relations that can be transcribed in a zone. How does one
become aware of this co-related contradiction? First of all, it may
be said that it is a paradox; secondly, a temporal barrier may be
introduced, that is to say, to situate this movement and say it is a
movement of drive. Every time a term is excluded, it will have to
return, and so on. That is exactly what Lacan proposed with the
topology of the unconscious, which incorporates drive, openings,
and closing of the unconscious. The subject of the unconscious may
also be transcribed according to Russell's paradox. In the third
place, finally, we have the inner eight that explains it, in as much
as the interior-exterior gets crossed up. This is the point at which
our term may be situated in the critical zone else it appear to have
no place. The inner eight is the simplest way to represent the self-
difference Sartre pursued: the self-difference of the signifier insofar as it cannot mean itself, and the self-difference of the subject

insofar as it is represented by a signifier in relation to another. In other words, the inner eight is not a supplementary complexity of topology introduced by Lacan; it is a simplification that frees us from 600 pages of rhetoric such as Sartre's in *Being and Nothingness*.

I would like to finish by addressing an area of topology where things are not apparent. I want to demonstrate the extent to which topology of the surface is essential to a text where there doesn't seem to be much importance, in *The Agency of the Letter*, for instance, the *princeps* and one of Lacan's best known texts. It is present in the letter, because the letter, as Lacan says, is the localized structure of the signifier, which is to say that it requires a space where the distinguishing features of the signifier can be found, features that used to be able to be materialized when the printers still used individual characters, with an individual place for each one. There you have a representation of the localized structure of the signifier. Lacan adds that the signifier is always composed according to the laws of a closed order, which means that the signifying units fit together—there are also relationships of involvement—and a topological substrate is needed for all this, as substrate that is the signifying chain of rings, and each necklace of rings is interlocked with another, and so forth.

You also know that Lacan says linearity is insufficient: the signifying elements must be arranged in a pentagram. It is obvious that the signifier could never be satisfied with the dimensions of a line; at the very least, it needs a surface. When Lacan speaks of a pillowing point (*point de capiton*), one might be inclined to believe that we now need thickness, the three dimensions. Nevertheless, he will situate the pillowing point on the diagram, on the flat two-dimensional plane.

I studied the Anglo-Saxon texts of language that appeared this year and last in the United States and England, in order to see where they were headed, and to see if I could find anything in them that relates to psychoanalysis. In Chomsky's book, one reads a phrase that appears to have been translated, with the addition of negation, from Lacan's text. The negation evidently changes everything, but I can say that the arguments of the latest Chomsky can be refuted in Lacan of 1957, point by point.[10] I simply used *The Agency of the Letter* to make a series with these texts and discuss them, and I found myself faced with a question that had bothered me for some time. You know that Lacan again took up the matter of metaphor and metonymy, particularly in *Radiophonie*,[11] in the third question. There he criticizes a philosophy professor who said interesting things, but at the same time had to be questioned. The professor would have been Lyotard, who wrote an article with the title, "The Work of Dreams Doesn't Think," a text that has as its merit the fact that it allows us a glimpse of Lacan's topology, there where it is almost invisible. Lyotard questions the very axis of Lacan's article, on the one hand the two mechanisms of the dream that are regarded as essential (condensation and displacement), and on the other the two functions so active in discourse (metaphor and metonymy). Lacan's thesis is that there is no difference between them, except that in the dream there is a supplementary condition, an Imaginary one, since one is dealing with images anyway. In dreams there is an Imaginary inertia, which accumulates, and a *mise en scène* composed of figures, all of which, to some degree, make the functioning heavier, but it is still always the same. The interesting thing about Lyotard's work is that he says exactly the contrary; that is, there are laws of the Imaginary, that belong to the figures of the dream, which are, in turn, autonomous with regard to the discourse.

Lacan, instead, remits the "illustrated ordering" to the signifying function. The gift is the incidence of the signifier. Lyotard bases himself on the fact that Freud himself differentiated thought and dreams, and work and dreams. There is no doubt that the thought of the dream exists, and similarly the work of the dream that fabricates this particular form of thought of the dream, and the essential thing in the dream is the work of the dream. In a note to the *Traumdeutung* we find this formula—the amusing thing is that, before Lyotard, Lacan hadn't used this text very much, but from now on it returns as a *leitmotif*—"the work of the dream doesn't think, it limits itself to transforming." Lyotard points out the value of this formula and suggests that the work of the dream, inasmuch as it is different from the thought of the dream, does not give interpretations, does not translate, does not mask; there where the work of masking of the dream cannot be restored through an interpretation, it is an operation sui generis on the image, on the figure, which requires extension and profundity. For example, condensation is like a physical process whereby objects occupying a given space are compressed to fit into a smaller space. In the dream, there is an element where the neutral space, in which the signifier and its localized structure are disposed, turns opaque. It is perturbed, and from this we get the example of the flag (which Lacan evokes in *Radiophonie*), where one can read "*Révolution d'octobre*" when it is fully unfurled in the breeze, and when the wind causes it to ripple and undulate, one can read, little bit by little bit, something like *Rêve d'or*.

This is the model of a Freudian condensation. If this is correct, then we need three dimensions; we need the folds in the flag. Lyotard is interested in showing that now there is a three-dimensional space in the picture, which has desire as a force operating in this third dimension. Lacan is not afraid to respond and again puts the figurative in its place. On the one hand he takes up Laplanche, who illustrated the unconscious through drawings that contained hidden objects, which have unclear outlines because other objects obscure them, but which we can see if we look at them in a given manner: Napoleon's hair for example. Laplanche had invented this example so that the unconscious could be well understood, something that clearly coincides with the unsubstantial character of the unconscious according to Lacan. On the other hand he borrows Lyotard's figurations. Lacan maintains that the only Freudian element that interests analysis is not what in fact exists, that which is of the order of the work of the dream in the thickness of the image; what interests analysis, the thing that is Freudian, is that which needs only two dimensions to sustain it, the typographical purely and simple.

This debate is very complex. Jakobson and Lacan never agreed on condensation and displacement in Freud. Lyotard adds his own point of view, and there are many ways to go in circles around this question. I will point out, anyway, still from *Radiophonie*, the position of the interpretive cut that Lacan constructs. He introduces the Möbius strip and brings it to bear on the question Laplanche used to ask regarding double inscription, about how a double inscription, on the one hand pre-conscious and on the other un-conscious, was possible. Lacan says: "*It will reveal the topology that governs a Möbius strip. Because it is only from this cut, this surface, where one has access at any point to the inverse, without having to cross any barrier (having only one face then), it later finds itself provided with a verso and a recto. The Freudian double inscription, consequently, could not be equated to any kind of Saussurean bar, but rather to the actual practice that proposes the problem, in other words, the cut, that the unconscious, when it gives up, testifies that it exists nowhere but in it . . .*"[12]

This situates the interpretive cut as a crossover for the Möbius strip, as it opens it up and makes a belt with an inside and an outside. This is the conclusion, almost in the conditional, since I would have liked to say that the unconscious arises only in the interpretation itself, that there is only something there to interpret because the interpretive cut occurred, and that the interpretation perhaps constitutes its own verification, as we are able to deduce at the end of the quote, "*. . . I mean to say, that the more the discourse is interpreted, the more the unconscious is verified. This is true up to the point where only psychoanalysis—on the condition that it be interpreted—could discover that there is an inverse side of discourse.*"[13]

ENDNOTES

1. Jacques Lacan, "The function and field of speech and language in psychoanalysis" (1953, "The Rome Discourse"), *Ecrits: A Selection*, trans. by Alan Sheridan, New York: W. W. Norton, 1977, p. 105.

2. *El Atolondradicho*, cf. *L'étourdit*, *Scilicet*, no. 4, 1973, pp. 5–52.

3. Sheridan, *Ecrits*, p. 105.

4. *Ibid.*

5. Jacques Lacan, "Position of the Unconscious" (1964), *Reading Seminar XI: Lacan's Four Fundamental Concepts of Psychoanalysis*, trans. by Bruce Fink, ed. by R. Feldstein, B. Fink, and M. Jaanus, Albany, NY: SUNY Press, 1995, pp. 259–282.

6. Jacques Lacan, "The agency of the letter in the unconscious or reason since Freud" (1957), *Ecrits: A Selection*, trans. by Alan Sheridan, New York: W. W. Norton, 1977, pp. 146–178.

7. Jacques Lacan, *R.S.I. . . .*, 1974–1975, *Le Séminaire XXII*, unpublished.

8. *The Seminar of Jacques Lacan: Book II: The Ego in Freud's Theory and in the Technique of Psychoanalysis* (1954–1955), ed. by Jacques-Alain Miller, trans. by Sylvana Tomaselli, with notes by John Forrester, New York: W. W. Norton, 1988.

9. Jean-Paul Sartre, *Being and Nothingness*, 1943.

10. Noam Chomsky, *Knowledge of Language: Its Nature, Origin, and Use*. New York: Praeger, 1986.

11. Jacques Lacan, *Radiophonie, Scilicet*, no. 2, 1970, pp. 55–99; *Ecrits*, ed. by Jacques-Alain Miller, Paris: Seuil, 2001.

12. *The Seminar of Jacques Lacan, Book XX: Encore*, 1972–1973, trans. with notes by Bruce Fink, New York: W. W. Norton, 1999; "The subversion of the subject and the dialectic of desire in the Freudian unconscious" (1960), *Ecrits: A Selection*, trans. by Alan Sheridan, pp. 314–315.

13. Jacques Lacan, *Le Séminaire, livre XVII, L'envers de la psychoanalyse*, 1969–1979, ed. by Jacques-Alain Miller, Paris: Seuil.

3

Lacan's Topological Unit and the Structure of Mind

ELLIE RAGLAND

This essay, "Lacan's Topological Unit and the Structure of Mind," invokes the last part of Lacan's teaching.[1] Even though one could take Lacan—the last one, the one who developed a psychoanalytic logic based on a topological structuralism he also called "a science of the real"[2]—to be a postmodernist, as have many academic readers of Lacan, Lacan was never a postmodernist or a poststructuralist. From the beginning of his teaching, he worked with the fact that every unit of two establishes a structure. Thus even undoing a structure presupposes a structure. As early as his "Report to the Rome Congress" in 1953, Lacan proposed that prior to "the serial articulations of speech" we can ascertain a structure between the serial and what is primordial to the birth of symbols. "We find it in death," he said, going on to give a topological sense to this statement:

> To say that this mortal reveals in speech a centre exterior to language is more than a metaphor; it manifests a structure. This structure is different from the spatialization of the circumference

or of the sphere in which some people like to schematise the limits of the living being and his milieu: it corresponds rather to the relational group that symbolic logic designates topologically as an annulus. If I wished to give an intuitive representation of it, it seems that, rather than have recourse to the surface aspect of a zone, I should call on the three-dimensional form of a torus, in so far as its peripheral exteriority and its central exteriority constitute only one single region. (Note No. 115: "Premises of the topology that I have been putting into practice over the past five years" [1966]).[3]

Even though Lacan worked with concepts such as the point of an annulus, the sense of which is exterior to language but which pokes a hole through a word as the limit of mortality itself, or later, with the proposition that fantasy brings the duality of alienation and the cut of separation ($\Diamond$ the poinçon) that constitute the lack in desire ($) into concrete language, both the annulus and the fantasy have precise terms, exact limits. These are structures whose formal terms Lacan taught and that his students studied and use(d) in a variety of fields.

I shall refer, then, to the period of Lacan's teaching from 1974 to 1981, the year he died. We know that in his first period Lacan elaborated an understanding of the mirror-stage effects of the process of identification as they come to constitute an imaginary order of normal narcissism and transference relations with others. In developing the dialectic by which an infant takes on its identity— what Lacan called a *symbolic order structure*, an ideal ego—through identifications with the others of its world, Lacan was able to challenge the notion of a unitary self, unitary ego or identity.

In the second period of his teaching he developed his theory of the Symbolic order which stressed the triadic function of the signifier, which Ferdinand de Saussure—the father of modern linguistics—had reduced to acoustic sound. In Lacan's reconceptualizing of it, the signifier was not simply acoustic sound. It became that which re-presents a subject for another signifier: $S_1 \rightarrow S_2$.

In Lacan's view, the signifier is dialectical. It has a triadic structure, even a quaternary structure. In other words, if *something* re-

represents something for something else—even if that something is a someone, the first something has a referent. In Lacan's teaching the primary referent(s)—the Ur-lining of the real that causes the subject to desire ($) —are minimal and invisible at the level of cause. They can only be analyzed or "observed" in their effects. Yet, they all refer to the body parts that first cause an infant to desire. Lacan named those parts—or partial objects-cause-of-desire-in 1960 "the mamilla, faeces, the phallus (imaginary object) and the urinary flow. An unthinkable list if one adds, as I do, the phoneme, the gaze, the voice—the nothing."[4]

The new phenomenology Lacan develops at this time valorizes the seemingly empty space in between the desiring subject and the object towards which it is drawn, thus giving formal properties and logical shape to "invisible" objects (the object *a*). You will not be surprised to hear the *nothing* valorized as a positivizable object if you have read *Laws of Form*[5] (1969) by the mathematician G. Spencer-Brown, whose work was greatly praised by Bertrand Russell.[6]

Spencer-Brown's work on the mathematics of logic was known for its separation of the algebras of logic from the subject of logic in order to realign them with mathematics.[7] At different junctures in his work, Spencer-Brown considers it to be psychoanalytic in that the illustration or injunction is not the thing itself:

> A recognisable aspect of the advancement of mathematics consists in the advancement of the consciousness of what we are doing, whereby the covert becomes overt. Mathematics is in this respect psychedelic. The nearer we are to the beginning of what we set out to achieve, the more likely we are to find there procedures which have been adopted without comment. It is arranged [. . .] that we shall write on a plane surface. If we write on the surface of a torus the theorem is not true.[8]

The theme of his book, akin to Lacan's topological work, is that

> a universe comes into being when a space is severed or taken apart . . . [This brings to mind Lacan's logic of the cut as developed in the 1960s.] By tracing the way we represent such a

severance, we can begin to reconstruct, with an accuracy and coverage that appear almost uncanny, the basic forms underlying linguistic, mathematical, physical, and biological science, and can begin to see how the familiar laws of our own experience follow inexorably from the original act of severance . . . Although all forms, and thus all universes are possible, and any particular form is mutable, it becomes evident that the laws relating such forms are the same in any universe. It is this sameness, the idea that we can find a reality which is independent of how the universe actually appears, that lends such fascination to the study of mathematics. That mathematics, in common with other art forms, can lead us beyond ordinary existence, and can show us something of the structure in which all creation hangs together, is no new idea. But mathematical texts generally begin the story somewhere in the middle, leaving the reader to pick up the thread as best he can.[9]

In 1969, it is Spencer-Brown's intention to trace that story from the beginning: to start with the fact that an indiction requires a distinction, making of the form of a distinction the form itself.[10] In the preface he added to his 1994 limited edition, Spencer-Brown attacks what he calls "the falseness of current scientific doctrine . . . [or] scientific duplicity: that appearance and reality are somehow different. Since there is no means, other than appearance, for studying reality, they are definitively the same."[11] This is what Lacan called the *seeming* adequacy of the Imaginary order of the visible to itself, its confusion of appearance or semblance with reality. Spencer-Brown writes:

> Since there is no means, other than appearance, for studying reality, they are definitively the same. But the scientist not only supposes they are different [. . .] he supposes also that awareness (which he mistakenly confuses with "consciousness") of the reality-appearance is something that is different again; and that the universe might have "existed" for "billions of years" amid total unawareness of what was going on. This I shall have to call scientific triplicity. Again by definition, there can be no appearance that is not an awareness of appearance, and, of

course, no awareness that is not an appearance of awareness. And since the scale of real-unreal cannot apply to appearance in general, whatever appears, *as appearance*, must be equally real and unreal. Reversing the false distinctions, we arrive at what I call the *triple identity*, notably the definitional identity of reality, appearance, and awareness. It is remarkable how all the "building blocks" of existence appear as triunions. (Compare the so-called "divine trinity" of Christianity, which is merely a summary of our perception of how to construct the formation of any thing whatever.) It is the triunion that apparently provides the magic inflatory principle that makes it all seem like it's really there.[12]

Spencer-Brown brings us squarely into the problematics Lacan takes up in his third period of teaching, problems which Charles Sanders Peirce, linguist and semiotician, had tried to solve by a system of logic beyond classical symbolic logic, decades before Lacan and Spencer-Brown (Compare Hippolyte Taine's triad concerning *race, milieu*, and *moment*). The structure of mind is not binary, Lacan argued, as early as the 1950s, as certain mathematicians and philosophers would claim, but triadic or trinary. And he said this is provable, but not via some arbitrary application of mathematics to psychoanalysis or philosophy, nor in a literary metaphorical world of would-be equivalences. Lacan proves his structure of mind through a use of mathematical topology: the study of surfaces of things on which lines, holes and spaces can be connected even though their functions may be paradoxical or contradictory. That is, topology is the study of the relations of contradictory elements at the surface of something.

Spencer-Brown alerts us to the problem Lacan takes up in the 1970s: the grounding of being or identity in a place—or a *where*—is an illusory exercise. We are grounded, rather, Lacan teaches, in the spurious Imaginary consistency of an unconscious ideal ego; in the fixity of traumatic inscriptions; in the language upon which we draw to represent ourselves as (desiring) subjects to others.

Although Derrida has sought to prove that being is made up of language, with its many forms and sounds, language is not the final answer to the question of what grounds *being*. In 1967, Spencer-Brown wrote in an introduction to *Laws of Form*:

> The subject matter of logic [. . .] is not, in so far as it confines itself to the ground of logic, a mathematical study. Its mathematical treatment is a treatment of the form in which our way of talking about our ordinary living experience can be seen to be cradled. It is the laws of the form, rather than those of logic, that I have attempted to record. In making the attempt, I found it easier to acquire an access to the laws themselves than to determine a satisfactory way of communicating them. In general, the more universal the law, the more it seems to resist expression in any particular mode [. . .] Some of the difficulties [. . .] are extending the analysis through and beyond the point of simplicity where language ceases to act normally as a currency for communication [. . .] To extend them back beyond this point demands a considerable unlearning of the current descriptive superstructure which, until it is unlearned, can be mistaken for the reality. The fact that [. . .] we have to use words and other symbols in an attempt to express what the use of words and other symbols has hitherto obscured [. . .] records itself and [. . .] that which is so recorded is not a matter of opinion.[13]

In *Seminar XX* (1972–1973), Lacan writes:

> Just because I have written things that serve the function of forms of language doesn't mean I assure the being of metalanguage [. . .] Mathematical formalisation is our goal, our ideal [. . .] but it only subsists if I employ, in presenting it, the language (*langue*) I make use of. Therein lies the objection: no formalisation of language is transmissible without the use of language itself. It is in the very act of speaking that I make this formalisation [. . .] ex-sist. It is in this respect that the symbolic cannot be confused with being.[14]

By adding the category of the Real and demonstrating how it cuts into imaginary *illusions* of wholeness, consistency and solidity of being, body, and knowledge, Lacan gave new meaning to the many tasks language must perform to negotiate desire and *jouissance*, while coping with the traumatic aspects of the Real.

What makes things seem as if they are really there when they are only our perception of how to construct a given formation? Spencer-Brown asks. His answer is that "the word 'there' supplies the trick. There exists in reality no 'where' for the 'there' to be. Nor is there any 'when'."[15] In Lacan's terms, the problem of (re-) constituting oneself as an "I" concerns the field of the gaze— where the eye is both seeing and seen. One is grounded as an "I" in reference to the other/Other for whom one *is* taken to be this or that, and slotted away as "being" "here" or "there" in the Imaginary/Symbolic terms of a given social order. Usually, a person's life does not change so much that he or she has to challenge the limits of the Imaginary ego by which one lives. Yet the history of histories and of politics shows such limits being continually challenged for groups of people, as well as individuals. Lacan's work, spanning the period of the two world wars, argues that we cannot *not* learn what constitutes the "I," with its spurious grounding, in this most barbaric of all centuries.

Spencer-Brown says that "there," "where," and "when" are all constructions of imagination, inventions of apparently stable formations for the apparent appearances.[16] No thing can be explained, he continues, except by defining two states. As early as *Seminar II* (1954–1955), Lacan taught that any two elements constitute a structure, that no dialectic can derive from one alone, even in functions of negation.[17] For example, any concept of an *un-unbewusste*, *unbegriff*, undone, deconstructed, unraveled, and so on, negates a first thing, a thing supposed as first (thus situated in place and time) even if it is the concept of a lack. Lacan gives numerous examples of his phenomenon. He says

> that the subject in his manifestation in this special guise of the production of an organised discourse, in which he is always subject to this process which is called negation and in which the integration of his *ego* is accomplished, can only reflect his

fundamental relation to his ideal ego in an inverted form. In other words, the relation to the other, in so far as the primitive desire of the subject strives to manifest itself in it, always contains in itself this fundamental, original element of negation, which here takes the form of inversion.[18]

As well, he says: "there is not one form of the perverse phenomena whose very structure is not . . . sustained by the intersubjective relation."[19] Later Lacan will map subject locations of "self" as "here" or "there" as topological references to the phallic signifier and castration.

"In reality," says Spencer-Brown, "there never was, never could be, and never will be anything at all . . . All I teach is the consequences of there being nothing."[20] Lacan, too, postulates nothing at the beginning. But it is a nothing which responds to something and which is, therefore, valorized by positive attributes: the loss of the object *a*, that might be named as the only *a priori*—even though its effects come from the outside, creating a hole or a cut—causes an infant to desire more, to desire again, to want a repetition. Like Spencer-Brown, Lacan was concerned to enumerate the consequences of there being a nothing with positive properties. Although psychoanalysis has traditionally focused on the concrete contents of childhood experiences or memories, Lacan linked early infant experience to the very structure of mind. Insofar as early memories, themselves, are irretrievable, Lacan taught that what is retrievable has a dual structure, the structure of metaphor. Influenced by Claude Lévi-Strauss's valorization of the symbol and Roman Jakobson's understanding that the two main tropes of poetry are the two principal anchors of language, Lacan focused on the laws of language, rather than on its grammar or syntax. The ego has a double structure and functions by substituting one thing for another, he posited, and this is the law of metaphor. When such substitutions cannot be made—as, for example, by the character played by Dustin Hoffman in the film *Rain Man*—one is on the slope of limitless *jouissance* where the Real of the body makes of metonymic contiguity something other than a static rhetorical principle, something that bespeaks psychosis.

Generally speaking, infants want the return of the mother's breast. But, Lacan taught, it is not the breast *qua* object that is in question in some phenomenological sense of *das Ding* or *das Ding an sich*. Nor is it a breast one can characterize in an object-relations sense as the part standing in for the whole, or by some moral attribution of "good" or "bad." What the infant wants is the return of a consistency—of warmth, of quietness, of touching, of oneness. Long after his or her hunger is satisfied, the infant stays at the breast or with the bottle. By valorizing the desire first created in reference to the primary objects that cause desire because they are lost, Lacan gave the logic of how they become desirable: not because the body is automatically programmed for desire but because the objects that satisfy are continually lost, taken away, moving from here to there in a dialectic dynamic of life motions. It is this way of understanding that places Lacan's work within the sphere of a topological structuralism. He links the when and where of consciousness to the tim(ing) of desire (lack) [$] and to the space of the demand for satisfaction (Ø), space created as an Imaginary set of signifiers imprinted on the surface of the body. In 1976, in *Radiophonie*, Lacan spoke of the body as the surface of a torus, imaginarizing it as the surface of an inscription that "can carry the mark required for arranging it in a series of signifiers."[21]

That objects must be refound, replaced and repeated tells Lacan that the structure of desire has the inverse face of lack. Although this is a seemingly contradictory dynamic, its structural middle point of overlap, or of two limits intersecting, marks an actual gap in thought. Linguist, logician, and semiotician Charles Pyle, characterizes three phases of a concept of "wild language" as typical of what appears in the concrete gap in thought. In his article "Proving Lacan: The Linguistic Point of View,"[22] Pyle opposes language proper, that is, as made up of symbolic signs, to wild language whose domain he depicts first as the animal and plant kingdom of the natural: undomesticated, savage, unrestrained, and unruly. Placing this division within Charles Sanders Peirce's logic of three types of signs—the iconic, the indexical, (the Symbolic), the latter two compared roughly to Lacan's Imaginary and Real, he concludes with the assertion that wild language is typical of the gap between primary and secondary processes, although Freud assigned no negative term to wild language.[23] Turning to Lacan's topological structuralism, one might claim that the negative term which enables an infant to babble at all, even like a virtuoso, is opposed to the silent autism of the child who never babbles. This is closer to what Lacan has called the minimal structure of a topology: the tiny gap between the opening and closing of a sphere, for example, which makes it dynamic, not static. This, one might add, is the experimental leap from closed circle geometry to dynamic process topology.

In "Rings of String" Lacan lays out the basic terms of his topological structure of the mind: "Being is . . . but a fact of what is said."[24] In other words, there is no *being* in Heidegger's sense of an ontological essence. Rather, being is *supposed* from certain words—which may produce the only *substance* of which Lacan will admit: *jouissance*. But *jouissance* is not reducible to being, nor is being equatable to the subject of desire. That we distinguish ourselves from the language of being implies verbal fictions (*fiction de mot*) in Jeremy Bentham's sense. Equating the language surrounding the being question with a "fiction on the basis of the word," Lacan points out that one has not assured the being of metalanguage but, rather, has brought ethics into the equation. Crediting Roman Jakobson with having drawn his attention to Bentham, Lacan points out that Bentham's use of the word "fictitious" is meant in the sense that every truth has the structure of fiction. Bentham's effort is located, Lacan maintains, "in the dialectic of the relationship of language to the Real so as to situate the good . . . on the side of the real." Later, he says that Bentham made no effort to reduce the progress of knowledge to transcendental or supernatural dimensions, but showed that it is man himself who approaches the question at the level of the signifier.[25]

The status of the unconscious is ethical, Lacan said in *The Four Fundamental Concepts of Psycho-Analysis*, not ontic.[26] There is a "sense" of something in language that is not strictly grammar:

> There is some relationship of being that cannot be known. It is
> that relationship whose structure I investigate in my teaching,
> insofar as that knowledge—which, as I just said, is impossible—
> is prohibited (*interdit*) thereby [. . .] We have to expose the kind
> of real to which it grants us access. It is a real that is always in
> the process of being shaped, formatted-*mise en forme*.[27]

Finally, Lacan gives the logic of how the drives are *mise en forme*,
as well as how the structurations of discourse include desire and
the excess in *jouissance* that bespeaks a *sinthome*, and how time and
space are integrated in the Borromean unit made up of the four
orders: the object *a*, and the three *jouissances*. We are far from
Plato's Ideas and closer to Spencer-Brown's sense that the laws of
form are ultimately the forms of experience. We have already suggested that, at one level, Lacan's logic of forms culminates in his
topological logic of the partial drives, each of which corresponds
to a different topological figure.[28] The sense of something else in
language that does not come strictly from grammar, but from some
combination of desire (lack) and the demand for *jouissance* to fill
the lack that places the particularity of fundamental fantasy at the
base of each person's thought—that is, a certain absolutism of
jouissance which has positive attributes even though it was constructed as a response to lack and loss—does not come from a form
of being that acts as a container to hold the contained.

If there were this supposed subject of being it would have to
exist alone, says Lacan. This would not be mathematically formal-
izable. That is, "one" alone cannot provide a structure from which
something else can be deduced. Mathematical formalization—Lacan's
ideal "metalanguage"—resides, rather, at the site of the Real which
I shall define here as the residue or what is left over from the effects
and marks of language. In *Seminar XX* Lacan calls this an *écrit*, or
that which has already been written and repressed in an Elsewhere
he names the Other. These residual pieces of the Symbolic order
subsist—still exist—as a kind of ex-sistence outside of the first things
that were said. While Peirce points to secondness, or the index of an
actual mark (such as the hoof print of a deer) as the effect of iconic

firstness, Lacan departs from the visible realm of typology that distinguishes Peirce's semiotics. In this, Lacan is closer to theologians of old. Some effect is left behind by a cause that is not identifiable with—or the same as—the cause. Between the cause and the effect, in the place of the gap, one finds not just shadow letters or phonemic traces, but unary traits of Real effects that cannot be remembered in narrative, which can be only "acted out" or performed in repetitions, keeping the dual sense of repetition in French as that which is performed as well as repeated. The effects that appear in the gap are not commensurable with the re-presentations of images or words, but act upon images and words to place *jouissance effects* within them. These effects return in the logical structure of the torus—the inside and outside reminiscent of one another in a strange proximity of transformation and displacement that anchors difference in similarity—precisely because they were previously structured in the logical time one recognizes in the return of the instant of the glance, the time for understanding, and the moment of concluding.[29]

To what are these effects bound that gives them a seeming existence that Lacan, like Spencer-Brown, says never goes beyond mere appearance or semblance? The answer is the object-cause-of-desire whose unspeakable effects are anchored in the Real and are, thus, translatable only in the Imaginary and Symbolic, and displaced enigmatically in the *sinthome*. When Lacan places the object *a* on the symbolic slope going towards the Real under the term of semblance in the chapter on "Knowledge and Truth" he is, nonetheless, saying that "the true [S(Ø)] aims at the real."[30] Appearance may *seem* to be the thing itself, but everyone senses or feels there is "something more than meets the eye," or something left unsaid. Indeed, the Real of flesh demands that affect be translated into language, giving us a way to think of affect as something, other than solitary feelings. In this context, one might describe affect as a discontinuity that ruptures the apparent consistency of the Imaginary ego. Rather than call this being, Lacan calls it the form of knowledge which fills the lack, while insisting that such form is far from Plato's Ideal Thought or any other philosophical absolute.

It is Real in the sense that it holds the being in its cut, but at the level of the edge. It is the discourse of the being supposing that being exists, and that is what holds it. Alongside such supposed knowledge, Lacan places the knowledge that is forbidden or censured. But, he says, such knowledge is not interdicted; it is *interdit*, said between the lines, in the place of the gap.

In this place of discordance between knowledge and being—generally called mind and self—Lacan places the subject desiring *jouissance*.[31] This opens not onto Bishop Berkeley's idealism in which we can know only our own representations, but onto the first confrontation each subject has in early childhood with the sexual difference that forever after links mentality and gender to identity and sexuality. We learn being in predominantly masculine or feminine identifications which are, nonetheless, joined in an enigmatic perception of the relation between man and woman, starting with the child's view of the parental couple in which the problem of the rapport between M ◊ W is not reducible to the formula for M ◊ F (even if the father in that couple is only represented by a signifier as distant as "the outsider," as in some tribes Freud described in *Totem and Taboo*).[32]

Again, we come to the intersection of Lacan the philosopher with Lacan the psychoanalyst, the man whose entire edifice is built upon his early discovery in the 1930s that psychosis is the refusal to accept the signifier for any father at all, even if the one who intervenes in the Father's Name is a woman. Lacan argued in his doctoral thesis, written for the Faculty of Medicine at the University of Paris, that psychosis is, however, logical and rational if one understands how it is structured.[33] The psychoses are caused by a foreclosure of the asymmetry or difference between the two biological sexes. Thus, Lacan shows that not only is psychosis not caused by poor environment, brain deficit, genetic abnormality, or loss of reality, but that it provides a structural/empirical base against which to study other functions of mind and language as structured by identifications made in reference to the oedipal triad. Lacan used in proof of his own discovery the fact that psychosis is the condition of refusing loss of the object *a*.

In this context Lacan used the terms *phallic signifier* and *castration*. Taking up his earlier point that there can never be only one if there is to be structure, he teaches that the very reference to a divide between the sexes evokes the split itself as a third term. Thus, the identifications one chooses in the early moments of fixing an ideal ego as unconscious formation, positivize certain traits of the feminine or masculine and negativize others. At whatever age or moment one chooses one's sexuation (identifies predominantly with one biological gender or other) one might be said to have accepted castration, to have admitted to a lack-in-being, or a lack-of-being-all (One sex).

We have returned to the value of triadic structure, then, as the means by which an ego is constituted in the oedipal experience of substituting identifications with masculine and feminine traits for loss of the primary objects. Triads do not exist only in mathematics, linguistics, semiotics, and religion. We might even say, as does Spencer-Brown, that these disciplines try to represent something whose basis conforms to the Real of experience. This would make of the Oedipus something far different from a myth whose basis is sheer fiction. The unconscious begins to be structured by desire in reference to the primordial objects that *cause* a person to desire *within* a transference to the primordial objects that *cause* a person to desire *within* a transference relation. But rather than stress the subsequent intersubjectivity of relations, Lacan stresses that the capacity to substitute objects for the primordially lost ones lies at the base of the capacity to think dialectically. The major identifications are finally made, adding up gradually to a gender identity, concerning the loss, not of a specific object that caused desire, such as the good or bad breast, or the good or bad mother of object-relations theory, but the loss of one half of oneself as a previously supposed whole, an androgyne.

The structural necessity in such topological logic shows the birth of the subject from the losses that beget desire, which leads to action and motivation. The Real trauma of loss valorizes certain traits of the lost objects—unary traits—positivizing them as identifications by which to fill in concrete places of lack. All the early lacks constituted by cuts between the object and the infant's experience of it, build up an unconscious set of traumatic inscriptions that place suffering at the heart of being.

In the final period of his teaching, Lacan advanced the fourth term of his Borromean unit of structure: the knot or symptom. The Imaginary, Real, and Symbolic are tied together by the symptom, which is the Father's Name referent on the basis of which one builds ideologies and beliefs. At the level of the particular experience of one's symptoms, Lacan used the medieval French spelling *sinthome* to stress the uniqueness of each person's symptoms. Lacan argued, then, that humans are Symbolic creatures whose identities are first structured by the outside world in a primordial *Fort! Da!* movement of having and losing, and later, encountering a sporadic return of the Real into the Symbolic. Most people protect themselves from the Real by identifying with what is predominantly valued by the Symbolic/Imaginary knowledge of their local (universal) cultural content. In this way individuals need not address the specificity of their symptoms. They merely "mouth" the conventions of the masquerade in play. At the other end of the fulcrum—away from the *realpolitik* of being "enjoyed by one's symptom"—is this: the most severe consequence of having something, losing it, and then having nothing, is that nothing is a concrete, Real object. It produces effects all the way from boredom and fear to the raw anxiety Lacan imputes to any direct encounter with the void place in being.[34]

In *The Four Fundamental Concepts of Psychoanalysis*, Lacan says we are usually protected from a direct encounter with the void by the ever-flowing chain of fundamental fantasies. While each person's fundamental fantasies are marked by the concrete imprints of life experiences, the object(s) *a* that first causes desire—and then seems to fill the lack that is the subject ($) from the outside—is at the center of each individual Borromean unit, units that are knotted in thousands of inter-linkages in a signifying necklace Lacan defines as memory/mind. These build up the myriad forms of "being" whose iconic forms and verbal names in turn mark the Real as an order of primordial repressions of single strokes (Freud's *Einziger Zugen*) which reappear—as in Dora's memories of her father's cigar smoke or of Frau K's "beautiful white body"—as a kind of non-linear rememoration. Lacan's unary traits, however, seem to have little in common with Derrida's concepts of the trace and the mark.

In his topological development of the structure of mind, Lacan may have borrowed, consciously or unconsciously, from Peirce's work on the categories of firstness, secondness, and thirdness which structure language in two categories. In my reading of Pyle's bringing together of Peirce and Lacan, wild language, which he also equates with Freud's primary processes, contains the marks of icons or first forms and the Real marks these make as indices of the brute effects of the marking. Peirce's category of thirdness, that of Symbolic naming, or language, would place him in the camp of Spencer-Brown, or any other thinker who gives a truth-functional logic to a third category outside the strictures of symbolic logic or classic entailment logic wherein only the binary logic of true and false tables is validated. Lacan used topology to show that in the place of the overlap of any of two categories—two sets from mathematical set theory, for example—properties from each category are inscribed so as to make up a third, seemingly paradoxical place, whose contradictions arise only in that it shares properties of the other two categories.

This only makes sense if one accepts that topology is a domain of science by which science takes account of its own failure in the matter of suturing the subject. Put another way, language cannot account for all that comes out in it. Language cannot account for affect, fantasy, intuition, and desire, to name a few. The science Lacan evokes does not work from the controlled experimental variables of empiricism, but includes within itself the negative principle as a part of the definition of the science, not as an object outside to be observed and then counted or measured in some way.

In the "Rings of String," Lacan sketches out the basic dimensions of the topological structure of mind or language, having earlier in the same seminar described topology as having a strict equivalence with structure. In "On *Jouissance*," he says that if we take that as our guide, what distinguishes anonymity from what we talk about as *jouissance*—namely, what is regulated by law—is a geometry. A geometry implies the heterogeneity of locus, namely that there is a locus of the Other. Regarding this locus of the Other, of one sex as Other, as absolute Other, what does the most recent development in topology allow us to posit? I will posit here the term "compactness" . . . [based on] the institution of a locus, which is not that of a homogeneous space—the equivalent of what I earlier posited as an intersection extending to infinity. If we assume it to be covered with open sets, in other words, sets that exclude their own limits—the limit is that which is defined as greater than one point and less than another, but in no case equal either to the point of departure or the point of arrival . . . it can be shown that it is equivalent to say that the set of these open spaces always allows of a subcovering of open spaces, constituting a finity (*finitude*), namely, that the series of elements constitutes a finite series.[35]

In chapter X of the same seminar, Lacan says that

Writing is thus a trace in which an effect of language can be read . . . One must ensure things by writing. The latter certainly is not metalanguage, nevertheless, though one can make it fill a function that resembles it. That effect is nevertheless secondary with respect to the Other in which language is inscribed as truth . . . When you scribble . . . it is always on a page with lines, and we are thus immediately enmeshed in this business of dimensions.[36]

With that Lacan gives his minimalist logic of the dimensions that obtain in language, giving language a triadic structuration which is topological. What cuts a line is a point which has zero dimension. At this point, those concerned with triadic structure talk of brute effects—Peirce's category of the index, Freud's trauma, Lacan's Real, Derrida's archi-trace—not of existence. The line has the dimension of one. When the line is cut in two places one can speak of the dimension of a surface. The body is a surface on which

Imaginary and Real effects are written by the interventions of the object *a*: the voice, the gaze, the nothing, and so on. Thus what cuts the surface is space which has three dimensions: the dimension of the Borromean knot.[37]

That minimal topological unit, says Lacan, has all the characters of a writing. It could be a letter, except when you write cursively you do not think about stopping your line before it intersects with another one for the purpose of making one thing pass under another. Lacan's earlier work on the objects that cause desire would show them as continually placing discontinuities in language, bringing in their wake the structure of the drives with their vicissitudes—reversal into the opposite, turning back onto the self, sublimation, repression[38]—as that which marks the Real of the flesh by deconstructing the logical consistency of an Imaginary body. That is, such effects pass under and over the words that try to represent such vicissitudes of the drives. That space has three dimensions is not the point of writing, Lacan insists. When one is writing or speaking—making a consistency out of language—the last thing one wants is to know that an Imaginary line between the eye and the object one desires has "material" dimensions precisely because the Imaginary line has already been cut by the *Fort! Da!* movement between the eye, the object desired, and the gaze which encompasses the eye and the object, which comes reflexively back onto the "self" from the gaze of the Other onto which one projects oneself as an ideal unity.

Having suggested above that the movement of the object *a* into language and identifications could be said to recall Freud's theory that the drives are structured by reversal into their opposite, turning around upon the subject's own self, repression, and sublimation, one can see that this simple structure of a dynamic reversal—where inside and outside are not antithetical one to the other but are joined in thought—has the shape of a torus or a doughnut. The object *a* fills the hole created between words, making sure that we do not encounter the lacks-in-being too often. Lacan says this structure places absence and presence as a matter of distance—an interior exterior—within language. Issues of perspective could be studied here as well as that which concerns proximity to the object that causes desire. At a more unconscious level, the lack is continually filled in fantasy ($\$\Diamond a$) ensuring that one have an ever-flowing dialectic of presumed satisfactions. If the fundamental fantasy is destroyed altogether or in the traversal of it, one encounters the raw angst of the Real in which the first traumatic cuts of having and losing objects were instituted. The hole in the Other (Ø) between the Imaginary and Real orders is (re)-opened.

At Yale University, in the Kanzer-Seminar given on November 24, 1975, Lacan said, "the most important thing, at least such as we, analysts, conceive it, is to say the truth. And, since we have a rather particular idea of this truth, we know that it is difficult."[39] The "truth" of the psychoanalytic subject is that he or she is in internal division from his or her object. The divided subject is, in other words, an equivalent of its own division by the signifier, which alienates a person from being a natural being or from being one with language by the forced choice that the Other qua signifying chain imposes when a person is born into it, at the price of giving the individual a lack-in-being for operating in the world via exchange and supplement. The subject is also, as we have seen earlier, divided by the object at the point where he or she hopes to receive a complement of being from the other.

Because of these two divisions, the Symbolic order of language functions by default around the structure of a central hole. The subject is a topology, then, that makes a double turn around the hole, ending up showing that even the Other of language is a guarantee of nothing. The Other as complete and consistent does not exist (Ø), but rather, this de-completed Other leads one to operate with a signifier which manifests the presence of difference as such. According to Pierre Skriabine, the Lacanian signifier is the correlative of a loss then, a loss of reference.[40] And what comes to replace it is the object a of fantasy, what Lacan called "the sign of object a—namely, the cause by which the subject identifies with his desire."[41] What the unconscious teaches is that nothing need be invented; no new need be sought after postmodernism. Everything we need to know is already there. What we continually fail to do is chart the terrain of our knowledge because such a trip confronts us with the lack and loss in whose wake lie doubt and anxiety. Any other trip is preferable at the level of feeling good. But Lacan argued that we can never make change—individual or social—unless we confront the truths of the Real, however discomforting and painful they might be. Nothing else works to sweep the chimney clean of dead, unconscious desire, as Anna O. described it to Breuer, and he to Freud.

ENDNOTES

1. "Lacan's Topological Unit and the Structure of Mind" was presented on September 26, 1997, as the keynote address at Lewis University, Romeoville, IL, in the Scholars Colloquium entitled "Introduction to the Basics of Jacques Lacan's Teaching: Hard Questions, Daring Answers" on September 26–27, 1997. During the two-day colloquium, panelists, made up of Lewis University professors and students, worked with speakers Ellie Ragland and Charles Pyle (a linguist and scholar of Peircian logic and semiotics on which he based his presentation "Lacan's Theory of Language") on Ragland's and Pyle's papers and the texts the students had read in preparation for the Colloquium (sections from the "Rome Discourse" and *The Four Fundamental Concepts of Psycho-Analysis*). On the evening of September 26, each Lewis University panelist presented a brief written statement regarding what each considered hard questions and daring answers in Lacan's teaching. On the morning of September 27, Ragland and Pyle worked with a small group of undergraduate students from the Scholars program who had chosen writing assignments to complete with their mentors, based on the specific questions raised for each of them by their reading and their experience of the two-day colloquium. The organizer of the colloquium was Elaine Ross, an English Professor at Lewis University.

2. "*Je rappelle que c'est de la logique que ce discours touche au réel, à le rencontrer comme impossible, en quoi c'est discours [psychanalytique] qui la porte à sa puissance dernière: science, ai-je dit, du réel.*" Jacques Lacan, *L'étourdit* (July, 1972), *Scilicet: tu peux savoir ce qu'en pense L'Ecole Freudienne de Paris*, no. 4 (Paris: Seuil, 1973), pp. 5–6.

3. Jacques Lacan (1977). "The subversion of the subject and the dialectic of desire in the Freudian unconscious" (1960), *Ecrits: A Selection*, trans. Alan Sheridan. New York: W. W. Norton, p. 315.

4. *Ibid.*

5. G. Spencer-Brown, *Laws of Form* (Portland, OR: Cognizer Co., limited edn, 1994) [first published in London by George Allen and Unwin Ltd., 1969; in the USA by Julian Press, 1972; Bantam, 1973; reprinted from Julian, 177; by E. P. Dutton, 1979].

6. In ". . .1965, a young mathematician, G. Spencer-Brown, pressed me to go over his work since . . . he could find no one else who he thought could understand it. . . . As the time drew near for his arrival, I became convinced that I should be quite unable to cope with it and with his new system of notation. I was filled with dread. But when he came and I heard his explanations, I found that I could get into step again and follow his work. I greatly enjoyed those few days, especially as his work was both original and, it seemed to me, excellent." Bertrand Russell (1978). *The Autobiography of Bertrand Russell.* London: Unwin, p. 664.

7. Spencer-Brown refers his interlocutors to George Boole, *The Mathematical Analysis of Logic*, Cambridge, 1847.

8. A practice Spencer-Brown finds wrong. (Spencer-Brown, *Laws of Form*, p. 86).

9. Spencer-Brown, *Laws of Form*, p. xxix.

10. *Ibid.*, p. 1.

11. *Ibid.*, Preface to the 1994 Limited Edn., p. vii.

12. *Ibid.*

13. *Ibid.*, p. xxviii.

14. *Encore The Seminar of Jacques Lacan: Book XX: On Feminine Sexuality, The Limits of Love and Knowledge* (1972–1973), ed. Jacques-Alain Miller, trans. Bruce Fink (New York: W. W. Norton, 1998), pp. 118–119.

15. Spencer-Brown, "Preface," p. vii.

16. *Ibid.*

17. *The Seminar of Jacques Lacan: Book I, Freud's Papers on Technique* (1953–1954), ed. by Jacques-Alain Miller, trans. with notes by John Forrester (New York: W. W. Norton, 1988). *Cf.* "A spoken commentary on Freud's *Verneinung*, by Jean Hyppolite," pp. 289–297.

18. *The Seminar of Jacques Lacan: Book I*, p. 61.

19. *Ibid.*, p. 214.

20. Spencer-Brown, "Preface," p. ix.

21. Jacques Lacan (1970). *Radiophonie*, in *Scilicet* 2/3, June 1970. Paris: Seuil, p. 61.

22. Charles Pyle, "Proving Lacan: The linguistic point of view," paper given at the University of Missouri Symposium on "Proving Lacan: Psychoanalysis and the Evidentiary Force of Knowledge" (June 4–5, 1996).

23. Charles Pyle, "The Gap in Lacanian Psychoanalysis and Linguistics," pp. 8–9, 10, unpublished paper, June 29, 1998. All rights belong to the author.

24. *Book XX: On Feminine Sexuality*, p. 118.

25. See *Book XX*, p. 118, note 2, for the reference to Jeremy Bentham's *Theory of Fictions*, noted in *The Seminar of Jacques Lacan: Book VII: The Ethnics of Psychoanalysis* (1959–1960), ed. Jacques-Alain Miller, trans. Dennis Porter. New York: W. W. Norton, 1992, pp. 12, 228.

26. See Jacques Lacan, *The Four Fundamental Concepts of Psycho-Analysis* (1964), ed. Jacques-Alain Miller, trans. Alan Sheridan. New York: W. W. Norton, 1977, ch. 3.

27. *Book XX*, p. 119.

28. Jeanne Granon-Lafont (1990). *Topologie Lacanienne et Clinique Analytique*. Cahors: Point Hors Ligne.

29. Jacques Lacan, "Logical time and the assertion of anticipated certainty: A new sophism," *Newsletter of the Freudian Field* 2, no. 2 (Fall 1988): 4–22.

30. *Book XX*, pp. 90–91.

31. *Ibid.*, pp. 108, 119, 120.

32. Jacques-Alain Miller, "To interpret the cause: From Freud to Lacan," *Newsletter of the Freudian Field* 3, nos. 1 & 2 (Spring/Fall 1989): 30–50; *cf.*, p. 36. See also Sigmund Freud, *Totem and Taboo*, SE XIII: ix–162.

33. Jacques Lacan, "De la psychose paranoïaque dans ses rapports avec la personnalité," Thesis of Docorate in Medicine, Faculty of Medicine of Paris (Paris: Le François, 1932); published later to include some other early writings. Paris: Seuil, 1975.

34. Jacques Lacan, *L'Angoisse: Livre X* (1962–1963), unedited seminar.

35. *Book XX*, pp. 9–10.

36. *Ibid.*, pp. 121–122.

37. *Ibid.*, pp. 122–123.

38. Sigmund Freud, "Instincts and their vicissitudes," *SE* XIV: 111–40, *cf.*, 126.

39. Jacques Lacan, "Yale University, Kanzer Seminar" (24 November, 1975), *Scilicet* 6/7 (Paris: Seuil, 1976): 8.

40. Pierre Skriabine, "La clinique de Lacan et la topologie," *Travaux* (June 1990): 65.

41. *Book XX*, p. 136.

II

Topology of Surfaces

4

Clinic and Topology: The Flaw in the Universe*

PIERRE SKRIABINE

FIRST PART: THE FAULT IN THE UNIVERSE

By way of introduction to the fundamental logic that renders clinic and topology solidary for us, I will make twelve remarks, the generic subtitle for which could be: "the fault in the universe."

1. Structure

The clinic operates on the basis of structure and, why not advance ourselves here as Lacan does in *L'étourdit*, it operates on structure.[1]

The term "structure," as conceived by Lacan, is the Real itself in play in the analytic experience.

Structure is what concerns the speaking subject: from the moment he or she inhabits language, is parasited by language, he

---

*Translated by Ellie Ragland and Véronique Voruz, from *La Revue de l'Ecole de la cause freudienne*.

or she is submitted to the logic of the signifier and to the specifications proper to language: in other words, to the order which is that of the register of the Symbolic.

Structure is what accounts for this seizing of the living body in the Symbolic. It is what supports the manner in which subject, Other, and object are articulated to one another, and by which language and *jouissance* are conjugated. It is also the way in which the three registers—the Real, the Symbolic, and the Imaginary—are knotted together for the speaking being.

Structure is thus also what allows one to orient oneself in the clinic.

And this structure is articulated in terms of places and relations: in other words, in terms of positions, and of properties which result from those positions. Consequently, structure is itself a topology since this last formulation is none other than Euler's, which in 1736 defined a nascent topology as a new domain in mathematics.

There is no subject, then, who is not a topologist, even without knowing it—and this is even more true of analysts—but the analyst might well want to know something about this topology in spite of everything.

This is where Lacan leads us, to pass beyond the effects of inhibition, even horror, that topology produces in us, in order to confront us with the very structure with which we are engaged.

2. The Fold

In order to try to make it immediately apparent that clinic and topology are indissociable, let us chance putting ourselves in the position of witnesses: that is to say—since it is the same thing, as Lacan reminded us—martyrs of this knotting of the subject to topology.

Let us begin, not with a topological object, but with an equivocal representation, starting with the Imaginary of the figure which is called the Necker cube.

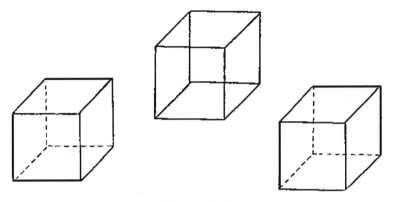

Figure 4–1.

An American specialist of what one can call scientific amusements, Rudy Rucker, has described this figure of an invertible cube in a work entitled *The Fourth Dimension*,[2] and noted the illusory effect it produces in the Imaginary. One of our colleagues[3] drew inspiration from it not long ago, and used it as a support and as a metaphor of the signifying equivocation in the vacillation it produces for a subject between two positions, between S_1 and S_2, and thereby drew attention to the effect of aphanisis—insofar as it is felt at the level of the body—of the subject represented by a signifier for another signifier, this effect of cut, of division of the subject by the signifier.

But we can just as well put the accent on a more fundamental aspect of what this figure introduces us to, which is not that of metaphor, but of structure. Thus we recognize, first, the effect of the object—here of the object-gaze—on the subject, we recognize the split of the subject by the object-gaze.

Indeed, this is what this equivocal perspective produces insofar as it puts the subject before a choice between two ways of bringing its gaze to bear in space, on the imaginarized cube: that is to say, a choice between two possible positions of this subject, determined by the object-gaze.

Otherwise said, it is the subjective division which is pre-sentified by the object-gaze.

These two positions of the subject are mutually exclusive; there is a radical discontinuity of the one from the other: between the two, there is no place for the subject. It is an untenable in-between, an effect of the aphanisis of the subject which seizes the body.

The Möbien structure—namely, the topology which accounts for the structure of the speaking subject, as Lacan shows in his Seminar on identification—unfolds on the basis of the way in which the subject gets hold of and frees himself from the object, if only to be caught by it otherwise; it unfolds on the basis of the subject's division by the object and of what already pertains to a choice and a consent of the subject with respect to this division.

To show this, one only needs two dimensions: those of a piece of paper represented on this sheet of paper.

Figure 4–2.

Seen in perspective, we can imagine this sheet as seen either from below or above: this is the choice that the gaze imposes on the subject, just as with the Necker cube.

We can however make these two ways of seeing, which are mutually exclusive, appear synchronically by folding the represented sheet.

Figure 4–3.

The function of the subject is what assures this coexistence as possible. We can see in this fold the very fold of the subjective division mentioned by Lacan in *Seminar XX, Encore*: "For every speaking being, the cause of its desire is, in terms of structure, strictly equivalent, so to speak, to its bending, that is, to what I have called its division as subject" (*Seminar XX*, p. 127 in the English).[4]

To make the topology of the subject appear—topology of the interior eight—namely, the Möbien structure, reducible to its cut which is also its edge, this interior eight where precisely the subject of the signifier and the object are articulated, it suffices to complete the drawing of the fold.

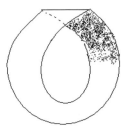

Figure 4–4.

Thus, what the Necker cube, as a representation, makes particularly apparent in the Imaginary and in the body, is nothing other than what Lacan has articulated, on the sole basis of this elementary and fundamental topological structure which the Möbius strip is. It is here that we find the topological advance made by Lacan in his Seminar on identification.

Indeed, this Möbius strip introduces us to Lacan's first development of his topology at the beginning of the 1960s, which corresponds to a period of his teaching, announced as early as 1953 in the *Rome Report*, which was specifically dedicated to emphasizing the Symbolic order and the notion of structure.

Lacan, in this sense, bases his progress on the topology of a-spherical surfaces, the elaboration of which culminates with the formulation he gives of it in *L'étourdit*. This topology, which articulates subject, object, and Other, which topologically articulates discourse itself, stems, as Lacan tells us in *L'étourdit*—"from the fault in the universe."[5]

3. Topology and Science

At this point, we can formulate a remark which can be phrased as follows: topology is a domain of science by means of which science accounts for its failure to suture the subject; this is in what topology and psychoanalysis are solidary.

This topology—which forms part of that which defines psychoanalysis as deriving from science, as correlative with science— is that of the subject, the very subject which science aims to foreclose, to suture, but it is precisely there that science fails.

The subject, as Lacan writes in his article "Science and Truth," "remains the correlate of science, but an antinomial correlate since science turns out to be defined by the deadlocked endeavour to suture the subject."[6]

This introduces the mode of the subject "for which the only index I have found is topological, that is, the generating sign of the Möbius strip that I call the 'interior eight'." Lacan adds that "the subject is, as it were, internally excluded from its object." (*loc. cit.*)

This is the divided subject, equivalent to its division:

- its division by the signifier in alienation, the forced choice of the Other and of the signifying chain, at the cost of a lack-in-being;
- its splitting by the object, there where it could find a complement of being.

4. The Fault in the Universe

It is essential to stress that language, the Symbolic, puts this "fault in the universe" into play in a fundamental and intrinsic fashion.

The function of the fault, of the lack, of the hole, is strictly equivalent to language; it supports all notions of structure: a structure is nothing else than a mode of organization of the hole—that is to say, a topology.

For example, with the Möbius strip, it is apparent that it closes back upon itself, that, like the torus, it puts a central hole into play. But one can see that it is necessary to circle the hole twice to return to one's point of departure while moving along the surface of the Möbius strip: it is a double-circuit topology of the hole.

First of all then, the hole is the fault in the universe which has to do with language and with nothing else. This means that the Other of language is fundamentally flawed, that it does not stand as guarantor for itself: there is no ultimate guarantor, there is no Other of the Other; and more fundamentally, the Other as complete, as consistent, does not exist. Lacan writes this fault in the universe Ø[A].

Ø is what makes the link between the topology of surfaces we just evoked with the Möbius strip and the torus, and the topology of knots.

Let us note that Lacan's topology of the 1960s starts from the Other to then succeed—precisely through these surfaces, torus, Möbius strip, cross-cap, Klein bottle—in putting into function the incompleteness of the Other, the structuring position of the lack in the Other. Starting from O, it ends up in Ø, while the topology of the 1970s, that of the knots, is explicitly founded on Ø.

This is where one finds the fundamental point of coherence: both of Lacan's topologies, of surfaces and of knots, are topologies of Ø which are grounded on the fact that the Other does not exist.

5. Ø

The fault in the universe, in the universe of the signifier—in other words what authorizes us to write Ø with Lacan—is based on this: that the signifier is only defined by difference, this being the very basis of linguistics.

Let us recall the differential definition of the signifier as it is formulated by Saussure in his course on linguistics (pp. 166–168):

> In language, there are only differences [. . .]. Applied to the unit—namely, a fragment of spoken chain corresponding to a certain concept—the principle of differentiation can be formulated as follows: the characters of a unit are confused with the unit itself. In language, as in any semiological system, what distinguishes a sign is the only thing which constitutes it. It is difference which constitutes a character, just as it gives value to the unit.[7]

To operate with the signifier is to operate with difference. Lacan insists that the signifier as such is used to connote difference in its pure state; at first, signifiers only manifest the presence of difference as such, and nothing else.

This entails consequences of different orders. The first one is immediate: the signifier is correlative with a loss, that of the reference. While a sign represents something for someone, the signifier, which is only worth something through the difference it introduces and through nothing else, implies that the relation between the sign and the thing be erased. It is at the cost of this loss, of the erasing of the trace which the sign was, that the signifier comes into being. The signifier as such is the product of a loss.

A second consequence bears upon the Other as the treasury of signifiers. I am going to try to summarize here the development made by Jacques-Alain Miller in his course entitled "Extimité."[8]

The Other is the treasury of signifiers, but does that constitute a set, can it make a whole, given that the operation which structures it is difference?

Let us take a set of four elements, a, b, c, and d, and the following operator of difference: of a we can say that $a \neq b$, $a \neq c$, $a \neq d$. Starting with a, we have a set $\{b, c, d\}$ defined through their difference from a. Similarly, starting with each one of the elements, we will obtain a set, that of the three other elements, defined by their difference with this element. In other words, we will be able to define a whole, a set, on condition that each time, one will not be there, that there will be an exception.

To obtain an exhaustive set, another operator would have been necessary, for example identity: $\forall x, x = x$. This yields a complete whole, but one which is founded on $x = x$, that is to say on a zero of meaning. It is because language aims at sense that the logic of the signifier which supports it is a logic of difference.

And since the signifier is differential, there is no possible whole of signifiers; one of them will always be lacking; and to make a whole, one must have one extra signifier [un de plus], which will not be there itself, which constitutes an exception. O [A] is thus incomplete; it includes a lack and, at this place, what makes Ø consist is this exterior signifier which draws its border, and which Lacan writes as S(Ø).

However, there is nonetheless a way of remedying the incompleteness and of integrating the signifier which makes an exception into the completed set: it consists, in the example we chose of a, b, c, and d, in accepting to write $a \neq a$, which transforms the function of the "one extra" [un-en-plus] into the function of the element which is not identical to itself.

These are logical functions. That any signifier whatever may come to this place does not change anything in this: that it is necessary either that one element remain excluded, or—and this is what can replace the preceding condition—that a heterogeneous element be introduced, one that would be different from itself. If it comes to complete the Other in this way, it also renders it inconsistent.

Incomplete or inconsistent, the Other only exists as barred.

And let us note with Lacan that each time the question of nomination is posed, each time, for example, that one tries to designate a signifier with itself, to write $a = a$, this signifier will come to the logical place of the point of inconsistency: there is no tautology.

"A signifier," says Lacan in *L'identification* (6 December 1961), "can be defined in no other way than through its not being what the other signifiers are. From the fact that it can only be defined precisely by virtue of not being all the other signifiers, there arises another dimension: it is equally true that the signifier could not be itself." In other words, one cannot write $a = a$. Lacan adds that "the signifier is essentially different from itself; nothing of the subject could identify itself with it without excluding itself from it."

6. $\mathcal{S}$

This brings us back to the subject—to the speaking subject—who is only a subject through the signifier.

It is thus only in the field of the Other, the Other which is always already there, the Other where it [ça] speaks of him or her, that a subject can come into being by recognizing him- or herself under a signifier, under the master-signifier S_1 of the fundamental identification.

S_1 designates the signifier inaccessible to the subject and which however supports the subject. This is why Lacan, in his formulation of the analytic discourse, writes:

$$\frac{S}{S_1}$$

S_1 is under the bar, forever separated from the subject, insofar as it constitutes the *Urverdrängung* spoken of by Freud, that is to say primal repression: the subject remains cut off from this signifier which nonetheless determines him or her as such.

In this logical and mythical time of the originary repression, the subject, who is nothing other than S_1, finds him- or herself excluded from this S_1 as he or she attempts to get hold of him- or herself in it. This pertains to the very structure of the Other, to the differential definition of the signifier which cannot get hold of itself, if not as different from itself, which can thus only grasp itself in its self-difference.

How, then, in this movement of the constitution of the subject, does one account for the originary repression by which the subject comes into being as lack of signifier, as one-minus [*un-en-moins*] in the very logical movement in which he or she is constituted?

It is as support of this logical time of the birth of the subject in this effort of self-grasping of the S_1, in this redoubling of the S_1 by S_1, that Lacan introduces the figure of the interior eight in *L'identification*.

Figure 4–9.

Lacan illustrates the logical time of the constitution of the subject as lack with the help of an operation of logic constructed on the basis of Euler's circles. This operation is that of symmetrical difference; that is to say the union minus the intersection: that is, either A *or* B, in which this *or* is exclusive.

In a conjunction of logic and topology, Lacan inscribes these figures on a torus and shows that on this condition, and thereby departing from the support of the plane and that of the sphere, logic continues to function, but otherwise: on the torus, union and intersection cannot be written, they do not stop not writing themselves. The torus excludes the intersection; there where one would expect to find it; one is outside the field.

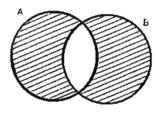
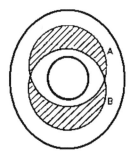

Figure 4–10.

The fields A and B cannot re-find themselves in a second moment.

A signifier which would try to get hold of itself in redoubling itself in the figure of the interior eight traced on the torus, can only subsist there in what becomes a field of self-difference, and only grasps itself at its limit, in its fading.

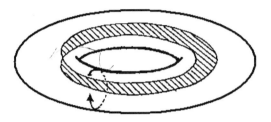

Figure 4–11.

One sees there that the signifier, in redoubling itself, only grasps a void, homogeneous with the field exterior to the signifier, and the subject designates itself there as an excluded field.

In order to account for the foundational entrapment of the subject in the signifier and the primal repression correlative to the emergence of the subject, we need a topology that is no longer that of the sphere, but constructed on the basis of the structuring function of the hole, in other words a topology of the *a-sphere*. The impossibility of saying $a = a$, in other words, that which founds the differential structure of the signifier upon this exclusion, is supported by the torus, insofar as the exclusion of the intersection is revealed there.

The Real of the signifier is homogeneous with the Real of the torus; it is, one could say, of the same order of Real: the impossible which is manifested there is the very one on which the subject founds itself.

Lacan writes in *L'étourdit* that "Structure is the real which shows itself in language." Its topology is this structure itself, such as the foundation of the subject in the signifier necessitates it.

Thus it is as a logical consequence of what the very characteristic of a language is—to wit, the differential definition of the signifier—that each speaking subject, parasited by language, thereby comes to answer this structure founded on the hole: it is at the very point of the lack in the Other, at the point where the signifier which could name him or her lacks, that the subject finds him- or herself suspended, excluded. For lack of being named, he or she can only be represented in the signifying chain.

The subject we first introduced as split by the object is thus found again here, divided by the signifier: $.

7. The Cut

Lacan had already laid the foundations of this topology, which he develops from the Seminar on identification onwards, as early as 1953, in the *Rome Report*, at the same time as he put the accent on the Symbolic. Those are the terms in which he developed it[9]:

> To say that this mortal meaning reveals in speech a centre exterior to language is more than a metaphor; it manifests a structure. This structure is different from the spatialisation of the circumference or of the sphere in which some people like to schematise the limits of the living being and his milieu: it corresponds rather to the relational group that symbolic logic designates topologically as an annulus.
>
> If I wished to give an intuitive representation of it, it seems that, rather than have recourse to the surface aspect of a zone, I should call on the tri-dimensional form of a torus, in so far as its peripheral exteriority and its central exteriority constitute only one single region. [Sheridan's translation, at 105]

In this center exterior to language where death dwells, this Real of which one cannot say anything, but where, however, the mortifying effect of the signifier attaches itself as an umbilical cord, let us recognize this structure of internal exclusion, the one of the *vacuole* which Lacan tells us about in *The Ethics*, and the scope of which Jacques-Alain Miller has shown in the different stages of Lacan's teaching under the term of *extimité*.

In starting with the torus, Lacan brings forth the three principal topological objects on which he will rely at the beginning of the 1960s.

Let us take the Möbius strip, precisely as Lacan makes it surge forth from the torus after the fact, in *L'étourdit*, on the basis of a cut in the form of the interior eight, and of a sticking together onto itself of one of the two edges thus produced.

The inverse operation, which consists in cutting a Möbius strip in its middle, produces a new edge—in the form of an interior eight—and makes the Möbien structure disappear: in this, the Möbius strip is this cut itself. There, the subject is designated, insofar as the signifier unveils its structure through its cut at the same time as it makes it disappear into what Lacan names the *ab-sense* of the Möbien void produced by the cut: it is the subject such as is constituted in alienation.

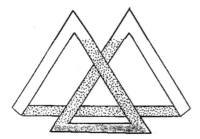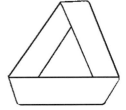

Figure 4–12.

Conjoining inside and outside in each of their points, the Möbius strip accounts for the question of the Freudian double inscription, conscious-preconscious on the one hand, unconscious on the other. This is what Lacan writes in *Radiophonie* (p. 70) concerning the Möbius strip:

> The Freudian double inscription [. . .] would thus be of the order [. . .] of the very practice which calls it forth as question, namely the cut: for in withdrawing from it, the unconscious attests to the fact that it consists solely in it; or again, that the

more discourse is interpreted, the more it is proved to be unconscious.

In this respect, the Möbius strip, as topological support, accounts just as well for interpretation and its effects—and thus for the analytic act insofar as it lays down the interpretative cut.

8. *"There Is No Metalanguage"*

Let us now try to approach the *a-spheric*, Möbien structure, which supports the Other, the subject, the unconscious, from another perspective, under an other angle.

The unconscious is structured like a language: this implies that any theory of psychoanalysis, any theory of the unconscious, would be a metalanguage. How, then, can we conciliate theory with what Lacan formulates when he states that "there is no metalanguage," and which we can just as well understand as follows, that there is no Other of the Other? What status are we to give Lacan's formalizations, whether they be logical or topological?

A formal language is not conceivable without the support of a common language: the common language is necessary for communication and for the introduction of any formal language, failing which it would only be a "cryptogram without a cipher." On this point, we can refer to an article by Jacques-Alain Miller, published in *Ornicar?* no 5, on the unique language, the "U language" of Haskell Curry.[10]

A language can always be considered as a metalanguage for the object-language of the preceding rank. This gives rise to a recurrent series, and at the beginning of this series, there is a language which is only pure object; its words are things—letters, drawings, and so forth—which signify nothing, which are only materiality. Miller noted that any formalized language, insofar as it is a being of writing, is in this sense an object-language, and that the common language, the "U language," is the metalanguage of writings. There is here an inversion of the starting position: a theoretical elaboration formalized on facts of common language—thus a metalanguage—is at the same time an object-language, the common language of which is precisely a metalanguage. Miller proposed to resolve this paradox—and it is here that we meet up again with topology—with the concept of the unique language, in the following terms: "There is no object-language, there is no metalanguage. The unique language is to itself both metalanguage and object-language which intertwine and interlace; not stratified, but coiled in a Möbien way, the unique language does not cease citing itself: autonymous, it is inconsistent."

There is no metalanguage then, not only because there is no Other of the Other, but more fundamentally because the Other does not exist; there is only a barred Other, marked by inconsistency or incompleteness.

There is thus cause for us to distinguish the formal constructions of the linguists and the logicians, which aim to make the Other exist, and Lacan's formalizations, logical or topological, which derive from a logic of $\emptyset$. In this respect, the logical formalizations of Lacan, like his topology, aim to encircle the place of what is not symbolizable, to circumscribe the point of inconsistency of language, the point of failure of the Other: they arise from the fault in the universe.

9. Logic and Topology

In this respect, how can we articulate logic with topology?

There is certainly a creationist effect in topology; with writing, the drawings, one achieves a small gain on the Real. This small gain pertains to the sole fact that such writings and drawings serve to apprehend a mathematical object, outside of any meaning; they serve to put some Symbolic on a pure structure, which ex-sists as Real.

We can indeed illustrate it by using the Möbius strip. The signifier could not account for this elementary structure, which however is its very own, before the intuition, the form, and the study of it were progressively uncovered by Gauss, Listing, and Möbius. And once this strip is invented, the signifier continues to remain below the Real of the structure which the strip incarnates.

Lacan is, without a doubt, making use of this creationist effect to encircle this Real, to circumscribe this structure. But he also warns us against what could become a mysticism of topology, against any fascinating effect or initiatory drift associated with it— through capture by the image, the putting into play of the Imaginary of the body. Is it not precisely on this point that we may recognize the reason of the tour de force accomplished by Lacan in *L'étourdit*, a text in which he articulates his topology for us with no other support than words, in which he shows us how discourse itself is topologically articulated?

What Lacan formidably demonstrates in this text—and this is what gives all its weight to topology in his teaching, in psychoanalysis, and simply for the speaking being who, like Monsieur Jourdain [in Molière's *Bourgeois Gentilhomme*] can only be a topologist, be it without knowing it—what Lacan demonstrates then, is that one can do without topology on condition that one make use of it. Is this to say that one should oppose, on the one hand, topology as structure, and the logical formalizations on the other hand, or would they not, rather, be homogeneous?

Let us stress first of all that Lacan's theoretical discourse is homogeneous with its object: just as language harbors within itself its point of lack, its point of inconsistency, the discourse which accounts for what happens for the subject of language is *a-spherical* topology, founded on the structuring function of the hole.

Likewise, let us note that it is because Lacan's formulations do not arise from a metalanguage disjoined from common language, but from a process of ciphering, substitution, and metaphor internal to this language, whose own structure is already Möbien, that they are homogeneous with his topology.

And indeed, topology stems from a combinatory and, more precisely, from the impossible in the combinatory: this is where topology emerges from, as *analysis situs*, with the problem of the bridges of Königsberg. The impossible is just as well what every signifying structure harbors, as Lacan demonstrates in *The Purloined Letter*, with the *caput mortuum* of the signifier, this remainder excluded from the operation, which makes a hole, and thereby takes its structural and causal value, exactly like the hole of the cross-cap, or of the Möbius strip.

This remainder, this fault in the universe, comes to parasite science and introduce scandal in its most elaborated constructions. We can evoke here, not only Gödel's theorem, but also what brings us even closer, perhaps, to the questions which preoccupy mathematicians; namely what one of our Japanese colleagues, Shin'ya Ogasawara, recalled last year[11]: in the rational mathematical universe, that of the set theory of Zermelo-Fraënkel, thus in a universe which presents itself explicitly as excluding the subject, there nonetheless appeared an extimate object where the subject could lodge itself, showing—as Lacan stated in *Science and Truth*, as we just recalled—that logic fails to suture the subject. In this universe, an indiscernible heterogeneous set slips in and conceals itself, and it is one which does not have any specific signifier. It is a kind of inevitable parasite, demonstrated by the mathematician Paul J. Cohen, who named it *the generic*: it is a mathematical version of the Lacanian myth of the lamella.

For one, this leads us to accentuate the solidarity and the continuity of logic and topology. There is no way for either to avoid the structuring function of the hole: indeed, on the contrary, both the one and the other arise from it.

And this is at the heart of Lacan's theoretical progress, of his advance on the basis of the Freudian discovery. Two essential points—essential for the orientation of the clinic—of this advance have been formulated by Lacan in his famous aphorism: "The unconscious is structured like a language" and in his elaboration of object *a*.

10. *"The Unconscious Is Structured Like a Language"*

In effect, when Lacan formulates that the unconscious is structured like a language, let us note that this implies and condenses three successive articulations.

- First of all, Lacan proposes that what Freud discovered—
  to wit, that there are some repressed representations which
  are produced on the basis of a repressed prototype, an *Urverdrängung*, namely the logical necessity of originary repression as foundation of the unconscious—is nothing other,
  for a speaking subject, than the primary consequence of the
  differential structure of the signifier. Primary repression and
  the constitution of the subject in the field of the signifier
  are equivalent.
- Secondly, Lacan formulates the consequence of his proposition: the unconscious and language have the same structure.
- And finally, the whole of Lacan's work of elaboration and
  formalization precisely targets this structure on the basis
  of this second consequence: namely that it is founded on a
  lack, on a hole, and that it is *a-spherical* topology.

11. The Object a

It is on this point of umbilical attachment of the structure that the
place of the object *a* is designated, in its double valence of lack, of
pure absence on the one hand, of cork on the other. Or, to say it
otherwise, the object as cause and the object as remainder, or again,
agalma and waste.

The object *a* is what comes to suture the lack of the subject in
a fallacious completeness which misrecognizes its division, in the
fantasy.

The object *a* is, just as well, what comes to split the subject,
to cause it, beyond the fantasy.

The object *a* is also, as correlate of the failure in the Other,
the logical consistency which comes to complete the inconsistency
of the Other.

That is why this object, which comes to close up the gap of
the Möbien structure of the subject as of the Other, also has the
interior eight for edge in Lacan's topology.

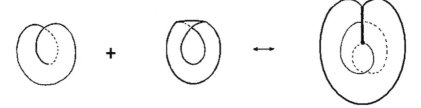

Figure 4–13.

It is this disc [*rondelle*] which can come to suture a Möbius strip along its unique edge, and this produces a new surface, the projective plane and, insofar as it derives from it, the cross-cap.

12. Identification, Drive, Fantasy, or the Topology of the Transference According to the Interior Eight

Lacan gives us an example of the fact that one can do without topology on condition that one makes use of it concerning the end of the treatment, in the last pages of the *Four Fundamental Concepts*.

Its topological structure is not immediately apparent, and this is what we can try to uncover, all the more so since this example evidences the solidarity of logic and topology on the one hand, and on the other shows in what way the clinic and its concepts—transference, identification, fantasy, drive—find their articulation in topology: namely, that clinic and topology are solidary as well.

Let us underline here that two major concepts of Lacan's concerning transference, the subject-supposed-to-know, and the enactment of the—sexual—reality of the unconscious find their coherence in their common reference to the function of the object *a* and to the status of the Other as barred: Ø. The Other does not exist. It is marked either by incompleteness or by inconsistency. The inconsistency of the Other implies that the reference to the signifier is not sufficient to situate transference.

The subject-supposed-to-know supposes that the Other does not know, that the Other in question is at the antipodes of the Other of knowledge, as Miller stresses in his course entitled *Réponses du réel*.[12] The knowledge in question pertains to what remains of unknown knowledge, unknown by the Other, a knowledge which does not flow from the signifier, but which has to do with the object.

Miller highlighted in this same course the very illuminating distinction between alienation-transference and separation-transference, which correspond very precisely to the couple alienation-separation introduced by Lacan in the Seminar on the *Four Fundamental Concepts*. In alienation-transference, it is truly the Other as incomplete, as amputated of a signifier, which is in play; it is, on the other hand, insofar as it is rendered inconsistent by the inclusion of the object *a*, which is not one of its elements, that the Other of desire functions in separation-transference.

The function of the subject-supposed-to-know, just like the enactment of the sexual reality of the unconscious, aims at the Other precisely there where it is lacking, where it is revealed as Ø.

We have seen how the gap of the subject, like the fault of the Other, can come to be filled by the object coming to suture, along its edge, the Möbius strip which supports their structure, thereby producing a cross-cap. Lacan topologizes the relation of the subject with the Other by drawing support from another surface, the Klein bottle.

2 Möbius strips   Klein bottle

Figure 4–14.

Lacan underlines in the Seminar that follows the *Four Concepts, Les Problèmes cruciaux de la psychanalyse*, the topology which accounts for the articulation of the subject with this Other, which is first of all the Other subject, as absolute Other which can make the subject itself disappear; this topology consists precisely in the articulation of two Möbius strips along their single edge. And what results from this is the surface called the Klein bottle.

In this conjunction, which is that of alienation, the subject is prey to the metonymy of the signifying chain, of the lack-in-being. But it cannot find its identity there as being; it can only disappear beneath the signifier which represents it for another signifier. This is the closed field of identifications and of the slope towards the idealizing identification, which is that of the transference.

So let us return precisely to the question of the transference and the end of the treatment, starting with these two facets of trans-ference which Lacan brings to the fore in the Seminar of the *Four Fundamental Concepts of Psychoanalysis*.

The side indexed by O [A], referred to the Other—the Other of Truth and the deceiving Other—is that of the supposition of knowl-edge, but also that of the deception of love and of the idealizing iden-tification. Here, transference is ordered between S and Ø [A], and puts into play a supposition of knowledge which only has to do with the signifier. The Other is there as Other of knowledge, and what is deployed is in the register of alienation-transference. Here, the sub-ject has no other choice than the register of the signifier; we are in the field, or the plane, as Lacan says, of identification.

The side *a*, that of transference as moment of closure of the unconscious, but which nonetheless remains referable to the subject-supposed-to-know, requires an Other therefore completed with the *a* as logical consistency, an Other to whom the subject will have entrusted the cause of its desire. Transference then puts into play the Other of desire, and supposes a knowledge which has to do with the object.

Here, separation is possible, and this is what the desire of the analyst allows, insofar as it brings demand back to the drive. The subject can then come to this place of the *a*, and the relation to the Other will play itself out at this point between *a* and Ø, on the axis of a subjectivization without a subject—acephalic, as Lacan puts it. It is the axis, the plane of the drive, and it is because the subject has been able to come to the place of the *a*, to identify itself with the object, finding there its complement of being in separation, that what Lacan calls the crossing of the plane of identification is possible.

There, thus, remains the fantasy to account for, which we evoked earlier: $S \diamond a$. When the subject in analysis has experienced this crossing, has passed through the place of the a, has felt him- or herself as being, in the a, "the experience of the fundamental fantasy becomes the drive," says Lacan, which is to say that it is played out beyond the pleasure principle (*Four Concepts*, p. 273 in my English edition). It is insofar as it has been able to occupy this empty place in the Other, that of the a and insofar as it has been caused by the a that the subject as a aims at itself in the Other, beyond the fantasy.

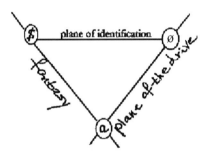

Figure 4–15.

As we saw earlier, it is on the basis of what makes for the articulation of subject and Other, of object and Other, on this curve of the interior eight that Lacan proposes to topologize transference in the Seminar of the *Four Fundamental Concepts*.

Thus, here is what could be the deployed schema of this interior eight, insofar as we can decline it, as Lacan does at the end of the *Four Concepts*, in reference to transference and to the operation of the analyst's desire. We can inscribe this deployed schema as a logical schema on the condition that we do not forget what has led us to it, and that what makes its essential coherence, we could even say its intrinsic coherence, is the topology of the interior eight.

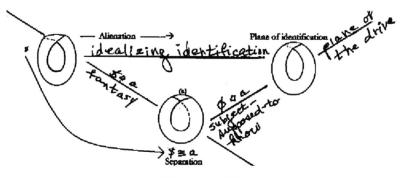

Figure 4–16.

Here we can read what Lacan announces at the end of this Seminar *The Four Concepts*:

"The transference operates in the direction of bringing demand back to identification. It is in as much as the analyst's desire, which remains an x, tends in a direction that is the exact opposite of identification" namely, it maintains the distance between the I of the fundamental identification and the object of the drive, *a*—"that the crossing of the plane of identification is possible, through the mediation of the separation of the subject in experience. The experience of the subject is thus brought back to the plane at which, from the reality of the unconscious, the drive may be made present" (p. 274).

Thus, to end these preliminary remarks and to continue resonating with the end of the Seminar of the *Four Fundamental Concepts*, we hope to have shown that topology is not to be classed among the obscure gods. It is not a mystique, nor is it an autarchic research, a topology for topology's sake. It is the structure of the clinic, the structure of the analytic experience, because it is above all valid for each speaking being.

This is why Lacan can say in *L'étourdit* that topology is structure, nothing other than this structure, that is to say, in his own terms in *L'étourdit*: "the *a-spherical* harboured in the articulation of language insofar as an effect of the subject avails itself of it."

Lacan developed this topology for us in his teaching, but, just as with structure, he made himself its dupe—something which he also exhorted us to do. Topology, he could do without it, because he made use of it: his practice was topology.

ENDNOTES

1. Jacques Lacan "L'etourdit," Scilicet, no. 4, Paris: Seuil, 1973, p. 34; Ecrits, ed. by Jacques-Alain Miller (Paris: Seuil, 2001).

2. Rudy Rucker, La Quatrième Dimension (Paris: Seuil, 1985).

3. Dominique Inarra, May 1989, unpublished exposé.

4. Jacques Lacan (1988 and 1998). The Seminar, Book II (1972–1973); Encore, ed. by Jacques-Alain Miller, trans. with notes by Bruce Fink. New York: W. W. Norton.

5. Jacques Lacan, "L'etourdit," Scilicet, no. 4, p. 34.

6. Jacques Lacan, "La science et la vérité" (1965), Ecrits, Paris, Seuil, 1965, p. 861; "Science and Truth," trans. by Bruce Fink, Newsletter of the Freudian Field, vol. 3, nos. 1&2 (Spring /Fall 1989), pp. 4–29.

7. Ferdinand de Saussure (1966), Cours de Linguistique Générale, Paris: Payot, 1972, pp. 166–168; Course in General Linguistics (1916), trans. by Wade Baskin. New York: McGraw-Hill.

8. Jacques-Alain Miller, Cours 1985–1986, Extimité (May 14, 1986), unpublished.

9. Jacques Lacan (1977). "Fonction et champs de la parole et du langage (1953)," Ecrits, Paris: Seuil, 1966, pp. 320–321; "The function and field of speech and language in psychoanalysis" ("Rome Discourse" of 1953), trans. by Alan Sheridan. Ecrits: A Selection. New York: W. W. Norton.

10. Jacques-Alain Miller, "U ou 'il n 'y a pas de metalangage'," Ornicar?, no. 5, 1975.

11. Shin-ya Ogasawara, "Du a en tant qu 'agent, une fiction mathematique," Actes de L'Ecole de la Cause Freudienne, no. 15, 1989.

12. Jacques-Alain Miller, Cours 1983–1984, Réponses du réel (January 11, 1984), unpublished.

5

Objet a *and the Cross-cap**

JUAN-DAVID NASIO

Now we will address three problematics in the field of psycho-analysis: the relation between the *inside* and the *outside*; the *cut* and what it signifies as a line that separates and reunites two heterogeneous parts; and finally, the quite specific problematic of one of these parts that Lacan identifies as *objet a*. In practical terms, the cross-cap represents or better yet allows three psychoanalytic concepts to be considered in material terms: the lack of a difference between the inside and the outside; the cut between the divided subject and the unconscious and *objet a*; and finally the particular characteristics of that object. The element common to the three concepts is that of the phallus, or the phallic signifier that is symbolized in the cross-cap, by a single point of the so-called self-intersecting line.

*Translated by David Pettigrew and François Raffoul, from J.-D. Nasio's *Les Yeux de Laure: le concept d' objet a dans la théorie de J. Lacan* (Paris: Aubier, 1987), pp. 193–217.

1. INSIDE/OUTSIDE

We have established that in its concrete and visible version, the sphere equipped with a cross-cap is a closed surface with an inside and an outside. This is exactly what the photograph shows. Let us note that the term "closed" is the name given to a surface that has no edge. The *torus* (tube) is also an example of a surface which, having no edge, is closed, and therefore its inside is distinct from the outside. In fact, if we were to paint the outside of the torus, its inside will always remain unseen, unless, in order to paint it, we opened the torus with scissors. In a three-dimensional space the torus and our sphere equipped with a cross-cap in its concrete version are both closed and bilateral surfaces, that is, with two sides: one facing the inside and the other facing the outside. But, unlike the torus, the sphere equipped with a cross-cap has an anomaly that we have called the suture line and that we now can call the self-intersecting line. It is *self*-intersecting to the extent that the two intersecting surfaces belonging to the same surface can be considered as a body that enters into contact with itself. Certain topological texts also name this line, the line of self-contact, or self-crossing. We insist on this: the line exists in the concrete cross-cap and does not with the abstract cross-cap.

We will see that depending on how this line is considered, we will attribute the property to the cross-cap of being either a bilateral surface, or a unilateral surface.[1] This can be clarified in what follows. If we conceive of the line as the place where the two surfaces meet (Nasio [1987], fig. 20), we would say that the cross-cap is closed and that it has two sides that remain distinct without any continuity between them: the inside is separated from the outside and the surface is bilateral. If, on the contrary, we attribute to the same concrete cross-cap the theoretical property of not having a self-intersecting line, by stating that the surfaces do not intersect, we would then say that the cross-cap has only one side: the inside is not separate from the outside and the surface is therefore unilateral. In this latter case we will claim that there is no border between the supposed inside and the supposed outside of the surface. In other words, if we recognize it as *theoretical*, the cross-cap has neither an inside nor an outside. This characteristic of the cross-cap of not having an inside or an outside is not, therefore, immediately perceived by the eye. One must think abstractly so that while observing the line that pinches the balloon we are able to think of it as simply not being there.

We see that the cross-cap relevant to psychoanalysis is not the concrete one that we have constructed in three dimensions, nor the abstract one that exists in algebraic formulas, but the conjunction of the two.

In order to understand this theoretical property of a cross-cap having neither an inside nor an outside, let us take the example of an ant following the surface that never encounters the so-called self-intersecting line. If the ant begins at a point on the outer anterior side of the right lobe of the cross-cap to go towards the place of the line, it will be surprised to arrive at the inner posterior side of the left lobe without having crossed any limit or border. That is to say, it passed from a supposed outside to a supposed inside without encountering any obstacle. The obstacle that it could have encountered, if we were to think of the cross-cap in only three-dimensional terms, would have been, for instance, another ant taking a symmetrical path, beginning from the outer anterior side of the left lobe and ending on the inner posterior side of the right lobe. In short, to recognize the theoretical property that renders the cross-cap without inside or outside, we must apply the following rule: two ants passing symmetrically at the same time and at the same place do not meet, for one is unable to get in the way of the other.

We note that the theoretical property of the unilateral nature of the cross-cap recalls the unilateral nature of the well-known Möbius strip. Indeed, if one follows this strip, one will always remain on its one and only side. That said, the unilateral nature of the cross-cap is much more interesting than that of the Möbius strip, because it is an open surface while the cross-cap is a closed surface; it is indeed more interesting to consider the unilateral as such in a closed balloon rather than in an open ribbon. Why? Because if we admit—according to a certain theoretical assumption, one recalls—that the supposed two sides of a closed voluminous body have only one face, one must also immediately accept that the so-called interior order of the body is perfectly continuous with the so-called surrounding milieu. The body is closed and yet the surrounding milieu is inside it. Or inversely, the milieu surrounds a closed body of which it is nevertheless the most intimate core.

The border between the inside and the outside is subverted: this is what the cross-cap teaches psychoanalysis and it is *on the basis of* that subversion that psychoanalysis conceives of space. There are three ways of treating the border between the inside and the outside. The intuitive manner recognizes it as a partition or a skin separating the inside from the outside of a closed body. The topological manner—the abstract cross-cap—considers it directly as a nonexistent border since the inside is continuous with the outside. In this case, clearly the words "inside" and "outside" have lost their raison d'être since they are no longer in opposition but rather continuous. And finally, the "psychoanalytic" manner, while considering the border as nonexistent, nonetheless maintains the use of the two terms inside (interior) and outside (exterior) but completely reverses their ordinary meaning. The psychoanalytic use of expressions such as outside (exterior) and inside (interior) in relation to certain very specific problems ultimately combines three moments of thought: first, the recognition that the inside is not the outside; second, the cancellation of this opposition; and third, the use of the same terms, finally, while radically subverting their initial meanings. Concretely, it is much more useful to subvert the relation between an inside and an outside than simply affirming their nonexistence. For example, the relation between intensive psychoanalysis and extensive psychoanalysis only achieves its fullest significance if one uses the inside/outside couple in a subverted manner. One must identify the furthest horizon of the analytic field at the edge of the most interior hole of analytic experience.[2] But the greatest psychoanalytic problem where it is indispensable to distort the inside/outside separation is the subject's relation with the two fundamental psychic agencies: the unconscious and *jouissance*. (This is addressed specifically in the chapter devoted to the formations of *objet a*.)³ What is essential is that the unconscious and *jouissance* are external to the subject who, through the event of a saying or an act, actualizes them. It only requires a saying or an act to recognize that at that moment—and only at that moment, the moment of the event—the unconscious and *jouissance* spread in the space assumed to be outside the subject, the bearer of what is said or done. The entire difficulty lies in being able to conceive of *jouissance* and the unconscious as external parasitic agencies, surrounding the subject while an event takes place in the cure. In other words it is with the cross-cap that we give thought to this unprecedented conception of a psyche external to the subject, when in principle it is its most intimate agency.

2. THE LACANIAN CUT OF THE "INTERIOR EIGHT"

> "*The one [the psychoanalyst] who can open* objet a *the right way with a pair of scissors is the master of desire.*"
> —J. Lacan

The other property of the cross-cap which interests us is found in the act of cutting. All the elements of our *topologerie*⁴ and particularly the spherical surface equipped with a cross-cap only demonstrate their efficacy as psychoanalytic mathemes, that is, their efficacy as a mode of transmission, on the condition that they are subjected to a certain kind of cutting. Our surfaces are only actualized by the cutting and only exist by the edges that the scissors confirm or create.⁵

Let us clarify from the outset that the cuts to be discussed later are to be imagined certainly as sections cut with scissors from the "concrete" cross-cap, but on the condition of respecting the following theoretical rule: when the scissors meet the so-called self-intersecting line, it would be necessary to act as if the line did not exist, as if the cross-cap that we are going to cut had no thickness or line that would be in contact with itself. Consequently if we abide by this rule we must accept that we will cut the concrete cross-cap with concrete scissors while following, however, a theoretical line.

The cutting practiced on the sphere equipped with a cross-cap that interests us are simply the closed curves, called Jordan curves.

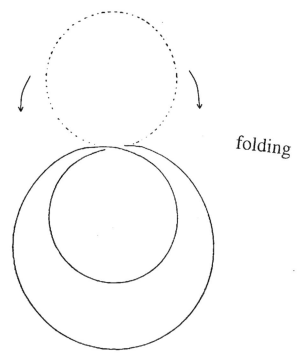

folding

Figure 5–1.

They can be classified in two types: those that separate the surface into two pieces and those that leave it in one piece. The first are really important to us and in particular the one Lacan used to account for the logic of the signifying repetition and its effects called "the cut of the interior eight" (cf. Fig. 5–1).

The cut of the internal eight divides our cross-cap in two: a nonorientable surface—the Möbius strip—identified with the subject of the unconscious, and an orientable surface—a disk—identified with *objet a*. We can add, moreover, that the difference between the cuts that separate the surface into two pieces and the cuts that do not separate them, resides in the fact that the separating cuts cross the self-intersecting line an *even* number of times, while the nonseparating cuts only cross it an odd number of times. As we will see, the interior eight crosses the line *twice*. By separating the surface into two absolutely heterogeneous parts, the interior eight confirms that the parts, although heterogeneous, compose nonetheless the unique piece that is the sphere equipped with a cross-cap. In other words it is necessary to cut the cross-cap to determine that the resulting orientable portion and the nonorientable portion—that is to say, *objet a* and the subject of the unconscious—were able to coexist in continuity in one surface.

But why choose the form of the interior eight to divide the cross-cap when with other closed sections with different shapes that also cross the self-intersecting line an even number of times, we obtain an identical separation?[6] This is due to the fact that the two loops of the cut called the interior eight represent—in a way that nothing else can—the different moments of the repetition of the signifier.

The importance in Lacanian theory of this figure of two loops, one encompassing the other, goes further than the problematic of the cross-cap. Independently of the theoretical contexts in which it comes into play, the interior eight responds to a specific task: in every case it supports the function of saying in its relation to the subject. There is a word to designate this fundamental relation: repetition. The interior eight, or the folded eight, graphically represents the logic of the repetition of the signifiers and its effect on the subject. Thus when we make an incision in the cross-cap, following a cut of this type, we do more than simply materialize the incidence of the words (not just any word) on a surface preexisting them: we inscribe in the Real the effect that these words provoke once they have been uttered. We take the folded eight; we *think* repetition *with* it; we apply it on our spherical surface; we verify that it crosses the self-intersecting line twice; and we recognize the effects produced as being effects of repetition.

Concretely, the cut of the repetition in the form of the folded eight involves three aspects: the deployment of the curve in two loops, its eventual closing, and its effects that are visible in the transformation of the cross-cap. Let us begin with a description of the two loops. The minimal unity of the repetitive movement is given by one vector with a progressive orientation and an other vector with a retroactive orientation.[7] The vector AB shows the two states of an event: before it is repeated: in A; and when it is repeated: in B. Nothing would authorize us to speak of repetition if we did not introduce a third trivial yet decisive element: the simple fact of counting. If we do not count a before and an after,

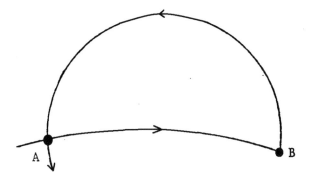

Figure 5–2. The schema of deferred action (*l'après-coup*).

or rather a first, a second and an *nth* time, there will never be repetition. In other words, the state of the event before being repeated becomes the repeated state on the condition that there was a count and someone who counted, understanding that the count is only verified once the repetition is accomplished in B. Before the repetition and consequently before the counting, A did not exist; A will only be first if a second B repeats it. We need to trace the vector BA in the retroactive orientation and indicate that B establishes A as an original event. The first loop schematizes simply the movement that we know as the *deferred affect*. A only becomes first by virtue of the deferred affect, after we count B as its repetition.

The large loop encompassing the small one represents the operation of counting itself, or more precisely, the element that makes calculus possible, that is, the trace of writing. This element—

the trace of writing—that is indispensable to the constitution of a series of numbers, is not, however, itself reducible to a number. It is outside the series, or, if you will, outside of the repetitive succession. It is as this external element that it bears the name given to it by Lacan: plus-One [*l'Un en plus*].

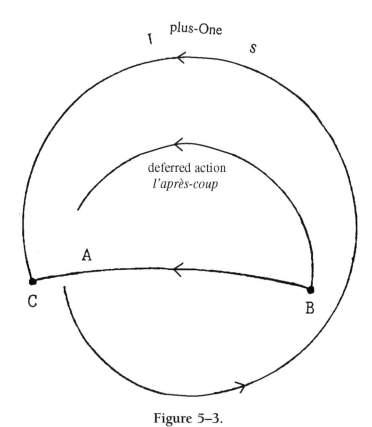

Figure 5–3.

We have said that with respect to the horizon of the counting, there is always someone who counts and calculates. But he or she counts or calculates without being able to count him- or herself. The radical powerlessness of the speaking being who undergoes *jouissance* is that it cannot recognize itself in the successive repetitions. The subject counts but does not count itself—or rather—it is counted as a minus-subject [*sujet en moins*]. The final looping of this double curve with the shape of an interior eight signifies that the repetition is accomplished and brings about the emergence of a new subject that we just described as the minus subject. The point C of Figure 5–3 thus reveals mark three: the closure of the movement of repetition, the closure of the operation of counting, and the emergence of a new subject.

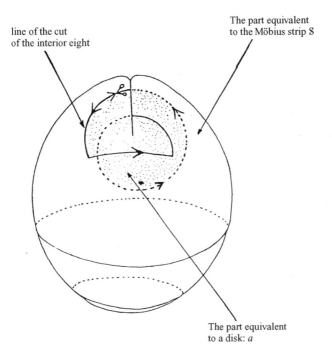

line of the cut
of the interior eight

The part equivalent
to the Möbius strip S

The part equivalent
to a disk: *a*

Figure 5–4.

If now by following the movement and orientation of the curve of the interior eight, we make an incision in the sphere equipped with a cross-cap (Fig. 5–4) at the end of the cut, we produce two surfaces: one equivalent to the Möbius strip that Lacan identifies as the new subject and the other equivalent to a disk identified with *objet a*. In short, to cut the cross-cap with scissors that follow the line of the interior eight constitutes the gesture that spatially materializes or represents the fact that the repetition produces a subject and leaves a residue.

Let us note two things, one concerning the details of the cut on the surface and the other concerning the resulting effects. Let us refer to Figure 5–4 and follow the trajectory of the scissors. The signifying scissors open their path at a point of the self-intersecting line to return to a new level slightly lower than that same line after having cut through the anterior face of the balloon following the form of a loop. Arriving at the second level of the line, they continue their cutting (represented in the drawing by a dotted line) but this time on the posterior face. Finally, they come to the line at the same point where they began their journey. At this precise moment where the loop closes itself, the surface is separated into two parts.

We turn now to the two parts that have been cut. In order to better understand their nature it is necessary—once again—to avoid the error of confusing the concrete and the abstract cross-cap. The effective cut of a thick surface with the metal scissors (our balloon for instance, but made of plaster) is only the allegory or spatio-temporal demonstration of a theoretical cut traced on a surface without any dimension, line, or points where it would enter into contact with itself (this last abstract surface does not therefore have the self-intersecting line).

If we take account of this concrete/abstract distinction with respect to the cut we will also be able to take account of the products of the cut. In fact, the two pieces detached after the spatio-temporal cut of a cross-cap plaster balloon take with them the portion of the self-intersecting line that originally pinched them when they belonged to the surface of the globe. Each of the two pieces thus carries the trace of the anomaly that constitutes the self-intersection. But now it is a question of looking at these two pieces while ignoring the portions of the line where each of them enters into contact with itself. If we consider them without the line of self-contact they could legitimately be considered as equivalent: one to a nonorientable strip and the other to an orientable disk. Still through this theoretical frame let us note that the sphere equipped with a cross-cap is, taken as a whole, a nonorientable surface. From the topological point of view, in the continuous coexistence of the orientable and nonorientable in a unique surface, it is the non-orientable that leaves its mark, and it is the strip that prevails over the disk. If we limited ourselves to looking at the cross-cap balloon without a topological prejudice, it is, on the contrary, the orientable—the sphere—that would prevail. In our opinion, Lacan maintained this contrast between the abstract and concrete cross-cap by speaking of the *a-sphere*[8] in order to refer to the abstract character of a surface that the Möbius strip rendered nonorientable, and speaking of the inflated part [*la gonfle*],[9] to refer to the spherical and closed aspect of the concrete cross-cap. Certainly the *a-sphere* only appears as *a-sphere* to us after the fact, that is to say, after we have observed that the Möbius strip was included in the inflated part, and after the cut has taken place and the piece equivalent to the strip has been detached. It is necessary to cut the inflated part to detach the piece equivalent to the strip from it and recognize then and only then that the concrete inflated part that we saw in three dimensions represented an *a-sphere* in four dimensions. It is necessary to cut to perceive the structure. For the inflated part (concrete cross-cap) to become *a-sphere* (abstract cross-cap), there must be a separating cut which detaches a Möbius strip and shows that the surface of the inflated part was a surface dominated by the non-orientable character of that strip.[10]

With respect to these two disjunctive pieces produced by the cut, we have already examined the case of the Möbius strip and its relation to the subject of the unconscious.[11] We will now consider the other piece (orientable) where Lacan situates *objet a*.

3. *OBJET A* AND THE DISK

Let us consider a particular characteristic of that central part of the cross-cap balloon (drawn in dots in Figure 5–4)

residue of the self-intersecting line

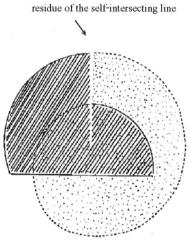

Figure 5–5.

that the cut of the interior eight just cored. To the eye this detached piece has the form of a conch and bears the mark of a small portion of the self-intersecting line. This surface seems to follow a spiraling movement upward, in the manner, if you will, of a small parking garage with two levels (Fig. 5–5).

But let us recall again that if we consider this same piece from a theoretical point of view it will not have the residue of the self-intersecting line and consequently neither will it have the shape of a conch; it only has that shape in three dimensions. From the theoretical point of view that we have already assumed on several occasions, the conch surface is equivalent and only equivalent to an orientable disk. But what led Lacan to identify this disk with *objet a* is not only its orientable nature, in contrast to the nonorientable strip that represents the subject of the unconscious. It has two other characteristics that are just as important.

a) The Conch and the Phallic Point

First, in the same way that the orientable disk turns out after the cut while carrying with it the residue of the self-intersecting line, *objet a* is marked by the characteristic of the phallic function. Lacan confers a great importance not so much on the small portion of the line of intersection that marks the shell as on the particular point where that portion of the line ends. This point—which is sometimes a hole or even a point hole—according to Lacan, gives consistency to the surface of the sphere equipped with the cross-cap, and to the point around which the two loops of the cut of the interior eight turn. Its role is that it allows us to specify the two parts separated by the cut: one, the conch retains the point within it, while the other—the Möbius strip—does not. But what does it mean in psychoanalysis to emphasize the value of this singular point situated at the lower extremity of the self-intersecting line? We say in psychoanalysis because, topologically speaking, the point of which Lacan speaks is no more privileged than the other singular point situated at the upper extremity of the line. From the strictly topological perspective this point merits no special mention. These two privileged points, one at the top and the other at the bottom of the line, only exist because the self-intersecting line exists, for example, exists in three dimensions. Outside our usual space in the abstract cross-cap there is neither line nor privileged point.

That being noted, let us attempt now to understand the psychoanalytic value of the singular point which is at the center of the surface—concrete cross-cap—and of the shell once it has been cored by the cut. This central point represents the phallic signifier stemming from the experience of castration, understood as the transformation into a signifier of this particular organ that is the penis. Lacan would say that the phallus is that which results from the elevation of the penis to the dignity of the signifier. But, the signifier of what? Since the desire that puts the penis into play is indeed sexual desire, or more exactly the desire of the Other, the phallus will be the signifier of that desire. The transformational process that psychoanalysis refers to as castration constitutes the matrix according to which all the other parts of the body will separate, even if none of these parts is able, like the penis, to become signifiers.

In sum, to speak of the phallic signifier means to affirm the primacy of castration and, correlatively, the primacy of the desire of the Other implicit in it over any other experience of separation. This is, in short, the premise that was necessary to recall in order to justify the interest that we have in the fact that the terminal point of the line effects the cored piece called the conch and through which we conceive of *objet a*. Also, the phallus invests *objet a* with meaning to make it an object of desire.

b) Objet a *as a Point*

The other noteworthy property which assimilates the *objet* to the conch or disk consists in its capacity for deformation. To clarify matters we will henceforth call *disk* what we have until now called *conch*. Among the possible deformations of the disk, two are noteworthy: one linked to the mirror and the other intrinsic to the very nature of the disk. We begin with the latter. We can deform this disk so far as to reduce it to a point, and, shrunk in this way, relocate it beside the Möbius strip. In fact, if we want to mentally join the strip with the disk that has become a point, that is, if we supplement the band with a point, we will arrive at the odd conjecture that the Möbius strip supports itself and organizes itself around a point. If it is necessary to imagine this abstract collage, we will then conceive the strip as linked to an external point through the array of lines that join that point to each of the points of the edge of the strip. Let us specify that this supplementary point is not only external to the strip but also external to usual space, as if that point was a vanishing point through which the strip would be sucked into the fourth dimension.[12]

Lacan used this property of the disk to be deformed into a point to show that indeed the subject of the unconscious only supports itself on its object—*objet a*—that becomes an excentric and vanishing point. If we wanted to accentuate the difference between the relation of the ego to the world and the relation of the subject of the unconscious to the world, we would conclude that the egoic world is spherical and concentric, while the world of the divided subject is punctual and excentric. Let us recall briefly how Lacan treated the relation between the strip and the disk in his text *l'etourdit*.

1. The Möbius strip is composed of a bundle of lines, each line being composed in turn of points that all have the particularity of being a place where the back is also the front. At every point of the surface of the strip we find this anomaly of a front which is indistinguishable from the back. Henceforth, any line of the bundle is a line of "pseudo" points, or, as Lacan says, a "line without points."[13] Let us note that it is possible to reduce the surface of the strip to a sole line without points and then qualify the Möbius strip with this expression, "*line without points*." We note also that condensed in a line in this way the strip corresponds exactly to the line of the cut of the internal eight. Hence the corollary: if the strip reduced to a line amounts to the cut of the interior eight, then the cut and the strip are one and the same thing.

2. With respect to the punctual disk that is external to the strip, and thus to the line, it is justified to consider it—with Lacan—as a *point outside the line*.[14]

3. In sum, the cross-cap is the conjunction/disjunction of a *line without points* and of a *point outside the line*.

c) Objet a *Is Nonspecular*

The other quite curious property, where the object meets the disk, involves the capacity of the latter to deform itself in such a way that its image in the mirror disappears. The disk can deform itself without tearing or scarring and adopt the exact same spatial disposition as the image in the mirror. At that point it no longer has an image. Imagine a rubber man in front of the mirror with a birthmark on the left cheek. Now imagine that his reflected image—with the birthmark on the right cheek—is frozen like a photograph. Let us suppose now that through a continuous deformation our man is able to achieve the same corporal disposition as the frozen image in front of him and superimpose himself there.[15] To do this he must first make a half-turn in such a way that by presenting his back to the mirror he enters it backwards. Being thereby included in the mirror he would still have a birthmark on his left cheek while the frozen image would still have the birthmark on its right cheek. In order for the superimposition of our man with his image to be perfect, it is still necessary that he manages to deform his rubber face until the left cheek moves the birthmark to the right cheek. At this moment, and thanks to this curious grimace, he will correspond exactly, point by point, to his frozen image in the mirror. The birthmark displaced now to the right cheek would correspond finally to the birthmark on the right cheek of the reflected image. At the price of a bizarre deformation of the face, the man succeeds in superimposing himself on his image as if it had absorbed him. We would say, then, that there is no longer a relation of alterity between the person and the image, or quite simply, that the person no longer has an image. We call that person who no longer has an image—because he is conflated with it—a *nonspecular* person.

It is precisely this result that Lacan obtains by manipulating the piece called a disk or conch. Seeking to justify the nonspecularity of *objet a*, he twists and deforms the piece of the orientable surface to make it coincide with its own image in the mirror. With respect to the other part of the cross-cap that is cut—the Möbius strip—such an operation is impossible. For one cannot superimpose the strip on its reflected image without causing it to tear. The strip retains the alterity of its image and is thus specular. In the vocabulary of topology we say that the disk is homotopic with its image—or in our terms that *objet a* is nonspecular while on the contrary the Möbius strip is specular.

The Lacanian thesis that affirms the nonspecularity of *objet a* thus seeks to define the nonimaginary nature of the drive. The drive is not an image and does not have an image even if it is through and thanks to the image that it functions. In this sense *objet a* reminds us in an amusing and strange way of the woman in Roman Polanski's film—"Dance of the Vampires"—who discovers her metamorphosis into a vampire at the moment when the mirror no longer reflects her image. Like the vampire of the movie, *objet a* is a kind of libidinal vampire without image.

ENDNOTES

1. In topology, a surface has two sorts of properties: on the one hand, intrinsic properties that do not depend on the nature of the surface and that are based on the rules of theoretical calculus: this is the case of an orientable or nonorientable surface; on the other hand, there are extrinsic properties that depend on the space in which the surface is situated— this is the case of being either unilateral or bilateral (having one or two sides). The same surface, unilateral in one space, can be bilateral in the other. Cf., Seifert, H., and Threlfall W., *A Textbook of Topology* (New York: Academic Press, 1978). We can note that these properties become more difficult to study when some part of the surface enters into contact with itself, as is the case of the sphere equipped with a cross-cap which, situated in a three-dimensional space, enters into contact with itself all along the self-intersecting line.

2. Cf., p. 15 of J. Lacan, "*Proposition du 9 Octobre 1967 sur le psychanalyste de l'École,*" in *Annuaire de l'École freudienne de Paris* where he states: "conforming to the topology of the projective plane, it is at the very horizon of psychoanalysis—*in extensio*—that the internal circle we are tracing as gap of psychoanalysis—*in intensio*—is tied."

3. Cf., Chapter III, pp. 75–106 of *Les Yeux de Laure.*

4. Translator's Notes: The coinage of the neologism *topologerie*—a term that Dr. Nasio has invented—in place of *topologie* echoes Lacan's occasional usage of *linguisterie* in place of linguistics, in order to convey the subversion or *détournement* of its traditional meaning. *Topologerie* therefore refers to both topology and to the twist its meaning receives at the hands of psychoanalysis. We would like to take this opportunity to thank Dr. Joseph Fields, Assistant Professor of Mathematics at Southern Connecticut State University, for his assistance with topological concepts and terms.

5. "We refer to as *cut* a section made with scissors on the surface starting from a point of an edge, and ending in a point of an edge (. . .). The cut will end when we arrive in a point of the edge, whether a point of an edge, or a point of the new edges determined by the path of the scissors." P. Appel, *Theory of Algebraic Functions* Vol. I (New York: Chelsea House, 1929), p. 100.

6. Let us note that if you cut a little window in our cross-cap balloon in a place that is far from the self-intersecting line, you produce the same two pieces that are obtained with the cut of the internal eight. Therefore a cut that does not go through the self-intersecting line divides the cross-cap into two distinct parts.

7. This schema of the deferred affect [après-coup] refers to the schema of the first version of the graph that Lacan constructed during the seminars Les formations de l'inconscient and Le désir et son interprétation (1957, 1958, 1959) in order to represent the two states of the signifier. The "father" of the folded eight seems indeed to be the minimal nucleus of the Graph of Desire.

8. Lacan "L'étourdit" in Scilicet 4 (1973), pp. 27–30, 39, 41–42.

9. Ibid., p. 30. Tranlator's Notes: Dr. Nasio has suggested that Lacan's neologism "la gonfle" (from the verb gonfler, to "inflate") be rendered here as "the inflated part."

10. From this same perspective, but in a slightly different sense, Lacan writes: ". . . but from its double looping [that is, the double loop of the cut in the form of the internal eight] it makes the sphere an a-sphere, or cross-cap" Ibid., p. 39.

11. Cf., Ch. VI, 151–163, Les Yeux de Laure.

12. This point must be placed in the fourth dimension.

13. "L'étourdit," p. 27.

14. Ibid., p. 27. The assimilation of objet a to this point outside the line echoes the expression of "outside-the-body" with which Lacan characterizes objet a. Cf., Ch. IV, Les Yeux de Laure, p. 86.

15. In a beautiful painting, Magritte paints a man from the back looking into a mirror that reflects the image of the man's back.

6

Floating between Original and Semblance

ZAK WATSON

How are we to apply topology to literature? This is no easy question. Lacan provides one answer via the *sinthome* in Joyce. The human sciences offer another answer that is perhaps only too obvious in hermeneutics—a technique for gaining understanding that takes place within a circle. This circle can be treated topologically and hermeneutics can be analyzed this way and clearly contrasted with psychoanalysis.

To this end I shall rely on references to Gadamer's *Truth and Method, the* twentieth-century statement on the human scientific process of understanding via hermeneutics.[1] The other side to the interpretation of meaning is its production by an author (this statement is more convenient than accurate, but necessary here as it allows hermeneutics as a practice to be separated from symbol and allegory as textual elements). We can think of these two tropes as the other side of the hermeneutical coin or as its mirror image. At any rate, it is difficult to talk about the process without bringing up these tropes—and indeed there may be no difference at the heart of the matter. The question of which trope—symbol or allegory—

is the better mirror image of hermeneutics will be left for later. My referent for allegory as production of meaning in this paper is Hermann Broch's *The Death of Virgil*.[2]

Why *The Death of Virgil*? First of all, the subject matter and compositional history make it rich ground for allegorical interpretation. Written partially as a dialogue with death in a German prison camp, it can be read as a commentary on the evils of totalitarianism. Second, and more importantly, Broch's account of the last two days of Virgil's life comes down to questions of holes and edges, which is precisely what topology is concerned with.[3] The plot of the work is simple. Divided into four parts, the first ("Water— The Arrival") details the ailing Virgil's arrival at Brundisium on the occasion of a great celebration for Augustus Caesar. Part two ("Fire—The Descent") tells of Virgil's fitful night spent—often in "visionary" (delusionary?) states—desperately agonizing over the mundane waste his life and work have been to this point. It is in this part that he decides to burn the *Aeneid*. The third part ("Earth— The Expectation") rounds out the last morning Virgil spends on earth, in which he speaks with various friends and is convinced not to burn his masterwork, instead, handing it over to Augustus. The fourth part ("Air—The Homecoming") is a completely visionary narration of Virgil's final journey into death and back to the source of creation itself.

What does all of this have to do with psychoanalysis? We might say that analysis is a search for meaning that takes place entirely differently than hermeneutics. By bringing in the Real as referent for language, we will see how psychoanalysis makes absence, non-knowledge, the void, a function in the interpretation of meaning. Already the gulf between psychoanalysis and hermeneutics yawns in the very terminology required by each practice— the understanding aimed at by the hermeneuticist is the hallmark of error for the psychoanalyst, who must suspend all understanding. To the end of further comparing hermeneutics and psychoanalysis, I will express each in terms of topological figures, thereby crystallizing their all-important differences.

What has the quest for a human science of understanding led to? Hermeneutical enterprises have always been plagued by the same problem—trying to locate the One of meaning somewhere in language, whether this be objectively through historical reconstruction (Dilthey), or subjectively by understanding what the author meant better than he himself did (Schleiermacher).[4] On one hand we have the view that signifiers line up with signifieds to produce meaning in a system and on the other the idea that there is a language of affect in the text that we can read if we are good enough readers.

With Gadamer we go beyond Dilthey's naive belief that historical reconstruction is possible, that we can situate ourselves at the same level as the author's original audience and thereby come closer to the intended meaning. Further, we get away from the objectivity of language which characterizes Dilthey's and Schleiermacher's work; rather than that, we have Gadamer's fusing or mixing of horizons. Certainly much deference is given to the interpreting subject in this notion.

However, to stop at the mere notion that the signifier does not match up with meaning and that these things can be different for each person—making prejudice part of the work of interpretation, for instance—is another mistake. Where this can lead is to some sort of Derridean notion that all language is empty of meaning, as any signifier is defined only oppositionally and such oppositions can be deconstructed. Opposed to this notion, I shall argue in this paper for the presence in language of something that is neither arbitrary nor binary. Certainly the charges of arbitrariness and binarity are applicable to the Lacanian Symbolic order, which is defined only by these very oppositions, but psychoanalysis suggests that there is something more going on in language, that it bites into the Real.

To back up a moment. What has this tradition of understanding missed? The entire project of a science of understanding can never come to be if we are to take science in its modern definition, exemplified by modern physics. By modern physics, I mean physics since Kepler, since the function of the center as it regards the rotation of the planets was proven different than what had been assumed before. "In physics we have adopted the law that we proceed from the idea that in nature nobody uses the signifier to signify."[5] What is at stake in any modern science are signifiers, not whether they mean anything to us or not. No one takes the signifiers of nature to be an expression of god's presence in any scientific sense anymore. If there is to be a modern science of understanding, it cannot proceed by the empiricism of Schleiermacher's hermeneutics nor can it stop with the simple notion of the binary signifier (the trap of deconstruction): "You must nevertheless not think that our physics implies the elimination of all meaning. There is a meaning at the limit, but there is nobody to signify it."[6] This word *limit* will be of great importance in distinguishing our two practices shortly. A modern hermeneutics would have to be based on the impossible to signify, which is precisely where psychoanalysis dwells.

If we stay within the empirical approach—philology and psychology—we are doomed to know nothing of the One of the signifier. "No empirical theory is able to account for the existence of even the first whole numbers."[7] All that this approach can tell us about is the One of meaning, which is the realm of the arbitrary relation of signifier to signified. It is an infinity based in masculine sexuation, which is to say an $\aleph_0$ infinity (of which the famed hermeneutic circle or the infinitely expanding horizon of meaning are perfect images). This is the idea of a closed set; it contains its own limits, and because of that, the set of meanings, the One of meaning, seems to be a totality. I hold that this is what Broch is referring to in *The Death of Virgil* when he makes his many references to "sham-infinity." The sham infinity is of a hermeneutics that cannot recognize that the only place we have access to meaning is at a limit point. This sham infinity of the symbolic order (defined solely by oppositional signifiers) bears only ex-sistence; it has nothing to say about being as such.

Thus, the so-called human scientific search for meaning is bound to tell us nothing in the way of truth about being, other than by the sorts of error from which truth always emerges. Rather, it will always be caught in the illusion that everything can be said, that it can come to be understood (even if this is at an infinitely far away point). This is the logic of masculine sexuation as put forth by Lacan in his *Seminar XX: Encore*, characterized by the semblance of being whole.[8] This logic of the "all" has no hope of attaining anything in the way of meaning as it pertains to lack, which is the only meaning at stake in psychoanalysis and is the meaning I shall argue Broch has recourse to in *The Death of Virgil*. What it is destined to miss is that the first cause is manifestly a lost cause—loss as cause.

The difference between this tradition I've been talking about and what Broch wants to say is based on the relation to the Other. For the hermeneuticist who believes in an infinite process of understanding, there is nothing missing in the Other (in this case, the Symbolic order of binary oppositions, rules, and language). It is possible to speak the truth, to get at a universally valid knowledge. Here the Other functions as guarantee; it is a perfect sphere in which everything is kept, even if the surface is infinitely far away from the center. In this way, even if the task of understanding is taken to be infinite, as with Gadamer, it is understood as an ideal point out there on the horizon. It is the very impossibility of attaining this asymptotic point that causes hermeneutics to fail.

Broch's project, on the other hand, is based on the proposition that the Other lacks something inherently (at least since man's fall from grace). For him, language cannot say it all. Hence, his dissatisfaction with mere allegory or symbolism, as both of these tropes are still caught in the sham infinity of existence. To put a Lacanian spin on it, divide that last word: ex-sistence. These tropes ex-sist to the truth, which, for Lacan (and for Broch as well, I think we shall see) is that the Other lacks. There is a truth that goes beyond words but, paradoxically, is in words in some manner, just as the point hole in the cross-cap seems to be an exclusion that is within, a void in the Other whose relation is extimate.[9]

Now I must lay out a few concepts active in Lacan and to be found in Broch. First of all, the object *a*. Evanescent is the adjective applied to it most often in *Seminar XI: The Four Fundamental Concepts of Psycho-Analysis*.[10] "By saying that *a* is that which causes desire, what I mean is that it is not its object. It is not its complement, either direct or indirect, but only that cause which . . . is always a lost cause."[11] The object *a* is lost as cause of desire, never to be refound. It falls from the field of the Other (in this case, the Real Other, primary caretaker, [m]Other) at a point of loss—the mother stops singing the lullaby, the child loses the voice as object. This is the point at which the fabric comes into existence by dint of the cut—the hole exists before the fabric itself.[12] The relation of the subject to the Other is one of loss. However, the object *a* also invests objects of this world with a *jouissance* value, with the caveat that these things are not what would satisfy desire once and for all, but only what the drive will accept as substitutes for the thing itself, *Das Ding*. The object can function as a lure, but what is aimed at is the impossible unity with the Other, the healing of all lack. Needless to say, when you get this object, it turns out that "that's not it. 'That's not it' is the very cry by which the *jouissance* obtained is distinguished from the *jouissance* expected."[13]

These cuts are the single strokes, what Freud called *Einziger Zugen* around which identities will be built up. The cut opens a hole in the Real, affect at the level of flesh. To this hole an identification will come to be tied because the absence of the object is unbearable for the subject—something must be done. To this first knotting—which Lacan refers to as the symptom—will the chain of signifiers that comes to be the Symbolic order be attached. Consider the Symbolic as a fabric. This fabric or signifiers can be worn down to the thread, the knot of the symptom. "The formula *wearing down to the thread* clearly alerts us sufficiently to the fact that there is no fabric without weave."[14] What is the point of this? That the Symbolic order of signifiers and the Imaginary order of identifications can be traced back to these threads knotted around the Real void in the Other. Regardless of the seeming seamlessness of the fabric, it is actually made of myriad rings, linked Borromeanly and therefore held together only by the infinitely small points of absence (*a*) they locate by wedging. Consequently, there is something of the *jouissance* of the cut that comes through in language—pieces of the Real are present there. This is what is at stake in the *Fort! Da!* game played by Freud's grandson with a bobbin reel. This making the Real (the unsymbolizable remainder of *jouissance*/latent referent of the signifier) present in language is what is going on in *The Death of Virgil*.

In order to compare the hermeneutic approach to meaning to the psychoanalytic (which I hold makes better sense of Broch), I will rely on an analogy. The crux of the analogy is that the search for meaning is an attempt to relate to the Other. I hold that this is valid because the treasury of signifiers is nowhere else but in the Other, and the subject as meaning only exists in the context of the Other. The analogy I am drawing is between these two different ways of looking for meaning and Lacan's account of the ways in which the two sexes relate to the Other in chapter one of *Encore*.

To start with the male side, hermeneutics approaches the Other as Achilles approaches the tortoise. Gadamer's scheme of the infinite task of understanding and the mixing of horizons is a representation of phallic *jouissance*. Just like Achilles, every time the hermeneuticist takes a step, he finds his quarry has advanced a little further; he may be ever so much closer to the meaning, but he will never actually get there. Why? Because the Other is not all; there is something missing in it, although Achilles the hermeneuticist does not realize this. The hermeneuticist progresses along toward a mixing of horizons, a point infinitely far away. The infinity of the horizon is the one of succession, $\aleph_0$, which is impossible to reach.[15] The hermeneutic depiction of the Other as a sphere, a totality, is incorrect because in order for the Other to exist, there must be a cut. This cut is what is ignored by the very positing of the spherical infinity of the task of understanding.[16] This approach, defined by the "all" of masculine sexuation, will always fail because there is no all to get. It's not that this approach is wrong per se, but it will always fail to get at the Other because of the very impossibility of the signifier fully representing something. There is always a latent reference that is missed; the Symbolic always overlaps the Real (except in a psychotic break).

On the other hand, we might characterize psychoanalysis as an approach that takes account of this not all. There may be a chance for this kind of approach to have some access to the Other. Rather than assuming that meaning is out there at some infinitely far away point on the horizon and that understanding should be based on unity, it aims for a more proximate infinity and a knowledge based on what is missing. This is an $\aleph_1$ infinity, which Cantor discovered in the transfinite, that says no matter how whole a set of numbers seems, you can always find another term between the ones you have accounted for. No matter how well hermeneutics has accounted for every signifier in a text, for every bit of meaning to be found there, there is always something else falling out in the gaps. What falls out is the object *a*, which is not meaning in the traditional sense of the term, but is the beyond meaning that is conveyed nonetheless in a text. To put it another way, the seeming smooth sphere of the other is actually found to have a one dimensional cut in it, making it a cross-cap. It is this dimension one that psychoanalysis and Broch are both aiming at. Ultimately, the importance of a text may not be what is written there in two dimensions on the page, but what is felt, what is one dimensional, the dialectic of the edge and hole present in the text—in short, the text's topological aspect. This is precisely the Real running into the text as an impasse in formalization, as what cannot be written. It is important to note, however, that in this scheme based on feminine sexuation, the access to the Other is no sure thing. Just as a finite subset may cover an infinite compact space without announcing itself as the one that will do so, we can't know for sure just when the Other has been grasped where it is. The relation is contingent.[17] That which cannot be written is, a fortiori, the sexual rapport. The absence of the sexual rapport is the fundamental hole for psychoanalysis; this is the hole topology seeks to account for.[18]

To turn from speculation to application, we shall look at *The Death of Virgil*. As a way into this dense text of Broch's, I will take a quote from an essay of his: "the infinite and death are children of one mother."[19] These are the points beyond which Broch wants to pass in *The Death of Virgil*, to get to some impossible knowledge.

Both infinity (that $\aleph_0$ infinity that strains always for an unreachable horizon) and death are results of the superego. The death resulting from the superego is castration and the infinity is the infinite push to enjoyment commanded by the superego. (Enjoy!)[20] With this kind of infinity, death (as an element that cannot be known) is some ultimate point out beyond where language might tread, an unreachable goal. The infinite and death are twins that cannot be expressed in language in any way, according to this scheme. In this wanting to pass over to death, to the unreachable point, Broch wants to go explicitly beyond language, but how is he to get there?

In *The Death of Virgil*, the signifying chain itself is traveled by Virgil throughout his revelation leading up to the point of the absolute void and finally to the creation (re-creation?). The reason this chain must be traced back to its absolute origin is so that unity might once again be achieved. Throughout the text there is a foreboding: "Not quite here but yet at hand" is repeated many times. Whether this is a movement forward or back will be addressed later.

> This objective may be defined as follows: to unify a succession of impressions and experiences, to force the current back into the unity of the simultaneous, to relegate time-conditioned elements to the timelessness of the monad; in short, to establish the supratemporal nature of the work of art in the concept of indivisible homogeneity.[21]

In this quote, Broch is referring to Joyce, but the objective he identifies in it could certainly be that of *The Death of Virgil* as well (as, indeed, much of this article can just as aptly be applied to Broch as to Joyce). What Broch is saying in this quote is that the objective of literature must be to locate the One, which Lacan tells us is "indeterminate between the phoneme, the word, the sentence, and even the whole of thought."[22] This is precisely what Broch tries to do in *The Death of Virgil*. Which One he succeeds in locating is to be determined.

The revelation of what lies beyond the sham infinity of existence begins as soon as Virgil reaches his room in Brundisium. As he lies there, the music of the night drifts in: "Oh motherly song of night, resounding through all nights, echoing from of yore, sought for again with the break of each new day . . . 'my mother was dead by that time, only the sound of her voice remained.'"[23] This is clearly the voice as object *a*. It is a question of Virgil's mother's voice, the voice of the Other. What is curious about it is that it is present rather than absent. Certainly the trace of the object may be present in memory, as a wisp, something fading. This passage points up very clearly the dual aspect of object *a*, as both primordially lost and as what comes to be substituted in the place of loss. What is lost, always looked for but never found is the "motherly song of night echoing from of yore." It is radically beyond Virgil's recollection but is nevertheless present as something looked for. His mother's voice is the form that the true voice, the "motherly song of night" takes. Further, this song of night is not the final truth. The book's last sentence would be the true voice, that of the creation, "the word beyond speech."[24]

Is this allegory? I don't think that is any longer a useful term here. Allegory, at least for Broch as I understand him, is a prisoner of the sham infinity of existence, not at all privy to Real reality.[25] What this passage evokes is that which is beyond signifiers, beyond binary splits—total unity that is completely lost. If we are to call this allegory, then the term will require a re-definition to require that it refer to something manifestly beyond language rather than simply beyond the text, some piece of the Real in language. A key difference between Broch's approach and that of psychoanalysis crops up here. Clearly both call for some kind of referent manifestly beyond language, but Broch would have it be a unified reference (God) while psychoanalysis would insist that it cannot be, that there are only pieces of the Real (*dits*).

Can we call this a symbol? Absolutely not. The literary symbol always has as one of its characteristics a relation of the part to the whole. An adequate symbol will necessarily reflect the whole in every part and all the parts in the whole. The symbol in this sense always exists within a perfect circle or sphere, nothing missing—a self-contradictory impossibility if this wholeness, the perfect circle, is based on a master signifier, an exception to the rule. Since we are dealing with something, this lost voice or song of night, that is not part of any whole, but rather, part of the not-whole of an open set, the connection of the not-whole to the parts might possibly exist, but the chances of finding it lie wholly on the plane of contingency.[26]

In this way too, at the risk of digression, I will venture that symbol, not allegory, is the trope most appropriate to hermeneutics, insofar as hermeneutics can be based on a relationship of whole to parts. This part/whole dilemma is endemic to the hermeneutical enterprise as we might define it as the very process of reconciling the parts with the whole. The image of the ever expanding field of understanding, the notion that nothing can be understood without recourse first to the rest of the text, then to the rest of the author's work and so on until the recourse is to the very totality of representation is just another version of the part/whole, which is another way of saying that it is running after the One of universal fusion that would stitch up the hole in the Other. What Broch is doing is putting his finger right into the wound that limits this would-be whole, this sham infinity, destroying the possibility of a true symbol by touting the point hole of the cross-cap.

To get back to Broch. The presence of the voice is the first inkling that something of Real reality is going to be revealed to him. It is significant that Broch should choose the voice to herald this. The voice, music, is precisely what can be made present by a written text that goes beyond any sense of signification. His lyricism brings together form and content, although in a totally different way than Joyce's *Finnegans Wake*. Broch stays within the bounds of what poetry has always done, using the written word to play with phonation while still maintaining something in the way of understandability. There is both form and content in Broch. With Joyce, "the ultimate symbol of expression becomes language per se, the magic quality of sound that is the culmination of every chain of similes and has grown mystically from remote origins, to which it returns . . ."[27] If *Finnegans Wake* actually manages to become pure voice in form, then *The Death of Virgil* at least describes the journey to the pure voice, the originary, mythical One that (impossibly) goes beyond any cut.[28]

However, I think these two authors do have somewhat different goals. If language is to become pure voice, as it would for Joyce, then any hope for meaning might be lost—or, rather, it might all mean too much. Language could be destroyed as long as we could still babble. For Broch, the efficacy of language is a major question. I don't think that he is as ready as Joyce to scrap the whole affair, to allow the pure voice to reign. With Broch, the *jouissance* of the voice is not everywhere, pressing in from all sides, but hidden within the words, something to be coaxed out of them. If Joyce's goal is to push language to the edge where it threatens to topple into pure *jouissance*, Broch's is to show that that same *jouissance* permeates language, punching through every gap in the sham infinity of the semblance.

This comes through in *The Death of Virgil* in the crisis Virgil has over destroying the *Aeneid*. The question that is actually being debated is whether Broch should burn his book, and it progresses along precisely the same lines of argument over whether Virgil should burn his. Why should it occur that *The Death of Virgil* should become a candidate for burning? In reference to Joyce, Broch states: "Certainly no present-day artist can avoid this dilemma, none can escape pessimism with regard to his own activity."[29] He goes on to talk in the same breath about the will to create and the will to destroy. A work must be held up to its own standards. If you are to write a work about something that is trying to go totally beyond language, to get out of signification, why write at all? Why not, for instance, write a sonata?

First of all, another medium would not be the answer. Broch doesn't only want to get past language, but to leave this world behind. The "motherly song of night"—let alone the voice of creation—is no more (and possibly less) present in a string section than in some lines of poetry. Both forms of expression are mere echoes of the Real reality, the lost reality of the time before division, before the loss of unity. This talk of "real reality" is Broch's terminology, not Lacan's, as the latter would never formulate a reality before the cut.

The second answer is along the same lines as the first as it regards the potential of expression. Why write? Why should art exist? Whether it is adequate or not, it is the best that we humans can manage within our sham infinite world; extimacy is the very measure of how close a work of art may dwell or how far it may stray from the lack in the Other. Virgil resolves to having his imperfect work survive because it is a work of humanity, and therefore must be flawed. It does announce the coming of Real reality, of the annunciation, not quite here but yet at hand, just as Caesar is the representative of a god, one who can usher in the return of the golden age of Saturn. The fabric of empire can be worn down to the threads by which its signification is tied to the absolute void of what existed (didn't exist?) before creation itself—the mythic golden age (lure) and even what came before it.

If we can apply this question of burning the *Aeneid* to whether Broch should have burned *The Death of Virgil*, then there are some interesting conclusions to be drawn. Assuming that Broch chose to save his work for the same reasons that Virgil found for saving his, then this thematic of going beyond this world of sham infinity is made even more clear. Further, as this goal is represented somewhat rationally, since this book can be read, it leaves less of a question of Broch's sanity (as opposed to Joyce's, which may be up for debate). And, finally, just as Virgil entrusts his work to Caesar, the emblem of empire, the epitome of this-worldliness, Broch can leave his work for this world, regardless of how it may be taken, because it holds the seeds of the truth that goes beyond this reality. Ultimately for Broch, this world and its creations are worth something because there is something of the Real reality that cuts through, just as the signifiable is split into the signifier and the Real latent reference of the impossible to signify.[30] "It is at this point that the mission of literature begins; the mission of a cognition that remains above all empirical or social modes of being . . ."[31] If modern science has held philosophy to the rigor of the signifier (as opposed to meaning) then it is up to literature to pick up what is no longer allowed to philosophy, such as the ethical domain.[32] In this we come back to Broch's striving for unity, which is essentially the same as striving to get beyond signification. The extra twist that a Lacanian reading of *The Death of Virgil* gives is that it is the One of the unary trait and not the One of universal fusion that is at the end of the signifying chain.

Getting back to which theme, going beyond signification, considering signifiers in their essentially binary form leads to some insight into many passages in *The Death of Virgil*. A reader is hard pressed to open to any of the less "rational" sections of the book without finding what seem to be complete contradictions liberally sprinkled on every page. I quote at random ". . . never-comprehended, always known . . ."[33] Might we say that what is at work here is the logic of the dream, which knows nothing of contradiction or perhaps some romantic collusion of opposites? I would say rather that we are moving along with Virgil down a path of less and less signfierness, to use an awkward term. As he comes closer and closer to the so-called Real reality, the division by the signifier into same and different or One and Other disappears. This is a further topological dimension to the work. Lafont writes: "*La topologie formalise les opérations qui sont à l'oeuvre et qui, à partir du trou et son bord, construisent la réalité.*"[34] Broch is articulating this very construction, only in reverse, as his Virgil travels the chain of signifiers.

This is the drama of what happens in the fourth part of the book, the homecoming. Consider the myth of creation we get from Genesis, which is at least some portion of what is at play in this last section. In the beginning, God is doing nothing but creating signifiers, which is to say cutting. Light, dark, earth, water. Man doesn't become a signifier until woman exists. Plotia is Virgil's Eve, her voice too functions as a thread in the weave of his reality; it too participates in that summation of voices that is more than all of them that ends the book. We see in the reverse creation that goes on throughout the final section that once Plotia has disappeared, ostensibly turned back into one of Virgil's ribs, he has been reduced to animality. Later this distinction drops off further until it ends in the final unity of the void, when time itself stands still. The weave of the fabric has been worn down to the final thread of the voice of the music of the spheres. Broch might have it that there is no longer a first stroke nor what will come to have effaced it (the knot of unary traits). Rather, we are in the place of absolute unity, perhaps even the womb in some cosmic sense of the word. However, the silence just before the end of the book is not the perfect void of null-unity but rather the silent compliment of the voice, not here but yet at hand, the hole that pre-exists the fabric into which it is cut. Broch strives to represent a mythic *jouissance* that psychoanalysis does not dare to promise the subject, the One of universal fusion. However, the One he finds is the unary trait of the voice in its originary necessary opposition to silence. This is the dimension one, the Möbien cut in the sphere that makes it an *a-sphere* or cross-cap. I refuse the union Broch offers because that's not it. It is an edge bound to a hole, the revelation that the cross-cap is the perpetuation of the Möbien cut. In this we see where Broch (and Joyce as well in a different way) would surpass what analysis will allow itself to do, as the latter is by definition concerned only with speaking beings, which is to say those inhabited by the signifier.

At exactly this point Virgil is allowed to turn around, so that creation might start once again. However, Broch has certainly reached the objective he applies to Joyce quoted above. This point in the book is the twist in the Möbius strip, the end (of the book) is the beginning (of creation) (not wholly unlike *Finnegans Wake*). This annunciation of the voice of creation is the unary trait, the single stroke that was calling out to Virgil in so many guises (the voice of night, his mother's, or Plotia's voice) throughout the book. From this point the descent (or perhaps ascent, since the Möbius strip is a non-orientable surface) into Caesar's empire can begin anew. Is this progress forward or back? Along the Möbius strip we can say both and neither.

To sum up, what effect does this reverse creation myth have for any theory of understanding, for allegory, symbol and hermeneutics? Broch's statement to us is that this reality must be tempered by the knowledge that it is attached to something else beyond what we can know as reality. Put another way, the semblance of the sphere world is attached to the cut of the Real, introducing the infinitely small point hole of the cross-cap. This attachment is not arbitrary; rather it is necessary (there is no fabric without weave) and cannot be binary as it is seemingly prior to signification but is really its product-remainder (the unincorporable, impossible to signify latent reference). Hermeneutics, and its trope, the symbol, are totally enmeshed in this world and its impossible ($\aleph_0$) infinity. They are, however, still echoes of the voice of creation, whether they realize it or not—just as truth arises from error. Broch is not antagonizing these things, just as Virgil does not hate Caesar, although it may seem that way to anyone who won't admit that there may be something beyond this reality. To put it another way, Broch is telling us that the seeming meaning, the semblance, is all well and good, but there is something else, the Other which lacks, that is at play as well. Because both Broch and psychoanalysis bring into play that dimension beyond the signifier, they cannot be formalized as science can be, but they both ascribe to an ideal that science would do well to achieve. The final question is, to just what extent can we bring the unsymbolizable into account in art (or science)—in other words, what is the status of a science of the Real?

ENDNOTES

1. H.-G. Gadamer, *Truth and Method*, trans. J. Weinsheimer and D. G. Marshall. New York: Continuum, 1998.

2. H. Broch, *The Death of Virgil* trans. J. S. Untermeyer. New York: Vintage International, 1972.

3. J. Granon-Lafont, *Topologie Lacanienne et clinique analytique*. Paris: Point Hors Ligne, 1990, p. 13.

4. See W. Dilthey, *Selected Works, Volume IV: Hermeneutics and the Study of History*, ed. R. Makkreel and F. Rodi. Princeton, NJ: Princeton University Press, 1996; and P. Szondi, *On Textual Understanding and Other Essays*, trans. H. Mendelsohn, Minneapolis, MN: University of Minnesota Press, 1986.

5. J. Lacan, *The Seminar of Jacques Lacan Book III: The Psychoses*, ed. J.-A. Miller, trans. R. Grigg. New York: Norton, 1993, p. 184.

6. *Ibid.*, pp. 184–185.

7. *Ibid.*, p. 185.

8. See J. Lacan, *The Seminar of Jacques Lacan Book XX: Encore*, ed. J.-A. Miller, trans. B. Fink. New York: Norton, 1998.

9. For a literary approach to this aspect of language, see Rilke's *Duino Elegies*, particularly the Ninth.

10. See J. Lacan, *The Seminar of Jacques Lacan Book XI: The Four Fundamental Concepts of Psycho-Analysis*, ed. J.-A. Miller, trans. A. Sheridan. New York: Norton, 1977.

11. J. Lacan, "Seminar of 21 January 1975" (trans. J. Rose), in *Feminine Sexuality* ed. J. Mitchell and J. Rose. New York: Norton, 1982, p. 165.

12. J. Granon-Lafont, *op. cit.*, p. 17.

13. J. Lacan, *The Seminar. Book XX: Encore, op. cit.*, p. 111.

14. J. Lacan, "Seminar of 21 January 1975," *op. cit.*, p. 163.

15. G. Morel, *La Jouissance Sexuelle dans les Ecrits et le Séminaire Encore de Jacques Lacan*, unpublished course, 1993, p. 75.

16. See H.-G. Gadamer, *op. cit.*, pp. 293–294: "The circle, which is fundamental to all understanding, has a further hermeneutic implication which I call the 'fore-conception of completeness' . . . It states that only what really constitutes a unity of meaning is intelligible."

17. For the concept of compactness, see G. Morel, *op. cit.*, Chapter IV, parts of which appear as "The hypothesis of compacity in Chapter 1 of *Encore: Seminar XX (1972–1973)*" in *Critical Essays on Jacques Lacan*, ed. E. Ragland. New York: G. K. Hall, 1999, pp. 149–160.

18. J. Granon-Lafont, *op. cit.*, p. 15.

19. H. Broch, "Joyce and the Present Age" in *A James Joyce Yearbook*, ed. M. Jolas, trans. E. and M. Jolas. Paris: Transition Press, 1949, p. 107.

20. G. Morel, *La Jouissance Sexuelle, op. cit.*, p. 78.

21. H. Broch, "Joyce and the Present Age," *op. cit.*, p. 82.

22. J. Lacan, *The Seminar. Book XX: Encore, op. cit.*, p. 143.

23. H. Broch, *The Death of Virgil, op. cit.*, p. 60.

24. *Ibid.*, p. 482.

25. Here we might define allegory as the putting into one to one relationship of two sets of signifiers.

26. See G. Morel, *Jouissance Sexuelle, op. cit.*, Chapter IV.

27. H. Broch, "Joyce and the Present Age," *op. cit.*, p. 81.

28. It is impossible for this mythical One to go beyond any cut because the supposedly unified fabric doesn't even exist before the cut.

29. H. Broch, "Joyce and the Present Age," *op. cit.*, p. 76.

30. G. Morel, *La Jouissance Sexuelle, op. cit.*, p. 52.

31. H. Broch, "Joyce and the Present Age," *op. cit.*, p. 99.

32. *Ibid.*, p. 104.

33. H. Broch, *The Death of Virgil, op. cit.*, p. 171.

34. J. Granon-Lafont, *op. cit.*, p. 14.

7

Interpretation and Topological Structure

DAVID METZGER

Given the recent Sokal affair and the publication of *Intellectual Imposters*, it is no surprise that some scholars who have invested heavily in the exposition of Lacan's difficult teaching should suggest that we can do without some such thing as a Lacanian topology. "Remember the phallus?" they tell us. "We had a difficult enough time explaining that away. Why bother talking about something that is sure to discourage people from reading (about) this important thinker?"[1] My argument is that, whereas other fields of inquiry might resort to a metalanguage in order to offer an interpretation, psychoanalysis requires the elaboration of a structure that is *like* a language, a structure that I will later call "a topology of language." The first section of this essay will introduce us to an evidentiary difficulty that Freud attempted to address in *The Psychopathology of Everyday Life*: How do we know psychoanalytic interpretations are not merely suggestions that the analysand is compelled to accept? The second section of this essay will then show how Lacan's topological orientation of language allowed him to respond to this important question regarding psychoanalytic interpretation.

LANGUAGE AND THE UNCONSCIOUS IN FREUD

Freud begins his *Psychopathology of Everyday Life* with an example of forgetting and misremembering: he forgets the name of a Fresco painter (Signorelli), and he misremembers the painter's name as either-Botticelli-or-Boltraffio. Although Freud entertains the possibility that this particular instance of forgetting/misremembering might simply be "an arbitrary psychical choice," he suspects there is more to it than that. Indeed, Freud has reason to believe that he might "follow the paths" of this "displacement" given the immediacy with which he recognizes that Botticelli and Boltraffio are misremembered and Signorelli is, in fact, the artist's name he has been searching for. Forgetting and misremembering—at least in this instance—would be something other than a matter of recalling a list of possible painters and canceling out those who, by virtue of time period, location, style, and medium, could not or would not have painted the fresco. That is, misremembering and forgetting are both expressions of a knowledge demonstrated by the immediacy with which Freud recognizes that neither Botticelli nor Boltraffio is the painter's name and Signorelli is. What is more, remembering and forgetting must be related insofar as Freud misremembered one thing in particular (Signorelli) as two things in particular (Botticelli or Boltraffio). But, and this point is crucial, we cannot assume there is something "special" about the terms under consideration simply because they may lead Freud to some "specialized" knowledge.

Of course, we can't simply take this last statement for granted, since it grounds the entire project of *Psychopathology of Everyday Life*. But before examining Freud's chain of associations in more detail, let's be clear about what Freud's project is. From the standpoint of its descriptive power, Freud's discussion offers the following: Botticelli and Boltraffio are "displacements" of "Signorelli" (Freud, p. 2). From the standpoint of its predictive power, Freud's model offers:

> The conditions necessary for forgetting a name, when forgetting it is accompanied by paramnesia, may then be summarized as follows: 1) a certain disposition for forgetting the name, 2) a process of suppression carried out shortly before, 3) the possibility of establishing an external association between the name in question and the element previously suppressed. [Freud, p. 6]

If we are to avoid constructing a circular argument, we cannot accept that the introduction of the term *displacement* can, by itself, authorize the development of a chain of associations or, by itself, authorize the development of a model for the production of those associations. So, what authorizes Freud's statements regarding the descriptive and predictive power of his deliberations? Freud clearly wishes us to see his model of explanation as a possible model among others; his delineation of the chain of associations is even prefaced by a consideration of alternate explanations, which he subsequently dismisses: "The reason why the name Signorelli was lost is not to be found in anything special about the name itself or in any psychological characteristic of the context into which it was introduced" (p. 2). Here Freud anticipates arguments that have been made by Sebastiano Timpanaro, who argued that Freud refused to accept simpler and more direct explanatory approaches because they did not support the psychoanalytic cause (p. 96). In this instance at least, Freud anticipates the argument for "more direct" explanations, and he suggests that the conditions for such explanations do not obtain.

The more productive point of contention between Freud's "argument for associations" and the "test of directness" concerns "possibility"—more particularly, the question, "In what way might we account for the actualization of a (linguistic) possibility?" Timpanaro–whom we will now treat as one spokesperson for the "test of directness"—wonders if a slip of the tongue or a moment of misremembering might be better explained, more directly/simply explained, in terms of the properties of language (i.e., phonic similarities) than the properties of some such thing as the unconscious (p. 98). Freud's argument does not dismiss this point out of hand; Freud anticipates and reorients the notion of possibility that grounds Timpanaro's approach by asking, "In what way might we account for the (linguistic) actualization of an error?" These two approaches to the "test of directness" lead Timpanaro and Freud to two different approaches to "error." Timpanaro treats "error" as if it were an actualization, the identity for a host of possible linguistic possibilities ("errors" as something that we can count); Freud treats "error" as if it were one (you can count it, but there is only one). We can see Timpanaro's approach to error and possibility in his construction of the following counterfactual series of associations, which he offers as his principal refutation of Freud's model of interpretation:

> Very well, then, let us suppose that instead of forgetting *aliquis*, the young Austrian [from an example provided by Freud] slipped up on *exoriare*, "arise." He would have had no difficulty in connecting the idea of "arising" with that of "birth" (*exoriare* can have both meanings): the birth, alas, of child—so feared by him. Next let us suppose that he forgot *nostris*; the Latin adjective *noster* would have brought to mind the Catholic *Pater noster*, . . . and he could easily connect God the Father with the saints, and—passing from saint to saint—eventually with San Gainer and the feared failure of the woman to menstruate. . . . Are these cognisance that I have amused myself thinking up (and which could be varied and explained at will) grotesque ones? Of course they are. But are the cognisance via which Freud explains, or rather makes the interlocutor explain, the forgetting of aliquis any less grotesque or less "random"? [pp. 99–100]

Timpanaro insists that Freud must account for the fact that a particular word and not some other word is forgotten or misremembered. And he suggests that Freud's description of a particular series of associations cannot ever provide such an account because any other word in the sample might have been used as thread for the analysand's associations, any other word might lead Freud to his proposed destination—after the manner of the American party game, "Six Degrees of Kevin Bacon." Timpanaro suggests, then, that there are a host of equally possible associations for any single word. What is more, given that Freud's choice of a prompt for the patient's associations is arbitrary, then it makes more sense for Freud to treat the point of association as the actualization of a linguistic possibility than as the exploitation of that linguistic possibility by some such thing as the unconscious. In other words, Timpanaro is questioning whether Freud can separate the operations of the unconscious from the operations of language. If Freud can't, then there's no need for the idea of the unconscious; it's *simpler* to talk about language. If Freud can, then there is no evidence whatsoever for some such thing as the unconscious; it's *simpler* to talk about what is than what is not.[2]

With Timpanaro and Freud, we have two very different views of language. Timpanaro understands that there are "metalanguages" and that "metalanguages" are a subset of "languages"; this understanding then leads him to compare "metalanguages" of error. Freud understands that there are interpretations and that interpretations are intersections of the properties of languages: the phoneme, the morpheme, the grapheme. But how is it possible to have an interpretation without a metalanguage, a way of transcribing a given X as Y? Lacan's answer is the matheme. Mathemes designate the turns in an analysand's language (understood as a chain of signifiers) that enable analysts to offer an interpretation—the interpretation being what can be heard of the Other's speech but in the language of the analysand. Interpretation happens despite the fact that there is no place for the Other in the analysand's language if the Other can become the place for the analysand's speech.[3]

Lacan used two figures (a Möbius strip and a torus) and three mathemes [ϕ, a, and S(A)] to respond to the evidentiary quandary identified by Timpanaro. Just above, it was suggested that there is no place for the Other in the analysand's language. Lacan is much more precise. The Ø reveals that in language one cannot be Othered except by way of castration. The object a fills the only place there might be for the Other in language. The S(A) is the mark of the Other's absence in language. What is more, if there is no place for the Other in the analysand's language, Lacan leads us to consider that there be might another dimension to language, which he calls *lalangue*, where one might catch a whiff of the Other.[4] One might then presume to speak about this Other dimension to language if an analysand's language (a Möbius strip) could be mapped as a topology of language that has a place for the Other (a torus); in fact, this topology may be shown to be the place of the Other for the analysand leading to what we might call a diagnosis: the analysand is structured as a neurotic, psychotic, or perverse relation to the Other.[5]

A TOPOLOGY OF LANGUAGE

What is the difference between a metalanguage and a topology of language? A metalanguage forms and validates claims regarding the meaning of particular utterances by encouraging us to accept that "bodies" are ontologically prior to "language." A topology of language provides a model of interpretation where "bodies" and "language" are coextensive precisely at the point where there is no other place for a signifier than in the analysand's body: S(A). As we will see, this simple assertion is not without its effect at the level of meaning. This signifier in the body makes it possible for us to mean something, to see how meaning is not simply the fulfillment of the sentential form "T in language-1 is P in language-2" (ϕ); meaning is also the "hole" (a) defined by all such translations/identifications in the analysand's particular language. ϕ, a, and S(A) delineate three conditions for a topology of language (X being a "topology of language"): 1) language is itself an element of X; 2) an empty set is an element of X; 3) the union and intersection of the elements of X are also elements of X. We will address each of these characteristics respectively.

Imagine that two parents ask their baby if she loves Mommy and Daddy. If the parents take their baby's "smile" as "yes," then they do so by means of a particular association: "'smile' in baby language means 'yes' in English." We might even extend this association to include languages other than English creating a lexicon of smile: smile, see yes, *oui, si, ken*. Now, imagine that a family friend tells the excited parents, "Actually, I think the baby just burped." The family friend might go on to talk about the gastrointestinal workings that produce a burp, explaining how the baby's facial muscles are delineated, all in order to prove that what the baby produced was not "'smile in baby language means 'yes' in English." The baby's smile, the family friend asserts, cannot be meaningful-as-language because it need not be placed in the metalinguistic series "X in language-1 means Y in language-2." "There is a simpler, more direct explanation," the family friend asserts. "Baby is a body; bodies burp; therefore, babies burp." Despite the fact that the parents would, no doubt, find their friend's explanation less interesting than their own, the family friend's explanation has a certain appeal: the assumption that "burp" is prior to "smile/yes." What is more, the phrase "a body" has logical priority over—is *more simple* than—such expressions as "smile" and "yes" since bodies are the objects about which language might presume to be.

But why should we assume that "burp" is prior to "smile" or even "Ayes" [Other/A]? After all, even if the baby had vocalized "Ayes," this would not have meant "Ayes" if the parents had not asked the question "Do you love Mommy and Daddy?" And, even in that case, we do not know if the baby's "yes" is "yes" or [yes]. This may seem quite logical, but a good deal of effort has been spent on determining the priority of burp/smile. We might even imagine a documentary in which we see a series of animal greetings: clips of lions and tigers and bears displaying their teeth at each other. Then, Desmond Morris (the author of *The Naked Ape*) jumps from behind a blind and tells us that "displaying teeth" in animal is "smile" in human; therefore, he continues, "smiling" means "Hello! And by the way don't try anything." "Smile," in these terms, is thought to be prior to "yes" because "smile is a display of teeth" and "displaying teeth is what animals do when they encounter each other."[6]

After Desmond Morris, one could say that language could be heard as one long burp or extended display of teeth: Morris assumes from the beginning that "smile" means something, that it serves a social function even among animals. Likewise, Timpanaro in his creation of a counterfactual free association assumes that language means something, that it serves a social function. Both Morris and Timpanaro respond to the problem of accounting for the effects of language in the body by subsuming the whole of the one into the whole of the other. Where Morris finds that language is the history of body, Timpanaro finds in the creation of a counterfactual free association that language is not the history of language; therefore, language must be something else, some other body than the one invoked by Freud (the unconscious).

Believe or not. Our subsequent development of a Lacanian view of language will start from the position of the family friend. The family friend assumes that the burp may have a social effect even if it has no social function inherent to itself. But the display-of-teeth, the slip of the tongue, and the burp are not simply not-language; they are null-language markers (places where one would speak if one could). On what grounds might we argue for such a thing as a "null-language marker?" The family friend might be compelled to accept that if the baby were languaged she might have used burp to mean "yes." That is, "burp" in baby language could mean the following in English: "Yes, I'm full of food, Mom and Dad; you are great providers; you have heard my call." The question is whether burp means something in English because the baby is a body (bodies burp when they're full of food) or because the baby is languaged. The family friend is disputing whether the statement "smile in body" is a simpler explanation than "burp is a null-language marker."

Now, why would I go on about this null-language marker? . . . because without it, there would be no such thing as interpretation in the Lacanian sense of the word. There would be no signifier; there would be no topology. What our family friend calls a null-language marker, Lacan would call the object little a.[7] That is burp/smile/

yes might not be languaged (an example of baby language) but the baby's burp/smile/yes nevertheless participates in a little game of make believe, what we might call a discourse. Discourse localizes the site for an interpretation (the null-language marker, object little *a*) as something that is also in language (ϕ).

In order to address the relationship of *a* and N more precisely, we will need to consider Lacan's distinction between *lalangue* and *langue*. With *lalangue*, Lacan positions the definite article "*la*" where there would be a space in written language. Without this space, *la* is no longer the promise that a noun is sure to follow; the predictive function of a grammar is thereby disabled, and we are left to consider how *lalangue* can, nevertheless, have the effect of meaning.[8] We might say that *lalangue* shows us where the metalanguage of grammar does not work: the parceling of language into units of action, units of being, and units for expressing the relation between the two. *Lalangue* parcels language as the necessity, possibility, and impossibility of expression. That is, *lalangue* may appear in discourse (the analytic discourse), but it marks the effects of this discourse on language (*a*) as language (ϕ).[9]

Lalangue is the (w)hole through which language flows—not a mouth, not a phoneme, not the object little *a* (which is a hole in language marked by discourse) but *lalangue*, a w(hole) in language. Where others might suggest there is a metalanguage, a syntax, a way of substituting one part of language for another, Lacan positions *lalangue*, the expression of the fact that language cannot fit into itself, that the identification of the whole of language in one dimension constructs a hole in another *dit*-mension (*dit*/says, said). Even if we had all of the elements of language at our disposal, it would not be possible for us to count all that is in language because there is always something more: the point of interpretation. How do we know this? . . . Because the whole of language is not one but two: language and discourse . . . Because this whole is (w)hole, not-all at the level of language, *lalangue* . . . Because the hole of language (*a*, discourse) might allow us to count the (w)hole of language (*lalangue*) as language (ϕ). How so? Here, Lacan introduces S(A), what allows us to assert that the union and intersection of the elements of a topology of language are themselves elements of a topology of language.

S(A) ties X (a topology of language) to language by showing where language might make do without the Other and its discourse (the unconscious) by becoming the Other, the point where language might function as a pseudo-discourse, where language serves as the promise of a picture without a gaze, language as a-structural but nevertheless not without structure. These designations of S(A) may seem impressionistic. But let's push these impressions a little farther by way of an illustration, the film *The Talented Mr. Ripley*. You may recall that Mr. Ripley tries to become someone else. His life— even the movements of his own body—are becoming more and more incomprehensible to him, so he attempts to orient himself in the world as someone else. If Mr. Ripley accomplishes his task, he will be both this someone else and the world, since the only way to accomplish this task (to be the Other) is to destroy those who see him as both "Mr. Ripley" and "Tom." Now, Mr. Ripley doesn't need to kill people at every given moment; he only murders when there is a chance that he will be in the same room as a person who sees him as not-Ripley and a person who sees him as Ripley. Otherwise, he can live as Tom Ripley on the Other's money. At the level of demand, he can be both Tom Ripley and someone else; only when he is called to be both at the level of the subject must he kill. Analogously, we might say that language, as an object, seems to be able to meet all of our demands; we can say anything in a language (that's what languages do), but the one thing that a language can't do is to be a subject of language. Something else must function to create this language of the both/and. This isn't a language; it isn't a language-object; it's a signifier in the real: the language-subject one finds in the psychoses.

Again, why is this S(A) necessary? There is with S(A) the assertion that where there was the possibility of one thing coming to identify another (the basic structure of a metalanguage: X in language-1 is Y in language-2), now there is only one thing, and that one thing is a signifier. "Thing" isn't used here in a generic sense, but as something that comes to mean not through its association with the presence of another signifier but the assertion of the absence of other signifiers. What we might first see as a problem of connecting (How do we connect these two ends together?) becomes "How do we separate them given that there is only one piece of string, only one chain of signifiers?" S(A) asserts that there aren't two ends; all is one. The how-to- disconnect can only occur in the presence of the Other; as we will see below, the one-ness of the Möbius strip can be mapped on one torus or two.[10]

We might summarize our argument in terms of a phenomenologically oriented narrative:

1) The moment when we recognize language in discourse and ask "Is there a language before discourse?"

2) The moment when we recognize that language might function as a pseudo-discourse (no before discourse, but an instead-of-discourse).

3) The moment when we recognize that the impossibility of using language to write the Other nevertheless scripts the Other as an impossibility (that is, we map narrative 2 onto a torus).

4) The moment when we recognize that a and ϕ do not create a one—despite the efforts of S(A). There may be a one-of-language but not a one-in-language (narrative 3 is seen as the intersection of two toruses, one bearing the burden of ϕ, another bearing the burden of a).

5) The moment when we recognize that the existence of a and ϕ is supported by something that passes through them as S(A) but continues to write itself along the surface of narrative 2. In terms of narrative 4, this something (the unconscious), by necessity, ex-ists.[11]

6) The moment when we recognize that if a and N are connected at the level of language by way of S(A), then a—at the level of *lalangue*–might be used to support ϕ as symptoms.

7) The moment when we recognize that it may be possible to create symptoms as we desire if only we knew who this "we" might be or how to create a signifier.[12] Then, we

recognize that, at some point, we must have made a choice
(*a*) that we're stuck with (ϕ). Behind Door Number One:
the "we" is the S that we can create. Behind Door Number
Two: the not-We is the S that "we" can create or recognize.

How is all this a topology, more specifically, a topology of
language? Three conditions are met:

1) Where there would have been a hole in the Other there is
   S (a signifier) which, in the presence of the Other, would
   be (a subject), but in the Other's absence, is language as a
   subject.
2) This absence of the Other—that is as it is scripted in language as $\phi(a)$—can function as the Other rendering S as a
   subject (S).
3) At the level of language, all are one; at the level of discourse,
   not-All are two.

Again, why is this a topology of language rather than the assumption of a metalanguage? Surely, with the not-All we might think
that there is a possibility of a metalanguage; after all, we now have
a two (an X and Y).[13] But this not-all (this two) does not create a
one and another one in language, and certainly it does not create a
one in one-language and another one in another-language. The not-
all (the two) requires that we consider a one-in-language and a not-
all in *lalangue*. So where does the two come in? The "two" can only
be supported (counted) in a discourse that rescripts $S \rightarrow A[\phi(a)]$
$\rightarrow \mathsf{S}$ as $a \rightarrow A[S(\sim\phi)] \rightarrow S$.[14] When push comes to shove, the assertion of a topology of language is a way of accounting for the ne-
cessity of a signifier in the Real. Charting the course of this signifier
cannot be a metalanguage since "meaning" is effected in the wake
of this signifier, not in the realization of this signifier as "meaning." Sense (one thing) leads us to signifier (another thing). But
because the "you can say anything in any language given that what
you're speaking is a language"), the whole of meaning, is made
possible at the level of structure (a hole), this pursuit of meaning

leads us to something (a fourth thing in the Real, not wholly circumscribed by the tertiary logic of the signifier: a signifier is a subject for another signifier) that only makes sense as a signifier (a
third thing). The twist that forces us to count "four" before we count
"three" is not something that can be identified by the mapping of
one space onto another; it is the possibility of space itself (the knot),
the structure Lacan identified with "topology."

ENDNOTES

1. Topology has also been associated with "doctrinal intolerance
among Millerians." An "intolerance" that, it is suggested, attempts to sys-
tematize psychoanalytic theory against itself:

> A further problem with topological formalizations of subjectivity is
> that they're cognate with the impulse to systematize psychoanalytic
> theory. Given this problem, it seems to me a virtue rather than a deficit
> that Lacan's use of topology remains as haphazard as it does, since
> his only rudimentary grasp of advanced mathematics makes it that
> much harder for us [non-Millerians? Anglophones?] to systematize
> his thinking. [Dean, p. 55]

We also find in Dean a sincere attempt to situate psychoanalytic thought
on the common ground of one human experience: "Looking unblinkingly
at a psychoanalytic theory of excrement offers the benefit of enabling us
to gauge just how incidental to Lacan's account of fantasy sexuality, and
desire, is the phallus" (p. 264).

2. With Timpanaro and Freud, we have two very different views of
language. Timpanaro understands that there are "metalanguages" and that
"metalanguages" are a subset of "languages"; this understanding then leads
him to compare "metalanguages" of error. Freud understands that there
are interpretations and that interpretations are intersections of the properties of languages (the phoneme, the morpheme, the grapheme). But how
is it possible to have an interpretation without a metalanguage, a way of
transcribing a given X as Y? As we will see, Lacan's answer is the matheme.

3. To legitimize the unconscious as a theoretical entity, one need
not demonstrate that there are no other responses to the question, "Did
you mean to say it?" leaving one to assert, without fear of contradiction,
"Oh, it must be that pesky unconscious again." The unconscious is not
the last resort for meaning, so psychoanalytic interpretation need not be
a response to the question, "Do you mean to say that? What is the mean-

ing of your meaning?" Rather, psychoanalytic interpretation is a response to the question, "Is X (a slip of the tongue, let's say) a topology of language?" Lacan will take this point even further: if X is a topology of language, then X may have something to tell us about the unconscious inasmuch as the unconscious is structured like a language. We will first address the idea of a "topology of language." We will then be in a position to examine what it means to say that the unconscious is structured like a language rather than that the unconscious is a language.

4. "We know that language is first acquired in relation to others and that the other of primary transference usually refers an infant to a third thing—to the desire for being desired. Lacan named this early layer of enigmatic 'knowledge' about the mother's desire *la lalangue*" (Ragland, p. 79).

5. For a discussion of diagnosis in the Lacanian clinic, see Colette Soler's "A Passion in Transference: Marion Milner and the Susan Case," p. 27 in particular.

6. The appeal of Morris's work is precisely the appeal of popular notions about the unconscious: there's something animalistic, untamed, that is howling to get out, and it does escape its social constraints from time to time revealing what we really want, what we want at the level of the body. But this appeal hardly cashes out in the psychopathology of everyday life. There we find slips of the tongue, misrememberings, forgettings. Are these forgettings and slips, then, merely the trappings of the unconscious? If so, what is caught by and what escapes from these sorts of utterances? Answer: the possibility that there is something that does not think. Family friends suggest that babies don't think; Desmond Morrises suggest that "not all" of the activities of naked apes are saturated by thought. Furthermore, this position of the "Anon-thinking" is situated in a past that is linked to "human" subjects by way of a history (human development or evolution) that does not require thought. In this way, thought itself might be historicized: here is a *before* thought; here is an *after* thought. At some point, we then assume something "human" managed to escape the body because we are surprised when that "something" is trapped again (that is, when "humans" are shown to be "naked apes").

7. We might say that the object *a* is situated between two signifiers— S(A) and ϕ. In the presence of the Other (that is, in analysis) these mathemes are taken as S_1 and S_2, affording us the following statement from the editorial collective of the European School of Psychoanalysis:

> Formalizer simplement le problème: soit un signifiant premier S_1 proposé comme supposé métalangage d'un deuxieme signifiant S_2, nous serons nécessairement conduit à la formule suivante: $S_1 (S_1 (S_1 (S_1 \rightarrow (S_2))$, qui reporte à l'infini tant le sens ultime que la position

hiérarchique du signifiant premier. C'est dans cette fuite même du sens que Lacan situera la fonction de l'objet *a* comme véritable agent de l'interprétation, soit dans l'intervalle qui se situe entre deux signifiants, jamais ailleurs. L'interprétation, réductible à une scansion du discourse, isole précisément ce signifiant premier qui se révélera nonobstant comme insensé. ["Le sens du sens, Ernst Kris," p. 251]

8. For an extended discussion of this point, see Miller's "A Reading of Some Details in *Television* in Dialogue with the Audience," pp. 19–24.

9. If we now identify *a* as the object cause of desire we might see how Lacan underscores this point in the following from his Seminar on *Les formations de l'inconscient*: "Le désir de l'homme est toujour pour lui à rechercher au lieu de l'Autre en tant que lieu de la parole, ce qui fait que le désir est un désir structuré dans ce lieu de l'Autre" (p. 442).

10. "It is the real that permits the effective unknotting of what makes the symptom hold together, namely a knot of signifiers. Where here knotting and unknotting are not metaphors, but are really to be taken as those knots that in fact are built up through developing chains of the signifying material" (Lacan, *Television*, p. 10).

11. Rosine and Robert Lefort provide a detailed discussion of this transformation of the body of the Other into a Möbius strip in their *Birth of the Other*, pp. 345–348.

12. We have here the production of a new signifier (S_1 as it is positioned in analytic discourse) and the beginning of the psychoanalytic cure, a beginning that we need not question because the obsessional will continually end his analysis before it has begun by accepting this interpretation as an answer (*l'Un*) rather than support for the enigma of sex (rather than the *l'On*, the "We" of the brother and sister from "The function of speech and language in psychoanalysis": On est à femmes. Imbecile, on est à hommes!" For further elaboration of the relationship of obsession and/in interpretation, compare Kaufmant's "Clivage de l'obsession par l'interprétation" (p. 51) with Valas's "L'effet de l'interprétation" (p. 38).

13. See Lacan's discussion of one and two in "Of structure as an inmixing," p. 192.

14. For a succinct discussion of this reinscription in terms of knot theory, see Lew's "Note de lecture," p. 195.

BIBLIOGRAPHY

Dean, T. (2000). *Beyond Sexuality*. Chicago: University of Chicago Press.
Freud, S. (1957). *The Psychopathology of Everyday Life*, trans. Lytton Strachey. New York: W. W. Norton.

Kaufmant, Y. "Clivage de l'obsession par l'interpretation." *Ornicar?* 40 (printemps 1987): 45–50.

Lacan, J. (1972). "Of structure as an inmixing of an otherness prerequisite to any subject whatever." In *The Structuralist Controversy*, ed. Richard Macksey and Eugenio Donato. Baltimore: The Johns Hopkins University Press, 186–195.

———— (1990). *Television*, trans. Denis Hollier, Rosalind Krauss, and Annette Michelson. New York: W. W. Norton.

———— (1998). *Le Séminaire, Livre V: Les Formations de l'inconscient*, ed. Jacques-Alain Miller. Paris: Seuil.

Lefort, Rosine with Robert Lefort. (1994). *Birth of the Other*, trans. Marc Du Ry, Lindsay Watson, and Leonardo Rodriguez. Urbana and Chicago: University of Illinois Press.

Lew, R. (1992). "Note de lecture." In *Plastique des Noeuds Rares*, ed. R. Haddad and J. Trentelivres. Paris: Association de la Lysimaque, 194–195.

"Le sens du sens, Ernst Kris," European School of Psychoanalysis (collective). In *Les Pouvoirs de la Parole*. Textes réunis par l'Association Mondiale de Psychanalyse. Paris: Seuil, 1996, 247–253.

Miller, J.-A. "A Reading of Some Details in *Television* in Dialogue with the Audience." *Newsletter of The Freudian Field* 4 (Spring/Fall 1990): 4–30.

Ragland, E. (1995). *Essays on the Pleasures of Death*. New York: Routledge.

Soler, C. "A Passion in Transference: Marion Milner and the Susan Case." *Newsletter of the Freudian Field* (Spring/Fall 1991): 21–49.

Timpanaro, S. (1976). *The Freudian Slip*, trans. Kate Soper. London: NLB.

Valas, P. "L'effet de l'interpretation . . ." *Ornicar?* 40 (printemps 1987): 33–38.

8

The Inside Out of the Dangerous Mentally Ill: Topological Applications to Law and Social Justice

BRUCE A. ARRIGO

1. INTRODUCTION

In recent years, a considerable body of literature has emerged, exploring the sociological,[1] psychological,[2] and legal dynamics[3] of persons identified as mentally ill and dangerous. The significance of this scholarship does not principally rest in what it tells us about psychiatric citizens and the manner in which they are repeatedly subjected to state-sanctioned, transcarcerative practices.[4] Instead, these investigations are relevant insofar as they both reveal and conceal something quite profound about the cultural and psycho-analytic conditions of a society that insists on de-pathologizing, normalizing, and homogenizing difference.[5] Thus, missing from much of the prevailing and mainstream literature is any detailed statement about the construction of identity, meaning, subjectivity, discourse, and fantasy for those engaged in medicolegal decision making and for those exposed to the brutalizing effects of these institutional practices.[6]

This chapter, then, represents a conceptual and speculative foray into the lived experience of persons clinically diagnosed as mentally ill and dangerous, as determined by psychiatric specialists and endorsed, through the legal apparatus, by a civil commitment hearing and judgment. To access this excursion into the forensic domain, selected topological constructions, as developed by Jacques Lacan, will be employed.[7] Specifically, his use of the Möbius strip and the Klein bottle will be appropriated in order to better comprehend the psychoanalytic and cultural meaning of designating individuals as disordered and dangerous.[8] To situate these more philosophically animated observations, the seminal and controversial court decision of In the Matter of Billie Boggs (1987) will be examined. This appellate case represents a "classic confrontation between the rights of a citizen against governmental authority to confront and remedy a pervasive societal problem."[9] The specific problem addressed in the Boggs ruling was the plight of the mentally ill (and dangerous) homeless.[10]

I begin my inquiry by providing background on the Boggs case, and the respective decisions reached at the lower and appellate court levels. Next, I explicate Lacan's use of topology theory as a sophisticated collection of conceptual (and methodological) tools for psycho-semiotically discerning the relationship between subjectivity and discourse. I then apply several of Lacan's key topological notions (i.e., the Möbius strip and the Klein bottle), to the Boggs matter. I conclude by tentatively exploring the relevance of topology theory for persons defined as mentally ill and dangerous, especially in regard to the future of social justice and cultural change at the law–psychology divide.

2. BACKGROUND ON THE BOGGS CASE AND DECISION

Joyce Brown (aka Billie Boggs) was a 40-year-old homeless woman who lived next to a New York City restaurant throughout much of

1987. In October of that year, she was civilly committed to Bellevue State Hospital based on a petition filed by Project HELP, a mobile, mental-health outreach unit providing "emergency psychiatric services for allegedly mentally ill homeless persons, who live[d] on the streets of New York City."[11] Project HELP consisted of a number of clinical teams, composed of psychiatrists, nurses, and social workers. The expressed purpose of these mobile outreach units was to canvass the city in search of persons suffering from persistent and severe psychiatric symptoms, requiring immediate hospital treatment because they were "in danger of doing serious harm to themselves or others."[12]

Based on the initial screening and evaluation of Dr. Hess, a psychiatrist associated with Project HELP, Ms. Boggs was determined to be in need of emergency mental-health services. Soon thereafter, arrangements were made to ensure Ms. Boggs's confinement. The day following her court-ordered civil commitment, however, Joyce Brown challenged the hospital's authority to hold her against her will, and requested a hearing to assess the matter. At the lower court level, respondents (i.e., the state and its agents, including Bellevue Hospital and Project HELP) offered testimony from four psychiatrists, a clinical social worker, the older sister of Joyce Brown, and a witness who photographed Ms. Boggs living in the streets of New York City. At the hearing, the petitioner (i.e., Billie Boggs through her court-appointed attorney) introduced the testimony of three other psychiatrists and was a witness herself. The lower court granted the petitioner's application for release from institutional confinement. On appeal, however, the case was reversed, effectively quashing Ms. Boggs's request. In what follows, I present selected, though relevant, passages from the appellate court ruling as these comments disclose not only the logic that was dispositive for the case but signify how the court valued Joyce Brown's reality and the reality that was assigned to her by the respondent witnesses testifying against her. This latter point is particularly salient for the Lacanian application that occurs in a subsequent section of this chapter.

The Language and Logic of the Boggs Decision

The pivotal question for the appellate court in *Boggs* was whether the respondent proved, based on "clear and convincing evidence, that [Joyce Brown] suffer[ed] from a mental illness . . . , requir[ing] her immediate involuntary commitment to a hospital for care and treatment since, allegedly, if such an illness [wa]s left untreated, it [would] likely result in serious harm to the petitioner."[13] The appellate court reversed the hearing court's decision. Summarily, it found that the petitioner was both mentally ill and dangerous. In substantiating its conclusion, the court asserted:

> . . . we find the clear and convincing evidence indicates that, while living in the streets for the past year, Ms. Boggs' mental condition . . . deteriorated to the point where she was in danger of doing serious harm to herself when . . . she was involuntarily admitted to respondent Bellevue for treatment; and we further find that clear and convincing evidence supports the continued involuntary confinement of Ms. Boggs to the hospital for treatment.[14]

The appellate court further argued that the lower court was in error when it effectively dismissed the conflicting psychiatric testimony. As the appellate court maintained:

> [T]he hearing court states, in substance, that the respondents' psychiatrists and the psychiatrists who testified on behalf of Ms. Boggs "are diametrically opposed in their assessment of mental condition and in their predictions as to whether she is likely to cause herself or others harm. Thus I [the hearing court] derive little psychiatric guidance from them and therefore place great weight on the demeanor, behavior, and testimony of [Ms. Boggs] herself". . . . We [the appellate court] find that the hearing court erred in placing "great weight on the demeanor, behavior, and testimony" of [Joyce Brown]. . . .[15]

The significance of these passages, juxtaposed as they are, is in how they anchored and legitimized the appellate court's rationale for sustaining Joyce Brown's civil confinement. Indeed, the court unconsciously activated its Imaginary construction of the petitioner's identity when it chose to find meaning for her emotional state and physical condition outside of or beyond the explanation supplied by Billie Boggs herself. Notwithstanding the considerable weight this commentary received at the initial hearing, the narrative constructed by the majority opinion on appeal, based on the testimony of respondents' witnesses, established a detailed portrait of Joyce Brown, one that symbolically conveyed the nature and extent of her troubling and debilitating psychiatric disorder. In three pivotal contexts, the Imaginary configuration of the petitioner as both mentally ill and dangerous was pre-thematically conceived and persuasively articulated.

Tearing up money—The finding of mental illness in *Boggs* was based fundamentally on the meanings Project HELP staff assigned to the behaviors of the petitioner while observing her in the streets of New York City. It was undisputed that Billie Boggs, on occasion, tore up or otherwise destroyed paper money, especially when it was given to her by strangers. What is intriguing, however, is how this behavior was linked to "common sense"[16] notions of appropriate behavior, suggestive of the petitioner's underlying mental illness. In other words, what rational person would willingly and knowingly deface money?

According to Dr. Sabitini, a psychiatrist testifying on behalf of the respondents:

> It's not a general phenomena [tearing up money] and the indications I got were that there was a meaning to the destruction of this money because it represented, when it was given to her, people saying things about her—negative things about her that had a sexual overtone . . . people . . . were trying to control her sexuality through money. And I think the destruction of money served to dispel that.[17]

In addition, Dr. Marcos, another witness for the respondents, concurred with Dr. Sabitini, indicating that "being given currency was equated with men trying to tell Ms. Boggs that she was a prostitute."[18] Further, Dr. Marcos interpreted the petitioner's "burning of the currency as evidence of her belief that she could gain respect and dispel the idea [that] she [was] a prostitute."[19]

Both physicians endorsed the continued involuntary hospitalization of Ms. Boggs. They regarded her behavior as unorthodox, attributable to deep-seated mental illness. Indeed, following their logic, the destruction of money symbolized psychopathology. It stemmed from a non-commonsense belief about currency and sexuality that was the product of an underlying psychiatric disorder.

Notwithstanding the psychiatric testimony concerning the petitioner's mental illness, involuntary hospitalization requires something more. In short, there must be a showing of dangerousness. The question, then, is how did the appellate court interpret the petitioner as harmful to herself?

Self-injurious behavior—A finding of dangerousness in the mental-health law context indicates that, based on the evaluation of clinical forensic experts, one is likely to harm others or oneself in the foreseeable future. The appellate court in *Boggs* maintained that Joyce Brown posed a threat to herself in three specific areas, thereby necessitating civil confinement. As the appellate court explained: ". . . the key issue in this case is dangerousness and the record shows three aspects of self-danger. . . . [These include] self-danger from neglect, from actively suicidal conduct, and self-danger from aggressive behavior that is likely to provoke an attack from others."[20] According to New York's statutory standard, each of these expressions of dangerousness is sufficient to sustain an involuntary hospitalization order. Consistent with the finding of mental illness, the language and logic employed by the appellate court to reach its determination of the petitioner's dangerousness is worth noting.

The finding of self-danger stemming from neglect was predicated on the testimony of several respondent psychiatrists. For example, Dr. Mahon claimed that Ms. Boggs was not "ready to be an outpatient, since she . . . had no capacity to comprehend her need for food, clothing, or shelter, and, in addition, [could not] comprehend obvious danger."[21] Additionally, the mobile mental-health outreach team indicated that Joyce Brown had "throw[n] away warm clothing she had received from personnel representing Project HELP."[22] In assessing this behavior, Dr. Hess concluded that the petitioner was a "danger to herself, since she was incapable of accepting food, clothing, and shelter."[23]

The determination of self-danger arising from angry affect and hostile behavior was based on the observations of Project HELP staff. When approached by members of the mobile crisis unit, Joyce Brown would "twirl . . . an open umbrella to avoid eye contact, curs[ing] and shout[ing] obscenities . . . , and us[ing] threatening gestures."[24] Respondent witnesses testified that, if misdirected or misinterpreted, these actions could prompt pedestrians, motorists, or other citizens to respond adversely to Ms. Boggs, including physically assaulting her.

The finding of self-danger, resulting from self-destructive behavior, was linked to the testimony of Dr. Mahon. Attention was drawn to Ms. Boggs's tendency to run into traffic and throw away articles of clothing given to her by Project HELP staff. The petitioner professed her right to engage in this behavior. However, Dr. Mahon stated that ". . . running in front of traffic and saying she ha[d] a right to endanger her life is suicidal and as a psychiatrist, I have to call that suicidal behavior and I have to treat it as a clinician."[25]

The proliferating population of the mentally disturbed homeless— Although a judgment that one is both psychiatrically disordered and dangerous is sufficient for purposes of civil commitment, the decision of *Boggs* is significant because of how the appellate court confronted the social climate and political dynamics in which the case unfolded. There is no question that Joyce Brown attracted considerable media attention and public scrutiny. Indeed, given that the petitioner waived her right to confidentiality, the case received "almost daily news reports, prompt[ing] a number of television and other media discussions . . . relating to the problem of the homeless."[26] Fueling this intense frenzy, however, was a recently enacted mayoral directive aimed at remedying or, at least, curtailing the burgeoning number of street dwellers inhabiting New York City's alleyways, parks, grates, and sidewalks. Thus, Billie Boggs became a "test case" of sorts for the fairness and reasonableness of the City's newly crafted homeless initiative.[27] As Judge Milonas noted in his dissenting opinion,

> This case has attracted considerable attention, since the petitioner's involuntary hospitalization represents the first known effort by the city to implement a highly publicized and controversial Mayoral policy directed at dealing with the proliferating population of the mentally disturbed homeless.[28]

These observations are revealing, especially when considered in light of how the appellate court described the petitioner's social standing and psychiatric state both before and after involuntary treatment was administered. As the majority opinion observed,

> . . . undisputedly [Ms. Boggs] held responsible employment and was a productive member of society until 1984 [when] her mental condition began to deteriorate. [She had a] continuous work history of almost a decade, in which [she] was employed in responsible positions . . . [and] at that time, besides a job, she had a home and a family [until] she suffered a severe psychosis.[29]

Following the effects of the petitioner's thought disorder,

> she live[d] next to a restaurant . . . and stay[ed] at that location. [S]ince there [wa]s a hot air vent . . . she indicated that she had never been cold; she panhandle[d] money for food and, in that fashion, ma[de] between $8 and $10 a day. . . . [S]he claim[ed] that she ha[d] adequate clothes, and that when she needed more she had "friends" who . . . suppl[ied] them to her.[30]

The appellate court noted, however, that when Joyce Brown was initially hospitalized against her will, she became "rational, logi-

cal, coherent . . . an educated intelligent person . . . displaying a
sense of humor, pride, a fierce independence of spirit, [and] quick
mental reflexes."[31] The appellate court asserted that these changes
in demeanor and behavior were attributable to the fact that the petitioner "had recently been bathed, was dressed in clean clothes, and
had just received approximately a week of hospital treatment."[32]

3. LACAN AND TOPOLOGY THEORY: THE MÖBIUS STRIP AND THE KLEIN BOTTLE

In this section, two of Jacques Lacan's topological constructs will
be summarily described, mindful of their relevance for facilitating
a critical, psycho-semiotic investigation of forensic decision making. Elsewhere in this anthology (see Part I), several commentators canvass the insights of Lacan, detailing his reliance on topology
theory for ongoing psychoanalytic studies and much needed cultural change. For purposes of this chapter, however, I wish to situate
the previous accounting of the *Boggs* matter within an admittedly
selective, though relevant, discussion of key topological constructs,
including the Möbius strip and the Klein bottle.

Preliminarily I note that application studies in topology theory
are limited. Moreover, representative examples in the law, crime, and
social justice arena are particularly sparse.[33] This notwithstanding,
the Möbius strip and the Klein bottle enable one to investigate the
relationship between subjectivity and discourse—a central concern
examined throughout much of Lacan's complex and detailed psycho-
semiotic formalizations.[34] Broadly speaking, the Möbius strip and
the Klein bottle are descriptive devices directing our attention to the
often hidden manner in which sense production occurs, revealing
the inseparability of language and desire.[35] Thus, they are conceptual tools that provide a graphic illustration (i.e., a method or mapping)[36] for better understanding the relationship between subjectivity
and discourse in particular contexts. As I subsequently argue, this
includes decision making in the "psychiatric courtroom."[37]

Möbius Strip

As understood within the physical sciences,[38] the Möbius strip is a rectangular strip that undergoes a modification without changing its essential properties. The figure is constructed by taking a rectangle, twisting it once, and then joining the edges. The Möbius strip enabled Lacan to demonstrate how "that which is interpersonal (conscious and spoken) is connected to that which is intrapsychic (unconscious and pre-spoken)."[39] Indeed, this topological device was Lacan's way of "indicating how an 'inside' (the unconscious) has continuity with an 'outside' (the conscious)."[40] The Möbius strip is instructive for explaining the internal dialogue of the subject, the operation of metaphor, and the reification of phenomena, including forms of domination in the sociolegal sphere.

Lacan observed that often "the sender receives his [or her] own message back from the receiver in an inverted form."[41] This repetition, as an example of the subject's internal dialogue, can also signify a question being posed to one's Other (i.e., the unconscious). For example, "Why do I want to address the problem of the proliferating population of mentally disturbed homeless?" And the answer commences with I want . . . [objet petit a].[42] In other words, desire is embodied in an articulated demand. This demand activates a drive (e.g., fear, loathing, suspicion), followed by psychic recognition and social action (i.e., performativity).[43] In the psycholegal sphere, the return of the message in inverted form indicates how internalized ideological constructs anchor speech when deliberating upon such matters as mental state, reasonableness, culpability, dangerousness, volition, and so forth.[44]

Relatedly, the Möbius strip is instructive for comprehending Lacan's algorithm for metaphor.[45] According to Lacan, the unconscious is structured like a language. One way in which speech production is coordinated is through metaphor. The Möbius strip, then, graphically illustrates how, through metaphors, "a master signifier 'crosses the bar' to the unconscious and is replaced with another, less substantial, signifier. . . . In each instance [of metaphor] there is a reduction of the subject . . . [T]hat which is unique . . . is replaced by that which is abstract. Thus, the uniqueness and fullness of [the subject] disappear[s] in language."[46] For example, consider the metaphors, "the petitioner is mentally ill," or "the petitioner is dangerous." One signifier (i.e., the petitioner) is replaced by another (i.e., mentally ill, dangerous) and, following the complete pathway of the Möbius strip and utilizing Lacan's algorithm for metaphor, the former signifier re-emerges. However, all that is left are the abstractions "mentally ill" and "dangerous," negating the uniqueness of the subject (i.e., the petitioner).

Thus, we see how the reification of phenomena takes place, including the legitimation of certain linguistic forms in the juridical field. Indeed, legal conundrums, empirical anomalies, and other contradictions, inconsistencies, or paradoxes are explained by (i.e., reduced to) exchange values (e.g., abstract clinical forensic categories) that obfuscate the subject's identity and lived experience. This notwithstanding, meaning is generated by crossing the bar, by traversing the Möbius strip, furthering our understanding of the inexorable relationship that exists between subjectivity and discourse.

The Klein Bottle

Similar to the Möbius strip's development in the physical sciences, the Klein bottle, as a geometric device, demonstrates the intrinsic continuity of shapes.[47] As applied to the psycho-semiotic topography of Lacanian thought, "[t]he Klein bottle is significant for underscoring the relationship between master signifiers (Lacan's S_1) anchoring speech and the sequencing of words or phrases (Lacan's S_2) used to give content to these key phenomenal forms."[48] Thus, the Klein bottle graphically depicts how consistency in thought is perpetuated within and throughout one's speech. Moreover, the Klein bottle demonstrates how this consistency in thought is circumscribed: that is, how the particular words or expressions chosen to convey the speaking-being's desire are always and already saturated with pre-configured meaning, embodying ideological content consistent with the discourse in use.

In relation to the Klein bottle, Lacan referred to master signifiers (S_1) as "unary" signifers.[49] Unary signifers are words or phrases that explain certain drives. For example, in the mental health law context, "expert witness testimony" is relied upon in which "clinical evidence" (i.e., evaluation, diagnostic, and treatment categories) is introduced, providing an opinion on or prediction of such forensic matters as "psychiatric disorder," "competency to stand trial," "dangerousness," "malingering," and "mental state during the commission of a crime."[50] When employed or otherwise articulated in the psycholegal sphere, these words and phrases (i.e., signs) contain deeply felt but unspoken desires. Indeed, in the mental health law arena the disease model of psychiatric medicine is operative.[51] It seeks to diagnose symptoms, identify treatment, and control behavior.[52] The assumption is that with enough "science" mental illness can be corrected,[53] and people can be made functionally well. These desires, activated as drives, insist within psycholegal discourse but are outside the speech chain. In this regard, then, they operate as that "lingering notion or 'whisper,'"[54] breathing meaning into all other signifers and their corresponding signifying chains.[55] Thus, unary signifiers are "the unspoken truth (and desire) of the speaking-being, veiled in the act of speech."[56] In the construction of mental health law discourse, the cloaked truths for the drives mentioned above include such things as the objectivity of reason, the truth of science, and the certainty of psychiatric intervention. Here, too, we see the inextricable and ineluctable association between discourse and subjectivity, language and desire.

4. TOPOLOGY THEORY AND THE *BOGGS* DECISION: TOWARD AN APPLICATION

The appellate decision in *Boggs* amply demonstrates the utility of Lacanian thought and his reliance on the Möbius strip and the Klein bottle. In this section, I return to the language and logic of the case in order to reveal the "inside out" of the dangerous mentally ill, as symbolically embodied in the demeanor and behavior of Joyce Brown and as narratively constructed by the appellate court. Table 8–1 is a 3 × 2 grid. It identifies the specific contexts in which the Imaginary configuration of the petitioner's identity and being was constituted (i.e., narrative markers) and the topological constructs that deepen our regard for the language and desire operative in the psychiatric courtroom. The intersection of any of the points within the grid discloses the psycho-semiotic processes through which meaning was generated in the case of *Boggs*. In what follows, I suggestively and provisionally examine each of these particular intersections.

The Möbius Strip

According to respondent witnesses (Drs. Sabitini and Marcos), the petitioner's destruction of paper money was linked to underlying psychopathology, arising from a noncommonsense belief about currency and sexuality. However, the observations by Dr. Gould, a psychiatrist testifying on behalf of Joyce Brown, provided a different interpretation for this behavior. According to Dr. Gould, Ms. Boggs "had no delusions about money, rather . . . when someone threw paper money [at her] and she found it insulting or degrading, she would destroy it."[57] This explanation was confirmed by the petitioner, who indicated that she "destroy[ed] paper money if it [wa]s thrown at her or given to her in an allegedly offensive manner [and that] she ha[d] no delusions about black persons giving her money for sex."[58]

Given this conflicting testimony, how are we to reconcile the appellate court's judgment of Ms. Boggs (i.e., as mentally ill and dangerous)? Following Lacan and topology theory, the tearing up of currency was a metaphor for the petitioner's seemingly inexplicable behavior and being. Relying heavily on the testimony of respondent witnesses, the court substituted the subject's uniqueness (as a fiercely independent and proud woman) with abstract signifers,

TABLE 8–1: The Topology of the *Boggs* Decision

Topological Construct	Narrative Markers		
	Tearing Up Money	Self-Injurious Behavior	Proliferating Mentally Disturbed Homeless
Möbius Strip	metaphor for delusional behavior; reification of clinical categories in legal sphere	metaphor for dangerous person; legitimation of clinical categories in legal sphere	demand = civic unrest; drive = neutralization, resolution, reconciliation; performativity = civil commitment
Klein Bottle	respect for money; the primacy of reason; and the value of commonsense behavior	respect for normative living; esteem-appropriate speech & thought; actions = identity	homelessness = deviance; mentally ill (and dangerous) need to be corrected; civil commitment = acceptable remedy

involving troubling sexual and racial signifieds. The appellate court's discourse regarding the petitioner was mobilized and coordinated through its use of metaphors that crossed the bar into the unconscious where they were replaced with marginalizing and oppressive signifiers. Indeed, given that the respondent psychiatrists were unable to integrate the defilement of currency into any acceptable mode of normative comportment, the actions of Billie Boggs were exchanged with clinical values or categories (i.e. the petitioner as delusional). Thus, the expression, "tearing up money," as linked to Joyce Brown, obfuscated and reduced her identity, creating meaning that ostensibly quelled her humanity as conveyed through psycholegal language. This meaning, as affirmed and legitimated in the *Boggs* court, reified the power of psychiatric discourse *to speak the subject*[59] in the juridical sphere.

Relatedly, the identification of Joyce Brown as dangerous to herself because of self-neglect, active suicidal ideation, and aggressive behavior assumed metaphorical proportions. Witnesses testifying for respondents indicated that the petitioner was gravely disabled, unable to comprehend her basic need for food, clothing, and shelter. Moreover, Billie Boggs was thought to be a danger to herself because she ran into New York City traffic, discarding items of clothing given to her by Project HELP staff. Finally, respondent psychiatrists indicated that the petitioner's anger (affect) and hostility (behavior) toward others subjected her to possible serious physical harm from unsympathetic or uninformed pedestrians. Dr. Gould, testifying on behalf of Billie Boggs, intimated that each of these instances of self-danger could be explained. In short, he observed that the petitioner did not want to be "disturbed by some individuals who invaded her privacy."[60]

Topologically speaking, the sign of self-danger, as metaphorically employed in the *Boggs* decision, functioned to reconstitute the identity of Joyce Brown. Unable to accept the possibility that the petitioner preferred to live as she did (i.e., in the streets, panhandling, securing food and clothing from friends, resisting assistance from intrusive others), the appellate court dismissed the subject's unique agency and identity (i.e., as a choice-making,

though homeless, citizen), preferring instead to replace her indi-
viduality with abstract and alienating signifieds regarding self-
danger. Moreover, as these meanings found their way into the
unconscious, they no longer were metaphors for the petitioner's
behavior and demeanor; rather, they became indicators of Joyce
Brown "true" psychological identity. In other words, the appellate
court's coordinated discourse on self-danger and grave disability,
activated unconsciously through metaphor, reconstituted Billie
Boggs as someone whose specific *actions* were self-injurious to
someone whose very *being* was dangerous. Thus, we see how the
sign of self-harm, and all the corresponding and circumscribed
psycholegal meanings associated with it, dismissed the humanity
of the subject and validated the power of clinical discourse to define the identity and reality of the petitioner in the legal arena.

The appellate court's specific reference to the proliferating
population of the mentally disturbed homeless can also be explained by employing the topological construct of the Möbius strip.
Unlike the two previous points of intersection discussed as metaphors legitimating certain linguistic forms in the juridical sphere,
the court's focus on psychiatrically disordered street dwellers is
topologically informative for other reasons.

The Möbius strip helps explain the internal dialogue of the
subject. Posed as a question and asked at the level of the unconscious, the appellate court jurists pondered: "Why do we need to
address the case of Billie Boggs, a mentally disturbed homeless
woman?" In other words, following Lacan, the court unconsciously
considered the objects of desire that mobilized its attention upon
the petitioner. Several factors warrant some mention here. First,
the case received widespread media exposure, detailing the plight
of the homeless. Second, large-scale public sentiment surrounded
the case, creating a national debate on this social malady. Third,
the case challenged the viability of the recently enacted and extremely controversial mayoral directive on street dwellers in New
York City.

Based on these influences, the appellate court's desire to respond was embodied in an articulated demand: namely, that legal

intervention was necessary because the social and political climate of the case produced increasing civic unrest. This demand activated a drive (e.g., render a decision that neutralizes the press, that satisfies the public's clamor for resolution, that reconciles the merits of city government's initiative on homelessness). This mobilization of desire gave way to performativity (i.e., sustaining the petitioner's civil confinement). Following the path of the Möbius strip, it is worth noting how the court's response to its own query demonstrated that internalized ideological constructs (e.g., a circumscribed or clinico-legal meaning for mental illness and dangerousness) would anchor juridical discourse when the *Boggs* court deliberated upon the petitioner's need for continued involuntary hospitalization.

The Klein Bottle

The Klein bottle reveals how consistency in thought is maintained within and throughout speech, endorsing pre-configured meanings embodying ideological content consistent with the discourse in use. The unary signifier, "tearing up money" (S_1), was linked to the petitioner's delusional thinking (S_2), a clinical category with restricted linguistic meaning (a), delineating the subject's identity as psychopathological ($\$$). In the *Boggs* decision, the desire both outside of this speech chain yet lodged deep within it was activated through the petitioner's behavior and the appellate court's narrative construction of her. The unspoken, yet lingering, truths for the signifier "tearing up money" included such desires as respect for currency, the primacy of reason, and the value of commonsense behavior.

The unary signifier, "self-injurious behavior" (S_1) was associated with the petitioner's grave disability, suicidality, and aggressivity (S_2), clinical forensic determinations with bounded meaning (a) delimiting Joyce Brown's identity as dangerous ($\$$). The unarticulated truths for the signifier "self-injurious behavior," veiled in the act of speech production, included such desires as respect for normative living; esteem for acceptable/appropriate speech, thought, and behavior; and one's actions are synonymous with one's identity.

The unary signifier, "the proliferating population of the mentally disturbed homeless" (S_1), was related to the petitioner's emotional state and psychological condition as disordered and dangerous (S_2), psycholegal judgments embodying circumscribed ideological content (a), constituting the identity of the petitioner as someone in need of sustained institutional care and treatment (S). The unstated truths of the appellate court, communicated outside of the speech chain (i.e., the legal narrative) yet situated deep within it, included such desires as homelessness is deviance, the mentally ill (and dangerous) need to be corrected, and psychiatric confinement is an acceptable social and public health remedy.

5. CONCLUSIONS

The future of social justice at the law–psychology divide must embrace critical and alternative modes of analysis. This is particularly the case when determinations of mental illness and findings of dangerousness potentially affect the lives of psychiatric citizens adversely, including their protracted involuntary confinement in hospital settings. Topology theory, as a detailed method for intuitively grasping the inseparability of language and desire, dramatically reveals the unconscious roots of cultural intolerance in the forensic domain. As this investigation of the *Boggs* case poignantly revealed, persons like Joyce Brown are normalized, de-pathologized, and homogenized because of their articulated and lived difference. The Möbius strip and the Klein bottle amply demonstrate how the desiring voice of the clinicolegal apparatus affirms the linguistic coordinates of its own sign system while silencing the agency and identity (i.e., uniquenesses) of psychiatric citizens.

The work that lies ahead, both in theory and in practice, is to resist those marginalizing, alienating, and oppressive categories of sense-making that speak the subject in the psychiatric courtroom. This entails a debunking of prevailing modes of speech that always and already announce the circumscribed desire of the speaking being in the juridical sphere. For example, reconstituting the petitioner as "a psychiatric survivor," "a consumer of mental-health services," "differently abled," or "a psychiatric citizen" arguably embodies a more complete expression of one's desire than what is communicated by prevailing medicolegal signifiers and their corresponding ideological contents.[61] This step is the first in the process of recovering the subject's identity, embracing a fuller sense of difference, and re-thinking justice at the crossroads of law and psychology.[62]

ENDNOTES

1. See, e.g., C. Warren, *The Court of Last Resort*. Chicago: University of Chicago Press, 1982; J. Holstein, *Court Ordered Insanity: Interpretive Practices and Involuntary Commitment*. New York: Aldine de Gruyter, 1993; B. Arrigo, *Madness, Language, and the Law*. Albany, NY: Harrow and Heston, 1993; and C. Williams and B. Arrigo, *Law, Psychology, and Justice: Chaos Theory and the New (Dis)Order*. Albany, NY: SUNY Press, 2001.

2. See, e.g., J. Monahan, *The Clinical Prediction of Violent Behavior*. Washington, DC: US Government Printing Office, 1980; R. Wettstein, ed., *Treatment of Offenders with Mental Disorders*. New York: Guilford Press, 1998; B. Arrigo, *The Contours of Psychiatric Justice*, New York/London: Garland, 1996; and J. Monahan and H. Steadman, *Violence and Mental Disorder: Developments in Risk Assessment*. Chicago: University of Chicago Press, 1994.

3. See, e.g., R. Levy and L. Rubenstein, *The Rights of People with Mental Disabilities*. Carbondale, IL: Southern Illinois University Press, 1996; M. Perlin, *Mental Disability Law: Cases and Materials*. Durham, NC: Carolina Academic Press, 1999; R. Reisman and C. Slobogin, *Law and the Mental Health System: Civil and Criminal Aspects*. St. Paul, MN: West, 1997; and B. Winick, *The Right to Refuse Mental Health Treatment*. Washington, DC: American Psychological Association, 1997.

4. Transcarceration refers to the continual routing of dangerous mentally ill offenders (MIOs) to and from disciplinary systems of speech-thought-behavior control. See B. Arrigo, "Transcarceration: Notes on a Psychoanalytically Informed Theory of Social Practice in the Criminal Justice and Mental Health Systems." *Crime, Law, and Social Change: An International Journal*, 27(1), pp. 31–48, 1997.

5. The critique of "identity politics" or difference continues to evolve in philosophical, feminist, and literary circles. My own position is more akin to the postmodern deconstructive agenda of Jacques Derrida, especially his critique of Western culture's *logocentrism*, and the psychoanalytically informed semiotics of Jacques Lacan, particularly his commentary on the Real, Symbolic, and Imaginary Orders. For relevant work by Derrida see, e.g., J. Derrida, *Of Grammatology*. Baltimore, MD: Johns Hopkins University Press, 1976; *Writing and Difference*. Evanston, IL: Northwestern University Press, 1978; and *Positions*. Chicago: University of Chicago Press, 1981. For relevant work by Lacan see, e.g., J. Lacan, *Encore*. Paris: Editions du Seuil, 1975; *Ecrits: A Selection*. New York: W.W. Norton, 1977; *The Four Fundamental Concepts of Psycho-Analysis*. New York: W.W. Norton, 1981; and *Feminine Sexuality*. New York: W.W. Norton, 1985.

6. The history of the mentally ill is replete with examples of how these citizens have been corrected and/or punished. For lucid philosophical and historical accounts of this treatment see M. Foucault, *Madness and Civilization: A History of Insanity in the Age of Reason*. New York: Pantheon, 1965; M. Foucault, *Discipline and Punish: The Birth of a Prison*. New York: Pantheon, 1977; and G. Grob, *The Mad Among Us: A History of the Care of America's Mental Ill*. Cambridge, MA: Harvard University Press, 1994. For more recent application studies in this area see B. Arrigo and C. Williams, "Chaos Theory and the Social Control Thesis: A Post-Foucauldian Analysis of Mental Illness and Involuntary Civil Confinement," *Social Justice*, 26(1), pp. 171–201, 1999.

7. The conceptual tools of topology theory can be viewed as one of several important approaches for engaging in a postmodern analysis, particularly in the law and social justice domain. As Milovanovic notes, the linguistic turn in the sociolegal arena includes such orientations as "catastrophe theory [psychoanalytic semiotics], topology theory, quantum mechanics, and constitutive theory which collectively provide alternative ways of critically examining forms of domination. . . ." D. Milovanovic, "'Rebellious Lawyering': Lacan, Chaos, and the Development of Alternative Juridico-Semiotic Forms." *Legal Studies Forum*, 20(3), p. 296, n. 2, 1996. This chapter considers the manner in which psycholegal domination is articulated as a coherent narrative, impacting the lived reality of persons defined as mentally ill and dangerous.

8. The selection of these two topological constructs is deliberate. First, space limitations do not make it possible to examine Lacan's use of other ideographs or geometric contrivances. Second, and more importantly, the Möbius strip and the Klein bottle dramatically reveal the "inside out" of the court's narrative construction for the dangerous mentally ill.

9. *In the Matter of Billie Boggs*, 132 AD 2d 340 (1987), pp. 336–337.

10. The significance of the *Boggs* decision within the social science literature is not to be underestimated. Indeed, a number of critical commentators continue to assess the impact of the case for ongoing medicolegal decision making. See e.g., C. Williams, "The Abrogation of Subjectivity in the Psychiatric Courtroom: Toward a Psychoanalytic Semiotic Analysis." *International Journal for the Semiotics of Law*, XI(32), 181–192. In addition, the concern for the mentally ill homeless remains unabated as these citizens find themselves inadequately placed in local lock-ups, jails, prisons, or are otherwise abandoned where they sometimes succumb to the physical and emotional ravages of the street dweller's existence. H. R. Lamb and L. E. Weinberger, "Persons with Severe Mental Illness in Jails and Prisons: A Review." *Psychiatric Services*, 49: 483–492, 1998; R. Isaac and V. Armat, *Madness in the Streets: How Psychiatry and the Law Abandoned the Mentally Ill*. New York: Free Press, 1990.

11. *Supra*, n. 9, p. 343.

12. *Ibid.*

13. *Ibid.*, p. 341.

14. *Ibid.*, p. 366.

15. *Ibid.*, p. 364.

16. The notion of "commonsense" practices regarding the mentally ill and civil commitment is largely drawn from the work of Warren. See Warren, *supra*, note 1, pp. 135–140; and Arrigo, *supra*, note 1, pp. 23–25.

17. *Supra*, note 9, p. 353.

18. *Ibid.*

19. *Ibid.*

20. *Ibid.*, p. 370.

21. *Ibid.*, p. 363. The decision in *Boggs* relied on the case of *Matter of Carl C.*, 126 AD2d 640 (1987), for its position on self-danger through neglect. As the court in *Matter of Carl C.* suggested, a threat of serious harm to a mentally ill person "can result from a refusal or inability to meet essential needs for food, clothing, or shelter." *Ibid.*, p. 643.

22. *Supra*, n. 9, p. 363.

23. *Ibid.*, p. 346.

24. *Ibid.*, p. 348.

25. *Ibid.*, p. 351.

26. *Ibid.*, p. 367.

27. For a more detailed examination of this matter, emphasizing the political context in which the *Boggs* case was decided see, *supra*, note 1, Williams and Arrigo, *Law, Psychology, and Justice*.

28. *Supra*, note 9, p. 367.

29. *Ibid.*, p. 366.

30. *Ibid.*, p. 343.

31. *Ibid.*, p. 366.

32. *Ibid.*

33. For some lucid accounts of topology theory's relevance in the criminological sciences, see D. Milovanovic, "Postmodern Criminology: Mapping the Terrain," *Justice Quarterly*, 13(4), pp. 567–610, 1996; and B. Arrigo and T. R. Young, "Theories of Crime and Crimes of Theorists: On the Topological Construction of Criminological Reality," *Theory and Psychology*, 8(2), pp. 219–252, 1998.

34. For a detailed and recent foray, exploring the interconnection between discourse and subjectivity in the crime and justice divide, see B. Arrigo, (ed.), "Law, Society, and Lacan." Special Issue of the *International Journal for the Semiotics of Law*. The Netherlands: Kluwer Academic Publishers, *passim*, 2000.

35. Arrigo, *supra* n. 33, pp. 25–28; Milovanovic, *supra* n. 33, p. 593.

36. Rather than drawing attention to the particular ideographic or diagrammatic constructs themselves, this section explains how Lacan (and others) appropriated them for purposes of developing a psycho-semiotic strategy in which the construction of narratives and the activity of sense making could be decoded. For a graphic depiction and assessment of the Möbius strip and the Klein bottle in relation to law and criminological inquiry see, Arrigo, *supra*, n. 33, pp. 236–240.

37. See, e.g., B. Arrigo, "Desire in the Psychiatric Courtroom: On Lacan and the Dialectics of Linguistic Oppression," *Current Perspectives in Social Theory*, 16, pp. 159–187, 1996; and B. Arrigo, "Toward a Theory of Punishment in the Psychiatric Courtroom," *Journal of Crime and Justice*, 19(1), 15–32, 1996.

38. See, e.g., J. Weeks, *The Shape of Space*. New York: Marcel Dekker, 1985; S. Barr, *Experiments in Topology*. New York: Dover, 1964; M. Frechet and K. Fan, *Initiation to Combinatory Topology*. Boston, MA: Brindle, Weber, and Schmidt, 1967; and D. Hilbert and S. Cohn-Vossen, *Geometry and the Imagination*. New York: Chelsea House, 1952.

39. Arrigo, *supra*, n. 33, p. 236.

40. Milovanovic, *supra*, n. 33, p. 593.

41. For example, "Why did you find troubling the patient's tearing up of money?". . . . "I found troubling the patient's tearing up of money because. . . ."; "How did the petitioner engage in self-injurious behavior?" . . . "The petitioner engaged in self-injurious behavior by. . . ." See Lacan, *supra*, n. 5, p. 312, 1977.

42. Milovanovic, *supra*, n. 33 p. 594.

43. See J. Lee. *Jacques Lacan*. Amherst: University of Massachusetts Press, pp. 75–79, 1990.

44. For example, as Arrigo notes in his inquiry regarding the construction of criminological and legal thought and the hidden cultural values pertaining to them:

> What are the *linguistic* conditions under which we come to say what crime is?, What are the *linguistic* conditions under which we come to say what factors contribute to crime occurrence?, What are the *linguistic* conditions under which we come to say how crime can be controlled? This more self-reflective activity not only questions the values embedded in the criminological discourse in use, it also acknowledges how diverse ways of knowing are often reduced to certain patterns of speech, certain expressions of criminological logic.

B. Arrigo, "The Peripheral Core of Law and Criminology: On Postmodern Social Theory and Conceptual Integration." *Justice Quarterly*, 12(3), p. 466, 1995.

45. Lacan's mathematical formula for metaphor was: $f(S'/S) S \sim S(+)s$. Alternatively, he depicted this algorithm as: $S/S' : S'/x \rightarrow S(1/s)$. Lacan, *supra*, n. 5, pp. 157–158, 164, 1977; D. Milovanovic, *Postmodern Law and Disorder: Psychoanalytic Semiotics, Chaos, and Juridic Exegeses*. Liverpool, UK: Deborah Charles, pp. 69–70, 98–100, 1992.

46. Arrigo, *supra*, n. 33, pp. 237–238. Milovanovic describes Lacan's algorithm for metaphor in the context of Marx's use versus exchange value:

$$\frac{\text{exchange value}}{\text{use value}} \quad \frac{\text{use value}}{\text{unknown}} \quad \rightarrow \quad \text{exchange value} \quad \frac{1}{\text{idea of use value}}$$

When the terms that repeat themselves are omitted, all that remains is "exchange value" over the *idea* of "use value; that is, the substitution of uniqueness for abstraction." As Milovanovic comments when applying this logic to the legal sphere: "Homologously, . . .the juridic subject becomes the equivalent to the exchange value (the 'reasonable man' in law), and the uniqueness of the subject, or use value (e.g., abilities, needs), disappears. . . ." Milovanovic, *supra*, n. 33, p. 594.

47. J. Granon-Lafont. *Topologie Lacanienne et clinique analytique*. Paris: Point Hors Ligne, pp. 930–1006, 1985; D. Milovanovic, *Postmodern Criminology*, New York/London: Garland, pp. 177–180, 1997.

48. Arrigo, *supra*, n. 33, p. 239.

49. Milovanovic, *supra*, n. 47.

50. For a critical psycho-semiotic analysis of these and other mental health law signifiers, see B. Arrigo and C. Williams, "Law, Ideology, and Critical Inquiry: The Case of Treatment Refusal for Incompetent Prisoners Awaiting Execution." *New England Journal on Criminal and Civil*

Confinement, 25(2), pp. 367–412, 1999; and B. Arrigo, "The Behavior of Law and Psychiatry: Rethinking Knowledge Construction and the Guilty but Mentally Ill Verdict." *Criminal Justice and Behavior: An International Journal*, 23(4), pp. 572–592, 1996.

    51. Arrigo, *supra*, n. 1, pp. 76–105; Arrigo, *supra*, n. 2, pp. 129–174; T. Szasz, *Law, Liberty, and Psychiatry: An Inquiry into the Social Uses of Mental Health Practices*. New York: Collier Press, 1963; *Psychiatric Slavery: When Confinement and Coercion Masquerade as Cure*. New York: The Free Press, 1977; *Insanity: The Idea and its Consequences*. New York: John Wiley & Sons, 1987.

    52. T. Szasz, *The Myth of Mental Illness: Foundations of a Theory of Personal Conduct*. New York: Harper & Row, 1974.

    53. T. Szasz, *supra*, n. 51, *Psychiatric Slavery*, pp. 40–62.

    54. Arrigo, *supra*, n. 33. pp. 239–240.

    55. D. Nasio, *Les de Laure*. Paris: Aubier, pp. 37–41, 151–158, 1987.

    56. Arrigo, *supra*, n. 33, p. 240.

    57. *Supra*, n. 9, p. 356.

    58. *Ibid.*, p. 358.

    59. This is a reference to Lacan's use of the Borromean knot (the joining of the Symbolic, Real, and Imaginary Orders), and the meanings that insist within and throughout discourse, providing circumscribed articulations of the subject's being. Borromean knots explain how sense production occurs, how it is reproduced, and how it ensures the stabilization of "hierarchically constituted discursive formations." D. Milovanovic, "Borromean Knots and the Constitution of Sense in Juridico-Discursive Production." *Legal Studies Forum*, 17(2), p. 177, 1993.

    60. *Supra*, n. 9, p. 356.

    61. Arrigo, *supra* n. 1, pp. 106–149; Arrigo, *supra* n. 2, pp. 175–202.

    62. For some preliminary studies along these lines, employing the conceptual tools of Lacanian psychoanalytic semiotics, chaos theory, and/ or critical deconstruction see, e.g., B. Arrigo, "Insanity Defense Reform and the Sign of Abolition: Re-visiting Montana's Experience," *International Journal for the Semiotics of Law*, X(29), pp. 191–211, 1997; B. Arrigo, "Martial Metaphors and Medical Justice: Implications for Law, Crime, and Deviance," *Journal of Political and Military Sociology*, 27(2), pp. 305–322, 1999; B. Arrigo, "Transcarceration: A Constitutive Ethnography of Mentally Ill Offenders," *The Prison Journal*, 81(2), pp. 162–186, 2001; C. Williams and B. Arrigo, "The Philosophy of the Gift and the Psychology of Advocacy: Critical Reflections on Forensic Mental Health Intervention," *International Journal for the Semiotics of Law*, 13(2), pp. 215–242, 2000; Williams and Arrigo, *supra*, n. 1; Arrigo and Williams, *supra*, n. 6; and Arrigo and Williams, *supra*, n. 50.

Psychoanalytic Semiotics, Chaos, and Rebellious Lawyering*

DRAGAN MILOVANOVIC

INTRODUCTION

Lacan's use of topology theory in exploring the relation of the subject to discourse has provided a profoundly important intellectual tool in doing critical analysis. Recent scholarly investigations have attempted to integrate the work of this *oeuvre* with chaos theory[1] and applying this integration to criminology and law.[2] In this chapter we would like to indicate how this integration and application could be applied in developing an alternative discourse, a replacement discourse, in doing critical law.

Critical legal theory has recognized that hegemony in law is maintained by way of restrictive discourses. An important task is to offer alternative models that counter the dominant discourse of

*This is a revised version of Dragan Milovanovic's, "'Rebellious Lawyering': Lacan, Chaos, and the Development of Alternative Juridico-Semiotic Forms." *Legal Studies Forum* 20(3): 295–321, 1996.

law and the restricted narrative constructions that are allowed. In this chapter we would like to integrate chaos theory with Lacanian psychoanalytic semiotics and apply this integration to doing alternative law.

Critical legal studies ("crits"), feminist critical legal studies ("fem-crits"), and critical race theory have recognized how certain narrative constructions, reflecting dominant understandings, can take place in law; other narratives, other voices, other desires remain denied, or find incomplete expression in legal discourse. Activist lawyers, those desiring social change through the construction of alternative narratives that provide better understanding of the various biases and prejudices embodied in law, are hard pressed in developing an alternative. More often, they are caught in the dialectics of struggle whereby dominant structures are inadvertently reconstituted. Activist defendants find that the allowable legal discourse renders politicized versions of the "what happened" nonjusticiable.[3] Other subordinated, disenfranchised people (i.e., low-income, women, people of color, elderly, homeless, gays, lesbians, etc.) in their everyday struggles are often recipients of the "regnant forms of law,"[4] a form of law where dominant constructions are exclusively applied. In each instance—activist lawyer, activist defendant, other subordinated people—dominant legal and symbolic forms are reconstituted.

We need an alternative way. This chapter will provide some suggestions as to how an alternative discourse may take form. This discourse will not be of the static legal form but more in the form of what chaologists conceptualize as a dissipative structure.

A central question here is how to conceptualize agency and how to provide suggestions for legal change, particularly as to how an alternative discourse could develop, a discourse that offers the potential for the better embodiment of the unique desires of a plurality of peoples. Needed in the critical literature are some suggestions as to how, for the activist lawyer, to better interact with various clients so that alternative, more politicized narrative constructions can take place, while recognizing the dialectics of struggle whereby the client is both empowered in law, but is also disenfranchised as her/his desire is provided a diminished possibility of embodiment.

Our analysis will draw heavily from Jacques Lacan and chaos theory. Both offer the possibility of a useful integration which then lends itself to critically examining what is, and to offering vistas for change and the development of a more just order. We shall make use of chaos's offering of the "bifurcation diagram" in combination with Lacan's "four discourses" and his Schema R in demonstrating how a monolithic legal discourse may be undermined by one that is collaboratively produced by lawyer and client, more in the form of what Paulo Freire has called a dialogical pedagogy.[5]

Psychoanalytic semiotics has already been effectively used in critically examining law.[6] Chaos theory, on the other hand, has yet to be widely utilized.[7] And certainly chaos theory and psychoanalytic semiotics lend themselves to being integrated for the development of new conceptual tools for critical inquiry. It is time to move forward.

Our analysis draws from the sensitive and grounded analysis by Gerald Lopez, an activist in law, civil rights, and grassroots organizations. His book, *Rebellious Lawyering: One Chicano's Vision of Progressive Law Practice* (1992), focuses on two diametrically opposed methods in dealing with conflicts. The *regnant form* consists of the imposition of the dominant legal symbolic categories and unilateral form of interaction between lawyer and client. The *problem-solving form*, on the other hand, is more in line with what Paulo Freire[8] identified as a "dialogical pedagogy" whereby the professional and lay person together work through the conflict at hand, each an equal in contributing certain knowledge. Lopez's grounded work lends itself to being modeled by the bifurcation diagram that chaos theory offers us, and by the insights concerning the inseparability of subjectivity from discourse that psychoanalytic semiotics provides us. We wish, therefore, to model his findings, particularly by the use of topology theory, and in so doing, provide some insights for strategic points of intervention in the hegemonic legal order, or as Butler has suggested, offer strategies for "subversive repetition."[9]

PSYCHOANALYTIC SEMIOTICS, CHAOS, AND ALTERNATIVE LEGAL FORMS

The task before us is to develop an understanding of how alternative discourses may reach a level of relative stability and provide a medium in which the *parlêtre* (or *l'être parlant*: the speaking, or the speaking being) may create narratives that better embody diverse desires. The dialectics of struggle, in which the subject is both empowered in law and at the same time dis-empowered, often inadvertently reconstituting dominant forms of power, must find a productive way out of the dilemma.

Certainly, in the literature, some powerful arguments have been made for a more passive form of overcoming various forms of domination. The whole notion of a "slippage of meaning" operating in discourse itself provides the necessary openings for transformative practice. Of particular significance here is Cornell's[10] brilliant development of Irigaray's[11] notion of *mimesis* and Lacan's[12] formulation of metaphor and metonymy. In a more active direction is Lacan's[13] theory of the "four discourses" that is suggestive for how alternative signifiers might develop, particularly in the *discourse of the analyst*.[14] However, we are in need of a more grounded analysis. Freire provides the grounding; chaos theory the novel conceptual terrain by which our Imaginary can be expanded.

Doing law will be understood in this study more in the tradition of storytelling.[15] As Lopez argues:[16]

> Law is not a collection of definitions and mandates to be memorized and applied but a culture composed of storytellers, audiences, remedial ceremonies, a set of standard stories and arguments, and a variety of conventions about storywriting, storytelling, argument making, and the structure and content of legal stories . . . [T]he legal culture . . . generates over time

its own way of doing things and injects that way back into the larger culture.

Jackson's[17] "narrative coherence" model has shown how doing successful law is more an exercise in constructing narratives that have plausibility in the eyes of criminal justice practitioners and the jurors. Accordingly, segments of the population that are disenfranchised find themselves more at risk in the diminished use of dominant symbolizations and constructions, whereas higher income individuals remain "beyond incrimination." And we find that certain narrative constructions already have been stabilized by various criminal justice operatives.[18]

Bifurcation Diagram: Construction

Chaos theory has offered us various ways of "mapping" complex, dynamic systems. "Phase maps" indicate the various moments in an ongoing dynamic system. The bifurcation diagram indicates the various "snapshots" of a complex system as it changes over time. Figure 9–1 represents a possible integration of Lacan with chaos theory. It indicates the various identificatory factors that are at play for the subject. In other words, Lacan's theory has it that subjectivity is constituted by various identifications, both Symbolic and Imaginary. The intersections of these identifications produce a subject that speaks.

In applying chaos theory we are instructed to take some explanation being offered and tease out the important variables said to be at play in the dynamic system. This is referred to as "dimensional reduction."[19] We may, then, develop three identificatory axes (x,y,z) and one control parameter. The control parameter will be identified as the movement from the "regnant form" of lawyering to the "rebellious form," identified by Lopez as problem-solving. The three axes will represent possible identifications in three registers. These three registers include Lacan's three orders: the Symbolic, Real, and Imaginary. The unique desire and identifications of various *parlêtres*, in other words, is embodied in various forms at these intersections.

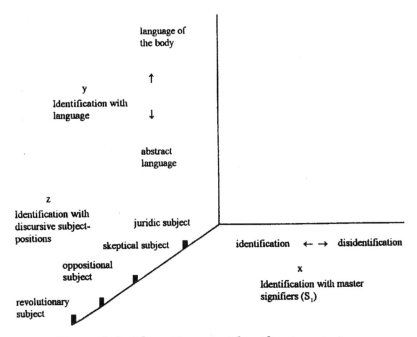

Figure 9–1. Phase Portrait: Identifications in Law

The x-axis—representing Lacan's Symbolic order—will be defined as the identification with master signifiers (S_1s). Master signifiers, for Lacan, are key signifiers or "identity-bearing words."[20] These are signifiers that can be traced to early socialization and entrance into the Symbolic order which are subsequently provided a more permanent basis (e.g., Lacan's *"points de capiton"*) within the Other, what Lacan calls the loci for "the treasury of signifiers." Later socialization, cultural forces, educational institutions, and other ideological apparatuses continuously reinforce more dominant forms of master signifiers. The relatively stable configuration of S_1s constitutes the ego-ideal ("I" in Figure 9–4 [Lacan's Schema R]). Thus the *parlêtre* can be viewed as having various dispositions toward her/his master signifiers. S/he may be very closely aligned with them, ambivalent, or, even in their expression, distanced from them. Accordingly, the x-axis will reflect a continuum from identification to dis-identification.

The y-axis—representing Lacan's Symbolic order, and here, for us, also the Real order (the primordial experiences that are beyond any congruent symbolization)—will be defined as identification with discourse. In constructing this axis we draw from Lecercle.[21] He indicates that we often embody desire in "abstract language," the formal language in which we must situate ourselves in order to construct narratives. Abstract language embeds knowledge (S_2), or constellations of signifiers tending toward the logic of equivalent exchange. In other words, they tend to take on more universal meaning in their use. These discourses, or linguistic coordinate systems, may take several forms, one of which is legal discourse. In Lacan's conceptualization, the existent phallocentric Symbolic order offers the potential for overcoming re-occurring feelings of *manque d'être* (lack-of-being). Signifiers, that is, may be selected to overcome "lack." This process "sutures," stitches over the *manque d'être*. And also produces *jouissance*; in this case Lacan makes a play on words, "j'ouir sens," I hear sense.

To speak "legally" is to make use of accepted legal signifiers (paradigm) and their appropriate linear ordering in syllogistic reasoning (syntagm). By so doing, one gains a momentary (illusory) feeling of completeness, experienced as *jouissance*, a phallic *jouissance*, represented by Lacan as JΦ. For Lacan, all signifiers in a phallocentric Symbolic order are tainted with the male's voice, expressed by him as: $\forall x \bullet \Phi x$ (to be read: all of x, e.g., behavior, signifiers, narratives, etc., are a function of the phallic signifier). Chaos theory, too, would suggest that abstract language is homeostatic.

On the other hand, Lecercle has also identified a "language of the body," having a closer approximation to the Real order, as a *délire*. Kristeva,[22] for example, talks about a dynamic, unstable and pre-verbal organization of the drives which precedes the child's inauguration into the Symbolic order. Chaos theorists would be quick to point out that here we have far-from-equilibrium conditions. Deleuze and Guattari[23] also point out how desire is "territorialized," inscribed on the body, by political economies. Poets, novelists, linguists, "insane," and often, in our studies, the disenfranchised, find themselves reverting to a discourse outside of the dominant forms. Its early more organized forms appear in "minor literature."[24]

Lacan's[25] insightful analysis of male and female discursive subject-positions indicates how women are deprived, are left-out, not-complete (*pas-toute*) in a phallocentric Symbolic order. In his matheme/algorithm:

$$\overline{\forall x} \bullet \Phi x$$

Here "woman does not exist." However, the person who takes up this discursive subject-position has access to another form of *jouissance*, an unspeakable *jouissance*. Lacan refers to this as the *jouissance* of the body, or *jouissance* of the Other, a supplementary *jouissance*, JO. Hence, our y-axis will represent a continuum moving from identification with abstract language to identification with the language of the body. In other words, the speaking being may find her/himself in various discourses and our y-axis represents a possible range.

Our z-axis—representing Lacan's Imaginary order—will be defined as various Imaginary identifications with discursive subject-positions (e.g., ideal-egos). These offer a discursively constituted location within which the subject can take up residence as an "I" in narrative constructions. At one end of our z-axis is the juridic discursive subject-position, the so-called "reasonable man/woman in law." Subjects before the law are required to use this as a background; for the juror, for example, it is the standard of reasonableness; for the defendant it is the basis of developing various defenses; for justices, the basis of interpreting various laws and their applications.

We see a range in the z-axis. Various discursive subject-positions can be identified: from accepting, to skeptical, to oppositional, to revolutionary.[26] In the accepting mode, the person upholds the ideal of the abstraction, the reasonable man in law, and identifies strongly with it. In the skeptical mode perhaps the person identifies with the "reasonable man" but does so with some degree of ambivalence. In the oppositional, perhaps the person resists close identification but nevertheless has no alternative, such as in Lacan's discourse of the hysteric. In the revolutionary identification, the person not only disidentifies with the abstraction of the reasonable man in law, but insists on every occasion with identifying with a more contextualized being. Those, for example, who attempt to politicize the trial are often offering alternative, more contextualized political constructions of events.

The complex interactions among the three axes, x, y, z, correspond to various "cuts" on Lacan's Schema R (see Figure 9–4). The *parlêtre* constructs various, fleeting perceptions of reality, conceptualized topologically by a Möbius strip, the "champ de la réalité," symbolized as R in Figure 9–4. This strip, or "cut" has one corner labeled $m(a'^{1-n})$ or the various ideal images of self, and the other corner, $i(a^{1-n})$, the Imaginary identifications with objects of desire which include signifiers. The various lines that can be connected between the two represent the various momentary "snapshots," or fantasies engendered in the unconscious, the Other, which become the bases of action. In other words, the embodied signifier (constituted by the interaction among the Symbolic, Imaginary and Real orders) now takes on a performative function. These various "cuts," for Lacan, represent fantasy, expressed by his matheme: $\$ \Diamond a$.

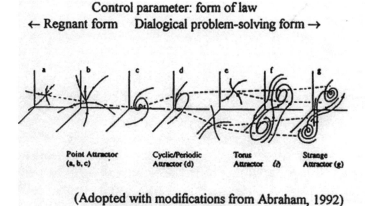

Control parameter: form of law
← Regnant form   Dialogical problem-solving form →

Point Attractor   Cyclic/Periodic   Torus   Strange
(a, b, c)   Attractor (d)   Attractor (f) Attractor (g)

(Adopted with modifications from Abraham, 1992)

Figure 9–2. Bifurcation Diagram, Forms of Problem-Solving, and Attractors

Figure 9–2 is a suggestive "phase map" of how our identified variables (x,y,z) interact with the control parameter (forms of delivery of legal services, from the regnant form to one that Lopez identifies as problem-solving). This phase map should not be interpreted with rigidity. It is suggestive and provides us with topological insights into complex processes in movement. It also provides a possible dynamic in the development of critical consciousness.

Figure 9–3 conceptualizes the development of a possible rhizomatic diagonal of *conscientization*. This term is a composite of various critical conceptualizations provided in the literature. From Paulo Freire[27] we draw the idea of *conscientization*, the development of a more critical consciousness. From Gilles Deleuze and Félix Guattari[28] we appropriate the idea of the *rhizome*, a non-linear movement, a line of flight of semiotic flow. Said differently, a rhizome represents a non-linear trajectory, not a straight line, but a "continuous line of variation," one which shows extreme sensitivity to initial conditions in its zig-zag development. Put in yet another way, the rhizome reflects much of quantum mechanics' notion of indeterminacy and string theory's representation in "trouser diagrams." Here, at best one can see at each point along a "line," a perpendicular "line" with a range of variation. Thus a pattern may emerge giving form to this tubelike structure in movement (global stability), but at any moment there is local indeterminacy, order and disorder as chaos theory tells us. In Figure 9–3 this rhizomatic diagonal of conscientization, we shall see, represents the development of a "border pedagogy" and a revolutionary consciousness.

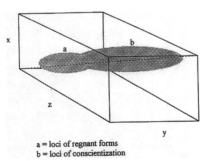

a = loci of regnant forms
b = loci of conscientization

Figure 9–3. Rhizomatic Diagonal of Conscientization

We are now ready to show how Lopez's work can be modeled and how an alternative discourse may begin to take form, in some cases, reaching a degree of stability. This developing discourse offers signifiers and discursive subject-positions that together provide the opportunity for alternative embodiments of desire in narrative constructions.

Regnant Forms of Lawyering

Our bifurcation diagram provides the various phase portraits in the development of a more critical discourse. Each of the three trajectories located in each of the cells of Figure 9–2 correspond to simultaneous differential equations that plot the movement along each of the three axes mentioned above. We shall first focus on the regnant forms of lawyering.

Figure 9–2a indicates that some subordinated person finds her/himself in conflict and/or crisis situations and in need of a resolution. S/he seeks the guidance of a professional, a lawyer. As Lopez has well argued, the lay person at this point enters a relationship with the professional in a state of relative powerlessness. He also quickly points out, however, "for all that they endure, battered women and low-income people of color still retain the capacity to work rebelliously with both stock and improvised stories—the capacity to resist victimization and subordination and to reverse its tendencies."[29]

In Figure 9–2a, we locate the "client" at the intersection of various trajectories. We can portray the various identifications induced by the functioning of the "regnant" form of lawyering, a form which separates the client or lay person from the professional, induces her/him to take up a discursive subject-position of a juridic subject, and subjects her/him to the violence of legal language. Our x-axis indicates that the lay person, in the regnant form of lawyering, is encouraged to embrace or identify with key master signifiers (S_1s) of law. Our y-axis indicates that the lay person is encouraged to identify with abstract legal language as s/he constructs various narratives of the "what happened." And our z-axis indicates that the subject is encouraged to imaginarily identify with the position of a "reasonable man in law."

In the regnant form of lawyering, whether encouraged by traditional law firms or by left lawyers, the *parlêtres* construct narratives that inadvertently reconstruct the dominant Symbolic order. They become, on the one hand, empowered legal subjects, but on the other, further disempowered as they relinquish the possibility of more fully embodying their unique desires, and inadvertently provide further legitimacy to the dominant Symbolic order. The trajectories in Figure 9–2a indicate that the tendency here is a homeostatic one: narrative constructions tend toward more prevalent forms of scripts. It is to engage in the production of a "readerly text."[30] We have here what chaos theory refers to as the *point attractor*. The logic of equivalence celebrates the point attractor.

Lacan has referred to this process as the dynamics inherent in the *discourse of the university*. Here, the initiator of the message provides some body of knowledge to the other who enacts it; that is, constructs narratives. The other, speaking within the legal discourse, however, finds much of her/his desire unembodied in the legal signifiers available. The *parlêtre* remains *pas-toute*, not-complete, left-out, not-all. And by not challenging dominant conceptualizations of law, s/he inadvertently gives further credence and legitimacy to the key master signifiers, the truth-claims that fuel the dominant body of knowledge (S_2). The *parlêtre* is interpellated[31] into discursive subject-positions. S/he becomes the "good subject"[32] or the spoken subject.[33] We have here a classic example of hegemony.

Figure 9–2b indicates that the trajectories are rather longer. This means that the lay person's increased contact with the regnant form of lawyering places her/him in an increasingly dialectical situation. On the one hand, s/he learns how to speak, legally, and how to construct narratives that will be listened to in law. But on the other, much of what s/he seeks to express is being denied. Disagreements with her professional lawyer may lead to the lawyer imposing what Lacan refers to as the *discourse of the master*. The lawyer insists that to be heard, certain narratives need to be constructed, certain master signifiers need to be expressed. To give a personal example, recently, when going through a "contingency" closing for a condominium, my lawyer, frustrated with the many questions and scenarios being offered, finally said: "Give me your thoughts and I will find the words." The dotted horizontal line in Figure 9–2b can be viewed as a time line connecting up the various phase portraits.

The x-axis in Figure 9–1 indicates that the *parlêtre* may on occasion distance her/himself from identification with the very master signifiers now being employed; the y-axis indicates that an oscillation begins to develop between embracing the legal discourse (discourse of the university) and reverting to a more nuanced, idiosyncratic discourse of the *parlêtre*. The z-axis indicates that the very discursive subject-position s/he is assuming is at times not wholeheartedly embraced. However, in Figure 9–2b the lay person, even with some distancing or dis-identification with master signifiers, abstract language, and the juridic discursive subject-position, nevertheless returns to a homeostatic position from which to construct narratives.

Figure 9–2c indicates that the subject's dis-identifications along the three axes may be greater, but yet the *parlêtre* still returns, after perhaps a lengthier time of consideration, to the point attractor. After all, where else is there to go?

Figures 9–2a through 9–2c indicate that the regnant form of lawyering will seduce the lay person to construct narratives within the dominant forms (Figure 9–3, shaded region "a"). We assume here that the lay person in a conflict and/or crisis situation has already been exposed to various discourses of the university and master (i.e., police, medical, insurance, child-welfare agencies, landlords, etc.) as s/he seeks to resolve a crisis situation. S/he has been offered discursive subject-positions within which to take up residence, master signifiers to express her/his plight, and often a bureaucratic discourse within which to create narratives that will be heard.

Beginning with Figure 9–2d, however, a different dynamic will be at play. At this moment, the problem-solving form of lawyering advocated by Lopez has a very different working philosophy and leads to different outcomes than in Figures 9–2a—9–2c.

Lacan, Schema R, and Borromean Knots

Let us pause for a moment before we continue onto Figure 9–2d, and apply some further Lacanian insights. Schema R has been offered as to how various perceptions of reality are constituted (see Figure 9–4). The Möbius strip represents the momentary stabilization of various identifications. We earlier noted, in Figure 9–4, that between "m," the ego, and "I," the ego ideal, various constructions of an ideal ego can be developed, $m(a^{\prime 1-n})$. And between "i," the Imaginary, or specular images, and "M," the primordial lost object of desire, the Mother, we see various Imaginary identifications with objects of desire (a), or $i(a^{1-n})$. In our conceptualization, the lay person is offered various legal master signifiers, here $i(a^{j})$, and an image with which to identify her/himself as an ideal ego, $m(a^{\prime j})$, the juridic discursive subject-position. The Möbius strip, too, has a nexus with the Symbolic order (the bottom triangle of Figure 9–4), indicating that the *parlêtre* must make use of the dominant discourse at hand. Legal semiotic production, then, can be viewed as entailing the production of a circumscribed constellation of "cuts" of the Möbius strip, a tendency for repetition of the same, that produces discourse with a performative function.

Lacan's RSI (Real, Symbolic, Imaginary orders), too, is implicated here. That is, discursive production always implies the intermixing of the three orders. We can reconceptualize this formulation with Lacan's notion of the Borromean knots (Figure 9–5). Here sense production is found at the confluence of the Imaginary and Symbolic orders. Here, too, phallic *jouissance*, JΦ, is found at the confluence of the Real and Symbolic orders. In other words, for those who assume the male discursive subject-position—and we will add, with our assimilation, those who take up the juridic discursive subject-position—overcoming *manque d'être* by the use

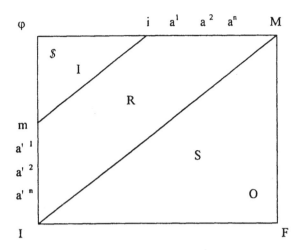

Where:

ϕ = small phi, imaginary phallus

I = Imaginary Order (imagoes, imaginary constructions)

S = Symbolic Order (culture, language)

R = *champ de la réalité*; perceived field of reality; framed by Symbolic and Imaginary order; represented here as a flattened Mobius strip; various "cuts"= fantasy or $\$ \lozenge$ a

I = lower left corner; ego ideal (symbolic identification)

O = Other; the unconscious "structured like a language"; repository of signifiers

F = law-of-the-father

M = Mother; primal object of desire (lost)

i = specular images; imaginary

a' = ideal egos

a = objects of desire

m = ego (imaginary)

$\$$ = divided subject; parlêtre; l'être parlant

i-M = where objects (a) are found; m-I = where imaginary identifications (a') are found

(Adopted with modifications from Lacan, 1977: 197)

Figure 9–4.

of dominant signifiers allows a momentary state of plenitude, experienced as *jouissance*. This form of *jouissance* finds an upper limit in the phallic Symbolic order. Note in Figure 9–5 what remains in potentiality: at the confluence of the Real and Imaginary orders there is indicated the possibility of a *jouissance* of the Other (JO), the inexpressible, but yet the loci from which an alternative

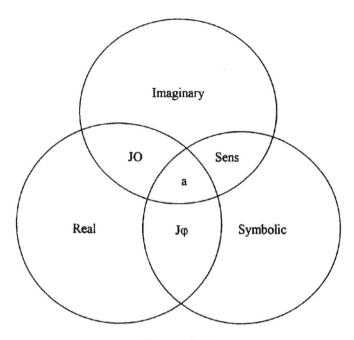

Figure 9–5.

discourse may evolve. Some postmodern feminists have argued that this is the locus from which an *écriture féminine* could arise.

We could also make use of Lacan's[34] late work on *le sinthome* and indicate that the "fourth order," which knots the three orders, RSI, functions, in the regnant form of lawyering, as a point attractor identified in Figures 9–2a—9–2c. In other words, *le sinthome* expresses quite well how the lay person's various identifications (x,y,z axes) tend toward a homeostatic point. The regnant form of lawyering, whether embraced by conventional or left lawyers, contributes toward the stabilization of this configuration. This contributes to relatively easy processing and resolution of various conflicts before the court. The linearity inherent in syllogistic reasoning, for example, is greatly aided by assuming stasis rather than continuous, non-linear change. In contrast, rather than deductive logic, rebellious lawyering often makes use of the more non-linear dynamic of "abduction" (we will return to this below).

TOWARD DIALOGICAL PROBLEM-SOLVING

Let us now return to the dialogical problem-solving form of rebellious lawyering and its effects (from Figure 9–2, phase maps 9–2d—9–2g). Again, we draw heavily from Lacan, Lopez, Freire and chaos theory; their integration, we suggest, is necessary for a better understanding of *conscientization*. Whereas the logic of equivalence and the celebration of universality is operative in the regnant form, in the dialogical problem-solving form two constitutive logics are involved: the logic of difference with the celebration of the particularistic, and the logic of "contingent universalities" which are contextualized, provisional, and historically specific.

At one necessary level of analysis, Lopez has sensitized us to how lay persons bring to the encounter with the professional, local, practical knowledges. In fact, "in the world of problem-solving, neither lawyers nor formal legal strategies are privileged."[35] For Lopez, then, "the lawyer need only treat them [clients] as capable, with a will to fight, and with considerable experience in resisting and occasionally reversing subordinated status."[36] Each person, the lay person and the lawyer, then, brings to the problem-solving encounter provisional expertise (*ibid.*). This relationship will necessarily remain in tension, Lopez tells us. This represents what chaos theorists refer to as far-from-equilibrium conditions.

The lawyer and lay person, each in turn, becomes teacher and learner. In this encounter each "learns to collaborate with another problem-solver. Together they bring what they are doing with one another under scrutiny and devise strategies for putting their ideas into action."[37] Unlike the regnant form where the *discourse of the university* prevails, often a disguise for the *discourse of the master*, in the dialogical problem-solving form of rebellious lawyering the activist lawyer "must combat monopolized conversations without abandoning her obligation to challenge her client—to critique as well as appreciate his understanding of his situation, the legal culture, and the strategies he pursues."[38]

This pedagogy has much in similarity with Paulo Freire's "pedagogy of the oppressed" and "dialogical pedagogy" (1972, 1973). It is also, with qualifications, somewhat in accord with Lacan's *discourse of the analyst*. Let us see how this approach produces not only mutually engaged problem-solving for the immediate crisis situation but also how it offers the potential for the development and relative stabilization of: new contingent master signifiers (S_1s'), the constitutive elements of a replacement discourse; various local knowledges; and ideal egos identifying with a more critical consciousness (e.g., Freire's notion of *conscientization*).

In Figure 9–2c, we note a splitting, or bifurcation has begun to develop (see the dotted horizontal lines that have begun to separate). Applying Lopez, Freire, and Lacan, we note that what has taken place is that the lay person has so alienated her/himself and dis-identified with given legal master signifiers (S_1s), the exclusive use of the legal abstract language, and the identification with the "juridic subject" that an alternative has appeared (e.g., portrayed by the bifurcation). How has this happened? Let us tease out the implications of Lacan's *discourse of the analyst* and Freire's work on the creation of "true words."

Lacan's discourse of the analyst reads as follows:

$$\frac{a}{S_2} \quad \rightarrow \quad \frac{\not{S}}{S_1}$$

According to Lacan, the analyst who assumes the position on the left offers to the other (the "hysteric," situated on the right) the left-out, the not-all (here little *a*, representing *pas-toute*). The hysteric is assumed to draw from a constellation of master signifiers that do not adequately embody her/his desire. The task is to replace dysfunctional master signifiers (S_1s) with new, more adaptive master signifiers (S_1s') that better embody desire. Lacan's process entails two steps: alienation and separation. This involves "dissolving and re-forming identifications in one or more of the three registers [Real, Symbolic, Imaginary]."[39] Preceding this alienation and separation, the analyst must engage in mapping (coding) previous master signifiers. The hysteric often begins with a *discourse of the university* in accounting for her/his situation in life.

In other words, sterile, bureaucratic discourses have been continuously offered and imposed. The skillful analyst will be a catalyst for a transformation from the *discourse of the university*, to the *discourse of the master*, to the *discourse of the hysteric*, to finally arriving at the *discourse of the analyst* where new master signifiers will evolve.[40] In this encounter, the analyst will continuously offer the little *a*, what is left out, to the other, who will—in the encounter that has brought the alienation and dis-identification (along the three axes) to its peak—begin to separate from the previous master signifiers. In other words, new signifiers begin to replace old ones. In short, the hysteric begins to construct narratives that lead to a heightened ability for problem-solving activity. S/he becomes a "border intellectual" negotiating the dialectics between sameness and difference and embracing emergent forms.

Paulo Freire's dialogical pedagogy has some similarities with Lacan's. In Freire's "pedagogy of the oppressed" the codification and decodification process entails deconstructing constitutive forms, "which, when transformed, can produce epistemic shifts that in turn are capable of generating other categorical changes and developing specific demands, programs, goals, etc."[41] The "space" created in the dialogical encounter engenders: distancing from the concrete, repetitive everyday world; critical reflection; and "an authentic process of abstraction" by the previously disempowered. This leads to a new form of subjectivity.[42] However, and critically, Freire's approach assumes a greater dialogical encounter whereby the "illiterate" and the "literacy campaign worker" work together to first code and then decode given existential situations. In other words, Freire's model is less unilateral in form and practice than Lacan's.

For Freire, the goal is to speak "true words."[43] The word has two dialectically related components: action and reflection. Absent either component in speech, the subject fails to engage in transformative activity: s/he engages in mere activism or verbalism; her/his words are inauthentic. For Freire: "to exist, humanly, is to *name* the world, to change it. Once named, the world in its turn reappears to the namers as a problem and requires of them a new *naming*. Humans are not built in silence, but in word, in work, in action-reflection."[44]

This process of naming can also be explained by a new form of *le sinthome*. Signifiers are knotted (*points de capiton*) to signifieds in various configurations of coupled iterative loops.[45] *Le sinthome* becomes the basis of the "writerly text."[46] Not merely repetition of the same, but the ever changing (the effects of iteration) is what now appears in semiotic production: Lacan's subject returns as the more-than-one.

As we can see, for both Lacan and Freire the creation of new master signifiers becomes a collaborative task. In our application, we redefine, with Bracher,[47] the meaning of "hysteric" to include those in opposition, those alienated, those in struggle against some order. We also lean more to Freire in seeing the dialogical encounter as a more symmetrical two-way encounter. The analyst must appear transparent to the hysteric. And this is what Lopez in fact encourages in his problem-solving form of rebellious lawyering. Each person, activist lawyer and lay person, becomes in turn teacher and learner. According to Lopez:[48]

> Like the client, the lawyer always teaches and always learns. In trying to understand the client's situation, she learns about the client's practices and about the relationships in which she intervenes. Even here she teaches when she lets the client see what she needs to learn, and, less obviously, when, as an outsider, she challenges thoroughly accepted ways of thinking and acting.

Returning to Figure 9–2. We note in 9–2d, 9–2e, and 9–2f that the lay person has increased her/his alienation and dis-identification along each of the three axes (e.g., away from abstract language, the reasonable man in law, and master signifiers of law) and has begun to produce new master signifiers (S_1s'). Following chaos theory, these moments can be identified as far-from-equilibrium conditions within which "dissipative structures" emerge. These new master signifiers, more holistic embodiments of the subject's unique desire, are then incorporated in narrative constructions in furthering the resolution of some crisis situation. This mutual problem-solving entails, again, an alienation, dis-identification, separation and a new identification and reconstruction. Lopez, too, suggests that the activist lawyer must often "challenge her client"[49] to re-examine often-used strategies for problem-solving, producing, no doubt, some anxiety in the process.

We now observe two separate outcome basins in Figure 9–2e. This indicates that the lay person is operating in two linguistic coordinate systems, one representing the old S_1s and S_2s, the other, the new S_1s' and S_2s', either of which can be the locus from which coherent narratives may be constructed. We no longer have a point attractor but a periodic attractor: outcomes oscillate between two loci. Figure 9–2e also suggests that these two loci are relatively static, and not connected.

In Figure 9–2f, however, the two outcome basins are now connected (e.g., coupled), indicating the more fluid interchange between the two discursive regions. Here, following chaos theory, we have a quasiperiodic torus attractor. There exists coupled os-cillations between two or more "truths" that remain incongruous with respect to each other. The more dominant forms of narrative production constituted by S_1s are being replaced by new forms.

In Figure 9–2g we note the emergence of the strange attractor (in a three-dimensional portrayal, the classic form would look like a pair of butterfly wings). We interpret this as both the lay person and rebellious lawyer expanding their respective stock of knowl-edge (S_2); first, by way of reliance on new master signifiers (S_1s'), and, second, by way of an expanded ability in constructing new forms of narratives that can better lead to problem-solving. In other words, each "wing" represents a locus where specific forms of nar-rative constructions can take place, given the form of the master signifiers (S_1s') in existence. There exist, therefore, two bases of knowledge.

And we are now in the position to comment on the develop-ment of the rhizomatic diagonal of *conscientization*. We had started our analysis by indicating that subordinated people consult pro-fessionals, including activist (left) lawyers often from a position of vulnerability (e.g., discourse of the hysteric) because of the crisis at hand. We also indicated, with Lopez, that the regnant form of lawyering, having much in common with the discourse of the university (many times, hiding a discourse of the master), is often the model embraced. And we see how hegemonic domination often results. The lay person is both empowered and disempowered. S/he inadvertently provides legitimacy for the continuation of the regnant form of lawyering.

The dialogical problem-solving of rebellious lawyering, on the other hand, is more in line with the discourse of the analyst *and* hysteric, and with Freire's pedagogy of the oppressed. Here, the activist lawyer and the subordinated meet in a joint undertaking where each learns and teaches. New master signifiers are being created. These new master signifiers "are less exclusive, restrictive, and conflictual . . . [they are of] a different style . . . a style that is less absolute, exclusive, and rigid in its establishment of the subject's identity, and more open, fluid, and processual: constituted, in a word, by relativity and textuality."[50] These S_1s' defy closure and remain in movement, in displacement that never stops.[51] These new master signifiers take the form that chaos theory refers to as "dissipative structures." This concept reflects both a deconstruction and a coming to be, a constant reconstruction in far-from-equilibrium conditions.

The upper right area of the rhizomatic diagonal of conscientization (Figure 9–3, shaded area b) represents a region, a locus, lying between the "wings" of the butterfly attractor, in the "saddle" region. It represents the "borderland"[52] where emergents are in flux. Here maximal indeterminacy prevails; emergents are fluid, ironic, and unexpected. Lacan's algorithms of metaphor and metonymy are at full play here: metonymy, because it is connected with the displacement of desire and engenders "a process of continual unmasking";[53] metaphor, because of the "slippage of meaning," the "disruptive excess"[54] connected with the "crossing of the bar," the "poetic spark" and the production of new meaning.[55]

Our diagonal in Figure 9–3 suggests that *conscientization* will follow a non-linear path. The three identifactory axes will witness movement outward toward dis-identification. But surmising that a mere diagonal line is the resultant is to fall victim to linear logic.

The rhizomatic diagonal of conscientization, rather, indicates that subordinated people and rebellious lawyers in struggle will find their journey dialectically constituted. The "truths" that they arrive at are but provisional, or "contingent universalities"[56] or to incorporate the idea of chaos theory, dissipative structures. Our rhizomatic diagonal of conscientization suggests that between the two coupled outcome basins identified in Figure 9–2g as constitutive of the strange attractor, a new way of discursive constructions develops which is conducive to resolving conflicts, and at the same time is better equipped to face various dominant forms insomuch as new narrative constructions better embody the plurality of desires, offer a better understanding of the given repressive order, contribute vistas for possible strategic intervention, and lead to potential social change and social justice. Problem-solvers at the local level, may, with further organization, become problem-solvers at the more global level. Social justice can indeed work from ground up.

Lopez's investigation also suggests that neither deductive reasoning (syllogistic reasoning), nor merely inductive reasoning should prevail. Better suited for the rhizomatic movement is the notion of "abduction," which draws from both. We shall continue with this notion below. We want to stress at this time that our analysis has led us to posit that an expanded space can be opened up within which alternative identifications may take place, and, consequently, alternative narratives may develop.[57] We would like to further suggest that this space is "fractal" insomuch as the traditional narrow integer space (e.g., 0, 1, 2, 3 dimensional space) with which we are all too familiar does not provide enough "room" to consider the continuous nature of phenomena. Dualities and dichotomies such as the Boolean logic embraced in legal proceedings are modernist assumptions that have restrictive notions of space. It would be premature and counterproductive to indicate the exact contours of this space or the definitive ideal end-point. The application of the problem-solving form to the immediate crisis situation has, then, a better chance for collaborative amelioration. And each "small" successful struggle may lead to a better understanding of larger forces of domination. There potentially exists, therefore, a grounded contribution to the development of social justice.

Rebellious Lawyering, Border-Crossers, and the New (Dis)Order

Rebellious lawyering, making use of the dialogical problem-solving method, offers an approach that empowers both the subordinated as well as the activist lawyer. Both become "border-crossers" engaged in a "border pedagogy."[58] As Giroux tells us,[59]

> . . . the concept of border pedagogy suggests more than simply opening diverse cultural histories and spaces to students [and other subordinated people]. It also means understanding how fragile identity is as it moves into borderlands crisscrossed within a variety of languages, experiences, and voices. There are no unified subjects here, only students [subordinated people] whose multilayered and often contradictory voices and experiences intermingle with the weight of particular histories that will not fit easily into the master narrative of a monolithic culture. Such borderlands should be seen as sites for both critical analysis and as a potential source of experimentation, creativity, and possibility.

Giroux's Freirian-driven analysis is well in accord with ours. Here subjectivity is recognized as multilayered, nonunitary, conflictual, marked by differences, with different degrees of awareness behind everyday action. The emerging identity is one in which "social agents become plural, that is, the discourse of the universal agent, such as the working class, is replaced by multiple agents forged in a variety of struggles and social movements."[60] Here signifiers reach temporary stability in historical struggle.[61] Through dialogical problem-solving, a "language of critique and possibility" will be a continuous emergent.[62]

The notion of "dissipative structures" once again seems an ideal conceptualization of this process. It is not that subjects will be cast adrift on high seas without navigational equipment. Rather,

provisional, contingent, and relatively stable positions can be formulated; or to use Butler's[63] formulation, "contingent universalities" may be developed which become the basis of further action.
Our dialogical problem-solving approach would seem to be one
strategy for "subversive repetition"[64] by which signifying practices
are denied stasis. Here, subjectivity is in continuous change. New
social movement theorizing which has integrated chaos theory[65]
has also shown the importance of the assumption of a continuous
persistence of resistance by dominated peoples, how it becomes the
basis for the proliferation of multiplicity, how differences and
sameness lie in a dialectical relation, and how new organizational
forms, reflecting polyvocal subjects and lifestyles, may develop.

Local, practical knowledges[66] provide, unlike the regnant form
of lawyering, an equal contribution to problem-solving. Rather than
syllogistic reasoning and deductive logic, what is called for is a form
of abduction,[67] whereby problem-solving works its non-linear way
between induction (local, practical knowledges) and deduction
(activists' global knowledge and understandings of various narratives of bureaucracies). It is a grounded pedagogy from the disenfranchised, an "outsider jurisprudence" that utilizes "contradiction,
dualism, and ambiguity."[68]

Lacan's schemas of the subject—Schema L, Schema R,
Schema I, Graphs of Desire, Borromean knots—and the four discourses can be productively integrated in explaining the subject-
in-process[69] in our dialogical problem-solving form of law. This
integration offers much explanatory power in pointing out the
possibility for the rhizomatic diagonal of conscientization emerging. Schema R, for example, indicates how alternative "cuts" of the
subject, or $\text{\$} \lozenge a$, are possible. In other words, we see that the
"champ de la réalité" will be constituted by contingent nexi between
m(a') and i(a). Here, along the three axes of Figure 9–1, the *parlêtre*
has dis-identified with conventional discursive subject-positions
of law (juridic subject), conventional master signifiers (S_1s, static
legal signifiers), and conventional abstract language (juridic linguistic coordinate system).

The dialogical problem-solving method of law engenders this process. The Symbolic, Imaginary, and Real orders find a knotting whereby repetition is subverted. This can be seen in the Borromean knots. It can also be seen in Lacan's late work on *le sinthome*. In our conceptualization, *le sinthome* takes on the form of an attractor, a strange attractor. It may also be a dissipative structure insomuch as stasis is continuously undermined. In other words, new master signifiers (S_1s') are more multi-accentual;[70] they reflect a plurality of voices in tension. The psychic apparatus in this view must be characterized as in "far-from-equilibrium" conditions rather than in equilibrium or homeostasis, as posited by structural function-alism—a core but questionable assumption of modernist thought.

Dialogical problem-solving in law, we have argued, provides the basis of alternative narrative constructions. New master signifiers will emerge which are grounded (Lacan's *"points de capiton"*) in historical struggles. They are of a provisional and contingent form. To speculate: it may very well be, too, that this process may entail the momentary transformation of Schema R into Schema I where the law-of-the-father has momentarily lost its hold on the subject. Here, previously sutured signifiers are released for the development of an alternative *points de capiton*. Nevertheless, the constellation of new master signifiers provides the basis of an alternative ego-ideal. A relatively stabilized replacement discourse, one built collaboratively from bottom-up, could provide the basis of more complete embodiment of diverse desires. And in this sense, following Lacan:[71] "a signifier represents the subject for another signifier."

CONCLUSION

The dialectics of struggle often produces inadvertent consequences. There always exists the possibility that frustrated activist (leftist) lawyers will insist on the discourse of the master (e.g., dogma) or the discourse of the university (juridic linguistic coordinate system) in their dealings with subordinated peoples. We have argued with Lopez that there is another way. A dialogical problem-solving methodology as opposed to the regnant forms empowers both the subordinated as well as the activist lawyer. Local, practical knowledges are respected for their everyday forms of coordination of action. In collaboration with the activist lawyer, a "border pedagogy" may develop. Here alternative master signifiers are provisionally knotted to signifieds producing a language of critique and possibility. As Lopez[72] has said, the dialogical problem-solving method of rebellious lawyering can "draw on marginalized experiences, neglected intuitions and dormant imagination to redefine what clients, lawyers, and others can do to change their lives." Yes, we do need our "utopian thinking,"[73] an expanded imagination, and new forms of master signifiers, to move beyond the present regnant form of conflict resolution.

ENDNOTES

1. For example, see the suggestive work by A. Cochet, *Lacan Geometre*, France, Europe Media Duplication S.A., 1998, pp. 171–181.
2. For example, see my anthology, D. Milovanovic, *Chaos, Criminology and Social Justice*, New York, Praeger, 1997a; and D. Milovanovic, *Postmodern Criminology*, New York: Garland, 1997b.
3. B. Arrigo, "Reason and Desire in Legal Education: A Psychoanalytic Critique," *International Journal for the Semiotics of Law*, vol. 11, no. 31, 1997, pp. 3–21; S. Bannister and D. Milovanovic, "The Necessity Defense, Substantive Justice and Oppositional Linguistic Practice," *International Journal for the Sociology of Law*, no. 18, 1990, pp. 179–198; D. Milovanovic and J. Thomas, "Overcoming the Absurd: Legal Struggle as Primitive Rebellion," *Social Problems*, vol. 36, no. 1, 1989, pp. 48–60; H. Stacey, "Lacan's Split Subjects: Raced and Gendered Transformations," *Legal Studies Forum*, vol. 20, no. 3, 1996a, pp. 277–293; H. Stacey, "Legal Discourse and the Feminist Political Economy," *Australian Feminist Law Journal*, no. 6, 1996b, pp. 1–21.
4. G. Lopez, *Rebellious Lawyering: One Chicano's Vision of Progressive Law Practice*, San Francisco: Westview Press, 1992.
5. P. Freire, *Pedagogy of the Oppressed*, New York: Herder and Herder, 1972; P. Freire, *Education for Critical Consciousness*, New York: Seabury Press, 1973; P. Freire, *The Politics of Education*, S. Hadley, MA: Bergin and

Garvey, 1985; S. Aronowitz and H. Giroux, *Postmodern Education*, Minneapolis, MN: University of Minnesota Press, 1991.

6. B. Arrigo, *Madness, Language and the Law*, Albany, NY: Harrow and Heston, 1993; B. Arrigo, "Desire in the Psychiatric Courtroom: On Lacan and the Dialectics of Linguistic Oppression," *Current Perspectives in Social Theory*, 1996, vol. 16, pp. 159–187; B. Arrigo, "Transcarceration: Notes on a Psychoanalytically-Informed Theory of Social Practice in the Criminal Justice and Mental Health System," *Crime, Law, and Social Change*, vol. 27, no. 1, 1997, pp. 31–48; D. Cornell, *Beyond Accommodation: Ethical Feminism, Deconstruction and the Law*, New York: Routledge, 1999; P. Goodrich, *Languages of Law*, London: Weidenfeld and Nicolson, 1990; H. Stacey, "Lacan's Split Subjects," *op. cit.*; H. Stacey, "Legal Discourse and Feminist Political Economy," *op. cit.*; V. Voruz, "Psychosis and the Law: Legal Responsibility and Law of Symbolization," *International Journal for the Semiotics of Law*, vol. 13, no 2, 2000, pp. 133–158; see also the special issue of *Legal Studies Forum*, 1996; and the *International Journal for the Semiotics of Law*, 2000, "2002."

7. With a notable exception, see B. Arrigo and C. Williams, "Chaos Theory and the Social Control Thesis," *Social Justice*, vol. 26, no. 1, 1999, pp. 177–207; C. Williams and B. Arrigo, "Anarchaos and Order," *Theoretical Criminology*, vol. 5, no. 2, 2001, pp. 223–252; D. Milovanovic, "Postmodern Criminology," *Justice Quarterly*, vol. 13, no. 4, 1996, pp. 201–244; D. Milovanovic, *Chaos, Criminology and Social Justice*, *op. cit.*; D. Brion, "The Chaotic Law of Tort," in R. Kevelson, ed., *Peirce and Law*. New York: Peter Lang, 1991.

8. P. Freire, *Pedagogy of the Oppressed*, *op. cit.*

9. J. Butler, *Gender Trouble*, New York, Routledge, 1990.

10. D. Cornell, *Beyond Accommodation*, *op. cit.*

11. L. Irigaray, *Speculum of the Other Woman*, Ithaca, NY: Cornell University Press, 1985.

12. J. Lacan, *Ecrits*, New York: W. W. Norton, 1977.

13. J. Lacan, *L'Envers de la psychanalysis*, Paris: Editions du Seuil, 1991.

14. M. Bracher, "Lacan's Theory of the Four Discourses," *Prose Studies*, vol. 1, 1988, pp. 32–49; B. Arrigo, "Reason and Desire in Legal Education," *op. cit.*; J. Schroeder, "The Hysterical Attorney: The Legal Advocate within Lacanian Discourse Theory," *International Journal for the Semiotics of Law*, vol. 13, no. 2, 2001, pp. 181–213.

15. L. Bennet and M. Feldman, *Reconstructing Reality in the Courtroom*, New Brunswick, NJ: Rutgers University Press, 1981; B. Jackson, *Law, Fact, and Narrative Coherence*, Liverpool, U.K.: Deborah Charles, 1988.

16. G. Lopez, *Rebellious Lawyering*, *op. cit.*, p. 43.

17. B. Jackson, *Law, Fact, and Narrative Coherence, op. cit.*

18. For the police, see J. Gilsinan, *Doing Justice: How the System Works—As Seen by the Participants*, Englewood Cliffs, NJ: Prentice Hall, 1982; for emergency response calls to the police, see P. Manning, *Symbolic Communication: Signifying Calls and the Police Response*, Cambridge, MA: MIT Press, 1988; for initial contact with the court, see B. Yngvesson, *Virtuous Citizens: Disruptive Subjects*, New York: Routledge, 1993.

19. F. D. Abraham, *A Visual Introduction to Dynamical Systems Theory for Psychology.* Santa Cruz, CA: Aerial Press, 1992.

20. M. Bracher, "Lacan's Theory of the Four Discourses," *op. cit.*, p. 23.

21. J. J. Lecercle, *Philosophy Through the Looking Glass*, London: Hutchinson, 1985.

22. J. Kristeva, *Desire in Language*, New York: Columbia University Press, 1980.

23. G. Deleuze and F. Guattari, *A Thousand Plateaus*, Minneapolis, MN: University of Minnesota Press, 1987.

24. G. Deleuze and F. Guattari, *Kafka: Toward a Minor Literature*, Minneapolis, MN: University of Minnesota Press, 1986.

25. J. Lacan, *Feminine Sexuality*, New York: W. W. Norton, 1985, pp. 149–161.

26. See also Jan Mohamed's discussion of a desirable oscillation between identification and disidentification with discursive-subject positions, "Some Implications of Paulo Freire's Border Pedagogy," in H. Giroux and P. McLaren, eds., *Between Borders*, New York: Routledge, 1994, p. 246.

27. See P. Freire, *Pedagogy of the Oppressed, op. cit.*; see also Giroux, *Border Crossings*, New York: Routledge, 1992.

28. Deleuze and Guattari, *A Thousand Plateaus, op. cit.*; they have defined a rhizome, p. 21, as "an acentered, nonhierarchical, nonsignifying system without a General and without an organizing memory or central automaton, defined solely by a circulation of states."

29. G. Lopez, *Rebellious Lawyering, op. cit.*, p. 41.

30. R. Barthes, *S/Z*, New York: Hill and Wang, 1974; K. Silverman, *The Subject of Semiotics*, New York: Oxford University Press, 1983, pp. 237–283.

31. L. Althusser, *Lenin and Philosophy.* New York: Monthly Review Press, 1971.

32. M. Pecheux, *Language, Semantics, and Ideology*, New York: St. Martin's Press, 1982.

33. K. Silverman, *The Subject of Semiotics, op. cit.*

34. J. Lacan, *Seminar 23, Le Sinthome* (1975–1976), text edited by J.-A. Miller, *Ornicar?*, vol. 6, 1976, pp. 3–20; vol. 7, 1976, pp. 3–18; vol. 8,

1976, pp. 6–20; vol. 9, 1977, pp. 32–40; vol. 10, 1977, pp. 5–12; vol. 11, 1977, pp. 2–9; for an application of the Borromean knots to law, see D. Milovanovic, "Borromean Knots and the Constitution of Sense in Juridico-Discursive Production," *Legal Studies Forum*, vol. 17, no. 2, 1993, pp. 171–192.

35. G. Lopez, *Rebellious Lawyering, op. cit*, p. 56.

36. *Ibid.*, p. 50.

37. *Ibid.*, p. 53.

38. *Ibid.*

39. M. Bracher, *Lacan's Theory of the Four Discourses, op. cit.*, p. 69.

40. *Ibid.*, pp. 69–71.

41. Jan Mohamed, "Some Implications of Paulo Freire's Border Pedagogy," *op. cit.*, p. 244.

42. P. Freire, *The Politics of Education, op. cit.*, p. 51; Jan Mohamed, "Some Implications of Paulo Freire's Border Pedagogy," *op. cit.*, p. 245.

43. P. Freire, *The Pedagogy of the Oppressed, op. cit.*, chapter 3; see also Peters and Lanskshear, *op. cit.*, p. 178.

44. *Ibid.*, p. 61; in law and critical race theory, see M. Matsuda, C. Lawrence, R. Delgado, and K. W. Crenshaw, *Words That Wound: Critical Race Theory, Assaultive Speech, and the First Amendment*, New York: Oxford University Press, 1993, pp. 10–13.

45. The actual dynamics among the various factors identified in this study can best be portrayed by what we have elsewhere referred to as COREL sets, or configurations of coupled iterative loops; see S. Henry and D. Milovanovic, *Constitutive Criminology*, New York: Sage, 1996; D. Milovanovic, *Critical Criminology at the Edge*, New York: Praeger, 2002, chapter 3, 10. That is, topological portrayals of various factors intersecting and having effects can follow suggestive work in chaos theory that suggests nonlinear development based on iterative practices. Various factors can be represented as dynamic, iterative (non-linear feedback) loops that are subject to continuous change. These iterative loops are often parallel, intersecting and mutually constitutive. Critical race theory, for example, has been especially insightful in indicating how subjugation is often more a function of the intersections of class, gender, and race biases; see Matsuda, *Wounds That Wound, op. cit.* It may never less be, however, that the resultant of these intersecting factors produces a movement, a tendency in a particular direction, as is the case with our rhizomatic diagonal of conscientization.

46. R. Barthes, *S/Z, op. cit.*; K. Silverman, *The Subject of Semiotics, op. cit.*, pp. 237–283.

47. Bracher, *Lacan's Four Discourses, op. cit.*

48. Lopez, *Rebellious Lawyering, op. cit.*, p. 53.

49. *Ibid.*

50. Bracher, *Lacan's Four Discourses, op. cit.*, pp. 72–73.

51. *Ibid.*, p. 73.

52. Giroux, *Border Crossings, op. cit.*

53. Cornell, *Beyond Accommodation, op. cit.*, p. 167.

54. *Ibid.*, pp. 147–148.

55. Lacan, *Ecrits, op. cit.*

56. Butler, "Contingent foundations: Feminism and the Question of Postmodernism," in J. Butler and J. W. Scott, eds., *Feminists Theorize the Political*, London: Routledge, 1992.

57. See also Jan Mohamed, *Some Implications of Paulo Freire's Border Pedagogy, op. cit.*, p. 245.

58. Giroux, *Border Crossings, op. cit.*; Freire, *Pedagogy of the Oppressed, op. cit.*; Aronowitz and Grous, *Postmodern Education, op. cit.*, pp. 199–200; R. Lippens, "Alternatives to What Kind of Suffering? Towards a Border-Crossing Criminology," *Theoretical Criminology*, vol. 2, no. 3, 1998, pp. 311–343; R. Lippens, "Into Hybrid Marshlands," *International Journal for the Semiotics of Law*, vol. 12, 1999, pp. 59–89.

59. Giroux, *Border Crossings, op. cit.*, p. 34.

60. *Ibid.*, p. 59; see also E. Laclau and C. Mouffe, *Hegemony and Socialist Strategy*, New York: Verso, 1985; Butler, *Gender Trouble, op. cit.*, p. 67.

61. T. Ebert, "The Romance of Patriarchy: Ideology, Subjectivity, and Postmodern Feminist Cultural Theory," *Cultural Critique*, vol. 10, 1988, pp. 22–23; Giroux, *Border Crossings, op. cit.*, p. 60; E. Laclau, *Emancipations*, New York: Verso, 1996, pp. 87–104; M. Zavarzadeh and D. Morton, "Signs of Knowledge in the Contemporary Academy," *American Journal of Semiotics*, vol. 7, no. 4, 1990, p. 156.

62. Giroux, *Border Crossings, op. cit.*, p. 77.

63. Butler, "Contingent Foundations," *op. cit.*

64. *Ibid.*, pp. 146–147.

65. For example, see R. Schehr, "Surfing the Chaotic," in D. Milovanovic, ed., *Chaos, Criminology and Social Justice, op. cit.*, pp. 57–78.

66. G. Lopez, *Rebellious Lawyering, op. cit.*, p. 56.

67. See J. Uusitalo, "Abduction, Legal Reasoning, and Reflexive Law," in R. Kevelson, ed., *Peirce and Law*, New York: Peter Lang, 1991.

68. M. Matsuda, *Wounds That Wound, op. cit.*, p. 19.

69. J. Kristeva, *Desire in Language, op. cit.*

70. V. Volosinov, *Marxism and the Philosophy of Language*, Cambridge, MA: Harvard University Press, 1986.

71. J. Lacan, *Ecrits, op. cit.*

72. G. Lopez, *Rebellious Lawyering, op. cit.*, p. 29.

73. D. Cornell, *Beyond Accommodation, op. cit.*

10

To Poe, Logically Speaking: From "The Purloined Letter" to the Sinthome

PHILIP DRAVERS*

> *Here is the well-rendered account of what distinguishes the letter from the very signifier that it carries with it—which is not to make a metaphor of the epistle, since the story consists in what of the message passes in it "hey presto," like a trick played in a conjuror's hands, while the letter goes on its way [fait péripétie] without it.*[1]

> *Thus, one verifies that the letter always arrives at its destination on condition that one considers it as disjunct from its dimension as message. For the destination in question is nothing other than the* jouissance *of whoever makes use of it. It is in this that the letter is* littoral, *tracing for the subject the contours of being.*[2]

Though it has been detained many times as it proceeds upon its circuit, "The Purloined Letter" continues to circulate in the interpretative elaborations of psychoanalysts, philosophers, and literary theorists alike. As the "Letter" is drawn up into such a process, it leaves a residue or material deposit in its wake which marks a relation to *jouissance*, a residue which we might refer to here as "literature," or quite simply as "writing." Lacan's "Seminar on 'The Purloined Letter'" certainly has its literary qualities, a dimension of style which allows him, through the effects of speech, to cipher the enigma that the letter inscribes. However, beyond its literary dimension Lacan's Seminar is also supported by a logic, one which unfolds from the analytic discourse and continues to evolve throughout his teaching. It is this dimension of a logic supported by the function of the letter in purely formal terms, thus divested

*I would like to thank Ellie Ragland and Dragan Milovanovic for the opportunity to contribute to this volume.

of any value of signification, that allows Lacan to formalize the structure of the subject and its relation to *jouissance*. It is thus the function of the letter that supports Lacan's topological elaborations. For, if what logic reveals most fundamentally is its failure to suture the subject of science and thereby draw it into the field of knowledge,[3] what arises to formalize this failure is a series of complex topological figures that fold around the empty place of its object only to turn themselves inside out in an involuted exposé of the impossibility that structures their domain—line but not ligature, cipher without sense, little letters writ large in the margins of science to figure the contours of its subject and outline its relation to *jouissance*.

Indeed, what topology reveals is that if the unconscious is a knowledge in the Freudian sense, in other words a network of signifiers bound up with *jouissance*, it is not, for all that, a knowledge with no edge, and this edge is the letter which divides the domains of knowledge and *jouissance* while at the same time knotting them within the text that it constitutes upon its own margin. For without the material support of the letter to structure its domain the *psyche* would be nothing but the hot air that its etymology implies, and the verisimilitude supposed of fiction nothing but the vanity of a misplaced mimetism, an imaginary captation content to beguile itself by building castles in the air. In fact, it is only through the function of the letter that the field of fiction can be said to be supported by a Real, a Real bound up with language and which is at once the Real of structure and also the primary instance of *jouissance* from which that structure derives.

Yet, if the letter is indispensable for psychoanalysis and literary studies alike, so too is breath, for without breath to give air to the aspirations of a body and lift the letter from where it lies latent, saturated with semblance and buried in a field of affect, neither poetry nor psychoanalysis could bring its narrow edge to bear upon the knot that binds the body with a thread borrowed from the unconscious and so effect the cut with which to separate the subject from his suffering. Indeed, it is only by passing through the effects of speech that a new mode of writing can emerge which is no longer content to circulate a letter in the name of what has gone before. Such a statement returns us once more to the question of style, for it is by bearing out the rigor of his topological elaborations that Lacan's style figures a relation to knowledge in which the figure itself forms the threshold between knowledge and *jouissance* and thereby becomes the mark of a stylistic effect.[4] Indeed, at the limit of his logical elaborations, it is only by linking the function of the letter with a mark of style that Lacan, in the final period of his teaching, will be able to make the innovations that allow him to make a definitive break with the Freudian unconscious with the emergence of a new mode of writing that he will ultimately name as his own.

Such a statement brings us to the central concern of this paper, which is to demonstrate how such a knotting occurs, and quite literally so, not only in a reading of "The Purloined Letter," but also in a *writing* that extends beyond such a *reading*. Indeed, if in what follows, the existence of the unconscious is to be taken as read, it will not for all that be taken as an excuse to leave it there, as the letter is not only what is read but also what is involved in a writing. For, although there is a great deal of truth, and no doubt too much truth, in the claim that a text is constituted in a reading—a reading, we must add, *of* the unconscious—such a "truth" does not exclude the possibility that there be a form of writing that is not based upon such a reading: a writing that is also an act of creation and invention which modifies the structure of the subject in its relation to *jouissance* and to knowledge. It is in exploring what is at stake in such a writing that we will move from "The Purloined Letter," and the critical debates that surround it, to the writings of Joyce and what Lacan himself was able to write by indexing himself upon what of the Real is inscribed therein. However, this will not cause us to leave "The Purloined Letter" behind, but rather to confirm its seminal status in Lacan's work. For although the text is essentially about a reading, the letter that it circulates also supports the possibility of such a writing. Indeed, it is only in taking up the question of what the letter inscribes, both as a logical function and as a mark of *jouissance* inscribed on the basis of a corporeal contingency—a duality rendered legible, that is audible, in English through what we can call, following Lacan, the $f(x)$ of the letter—that Lacan is able to go beyond the Freudian unconscious, and the reading that sustains it, to a writing of the Real.

I. A READING OF THE LETTER

The story before us concerns the movements of a letter as it is relayed between the four positions of a tetradic structure which once formed will henceforth determine what can be written of the positions of speech. As we shall see, this tetradic structure provides the elementary topology that frames a reading, while at the same time serving as the apparatus for what circulates therein. For although we are not given any description of the letter beyond the mere fact of its materiality, it nevertheless supports what unfolds within the story as a structure of repetition in which the letter comes to index what is at stake, within the positions of speech, for whoever makes use of it. In Poe's tale this stake is clear even if it is not strictly speaking legible as such, for beyond any question of the knowledge supposed in reading what is there to be read in the story is the letter insofar as it inscribes a relation to *jouissance*. Indeed, what the "The Purloined Letter" demonstrates, through its exemplary economy and form, is how the relation to *jouissance* that the letter inscribes comes to be organized through the structure of fiction and married to the truth it supposes. For while the contents of the letter are never divulged, we are nonetheless led to believe that its discovery by an interested party will lead to a right royal scandal. Indeed, it is through the transferential effects of such a supposition, and also of what remains illegible therein, that our own interest is aroused. In this way, we begin to see that the royal road to the unconscious is paved by a reading.

1. The First Scene

The initial scene, which we can refer to here as the primal scene of language insofar as it installs the structure of repetition from which the subsequent events of the story proceed and which is manifestly a scene of reading rather than of writing, concerns the royal couple and one of the King's ministers. The scene unfolds as follows: the Queen receives a letter in her apartments, the King and then the minister both enter before the Queen has been able to conceal the letter, the discovery of which would compromise discretion. The Queen thus leaves the letter exposed before the blind gaze of her partner, placing it nonchalantly on the table with its address uppermost. However, sheltered by the shadow cast by the unseeing gaze of his master, the watchful gaze of the minister *reads* the significance of the letter to the Queen in her behavior before her partner. Thus, from the first, the letter marks a certain non-rapport between the couple that the minister thinks he can use to his advantage and in so doing he attaches a signification to the letter. The minister then takes out a letter of his own, placing it beside the letter that the Queen has left exposed, only to then take up the Queen's letter before taking his leave, his own letter in its place as a substitute. Crucially, the Queen now knows that the minister has the letter and the minister knows that the Queen knows. However, beyond the questions that arise with this supposition of knowledge and what it is possible to find therein, Lacan also stresses the importance of the fact that the operation of substitution constitutes a residue which no psychoanalyst can afford to overlook, namely the discarded letter that the Queen's hand is now free to roll into a ball, confirming the dual aspects of the letter suggested by the Joycean pun that slides from *Letter* to *Litter*, which Lacan first makes use of in this Seminar.

2. The Letter and Its Envelope of Fiction

Before proceeding in our reading, let us arrest its flow of signifiers and take advantage of the letter's capacity to mark places by providing a schema for the tetradic structure as it is sketched out in this initial scene. For although the characters for this little *mise en scène* will change, it is this structure which supports and frames what can unfold in a reading of "The Purloined Letter," as well as what can be inscribed therein as a relation to *jouissance*. Let us therefore call this figure, quite simply, *the letter and its envelope of fiction*:

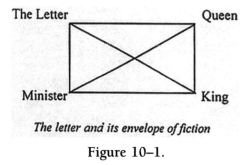

The letter and its envelope of fiction

Figure 10–1.

What this structure represents, in a form whose rigor will only become apparent in what follows, is the letter and its envelope of fiction insofar as this latter is constituted through the conjugation of the letter with the positions of speech. Indeed, on this schema, we see the structure which supports the subject's most fundamental relation to language, though here it remains masked by the so-called intersubjective positions that give body to the narrative and provide the dimensions of its drama, thereby sustaining the doleful semblance of a "family romance." As we can see, it is the envelope of fiction which covers the field of the reality sustained between the characters as well as the many readings that this "private theater" is heir to. The drama continues to unfold as follows.

3. The Second Scene

The second scene identified by Lacan in his reading of the story retains the structure of the first while redistributing the effects inscribed therein. Indeed, as we shall see, the format of the letter remains identical throughout. The redistribution in question begins with the second moment of the drama in which the police are called in to recover the letter, their path lit by the prospect of the considerable remuneration that their moonlighting will bring them if they can satisfy the Queen's request. Moreover, if this latter remains enigmatic, it is because we will never know the import of the letter beyond the itinerary it traces. Indeed, despite her relative absence from the tale after the initial scene, the contours of the letter continue to circumscribe the enigma of the Queen's desire, thereby designating it as "a place in reserve" existing beyond the details of the drama—for after all, what does she want with the letter?[5]

Meanwhile, the minister, who has now succumbed to the effect that a reading of the letter confers upon those who believe they can embody its power, leaves his apartments open to the gaze of the police. He is satisfied with the little knowledge he has of their techniques, for he knows that a little knowledge will suffice to fool the prefect of police—the PP to those who know him.[6] Indeed, through the "realist imbecility" with which they pound their beat, the police nevertheless demonstrate their fidelity to the elementary topology that marks out the area of their jurisdiction, namely reality insofar as it is framed by fantasy. For although they turn the minister's apartment inside out looking for the letter, they nevertheless remain blind to the hole in which the letter, in its ex-sistence, subsists. Indeed, the letter eludes them precisely through the effect of the simple reversal that its topology performs.[7] In this way the attempt to re-find the letter in its original form fails and the investigation continues to trace itself upon a surface that is searched in vain, returning the prefect to his starting point with for his only proof: *impossibility* and the *necessity* of a renewed search. His charge thus dissipates itself before the pleasure he hopes to attain.

It is in this way that the prefect of police is led to enlist the help of Dupin, whose knowledge, he believes, is not only supposed. He thus places his trust in Dupin's artfulness and recounts the fruitless experience he has gained in pursuit of the letter, all the while attesting to his consternation that things have not turned out for the best. From this short preliminary interview, Dupin is certain that the contours of the letter have been outlined in what the prefect has told him and thus has an impression of where it lies buried. After the prefect has departed, his rose-tinted spectacles rather cloudy, Dupin dons his own green pair and calls on the minister, whom he finds in the grip of a "narcissistic relation": namely, the "reciprocal fascination, established between himself and the Queen."[8] When he is there, Dupin, his own gaze now shaded by its somewhat garish attire, immediately identifies the letter, for although its external appearance has changed he is able to see that its elementary format remains the same. Returning later to pick up the snuff box he has left behind as a pretext for a second call, Dupin takes advantage of a diversion that he has orchestrated for the occasion and steals the letter from where it lies hanging from the mantelpiece, taking care to cover its lack with a letter he has prepared earlier. Of course this new letter has the same format as its predecessor, but it now comes complete with a literary appendage borrowed, appropriately enough, from a monologue rehearsed in another family romance: ". . . *Un dessein si funeste/ S'il n'est digne d'Atrée est digne de Thyeste.*"[9]

In fact, for all his ability to read the transference operating within the so-called intersubjective triad that constitutes the drama, it is clear that Dupin does not occupy the position of analyst in the analytic discourse as Lacan has defined it. For although his act intervenes within a transferential structure of repetition by plucking the dandy feather of the minister's *politique de l'autruiche*, he nevertheless uses it to cipher his own message upon a letter whose address will forever remain his own. He is not content to embody the enigma of the letter and become the wastebasket of its littering, but rather uses it to cipher his own enjoyment, thereby stepping into the circuit of the signifier as it returns to itself via the production of a surplus, or remainder, that it will never recover. Moreover, as Lacan states in Seminar XVIII, "*Dupin jouit,*" for he enjoys the interpretation he confers upon the letter and thus its envelope of semblance remains intact by redoubling its address. Indeed, this is exactly what is at stake in a certain type of reading. For Dupin's writing is structured by a reading and the repetition it implies. Furthermore, what he aims at in his counterpart reveals itself to be both the surest and the shortest way to being, and this is the definition of hatred.[10]

II. WHAT IS AT STAKE IN A READING?

From this rather summary account of a story which generates itself by following the movements of a letter as it passes through the turning circle of a repetitive sequence—in other words a story that is manifestly constituted through the scansion which organizes a reading[11]—it is clear that the dimension of its drama is constituted as each of the characters takes up a signifying position within the field of speech. In so doing, the characters relay each other through a series of positions which derive their value solely in relation to the letter and it is this that constitutes the reading that they each perform as they address themselves to the enigma that the letter inscribes in their experience, as well as to what comes to answer and obscure it for each: namely, the symptom and fantasy.

In this way, the letter comes to index what is at stake in taking a position within the field of speech for whoever makes use of it. For although it might appear self-evident that each *subjective* position relays itself through others in order to construct a reading—a theme which keeps returning in literary circles in the name of intersubjectivity and the intertextuality of desire and their interpretative counterparts, the plurality of meaning and the relativity of truth—what is more radically at stake for psychoanalysis is the subject's relation to the letter as such, as it is relayed through a series of positions which remain purely *structural*. Indeed, beyond its textual surface of intersubjective effects, it is the letter alone which interests the characters in the reality it constitutes and the letter alone which motivates their actions. The characters thus find themselves reduced and distributed as so many terms in a structure which envelops them as the action unfolds through a transferential structure of repetition operating in relation to the letter. The story thus demonstrates, in a remarkably "analytical" fashion, the subordination of the subject to the structure which supports a reading; for if the letter is what is read in the story, it is also, more radically, what reads, or, as Lacan puts it with characteristic economy and precision in 1955: *"for each of them the letter is his unconscious."*[12]

Although this definition is proposed in the early period of Lacan's teaching, it also holds, at least provisionally so, for the later period of his elaboration where Lacan's definition of the letter changes to accommodate the problematic of *jouissance*. In his original seminar, as in the re-written text of the reading which frames his *Écrits*, the letter is conceived as being entirely identical to the structure of the signifier. Indeed, Lacan states his purely propaedeutic aim to be that of illustrating the "truth" of the Freudian discovery, "namely that it is the symbolic order which is constitutive for the subject—by demonstrating in a story the decisive orientation which the subject receives from the itinerary of the signifier."[13] Here, as in "the instance of the letter in the unconscious," the letter is taken to embody "the essentially localised structure of the signifier."[14] It therefore evokes the entire differential structure within which it operates: namely, the unconscious, which, according to Lacan's formula, "is structured like a language." It is therefore the unconscious which inscribes itself in the displacement and successive substitutions of the letter throughout the story and in the repetition which exposes the identifications that organize the field of desire. Indeed, as Joël Dor explains in his aptly named study, "the actions of each of the characters are determined in relation to the letter in the same way that the subject, without being aware of it, is acted upon by the signifiers of the unconscious."[15] It is thus the linguistic operations of metaphor and metonymy which dominate in Lacan's initial reading of the "Letter" and, as such, it foregrounds the mechanisms which operate in both repression and the return of the repressed in the formations of the unconscious—formations upon which, as Freud never ceased to write, literature depends for its powers of creation. And if Lacan adds his own stylistic touch to psychoanalysis here, it is by returning the "truth" of the Freudian unconscious to the fundamental equivocation through which it emerges to proclaim itself as true.

However, beyond the value of enigma conferred upon the letter under the auspices of the signifier, the letter also has another aspect which only appears much later in Lacan's teaching: namely that it inscribes a relation to *jouissance*. This redefinition emerges with the topology that Lacan develops to circumscribe the subject's relation to *jouissance*, initially through the logic of the fantasy, written with the formula $\$ \lozenge a$, which places the subject in relation to what is effectively its value as *jouissance*, and later through that of the symptom, written by Lacan with the Greek letter: Σ—"one sole trait," as Jacques-Alain Miller explains, to write the "signifier and *jouissance*."[16] In fact, from the perspective of the later Lacan, we can say that what is at stake in a reading of the letter is ultimately the *jouissance* of whoever makes use of it, and this beyond any question of the signification that comes to be attached to it.[17] In this way the letter appears as the very cipher of *jouissance*, the ciphering of which is supported by every act of interpretation both inside and outside the text.[18]

Thus, in addressing ourselves to the letter, we must also address the question of what of *jouissance* circulates in a reading as the mode of enjoyment of the unconscious insofar as it is supported by the symptom and the structure of the fantasy. In other words, we must address ourselves to the question of how the unconscious comes to knot the body to the real of its enjoyment by passing through the equivocations of speech.[19] For it is only through the "pneumatic dispatch" of the signifier that the letter—as that which has fallen from the body of language—can take flight [*volée*] upon an air drawn from the aspirations of a body already resonating with the effects of speech, while at the same time knotting it through the itinerary it traces. In fact, if the letter can be said to circulate within the story, it is only because it is supported by a reading in a movement which attaches a signifier to the letter, thereby allowing it to be displaced.

Indeed, from the perspective of the later Lacan, we can say that each subject reads according to the "truth" of his symptom and it is this that must be elaborated and reduced in analysis through a process of construction which separates the letter from the signifiers of the unconscious which determine it—that is from the identifications which "articulate [. . .] the symptom with the subject in the place of truth."[20] Moreover, if the unconscious is elaborated in the dimension of "truth," and if the story demonstrates "so perfect a verisimilitude that it may be said that truth here reveals its fictive arrangement,"[21] then the letter alone is on the side of the Real. Thus, the letter not only designates what of the Real is elaborated by the signifiers of the unconscious, but also what of the unconscious is Real.

Such a perspective opens up new ways of approaching "The Purloined Letter" and the debates which surround it, as well as new ways of reconsidering the relationship between literature and psychoanalysis, particularly with regard to the position that one occupies in relation to the letter and the question of what interpretation can support through the function of equivocation.[22] Indeed, such a perspective will allow us to comment briefly on certain differences between Lacan and Derrida with regard to the "Letter." However, beyond the thematics of a character analysis— that is, beyond the analysis of character or critique—the use of the letter, and also the reading through which the story is generated, must ultimately be referred to Poe. It thus concerns, as Lacan states in *Lituraterre*, "what Poe made of being a writer in order to form such a message on the letter."[23] In other words, it concerns what Poe was able to construct, as an individual and through the savoir faire of the artist, in relation to what, for him, the letter inscribes as a relation to *jouissance*.[24] Indeed, from such a perspective, art can be considered as nothing but a fashioning of "the formal envelope of the symptom," a symptom thus *prêt-à-porter*, ready to capture the Other's *jouissance*.[25] The story of "The Purloined Letter" thus appears as a fictional elaboration of the *jouissance* that the letter inscribes of the mode of enjoyment of the unconscious.

III. THE RELATION TO *JOUISSANCE* AND THE THREE TIMES OF THE REAL

1. *The Relation to* Jouissance

Where does this relation to *jouissance* come from? It arises as a result of the traumatic encounter which, as Freud's analysis in *Beyond the Pleasure Principle* bears out, gives rise to a compulsion to repeat which attempts to integrate it within the unconscious, defined as a system of associative facilitation which aims at homeostasis. Following Lacan, and in view of his elaboration of the unconscious as a structure, we can describe this initial trauma as that of the encounter with language as such.[26] It is the repetition of the unary trait, as the mark of this primary instance of *jouissance*, which comes to support the unconscious and the elaboration of language as structure in an attempt to master what was imposed in the initial encounter with language.

Lacan takes up the question of the topology generated in this elementary structure of repetition in a lecture delivered at Baltimore in 1966.[27] Here, Lacan defines this topology on the basis of the logic which supports the generation of any structural sequence; in fact, it concerns the generation of number as defined by Frege. It is thus a question of "the logic of the signifier" and as such it is an affair of the subject, since for Lacan the subject arises as the precondition of the elaboration of any structure: which is not to say that Lacan falls back upon any intuited notion of the subject here, but rather that he deduces the subject on the basis of the facts of structure alone. At the same time it is also an affair of the One, since the One does not exist in and of itself, but emerges only in the repetition of an initial trait, therefore at the level of two, from whence it retroactively installs itself as the origin of the chain. At the same time something is effaced, erased, rubbed out, or barred in the very structure of this movement and it is here that the split subject, the subject of the unconscious, emerges to subsist as the precondition for the elaboration of any structural sequence.[28] Indeed, as Lacan says in his lecture, although the "unconscious subject is something that tends to repeat itself, . . . only one such repetition is necessary to constitute it."[29]

This elementary movement of repetition—a movement which we can refer to, following Lacan, as an elective act of *reading* which takes place before there are the signs of writing[30]—can be written in topological terms in the figure of the interior eight, which derives from the Möbius strip. This figure can be understood as the most elementary form of the topology of the subject as Lacan defines it in 1966:

It is thus through an initial act of reading that the body comes

Figure 10–2.

to be caught within the structure of the signifier and it is from such a reading that the letter takes form as the figure itself. It is therefore only in this sense that Lacan's topological figure "can be considered the basis of a sort of essential inscription at the origin, in the knot which constitutes the subject."[31] It is precisely here that Poe's story of "The Purloined Letter" reveals what, in his seminar on "Desire and the Interpretation of Desire in *Hamlet*," Lacan refers to as the "most vivid dramatic sense of a topology."[32] Indeed, the topological

figure of the interior eight is clearly outlined in the presentation of
the story given above.[33] Thus, what Lacan extracts from Poe's tale is
a structure of repetition which bears out the repetition compulsion
that Freud analyzes in *Beyond the Pleasure Principle*.

Here we can recall Lacan's "Introduction" to his "Seminar on
'The Purloined Letter,'" included in the French *Écrits*, in which he
elaborates on the generation of a structural sequence that effectively
establishes the scansion which determines what can follow from
it.[34] It is a scansion which organizes a reading, a reading that in
one sense the unconscious is, while it also organizes the reading *of*
the unconscious, conceived as a movement of articulation and signification which passes through the unconscious circuit defined
as a constantly repeating chain in which a signifier is always lacking.[35] What Lacan stresses in the "Introduction" to his Seminar is
that such a scansion organizes its own impossibilities, introducing a hole, a residual place within the chain which thereby becomes
the cause of the structure itself.[36] Here, Lacan defines this process
as the *caput mortuum* of the signifier, thereby referring to the residual deposit—one which we can retroactively designate as that
of *jouissance*—produced in the process of symbolization, while also
indicating the deathly effects inscribed by the phallic function.
These effects are identified by Lacan as the purloined letter itself,
a letter *en souffrance* operating on the border between the Symbolic
and the Real and it is this that distinguishes the letter from the
effects of signification which surround it.

There are thus two aspects of the letter here, one which
emerges in Lacan's initial reading of "The Purloined Letter," namely
the letter as that which designates the place of the subject, $\mathcal{S}$; and
one which emerges later in his teaching, the letter in its value as
jouissance: the object *a*. Hence, the dual aspects of the letter as a
signifier introduced into the Real where it remains ensnared, and
also as a bit of the Real caught within the defiles of the signifier.[37]

In this way we can see that the structure of the unconscious
as a network of signifiers can itself be seen as a defensive, and
even a fictional elaboration in relation to the Real. Indeed, in the
final period of Lacan's teaching, language comes to be seen as an

apparatus with which to support the radical alterity that the letter inscribes of one's fundamental relation to language. This will profoundly modify Lacan's conception of the Real. However, before discussing "the three times of the Real" in Lacan's teaching, we can gloss the development of the problematic that will take us there as follows.

2. Paper Cuts: from Schema L, Schema R, to the Topology of Surfaces

Lacan's initial reading of "The Purloined Letter" is coextensive with his structural reading of the Oedipus complex. This reading begins by formalizing the positions at stake in the child's relation to the Mother. Even in this initial cell of the Oedipus complex there are already three structural positions: the child, the Mother, and a third term that designates what the Mother lacks through the very fact of her desire. Though this third term gathers its consistency in the Imaginary, it nevertheless implies an already latent Symbolic dimension. This position is that of the Imaginary phallus (φ) and it is with this that the child first identifies in order to be inscribed in the circuit of the mother's desire. In very rudimentary terms it is in his identification with the phallus that the child seeks to identify himself with what the mother lacks. It is a narcissistic identification which, in relation to Poe's tale, we can conceive of as an imaginarization of the letter: the letter as latent as a sign suspended in an Imaginary mode. This can be figured in the first of two triangles (A), which can be written as follows:[38]

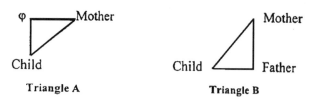

Triangle A   Triangle B

Figure 10–3.

In a second time, a second triangle (B) emerges which bears out the more classic form of the oedipal scenario, that of the relation between the Mother, the Child, and the Father, whose function Lacan will later reduce to that of the Name and thus to the act of nomination that it implies. These two triangles can be placed in conjunction with one another to form Schema R and it is here presented alongside the more familiar Schema L from which it derives and which Lacan names in his "Introduction" to his "Seminar on 'The Purloined Letter'" as the schema of the "Letter" itself.

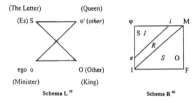

Figure 10–4.

The first of these two schemas presents the so-called inter-subjective dimension of the drama as it unfolds within the four-termed structure that we referred to above as "the letter and its envelope of fiction." Here the three terms of the Oedipus appear as signifiers whose articulation in the three times of the Oedipus complex will produce the paternal metaphor, or metaphor of the subject.[41] Although we will later have to modify the designation of terms mapped out on this framework in order to account for subsequent developments in Lacan's thinking, it is clear that the relation between the King, Queen, and minister is structured by the letter as a fourth term which designates the subject of the unconscious. For though the individual addresses his counterpart at the level of the ego, it is really the relation to the letter and its ectopic position in relation to the field of the Other that *counts*. The letter thus designates "the *ex-sistence* (or: eccentric place) in which we must necessarily locate the subject of the unconscious if we are to take Freud's discovery seriously."[42] However, this position is also that of the phallus, the lure which provides both the stake in the

game and the resistance necessary for its metaphorical structure
to unfold and then secure itself in a resolution which reveals the
subject bereft of signification and at the same time separated from
the signifier which represents him in the Other. The letter is thus
"already metaphorical" from the perspective of the signifier, since
its position at the summit of the first triangle implies the signifier
of the Name-of-the-Father in the second. As the drama unfolds
the three terms of the Oedipus complex are relayed as a series of
signifiers, a kind of "collective calculus" in which it is only possible to "calculate because one element is missing: the phallus. No
one has it, but the three of them have to take that symbol into account to define their positions . . . If any one of them makes an error,
thinking that he or she is the one that is missing . . . then they all
get stuck in their calculation. No one will find a way out."[43] Such
is the stake of the game engendered by a gap in the Imaginary, the
resolution of which provides the solution for the impasse of sexual
difference: "the fact that there is no inscription of man or woman
in the unconscious."[44]

The development of this initial schema of the letter into
Schema R demonstrates how the field of reality comes to be framed
by the Imaginary and Symbolic investments which support the field
of desire. The four terms that form the central strip that constitutes this framework are the ego and the image of the counterpart
(the Imaginary terms of the narcissistic relationship), the Mother
as primal object, and the ego-ideal formed through an identification with the unary trait. In his discussion of this schema in *Écrits*,
Lacan emphasizes the function of the Name-of-the-Father in sustaining the field of the Other in relation to the primordial object
and the ego-ideal and identifies the position of "the subject S under
the signifier of the phallus."

Though there is much that could be said about this schema as
it stands, what is crucial for this present study is the way that Lacan
develops it in a footnote added in 1966 in relation to the structure
of fantasy and the topology that supports it. To obtain this topology from the central strip one simply connects M to *e* and I to *i*.
The resulting figure is that of the Möbius strip. Lacan indicates that

the cut that forms this strip is identical to that of the split subject and what falls away through the operation of this cut is the object a: hence the structure of the fantasy ($\mathcal{S} \diamond a$) which, henceforth, comes to frame the field of reality: "it is as the representative of the representation in fantasy . . . that is to say as the originally repressed subject that $\mathcal{S}$, the barred S of desire, here supports the field of reality, and this field is sustained only by the extraction of the object a, which, however, gives it its frame."[45] It is to this topology that Lacan refers in his "*Ouverture*" to the *Écrits* when, in referring to the reading of the "Letter" that frames it, he says:

> For we decipher here in Poe's fiction, so powerful in the mathematical sense of the term, this division where the subject is attested to by the fact that an object traverses him without them penetrating each other in the least, and this division is the principle of what emerges at the end of this volume under the name of object a (to be read: little a).[46]

Through this topological analysis, borne out in the above presentation of the story, it is possible to see, though the Prefect of Police does not heed the warning, "that in the Möbius strip there is nothing measurable to be retained in its structure, and that it is reduced, like the real with which we are concerned here, to the cut itself."[47] It is thus not with just measure, but with good reason that in psychoanalysis interpretation is reduced, at its most extreme point, to the function of the cut.

In his presentation of this development in *Reading Seminar XI*, François Regnault presents this development in terms of the entire structure of Schema R as follows:[48]

Figure 10–5.

Figure 10–6.

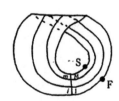

Figure 10–7.

What he stresses here is that while on the projected plane of Schema R the Name-of-the-Father appears as "a fixed point which orients the subject's relationships. On the strip, on the contrary, F and S are borders constituting only one side, but [also] a hole as well."[49] It is in exploring how the function of such a hole is secured in relation to a supplementary function of the letter that Lacan will later be led to develop the topology of the Borromean knot as a knotting of the Imaginary, the Symbolic, and the Real with a fourth term, that of the *sinthome*.

3. The Three Times of the Real

In *La Troisième* Lacan gives three definitions of the Real according to three different periods of his Seminar and it is in reviewing these three times that we will establish the trajectory which will take us from "The Purloined Letter" to the *sinthome*:[50]

1. The Real as that which always returns to the same place,
2. the Real insofar as its impossibility can be formalized through logic, and
3. the Real as the symptom.

Although these definitions describe three distinct periods of Lacan's elaboration, they nevertheless outline a certain continuity in his thinking, while at the same time they each come to redefine the relationship operating between fiction and the Real in Lacan's elaboration. In the first definition, one which is contemporaneous with the Seminar on "The Purloined Letter," the Real always returns to the same place because it is caught within the defiles of the signifier. The Real is in fact "always in its place, it carries it glued to its heel, ignorant of what might exile it from it."[51] Indeed, if the letter is subject to a form of Symbolic displacement, it is because it is coupled with a signifier, for as Lacan later declares, "writing, the letter, is in the Real, and the signifier in the Symbolic."[52] It is thus through this decidedly *odd* coupling and the impossibility inscribed within it that the letter "always returns to the same place," but as Lacan adds, in a way which redoubles its address; this place is "the place of the semblant." A *semblant* is that which covers over the hole introduced into the Real through the function of the letter, while at the same time locating a relation to *jouissance*, localizing it at a point of fixation within the structure and as Lacan declares in *Lituraterre*, the signifier is "the *semblant par excellence*."[53] Here we can see how the purloined letter itself comes to be clothed in semblance and thereby localizes a relation to *jouissance*, while at the same time sustaining the field of desire, the field of fiction, as a defense against *jouissance*.

In the second definition, Lacan uses logic to grasp more clearly what is at stake in the hole introduced into the Real by the letter by defining it in terms of the logical function that it supports. Lacan's recourse to topology is a direct result of this attempt to locate the void through the function of the letter and it is in this way that he isolates the function of the *semblant*. As a result of the failure of logic to suture the subject, it arrives at its own impasse, a hole in logic, here conceived in propositional terms, which gives rise to the structure itself and what is possible within it. However, in *Lituraterre*, Lacan reminds those who read him that it is not enough to simply evoke the void and flood it with *jouissance*, for one must also know how to locate it and operate upon the structure that encloses it in order to create a new topological consistency to support the subject's relation to *jouissance*. Such a process implies the construction of the fantasy and thus an isolation of the function of the *semblant* in the form of object *a*. The relation between surface topology and the fantasy is made explicit by Lacan in 1966 with his revision of Schema R in which, as we have seen, the frame of the fantasy that supports the relation between the subject and the Other is folded upon itself to create a Möbius strip whose cutting constitutes the fall of its object. Such a fall also constitutes the end of analysis in the clinic of neurosis, which occurs after the *semblant* which structures the fantasy has been isolated in relation to the presence of the analyst and his position as object within the transference, while also confirming, contrary to the

Derridean critique, that if a letter is cut, it remains the letter it is, but with a new topological consistency. However, this does not resolve the impossibility that topology itself implies. This impasse is ultimately rendered in Lacan's famous formulation of the sexual non-rapport, which demonstrates how the function of the letter inscribes only the *impossibility* of writing the sexual relation. In other words, at the level of *jouissance*, the letter does not support a relation to the Other sex other than by way of fiction.

This definition eventually gives rise to the final definition of the Real as the symptom, in other words the ciphering of the mode of enjoyment of the unconscious in its formations. In this period of Lacan's elaboration we see that, if the letter is the elementary term of the knot, the text it constitutes is nothing but "the fiction of surface within which the structure clothes itself."[54] For the letter not only determines the possibility of a cut being introduced in such a surface, but also the possibility that a new kind of topology can emerge beyond the surface effects that had previously enveloped the structure of the subject in its relation to the Other and the object through the structure of fantasy. This new topology is, of course, the Borromean topology that emerges in the 1970s. The shift from surface topology to that of the Borromean knot can thus be considered as a shift from the logic of the fantasy to a logic of the symptom in a re-elaboration of the fundamentals of the clinic, departing not from the subject's signifying subjection in the field of the Other, but from the primacy of the relation to *jouissance*. However, before going on to a discussion of the *sinthome*, the question that we must now address is, therefore, how does this relation to *jouissance* come to be organized through the structure of fiction?

IV. HOW THE *JOUISSANCE* INSCRIBED BY THE LETTER IS ORGANIZED THROUGH THE STRUCTURE OF FICTION

Such a question returns us to the "frame of reference" that we have extracted from the story to demonstrate how the *jouissance* inscribed by the letter comes to be conjugated with the positions of speech, namely the tetradic structure that we have referred to as the letter and its envelope of fiction. However, we must now re-duce this envelope to its elementary structure by casting off its so-called intersubjective dimension and introducing a different form of notation which will reveal that this tetradic structure which fig-ures the subject's most fundamental relation to language, while at the same time sustaining it through a structure of fiction, is in fact the structure of discourse.[55] Indeed, in *Seminar XVIII*, Lacan dem-onstrates how one can extract the structure of discourse from "The Purloined Letter," while at the same time taking the opportunity to push his elaboration further. In fact, Lacan stresses that what he develops here is merely a further elaboration of the structure es-tablished by his earlier reading and what it inscribes of the effects of speech. For recalling his presentation of the story in *Écrits*, he states: "In these pages I speak very precisely of the function of the phallus insofar as it is articulated within a certain discourse."[56]

Here, Lacan presents the structure of discourse in its elemen-tary form, in other words as the discourse of the master, also that of the unconscious, as follows:

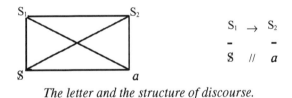

The letter and the structure of discourse.

Figure 10–8.

In this revision of our earlier schema it now appears that there are two positions to which we could assign the function of the let-ter: S_1 and a. In the figure above we therefore have the two aspects of the letter as it is presented in the story, the letter as S_1, the unary trait of the first identification of the subject, in other words the letter that the minister steals from the Queen and takes as signifier of her desire; and the letter insofar as it is produced as a residue of the process of identification, the letter as *a*. Here we see the subject's identification with a letter, or rather a unary trait, S_1, which is raised to the status of a signifier through its articulation with a second signifier, S_2, in an operation which splits the subject and produces the object *a* as the residue formed in the process of symbolization.

In this way, the structure of discourse demonstrates that it is logically derived from the operations of conjunction and disjunction defined by Lacan in *Seminar XI* as alienation and separation, an articulation which is figured in the lozenge in the formula of the fantasy ($S \lozenge a$).[57] In fact, it is the inclusion of the object *a* within the structure of discourse that marks the failure of Lacan's earlier attempt to reduce the Freudian libido to an effect of the signifier,[58] while at the same time revealing this structure to be in continuity with his previous topological elaborations. The subject's alienation in signification is figured by the articulation between S_1 and S_2 on the top line of this structure, while separation is constituted with the production of the drive-object and its recuperation in fantasy on the bottom line, thus sealing the letter by marking it with the stamp of the unconscious. Indeed, as Lacan says in "The Position of the Unconscious": "This secondary subordination not only closes the effect of the first in projecting the topology of the subject into the instant of fantasy; it seals it."

In returning to his exposition Lacan takes up what he had earlier defined as "the decisive orientation which the subject receives from the itinerary of the signifier"[59] by defining the letter, no longer as the split subject, but as S_1, "the letter of the master signifier, insofar as it carries it in its envelope."[60] The S_1 is thus the signifier which governs, its envelope being that of the semblance from which it derives its authority, and its path is facilitated by the police who ensure its free passage without knowing that it is passing through their hands. Indeed, in *Seminar XVIII*, and then in *Seminar XXIII*, Lacan takes up Hegel's affirmation of the identity of the police with the function of the state and the legitimacy they derive from the tetradic structure supported by the letter, while at the same time suppressing the enunciative position of the subject.

In the latter Seminar, the police are asserted in their function of assuring the circulation of the letter in the dimension of speech, as it continues to trace out the contours of the hole that it introduces.[61] However, the consistency that secures this hole is to be found elsewhere, and no doubt the minister's dual role of mathematician and poet can show us the way, for to paraphrase what Lacan states in the *Sinthome*, one needs a bit of imagination to make the hole thing hold together.[62]

Thus, the S_1 is a signifier that, in the discourse of the master, imposes itself in the place of the semblant, having substituted itself in the place of the subject. However, at the same time we must recognize that it also imposes a certain relation to *jouissance* and thus a certain mode of inscription thereof. The *jouissance* in question is the *jouissance* of the unconscious as it ciphers itself through a structure of repetition, returning to itself via the production of a surplus-enjoyment which it cannot recuperate. The *jouissance* of the unconscious is an auto-erotic and above all idiotic *jouissance* and this is borne out by the fact that I now designate it as the place of the King.[63] Indeed, the wax seal of the King bears the insignia of this idiocy in the outline of the phallus (Φ) and if we look closely enough we will find its profile on the letter addressed to the Queen. However, if our pursuit is not to share the fate of the prefect, we must hold back for a while, and continue our elaboration. For from Hegel we also learn that the *jouissance* of the master is really the *jouissance* of the slave. We must therefore turn our attention to the minister and ask once again, what is at stake in a reading?

From the figures above, we can see that the minister is in the place of the subject. If we read (. . .) the above diagram as a movement of articulation we can see that in addressing himself to the Queen, the minister is more secretly ciphering the *jouissance* of his own unconscious, the S_1 in the place of the King, which returns to itself via the surplus enjoyment with which he masks his subjective division and his alienation in the field of language. Indeed, this movement is a reading of the knowledge supposed in the Other (S_2), a knowledge supported by the object *a* as that which is *illegible* therein. This knowledge might be any knowledge, but as such, and because the structure of discourse is founded upon a positional articulation, it is also the knowledge supposed in the unconscious, a knowledge supported by the structure of the fantasy as a delirious elaboration of the initial mark of *jouissance*.

It is thus this knowledge that is at stake in the minister's supposition of knowledge in the Queen, and this is how we can read "the robbers knowledge of the losers knowledge of the robber"; indeed, it is the very principle of a certain type of reading, and as Lacan says in *Seminar XVIII* this knowledge "imposes a certain fantasy." It is this fantasy that frames the subject's relation to the drive while masking it with the Imaginary through a phallicization of the object. In the discourse of the master such a reading is supported by the subject insofar as he occupies the position designated as that of "truth," and this is ultimately the "truth" of his subjective division in fantasy. Indeed, here we see that the subject is split by the *jouissance* at stake in taking a position within the field of speech. For, as Lacan underlines, "the letter only arrives at its destination to find what, in my discourse on 'The Purloined Letter,' I designate with the term subject." Moreover, he later adds, in a way which returns us to his earlier elaboration of the "oddity of a letter marked with the recipient's stamp,"[64] which thereby becomes "a sort of love-letter he's sent to himself":[65]

> The letter, of course, is not to the woman, to the woman whose address it bears, whom it satisfies in arriving at its destination, but to the subject, namely, very precisely, in order to redefine it, to that which is divided in fantasy, in other words, to reality insofar as it is engendered by the structure of fiction.[66]

Indeed, when the neurotic subject reads he ciphers the *jouissance* of his own unconscious according to a symptomatic truth, creating a fictional Other to answer to the requirements of his symptom. In this sense, the inertia of the minister's relation to the letter can be read as resulting from a fantasy which forges a supposed identity between a semblance of knowledge and a *jouis-*

sance he claims as his own, thereby suspending the fictional possibilities of the letter by covering over the alterity that it inscribes. Indeed, if the letter supports the signification of "a wandering truth" that "shuts your trap," it is because it indexes the drive satisfaction which supports it on the basis of the symptom. Indeed, to be somewhat prescriptive, what the minister is clearly in need of is the "cease of castration as possibility," namely, as Lacan tells us in the *Sinthome*, that which "*ceases, to write.*"[67] For while the minister's fantasy continues to be, *to write with majesty*, and thus instate the sexual rapport, his desire will remain an impossibility and his fate will be bound to that of the King (Φ), the Queen remaining forever an impossibility. Far better then for the minister to give up his *politique* and return to *poetry*, for only then will his song have a chance to rise up into the royal chamber in a lyrical testimony both to the impossibility of writing the sexual relation and to the uses of fiction in allowing us to make something of it.

If the minister has got stuck in a reading and thus "holds the threat of a profound, misrecognised, repressed disorder,"[68] we must add that reading also offers the possibility of engaging in a process of construction which aims at drawing the letter from its place of semblance. Such a process of construction aims at extracting the letter in its alterity from the narcissism of the drive as it is elaborated in the fantasy. In other words, what is at stake in a reading is the possibility of attesting to the alterity that the letter inscribes in one's fundamental relation to language. Moreover, an attestation of this alterity will inevitably also be a testimony to the uses of fiction, for it is only fiction that allows *jouissance* to inscribe itself in the relation with the Other sex. And this is where we take up our reading of "The Purloined Letter" again, as a drama generated by the letter insofar as what the letter inscribes as the subject's relation to *jouissance* is indexed upon the impossibility of writing the sexual relation. In order to grasp this we can continue to elaborate our four term structure by adding a propositional dimension to it as follows.[69]

V. THE FUNCTION OF THE LETTER
AND THE FIELD OF FICTION

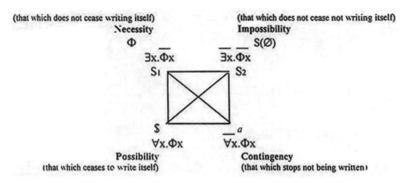

Figure 10–9.

Here we see that the S_1 is defined on the basis of the *necessity* of a repetitive instance of inscription which arises through the *impossibility* of its transcription into the field of the S_2. It is the mode of *jouissance* that Lacan will link to the symptom as phallic *jouissance*, which parasites the body and enjoys in the place of the subject. The *impossibility* in the second position arises through the failure of establishing a rapport between the respective fields marked out as S_1 and S_2. Here we see that the famous sexual non-rapport is founded upon a disjunction between the sexes which is at the same time a disjunction between "signifier and signified" and between "*jouissance* and the Other."[70] As S(Ø), it also designates "the impossibility of telling the whole truth" and thus of suturing the field of knowledge.[71] This impossibility of transcribing the *jouissance* of the S_1 into the field of the S_2 leads the subject to the *possible*. The subject thus comes to place himself under the bar of the universal law of castration, a consequence of the identification which constitutes the S_1, which sustains the fiction that all men are equal before its law. However, we can also say that in this way the subject is led to what it is *possible* to recuperate of a relation to *jouissance* through the structure of the fantasy, while remaining parasited by the phallic *jouis-*

sance of the symptom. However, more radically, and as indicated above, this position also designates the "cease of castration as possibility," namely the possibility of attesting to one's castration and thereby ceasing to enjoy it via the phallic *jouissance* of the symptom. Initially, Lacan conceives this simply in terms of a voiding of *jouissance* or a "ceasing to write," adding the vital comma only in the *Sinthome* in order to indicate the possibility for a subjective inscription of *jouissance*. Finally, at the bottom on the right we see *jouissance* inscribing itself on the basis of a corporeal contingency. It is here that the famous sexual rapport "stops not being written," which is not to say that the sexual rapport can finally be written as such, but that *jouissance* can inscribe itself on the basis of a corporeal contingency.[72] Indeed, in attesting to the inexistence, or rather the impossibility of the Other, S(Ø), one can nevertheless affirm the alterity that arises in its place. Thus, we see our path clear for a shift to a discussion of the topology of knots, for what this structure demonstrates is how *necessity* knots itself to *contingency*, by passing through the *impossible*, S(Ø).

    First, however, let us acknowledge that what this modal square demonstrates is how a relation to *jouissance* comes to be organized through the structure of fiction and supported by the function of the letter. Here we see the envelope of fiction performing its own logical reduction, by demonstrating that it is founded upon a certain use of the *semblant* and the various modes of affirmation and negation that support it as a *function of make-believe* (Φx).[73] It also reveals that at its limit the field of fiction runs up against the Real as an impasse in formalization graspable only through the function of the letter. From this follows the disparity which entails that any fictional organization will always fail to subsume *jouissance* within the order of the signifier, and thus will continue to run up against the radical alterity that the letter inscribes of one's relation to *jouissance*. Indeed, in Poe's tale we see how this disparity is secured only in a makeshift form through an identification with the phallus as Imaginary. However, if the envelope of fiction does not enclose the vein painted nakedness of the letter as such, what then does it fold around? The answer, of course, is being, for, above all, fiction concerns being, or as Lacan puts it in *Encore*, "*ce qu'il en est de l'être*."[74] Fiction is the envelope of being.

In fact, the modal square above marks a "substantial" modification of Aristotle's existential logic, a logic which proceeds from an unpostulated predication of existence by integrating the function of the *copula*, a function Lacan attributes to the phallus, into the mode of attribution in question.[75] However, existence is, as Bentham pointed out, a "fictitious entity" supported by a predicative articulation in the field of language and as such is founded upon a distribution secured through a function of semblance and make-believe: a function of the phallus we can say, but *not alone*. Indeed, to Aristotle's question "What makes man one?" we can respond that even though it may have something to do with the *idea* he has of his body, the answer is not to be sought in *essence*, but only in what speech can support of a relation to the Other sex.

Indeed, when Lacan considers the story in the light of the inexistence of the sexual relation, he reaffirms his earlier insistence that "the letter always arrives at its destination," but here he identifies this place more clearly as the place of the subject, adding that this place is occupied by the King. Lacan thereby interprets the story as a story of the non-rapport which unfolds according to the logic of the partner-symptom in which the Queen returns the King's letter to him, either by guile or misadventure, as his truth in the form of his castration, and the mark of this castration is, of course, the cuckold's horns he wears upon his crown. The Queen thus ruptures the supposed identity between semblance and *jouissance* (Φ) upon which the King's authority is founded, but it is an identity which will be taken up as necessary by all the subsequent discourses that this revolution gives rise to. In defining the minister as quite literally the subject of the tale and the King as the S_1, my reading does not contradict Lacan's, but rather places the emphasis on what is at stake in the reading conducted by the minister and thus what is at stake in the function of interpretation per se. Indeed, one could say that where the King is the subject of the tale, the King's King is his own unconscious, or as Louis XIV put it:

"*L'état, c'est moi*"—to which we can imagine the Queen replying by adjusting her postiche, with a little nod at the *not-all* and the *noeud beau* of her partner.

VI. FROM READING TO WRITING

Thus, what is at stake in a reading of "The Purloined Letter" clearly concerns how the *jouissance* inscribed by the letter comes to be organized through the structure of fiction and married to the truth it supposes. However, we must now pass from a *reading* to a *writing* by returning to the question of the symptom and its mode of inscribing *jouissance*. As a reference for this shift we can refer ourselves once again to Lacan's *Seminar* where, when speaking of the letter and the identifications that it gives rise to, he declares, "in determining the scope of what speech repeats, it prepares the question of what symptoms repeat."[76] For what is in question in the passage from which this is drawn is precisely the relation between the two functions of the letter, between the identification which supports the alienation of the subject and the object: S_1 and a.[77] And here we can reverse our earlier formula by saying that if the letter is what reads in the story, it is also what is read; and what is read is also what is at stake in a writing. For if the S_1 is what reads in the story, thus ciphering the mode of enjoyment of the unconscious, what is read behind the reality it constitutes is the object a, insofar as it alone supports the libidinal investments of the subject in a ciphering of $1+a$.[78]

We must now distinguish two different aspects of the letter as they are introduced by Lacan. For although the letter supports both a reading and a writing, the two functions are not the same; in fact, they must be radically distinguished, the one from the other, as they are not inscribed in the same register. Indeed, their only point of convergence lies where what is read remains, at least in part, illegible. Insofar as it can be read, a letter provides a support for signification. Signification is founded upon the order of the signifier, namely that which "represents a subject for another signifier" according to the laws of metaphor and metonymy, which Freud referred to under the auspices of condensation and displacement, and which, as we have seen, constitutes the framework for Lacan's initial reading of "The Purloined Letter." The Freudian unconscious lies entirely in the thematics which organize such a reading, and it is one which establishes the dimension of psychical reality as a signification supposed in the Other, supported by fantasy, and revealed through slips of the tongue, in *parapraxes*, and in dreams. In this way, the Freudian unconscious reveals itself to be founded upon the subject's alienation in language in relation to a phantasmatic knowledge absolutely correlative to the value Freud gave to interpretation as a recuperative elaboration of a meaning supported by an oedipal truth.[79] Indeed, one could even say that it is because Freud chose to interpret the irreducibility of the symptom at the end of an analysis that the Real of castration itself came to be installed in the dimension of the Freudian truth, a dimension which Freud himself had named through his very invention of the concept of unconscious as that of psychical reality. Indeed, here we must recognize that Freud's discovery of the unconscious is also of the order of invention,[80] and as such provides the basis for a conceptual knotting which allowed Freud to tie his own three registers—the Ego, the Id, and the Superego—together with a fourth term, that of psychical reality.[81]

It is in taking up the question of what remains illegible in what is read of the unconscious, that Lacan gives a new sense to what is meant by a reading and also to what interpretation can support through the function of equivocation. To say as much is to say that there is a poetics which operates not only in a writing, but also in a reading of texts and in the transference that sustains such a reading, a poetics of interpretation which must be taken at its word, but also to the letter. For it is only by taking interpretation to the letter that it will ultimately be able to pass to a limit which can only be crossed when it reverses itself in effects of creation. In this way, reading passes to a mode of writing which is also an act of creation and invention which modifies the structure of the subject and its relation to *jouissance* by returning the subject to what after a long period of elaboration has proved to be absolutely irreducible in what has been imposed in his fundamental relation to language. Such a process of reduction operates upon the fictional elaboration that has hitherto supported the subject's alienation in language.

Here we can begin to distinguish the two modes of writing which Lacan outlines in *Lituraterre*, and then identifies more clearly in the *sinthome*. These two modes of writing are indexed by Lacan with two separate letters from our above schema: $ and *a*. There is thus a writing indexed upon the split subject, the subject of the signifier, and a writing indexed upon the object *a*. In other words there is a writing indexed upon the subject's alienation in a non-totalizable field of difference and a writing indexed upon what the letter condenses of a relation to *jouissance*. For while the signifier is always different from itself, the letter is always identical to itself insofar as it is not answerable to any effect of signification. Indeed, Lacan places Derrida's notion of *écriture* on the side of $, on the side of what we can call reading in its most radical form, for its mode of textual engagement concerns "the precipitation of a signifier" in a field founded upon impossibility. However, as we have seen in relation to "The Purloined Letter," in such a field it is the reader who occupies the position of truth, and this is exactly where Lacan appears to place Derrida in his brief repost to the philosopher's critique in *Lituraterre*.[82] Indeed, in relation the opening remarks of Derrida's essay,[83] truth is only ever to be "supposed" in a reading—but what is it that "finds itself" in such a supposition, in such a reading, if not the *jouissance* inscribed by the letter for whoever makes use of it. Indeed, if Lacan speaks of "the fiction of the incomplete text" it is not because he is holding out on the possibility of textual closure, but because one cannot ignore the fact that the field of textuality, a field which is manifestly founded upon impossibility, is nevertheless supported by *jouissance*.

Lacan's own notion of writing, based upon the letter rather than the signifier and constructed through a reading of Joyce, is indexed upon a supplementary knotting produced in relation to, or rather *in the wake of* the letter and its conjugation with the positions of speech. Indeed, such a writing can only occur *in the wake of* a reading, for what one reads in the analytic discourse is the letter per se in the form of object a.[84] In *Le sinthome*, Lacan places the object a at the heart of the knotting of RSI, as follows:

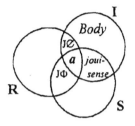

J∅ = *jouissance* of the Other (which does not exist)
JΦ = Phallic *jouissance* of the symptom parasites the body
joui-sense = enjoyment in sense

Figure 10–10.

Here we see that the three dimensions of *jouissance* are produced at points of intersection on the Borromean knot, and that they are all attached to or as Lacan says "plugged into" the object a. However, in *La troisième*, Lacan also states that the object a is precisely the form in which each register intervenes to interrupt the *jouissance* produced by the intersection of the other two. Thus: as Real, the letter intervenes to rupture an enjoyed sense produced between the Imaginary and Symbolic; as Symbolic, it intervenes to curtail the *jouissance* ascribed to the Other in anxiety through the intrusion of the Real into the Imaginary; and it intervenes in the phallic enjoyment of the symptom, produced through the intrusion of the Symbolic into the Real, in an Imaginary form, or more precisely through the function of equivocation. It seems to me that there is no simpler and no more practical way of demonstrating what is entailed in the cutting and splicing that constructs a different mode of knotting the subject's relation to *jouissance* other than by evoking the different uses of the object a in an analysis, and thus the different registers in which the analyst can "act with his being" in order to intervene in what is being ciphered by the One on the couch. Indeed, analysis is all about the ciphering of $1+a$ in which truth knots itself upon a scansion which instantiates itself as true, only for its effects to dissolve with its object, while what remains is the knotting that has been left in its wake.[85] In this way the knot reveals that it has all the properties of writing in the Lacanian sense: a material residue with a palpable consistency which inscribes a relation to *jouissance* left in the wake of a flow of speech, while at the same time being completely dissociated from the effects of phonation which support the dimension of meaning as a signification supposed in the Other.

> To tell the truth, the "*noeud bo*" in question completely changes the meaning of writing. For, to the said writing it gives an autonomy and it is an autonomy all the more remarkable in that there is another writing which is that upon which Derrida has insisted, namely that which results from what could be called a precipitation of the signifier. Derrida has insisted, but it is quite clear that I showed him the way [*la voie*]; indeed the fact that I found no other way of supporting the signifier than by writing S is already a sufficient indication. But what remains is that the signifier, in other words what is modulated in the voice [*la voix*], has nothing to do with writing. In any case this is what my "*noeud bo*" demonstrates. It changes the meaning of writing, it shows there is something to which signifiers can be attached . . . by passing through the dimension of speech.[86]

On his 75th birthday, Lacan speaks of his relation to Freud. This relationship is founded upon a reading of the Freudian text and upon the transference that sustained such a reading. However, here Lacan marks a point of separation with Freud by announcing the point of departure for a new mode of writing that he names as his own, a writing of the Real that is not answerable to the effects of sense.

> I have circulated (*véhiculé*) a great deal of this thing that one calls Freudian. I have even entitled one of the things I have written "The Freudian Thing." But in what I call the real, I have invented, I have invented something, not because. . . , it imposed itself upon me.[87]

Here we see an act of nomination conducted in relation to the Real, announcing a mode of invention which is achieved through a forcing in relation to *jouissance*. It is a forcing which has resulted from the logical reduction which is also a process of construction of what is at stake in a reading. However, this moment of invention is also a moment of creation that takes up what, after a long period of elaboration and a long time of reading Freud, has proved to be absolutely irreducible in what has been imposed as a relation to language. For what is at stake in a reading is ultimately that one stops circulating a letter in the name of what has gone before, and allows it to pass to the order of creation and invention that one can finally name as one's own. Here we could finally speak of Joyce and what he manages to construct in the course of his own experience as a writer by reducing literature to the Real that supports it, while at the same time reconstructing a relation to the body through a very particular practice of the letter. But this, of course, is another story, one which attempts to break the bounds of representation by exploring what is absolutely singular in what is inscribed through the function of the letter, and this leaves our elaboration to be continued elsewhere, beyond the bounds of this present study.[88]

ENDNOTES

1. "*Voilà le compte bien rendu de ce qui distingue la lettre du signifiant même qu'elle emporte. En quoi ce n'est pas faire métaphore de l'épistole. Puisque le conte consiste en ce qu'y passe comme muscade le message dont la lettre y fait péripétie sans lui.*" Jacques Lacan, *Lituraterre, Littérature* 3 (1971), p. 4. (In its literary guise *péripétie* also refers to each of the changes that effect a situation in a narrative work and thus *fait péripétie* refers to the letter as that which causes the transformations within it).

2. Philippe Hellebois, "Les mots tombent de haut," *La Cause Freudienne* No. 43 (1999), p. 50.

3. Pierre Skriabine, "Clinic and Topology" [section 9 (pp. 93–953 here); "Clinique et topologie," *Revue de la cause freudienne* 23 (1993), pp. 117–133.

4. "The letter is it not . . . more properly *littorale* [coast-line], figuring that one domain in its entirety makes for the other the frontier of

what is foreign to it, without being a reciprocal relation. The edge of the hole in knowledge, is it not this that it draws." Jacques Lacan, *Lituraterre, op. cit.*, p. 5.

5. It is clear from Poe's tale that the enigma of the Queen's desire is bound up with the problematic of *jouissance*. Indeed, in speaking of the place occupied by the Queen, Eric Laurent declares, "it suffices that this enigmatic place be a place in reserve. In this respect the place of *jouissance* rises up both as enigma, a hole in sense and, at the same time, as this place of *jouissance*." Eric Laurent, "La lettre volée et le vol sur la lettre," *La Cause Freudienne* No. 43 (1999), p. 35.

6. This is, of course, an allusion to the pleasure principle.

7. There are thus two aspects of the letter in play here: the letter insofar as ex-sistent and the letter insofar as it can be repeated. As we shall see, the structure of this topology can be rendered as that of the Möbius strip and its associated forms, the interior eight and the torus.

8. Jacques Lacan, *Seminar II, The Ego in Freud's Theory and in the Technique of Psychoanalysis* (Cambridge: Cambridge University Press, 1988), p. 200.

9. Edgar Allan Poe, "The Purloined Letter," *The Purloined Poe*, ed. John P. Muller & William J. Richardson (London: Johns Hopkins University Press, 1988), p. 23. The quotation is from Crébillon's play *Atrée*.

10. Jacques Lacan, *Seminar XX, Encore*, trans. Bruce Fink (London: W. W. Norton, 1998), p. 146.

11. The mechanism of this scansion is elaborated by Lacan in his postscript to his seminar on "The Purloined Letter"; also cf. Gilbert Chaitin, *Rhetoric & Culture in Lacan* (Cambridge: Cambridge University Press, 1996), p. 97 and p. 236.

12. Jacques Lacan, *Seminar II, op. cit.*, pp. 196–197.

13. *The Purloined Poe, op. cit.*, p. 29.

14. Jacques Lacan, *Écrits: A Selection*, trans. Alan Sheridan (London: Routledge, 1977), p. 153.

15. Joël Dor, *Introduction to the Reading of Lacan: The Unconscious is Structured Like a Language* (Northvale, NJ: Jason Aronson, 1997), p. 49.

16. Jacques-Alain Miller, "The *Sinthome*: A Mixture between Symptom and Fantasy," *The Psychoanalytic Notebooks of the London Circle*, 5 (2001), 9–31. To obtain this article and other indications of the contemporary Lacanian orientation write to LCESPNotebooks@aol.com or visit the website www.londonsociety-nes.org.uk.

17. As Eric Laurent insists, one cannot read Lacan's Seminar without distinguishing the place of *jouissance* from the effects of sense produced through the itinerary of the signifier; *op. cit.*

18. This perspective, which has profound consequences for the

theory of interpretation, is advanced by Jacques-Alain Miller, in "Interpretation in Reverse," *Psychoanalytical Notebooks of the London Circle* 2 (1999), pp. 9–16.

19. This formulation is based on Lacan's third Rome discourse: "*La troisième*," Lettres de l'EFP No.16 (1975). This formulation will ultimately lead us to the topology of the Borromean knot, which demonstrates the way in which the Symbolic, the Imaginary, and the Real are knotted in the experience of the subject.

20. Jacques-Alain Miller, "The *Sinthome*: A Mixture between Symptom and Fantasy," *op. cit.* Miller's formulation here is based on Lacan's comments on the discourse of the master in *Le sinthome* (18.11.75).

21. Jacques Lacan, "Seminar on 'The Purloined Letter,'" *The Purloined Poe, op. cit.*, p. 34.

22. For, as Lacan states in *Le sinthome*, equivocation is "the only weapon we have against the symptom."

23. Jacques Lacan, *Lituraterre, op. cit.*, p. 4.

24. Here, one could even reconsider the very pertinent comments which Marie Bonaparte makes about *anxiety* and *affect* in Poe's writing in this regard (Marie Bonaparte, "Selections from *The Life and Works of Edgar Allan Poe: A Psycho-analytic Interpretation*," *The Purloined Poe, op. cit.* pp. 101–132).

25. See the discussions on art and the symptom in Jacques-Alain Miller's "Seminar of Barcelona," *Psychoanalytical Notebooks of the London Circle* 1 (1998), pp. 11–65.

26. Jacques-Alain Miller, "Lacan avec Joyce," *La Cause Freudienne*, No. 38 (1998), p. 20.

27. Jacques Lacan, "Of Structure as an Inmixing of Otherness Prerequisite to Any Subject Whatever," in *The Structuralist Controversy*, ed. Richard Macksy & Eugenio Donato (London: Johns Hopkins University Press, 1970), pp. 186–200.

28. Lacan will later take up structure of this elementary topology and also the erasure which constitutes it in the very title of his short contribution to a discussion of the relation between literature and psychoanalysis: *Lituraterre, op. cit.*, pp. 3–10.

29. *Op. cit.*, p. 191.

30. Jacques Lacan, *Seminar IX, L'Identification*, unpublished (10.1.62).

31. Jacques Lacan, "Of Structure as an Inmixing. . . ," *op. cit.*, p. 192.

32. Jacques Lacan, "Desire and the Interpretation of Desire in *Hamlet*," *Literature and Psychoanalysis*, ed. Shoshana Felman (London: Johns Hopkins University Press, 1982), p. 11.

33. See note 7, above.

34. The scansion referred to here is elaborated by Lacan in his "Introduction" to his "Seminar on 'The Purloined Letter,'" *Écrits* (Paris: Seuil, 1966), pp. 44–61.

35. This itinerary is clearly marked out on the completed form of Lacan's graph of desire, in the articulation which passes through the unconscious circuit running between *jouissance* and castration. See *Écrits: A Selection, op. cit.,* p. 315.

36. For an extremely lucid account of this aspect of the "Introduction" see Bruce Fink, "The Nature of Unconscious Thought," *Reading Seminars I & II*, ed. R. Feldstein, B. Fink, & M. Jaanus (Albany: State University of New York Press, 1996), pp. 173–191; and also his book *The Lacanian Subject: Between Language and* Jouissance (Princeton, NJ: Princeton University Press, 1995), pp. 153–172.

37. Eric Laurent, "La lettre volée et le vol sur la lettre," *op. cit.*

38. Since this is a retrospective presentation of the developments of Lacan's thought, I will use the terms Mother, Child, and Father rather than Queen, Minister, and King in order to resist the tendency to reify the story in terms of the phantasmagoria of the Oedipus. For what is crucial here is not the oedipal drama, but rather the structure of the topology that follows from it.

39. Jacques Lacan, *Écrits* (Paris: Seuil, 1966), p. 53. Note that the subject is here presented as unbarred for reasons which will become apparent in what follows.

40. *Écrits: A Selection, op. cit.,* p. 197.

41. See Lacan's development of Schema L in the context of his discussion of the three times of the Oedipus complex in *Seminar V: Les formations de l'inconscient* (Paris: Seuil, 1998).

42. Jacques Lacan, "Seminar on 'The Purloined Letter,'" *op. cit.,* p. 28.

43. Eric Laurent, "Alienation and Separation (I)," *Reading Seminar XI, op. cit.,* p. 23. It should be noted that in this early schema neither the subject nor the Other is presented as barred. It should also be noted that the King is not identical to the Big Other; however his role as third term supports its structure. Indeed, the "King" can be considered, according to the logic of the early Lacan from which the schema derives, as "the signifier which, as locus of the signifier, is the signifier of the Other as the locus of the Law" (*Écrits: A Selection, op. cit.,* p. 221). Lacan will later modify this logic by indicating that the Other does not *include* such a signifier and this can be seen in the subsequent distinction between S_1 and S_2.

44. *Ibid.*

45. Jacques Lacan, footnote 18 of "On a Question Preliminary to Any Possible Treatment of Psychosis," *Écrits: A Selection, op. cit.* p. 223.

46. *Op. cit.*, p. 10.

47. *Ibid.*

48. François Regnault, "The Name-of-the-Father," *Reading Seminar XI, op. cit.*, p. 71. The source quoted for these diagrams is given as Vappereau, *Étoffe*, pp. 240–241.

49. *Ibid.*, pp. 71–72.

50. Jacques Lacan, *"La troisième," op. cit.*

51. Jacques Lacan, "Seminar on 'The Purloined Letter,'" *op. cit.*, p. 55.

52. Jacques Lacan, *Seminar XVIII, D'une discourse qui ne serait pas du semblant*, (12.5.71).

53. *Op. cit.* p. 7.

54. Jacques Lacan, *L'étourdit, Scilicet* No. 4 (Paris: Seuil, 1973) p. 41.

55. In this way, we proceed by means of analogy to that which lies beyond it. In this we must not succumb to an Imaginary mirage which would make the characters identical to their respective positions on the first schema.

56. Jacques Lacan, *Seminar XVIII, op. cit.* (session of 17.04.71).

57. Jacques Lacan, *The Four Fundamental Concepts of Psychoanalysis*, trans. Alan Sheridan (London: Penguin, 1977), p. 209.

58. Jacques-Alain Miller, "Interpretation in Reverse," *op. cit.*, p. 12.

59. Jacques Lacan, "Seminar on 'The Purloined Letter,'" *op. cit.* p. 40.

60. Jacques Lacan, *Seminar XVIII, op. cit.* (12.5.1971).

61. This reference places "The Purloined Letter" in *Le Sinthome*, while also linking it to its previous re-elaboration in *Seminar XVIII*.

62. Jacques Lacan, *Le sinthome* (18:11:75). Here the topologist Soury demonstrates that he shares something of the dual talents of the Minister, for he demonstrates the necessity of enveloping the hole introduced by the function of the letter with a bubble-like structure or torus in order for the holes that it envelops to consist. This is a function that Lacan gives to the Imaginary at this point in the seminar.

63. The King is thus now in the place of the master signifier and the letter in that of object *a*. This redistribution, or dare I say twist, derives from the theoretical shift which takes place in Lacan's development of the structure of discourse and also from my own somewhat playful use of these terms, which aims at what might be called *the sovereignty of the unconscious* that the discourse of the master bears out in effacing the subject that it enthralls. In fact, in *Seminar XVIII*, Lacan identifies the King as the subject of the story for reasons which will become apparent in what follows.

64. Jacques Lacan, "Seminar on 'The Purloined Letter,'" *op. cit.*, p. 47.

65. Jacques Lacan, *Seminar II, op. cit.*, p. 199.

66. Jacques Lacan, *Seminar XVIII* (18.05.71).

67. Jacques Lacan, *Le sinthome* (18.11.1975).

68. Jacques Lacan, *Seminar II, op. cit.*, p. 200.

69. In *Seminar XVIII* Lacan develops the positional articulation of the structure of discourse in the context of a form of propositional logic which anticipates the formulae of sexuation. However, my mapping of the formulae of sexuation onto the discourse of the master is in no way meant to be definitive, as there are other, of course, ways of articulating the schema. My rendition of the modal square itself is based upon Elie Doumit's logical contributions to *L'Apport Freudien*, ed. Pierre Kaufman (Paris: Bordas, 1993).

70. Jacques-Alain Miller, "Les Six Paradigmes de la Jouissance," *La Cause Freudienne*, No. 43, p. 25.

71. Jacques Lacan, *Encore, op. cit.*, pp. 94–95.

72. Thus "the apparent necessity of the phallic function turns out to be mere contingency." In the analytic discourse what comes to be inscribed in this position, and one could perhaps also say littered here, is the S_1.

73. Since the phallic function sustains the field of fiction as a field of desire and thus supports what can unfold in a suite of signifiers, we could also perhaps write this *function of make-believe* in an approximate form as ΦxSn or PhixSn.

74. The pun slips between *l'être* and *lettre*, i.e., between *being* and the *letter*; see *Encore*, p. 3.

75. As I understand it in Aristotle's spoken language, ancient Greek, the function of the *copula*, the function that confers being, was concealed in the "signifierness" of the name of the entity in question: cf., *idizwadidiz*, *Encore*, p. 31.

76. Jacques Lacan, "Seminar on 'The Purloined Letter,'" *op. cit.*, p. 35.

77. For a precise elaboration of the relation between the S_1 and the object *a* in the constitution of the *sinthome* see Jacques-Alain Miller "The Sinthome: A Mixture between Symptom and Fantasy," *op. cit.*

78. Jacques Lacan, *Seminar XX: Encore, op. cit.*, p. 49.

79. Jacques-Alain Miller, "Interpretation in Reverse," *op. cit.*

80. Lacan describes the unconscious as Freud's invention in the "Geneva Lecture on the Symptom," *Analysis* 1 (1989), p. 15.

81. Jacques Lacan, *Seminar XXII, RSI,* (unpublished).

82. *Op. cit.*, p. 5. Having said this, one could perhaps also define Derrida's position, more generously, as suspended in the analytic discourse, or then again elsewhere.

83. Jacques Derrida, "The Purveyor of Truth," *The Purloined Poe, op. cit.*, p. 173.

84. Cf., *Encore, op. cit.* p. 37. In the discourse of the analyst the S_1 no longer supports the alienation of the subject by imposing itself in the

place of the semblant but rather inscribes itself as letter, and even as litter, as it passes from the necessary to the contingent.

85. For this mode of ciphering and for an indication of the way the
other intervenes, beyond any intersubjectivity in the knotting that constitutes the subject, see Lacan's revision of his thesis of "Logical Time,"
and which is equally valid for "The Purloined Letter," see *Encore, op. cit.*,
p. 49, and also the final session of *Le sinthome* (11.5.76).

86. Jacques Lacan, *Le sinthome*, (11.5.76); my translation has ignored
the pun on "*dit-mension*" here.

87. Jacques Lacan, *Le sinthome* (13.4.76).

88. See my article, "In the Wake of Interpretation" in *Re-inventing
the Symptom*, ed. Luke Thurston (Other Press, 2002).

III

Topology of Knots

11

The Clinic of the Borromean Knot*

PIERRE SKRIABINE

The clinical pertinence of Lacan's topology will here be illustrated with a number of examples, referring to what we can call a clinic of the Borromean knot, a clinic of supplementations [*suppléances*], which paves the way for a new differential clinic.

GENERALIZED FORECLOSURE
AND SUPPLEMENTATIONS

If Lacan considers, as early as his article "On a Question Preliminary to Any Possible Treatment of Psychosis," that a supplementation to the "void suddenly perceived of the inaugural *Verwerfung*"[1] (p. 221, Sheridan, *trans. mod.*) is conceivable, it is only at the end of his teaching that he gives full extension to this term, to this function of supplementation. This emphasis, this generalization

---

*Translated by Ellie Ragland and Véronique Voruz, from *La Revue de l'Ecole de la cause freudienne*.

of supplementation, is indeed correlative to the displacement of the status of the Other effected by Lacan when he no longer takes his bearings from the Other, but from the One, that is to say, from an axiomatic of *jouissance*.

In Schema L, as in the formulations of the *preliminary question*, Lacan still relies upon the hypothesis of a dialectic subject/Other; and the Other, in this respect, is complete and consistent, it is the true and absolute Other which could annul the subject itself; it includes its own guarantee. The Other of the signifier is completed by the Other of Law. There is an Other of the Other which lays down the law for the Other. Its signifier is the Name-of-the-Father: "That is to say, the signifier [which] in the Other, as locus of the signifier, is the signifier of the Other as locus of the law" (Sheridan 221, *trans. mod.*). At this point in Lacan's elaboration, the Other thus contains its own signifier; the Other of the Other exists.

It is from his Seminar on *The Ethics* onwards that Lacan brings out that in the process of symbolization, of absorption of the Thing in the Other, where language erases *jouissance* and soaks it up, there is a remainder; this remainder is the object *a*, surplus-*jouissance* [*plus-de-jouir*], irreducible to a signifier.

In this respect, *a* is not an element of the Other, but it must be conceived as included in the Other, like the *agalma* within the Silenus to which Alcibiades compares Socrates in *The Symposium*.

The Other thus becomes a concept organized around a kernel, a vacuole of *jouissance* which lodges itself there in a point of extimacy [*extimité*], at the most intimate point, which nonetheless remains radically heterogeneous.

From then on, the Other is marked by a central lack: that of *jouissance* as signifier. Lacan introduces S(Ø) in this place, the signifier of the lack in the Other, a signifier which is different from the others; it is the signifier without which the others would represent nothing, but it can itself only be conceived as extimate in relation to the Other, as J.-A. Miller underlined.[2] Consequently, the Other can but be marked either by inconsistency—due to the fact that only a heterogeneous element can come in the place of its lack—or by incompleteness.

Lacan can then formulate, in *Subversion of the Subject and Dialectic of Desire*, that the Other does not exist—with respect to *jouissance*—and that there is no Other of the Other. This amounts to bringing out the foundational function of the fault in the universe, as we emphasized earlier.

From then on, what remains as Other in the Other, what founds the alterity of the Other, is the object *a* as non-symbolized remainder of the Thing.

The path followed by Lacan takes him from an axiomatic of desire, from a point of departure in the Other, to an axiomatic of *jouissance*, which, for its part, is fundamentally acephalic, autistic. By the same token, this also leads him to think of speech, no longer as addressed to the Other, as a vehicle of communication, but as a vehicle of *jouissance*. It is in this respect that Lacan proposes the concept of *lalangue* at the end of the Seminar *Encore*, namely a Symbolic disjoined from the Other and referred to the One. To lay emphasis on the One, on this "There is such a thing as One" ("*Y a d'l'Un*, cf., *Seminar XX*, English trans. p. 5) which Lacan formulates, and which marks the last period of his teaching, amounts to posing *jouissance* and *lalangue* as prior to language as structure, prior to an Other which henceforth becomes problematic.

It is then that Lacan can draw the ultimate consequences of the division of the Other, of Ø, and of the function of S(Ø). From then on, the Name-of-the-Father appears as a stopper of this Ø; the function of the father, however operative it may be, is only a Freudian myth. It is not unique. Hence the pluralization of the Names of the Father as supplementations to the structural fault in the Other.

In other words, that its own signifier should lack in the Other, be foreclosed, is a fact of structure. This amounts to a generalization of foreclosure as something structurally lacking. In this respect, the Name-of-the-Father appears as an addition [*en plus*], a complement. And should it fail, a supplementation, which is always a supplementation [*suppléance*] of a supplement [*supplément*], can come to remedy this fault. Thus, supplementation is correlative to a universal clinic of delusion.

THE BORROMEAN KNOT

And indeed, this is what is presentified by the topology of the Borromean knot, with which Lacan reformulates the very concept of structure solely on the basis of the categories of analytic experience: Real, Symbolic, and Imaginary.

The Borromean knot is an effort to think structure, the Symbolic, without any reference to the Other. It is also, as noted by J.-A. Miller, a reformulation of the structure of the Other as the condition of possibility of the analytic experience itself: this is what Lacan indicates in R.S.I. (18/03/75):[3] "If there is a real Other, it is nowhere else than in the knot itself, and this is why there is no Other of the Other."

Lacan's aim thus consists in circumscribing the One, *jouissance*, on the basis of the three registers: Real, Symbolic, Imaginary, insofar as they are fundamentally three heterogeneous registers. Yet, the speaking being is supported by these three registers, and as a result, something of a *jouissance* finds itself enclosed, wedged. It is to account for this that Lacan used the Borromean knot, as indicated in his Seminar *Encore* (p. 101).

His problem thus lies in elaborating, in situating the common measure necessary to these three absolutely heterogeneous registers. It is on this point that a fourth term intervenes; the four is already there, in the Borromean knot.

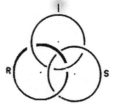

Figure 11–1.

Each one of the rings which support R, S, and I is not linked to any one of the other two. When taken two by two they are free, yet in the Borromean knot they hold together.

The common measure between the three resides in the possibility of their being knotted, knotted in a Borromean manner, and the knotting, the Borromean knot, is a fourth, new entity: it is the common measure *a minima*, in a way the perfect solution. But this does not imply that it be the only one, or even that it should be placed at the level of an ideal, or even mythical solution.

Lacan points out that in Freud's work, these three registers are left independent from each other, adrift; and to make his theoretical construction hold, Freud needs something which he calls "psychical reality," and which is nothing other than the Oedipus complex: namely a fourth term which knots the three independent terms, the three discrete rings, R, S, and I (*R.S.I.*, 14/01/75).

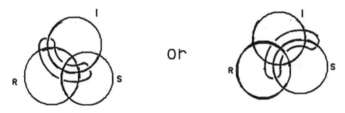

Figure 11–2.

What the Oedipus complex accomplishes here, in this figuration of the four-ring knot, is what the Borromean knot implicitly realizes in the three-ring knot.

The fourth ring, as an explicit fourth, comes here to remedy the unknotting where foreclosure is designated.

In the unknotting, it is the Borromean character which is foreclosed; the unknotting, as -1 of the knotting, is structural: it is exactly equivalent to posing the function of S(Ø).

The Borromean knotting of the three as implicit, ideal fourth, being de facto foreclosed, an explicit, supplementary fourth is required to restitute the structure of Borromean knotting, and this term is a supplementation.

This is what the fourth ring achieves, as Oedipus complex in Freud and Name-of-the-Father in Lacan, but also with reference to "the radical function of the Name-of-the-Father, which is to name things with all the consequences that it implies, including notably with regard to enjoyment [*jouir*]" (6, *R.S.I.*, 11/03/75), as nomination, as naming [*le donner-nom*]: Lacan says that this is where "speech knots itself to something of the real."

In the perfect solution of the three-ring Borromean knotting, "the Names of the Father are the symbolic, the imaginary and the real; these are the primary names insofar as they name something." That is to say that not only is each one of them a name, gives a name, but it also knots the other two, and as a third it equally carries the efficiency of the knotting as the implicit fourth.

In the four-ring knot, Lacan complements, supplements one of the three in its primary function, which is naming, nomination. To say it otherwise, it is in naming, in nomination, that supplementation truly resides: in other words, supplementation insofar as it responds to S(Ø), to the failure of the Other.

Thus Lacan can propose "three forms of the Name-of-the-Father, those that name the imaginary, the symbolic, and the real" (*R.S.I.*, 18/03/75). He then specifies that "It is not only the symbolic which has the privilege of the Names of the Father, nomination does not have to be conjoined with the hole in the symbolic" (*R.S.I.*, 15/04/75).

Inhibition as nomination of the Imaginary and anxiety as nomination of the Real are thus added to the symptom as nomination of the Symbolic: this is what Lacan indicates at the end of his Seminar *R.S.I.*

Here is another figuration of the four-ring knot, which helps us grasp better how this fourth as supplement to one of the three, R, S, or I, can restitute a Borromean knotting.

Figure 11–3.

MODALITIES OF FAILURE, MODALITIES
OF SUPPLEMENTATION

The general law then is that it fails, that it fails to constitute a three-ring Borromean knot; in other words, foreclosure is structural. This is what turns out to be the case for the neurotic; it is also what is revealed when psychosis is triggered, and it is what shows in different clinical notations on any given case.

There are many ways in which the Borromean knotting of the three registers of the Real, the Symbolic, and the Imaginary can fail, and there are as many ways of supplementing this failure: the four-ring knot we have just seen is only one among many others, if we consider that any means of securing R, S, and I is a supplementation.

What can we say of this failure with a degree of certainty?

Let us note first of all that this failure can be translated into different sorts of arrangements or rearrangements of R, S, and I:

- R, S, and I, which are fundamentally separated, disassociated, remain not knotted, or come undone: this is common madness, the "all mad" underlined by Lacan in *Les non-dupes errent* and in *R.S.I.*
- A Borromean knotting can be constituted, but a fourth element will then be required, which is fundamentally the naming, nomination: this is how Lacan defines the symptom in the four-ring Borromean knot which supports the most common case, neurosis: as nomination of the Symbolic. The fourth ring then intervenes as a supplementation of the unknotting of R, S, and I, which is structural in the generalization of foreclosure, Lacan's point of departure at the end of his teaching.
- A fourth element comes to repair the unknotting, the total or partial failing of the knotting, at the very point of error: R, S, and I remain knotted, but the knot is no longer Borromean. This is the function of the *sinthome* as fourth ring which Lacan brings forth on the basis of the case of Joyce.

- Two of the consistencies remain interlaced, and the third does not hold: taking the ideal solution of the three-ring Borromean knot for reference, this is what a single error produces—localizable at the point of overlapping in the flat [*mise à plat*] version of the knot. This is, for example, what the thrashing episode reveals of Joyce's structure prior to the production of the *sinthome*, which will prevent the slipping away of the Imaginary, that is to say, of the relationship to the body.
- There is a three-ring knot of R, S, and I that is not Borromean: this is the case for the Olympic knot, which Lacan situates in *Les non-dupes errent* as the characteristic of the neurotic insofar as it illustrates its indestructible dimension. One can cut R, S, or I, he says, but it holds together anyway. Let us however note that between *Les non-dupes errent* and *R.S.I.*, Lacan's construction has evolved.
- By putting R, S, and I in continuity with each other, the knotting transforms itself into diverse forms of knottings or unknottings with only one or two consistencies, with potential sinthomatic repairs occurring here too. For example, simply putting R, S, and I in continuity with one another, starting with the three-ring Borromean knot, leads to the trefoil knot which, as Lacan indicates, supports the structure of personality, which is nothing other than the paranoiac position.

These are only a few of the possible rearrangements of R, S, and I, among many others indicated by Lacan in the Seminars which follow Joyce, *Le sinthome*.

These remarks lead logically to some questions on the different orders of causality for the failure which they suggest, and on the distinction between what is the cause and what is the agent of this failure.

Indeed, the three- or four-ring Borromean knotting may fail:

- because one of the registers no longer holds and lets go, ruptures, or becomes inconsistent (which can be the case for R, S, I or the fourth element). This is how Lacan puts it in *Les non-dupes errent*, concerning the way in which the Symbolic comes undone when the psychotic subject encounters the deficiency of the Symbolic, with the call for the foreclosed signifier;

- because some "errors," which are effects of the paternal deficiency, of the paternal failure, were produced in the constitution of the knotting itself. This is what Lacan evokes concerning Joyce;
- finally, because there is confusion, lack of distinction between the registers R, S, and I; in other words there is a putting in continuity, an homogenization of two—or of the three—consistencies.

All this, of course, presents us with a great many questions concerning the clinic, and requires that we specify in each case how clinical phenomena account for these modes of failure.

Lastly, let us note that these modes of failure also signpost the possible modes of repair, of sticking back together, of rearranging things. Logically indeed, we must draw the consequence from this topology of knots to which Lacan leads us, and grasp that what operates has to do precisely with the tools of "practical topology."

- scissors, which effect the cut;
- glue, which performs a sticking back together, suture, and putting in continuity;
- thread, which, as consistency, allows for supplementation by means of a fourth element, and the local repair of the "error" through the *sinthome*.

All these operations can contribute to supplementing the failed reference, namely the three-ring Borromean knot.

They are produced by the subject:

- as symptom—supplementation, fourth consistency of the knot—by the neurotic subject;

- as *sinthome*, as constructed by Joyce;
- as suture and putting in continuity: this is, for example, the paranoiac solution;
- as delusional metaphor which, broadly speaking constitutes, in psychosis, an attempt at localizing *jouissance*, at instituting a supplementation in the place of the faltering supplementation of the Name-of-the-Father; like the symptom, it is on the side of the letter, a literal metaphor which condenses *jouissance*.

It is also there that the analyst operates with his or her act:

- through interpretation, which operates a cut, and through scansion;
- through interpretation insofar as it bears on equivocation and puts the function of the hole into play through the Möbien structure;
- through the symbolic act, which can operate either as suture or as supplementation;
- through the construction, the grafting—more or less forced —that he/she can institute (that is what Melanie Klein did with Little Dick, for example).

Cut, sticking back together, supplementation, these are the topological interventions operated by the analyst—with his act— but also realized by the subject by way of his or her "know-how" (savoir faire) with the signifier. And we can illustrate this with what Lacan brought us, around these three terms: symptom, *sinthome*, Symbolic graft.

THE SYMPTOM AS NOMINATION OF THE SYMBOLIC

In the topology of the Borromean knot as developed from *R.S.I.* onwards, let us only recall that Lacan evidences the symptom as fourth ring, as a supplementation to the function of the Father, as one of the Names of the Father which are necessary to remedy the structural failing of the Other, and to effect the knotting of R, S, and I.

This four-ring knot, and Lacan emphasizes this in his Seminar on Joyce, indicates a kind of inflection, or renewal of the status of the Symbolic itself.

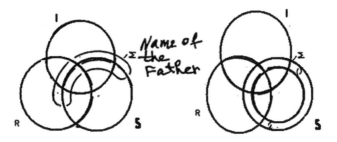

Figure 11–4.

The ring of the Symbolic is replaced by a binary, S + Σ. "The fourth element is what the symptom realises, insofar as it makes a circle with the unconscious. [. . .] It makes a circle, S + Σ: this is what makes a new kind of S," Lacan specifies in 1975 in his conferences in the United States.[4] This binary corresponds to the two sides of the Symbolic: the signifier insofar as it is able to couple itself with another to make a chain, and the letter. In other words, and as proposed by J.-A. Miller, it corresponds to the two functions applicable to the One of the signifier: the function of representation and the function of symptom. We can recognize here what Lacan evokes in *L'étourdit* regarding "these two *dit-mensions* [*dimensions of speech*] of the foranyman [*pourtouthomme*], that of the discourse thanks to which he foreveryones himself [*il se pourtoute*], and that of the places from which it mans itself [*ça se thomme*]."

On the one hand then, there is what pertains to the signifier insofar as it is articulated with another; in other words, what pertains to the structure of language, the unconscious and discourse, what is dialecticizable and can be elaborated in a knowledge. On the other hand, there is what pertains to the S_1 all-alone, from the letter insofar as it condenses *jouissance*, from *lalangue* as a vehicle of this *jouissance*: it is the non-dialectical, the symptom insofar as it is not analyzable; to put it another way, it is the symptom as Real.

By identifying with his symptom, the subject constitutes himself as a response of the Real. The symptom, as Real, is a supplementation.

In psychosis, unlike neurosis, in which they are opposed, the effect of sense disappears in enjoyed sense [*sens joui*], which is indexed by the Other. *Jouissance* is identified with the place of the Other, of an Other that enjoys. This is what the phenomenology of psychosis attests to.

The symptom is what co-ordinates *jouissance* and sense: this holds for both neurosis and psychosis.

In this respect, the delusional construction, taken as a psychotic symptom, is what allows one to master *jouissance*, to tame it, by separating it from the signifying chain that it invades in order to localize it, stabilize it in the delusion as symptom. It condenses it as writing, as letter which as such is non-analyzable insofar as it is a reject of the unconscious. If in neurosis the symptom as supplementation comes to complement the unconscious and constitutes the necessary supplement to the flawed Other by attesting to a fixation of *jouissance*, in psychosis, the symptom as contingent comes to separate *jouissance* from the Other, the gaping fault of which had caused *jouissance* to rush in, in a massive rejection of the unconscious.

As such, if psychosis is pure symptom, the delusional metaphor as psychotic symptom, as supplementation—albeit a contingent supplementation—comes to condense this rejection of the unconscious by localizing it.

JOYCE AND THE *SINTHOME*

Let us examine, apropos of Joyce, the way in which Lacan situates and constructs a clinical observation on the knot. It is one of the completely illuminating examples Lacan gives us of what the articulation of topology with the clinic can amount to in the analytic experience.

Lacan tells us that the *sinthome* comes to repair the fault, the slip of the knot, of the knotting of R, S, and I, at the very point of its occurrence. Lacan shows it to us on the knot in relation to the episode, taken as a clinical fragment, of the thrashing received by Joyce in which he has occasion to feel a kind of detachment from his own body, which seems to him to fall from him like the peel of a ripe fruit. In this effect of the dropping of the relation to the body itself, which is set adrift in this letting-drop, Lacan invites us to recognize the slipping of the Imaginary which does not hold, owing to a fault in the knotting.[5]

It is from then on possible to localize, to circumscribe this fault on the knot of R, S, and I, and it is there, at the point at which it occurred, that Lacan situates—this is how he formulates things in the case of Joyce—the ego as *sinthome*, as corrective repair.

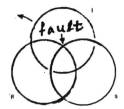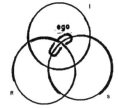

Figure 11–5.

Here, the ego designates what is constituted through the arti-fice, the art of Joyce, which produces an enigmatic writing, which undoes language, and which, as Lacan tells us, constitutes a pure symptom "which Joyce succeeds in raising to the power of language without for all that any of it being analysable."[6]

This ego as *sinthome*, as supplementation, restores a second link between the Symbolic and the Real, and makes the Imaginary hold. But this minimal fashion of repairing the fault, of making R, S, and I hold together, retains the memory, the trace, of the initial fault: R and S remain entwined, and the epiphanies are the mark of this in Joyce's work.

THE NOMINATION OF THE REAL AS SYMBOLIC GRAFT: MELANIE KLEIN'S CASE OF LITTLE DICK

How could we grasp something of what this other form of the Name-of-the-Father would be as nomination of the Real—namely as anxiety—coming to supplement the ring R and realize the Borromean knotting with I and S?

Let us try to approach this question by relying on Melanie Klein's case of Little Dick. She published this famous case in 1930, in an article entitled "The Importance of Symbol-Formation in the Development of the Ego,"[7] and Lacan referred to this case, extensively re-articulating it in his *Seminar I: Freud's Papers on Technique*, in 1953, at the beginning of his teaching.

When Dick, who is four, comes to see Klein, he lives wholly in an undifferentiated world and, unlike neurotic children, he manifests no anxiety: everything is equally real to him, equally indifferent: he lives in the Real, and in a non-anxiogenic manner. He is a child who does not respond, and who addresses no call. He does not have access to the Other, he does not have access to human reality.

However for Dick, the Real, Symbolic, and Imaginary are there, perceptible, just beneath the surface, notes Lacan. Dick is in the Real, but Klein's speech, in the Symbolic, will be able to operate and the objects, in the Imaginary, are already constituted; there is the beginning of an imaginification of the exterior world.

But Real, Symbolic, and Imaginary cannot interact with one another. They are lacking a common measure. "The whole problem is that of the conjunction of the symbolic and the imaginary in the constitution of the real," says Lacan—the Real is here to be understood as reality. That this conjunction should fail to occur is to be attributed to a fault in the situation of the subject insofar as it "is essentially characterised by its place in the symbolic world, in other words in the world of speech" (*Seminar I*, p. 80).

Lacan illustrates the mechanism of this conjunction in *Seminar I* with Bouasse's experiment, known as the experiment of the inverted bouquet. This optical experiment shows how Real and Imaginary objects can be conjoined, be included in one other, and that this works both ways. Lacan indicates that this experiment is a new presentification of the mirror stage: the image of the body, if we locate it in our schema, is like the Imaginary vase which contains the bouquet of Real flowers. That's how we can portray for ourselves the subject of the time before the birth of the ego, and the appearance of the latter (*Seminar I*, p. 79).

For Dick, this free play, the conjunction between the different forms of objects, Imaginary and Real, is what does not occur: the bouquet and the vase cannot be there at the same time. For Dick, the Real and the Imaginary are equivalent (p. 84). And that, Lacan tells us, is because the subject is not in the right place in the Symbolic. The coupling of language and the Imaginary has not taken place, namely, that which would allow Dick to enter into a system of equivalence where objects would be substituted for one another, in other words, in the process of symbolization, in the signifying chain. This is what will allow for Klein's intervention.

But let us return to the point of departure for Dick.

He lacks the signifying chain, S_2. Alienation—the choice of the Other, of speech—has not taken place. Dick only has at his disposal "an anticipated, fixed symbolisation," says Lacan, "with a single and unique primary identification with the following names, the void, the dark"—the body of his mother as container. "This gap is precisely what is human in the structure peculiar to the subject" (p. 69).

To say it otherwise, Dick remains fixated, petrified, under this primary S_1.[8] In this position indeed, he can spare himself the cost of anguish, of the anxiety which arises with "every new re-identification of the subject" (*Seminar I*, p. 69), an anxiety which, Lacan specifies, as loss of the subject in the signifying interval, as a signal of this loss, can be found at some extremely primitive levels. But Dick does not lose anything in the signifying chain; he fixes his being as subject in this S_1 of the primordial identification. What has not taken place for him is precisely the fall of this S_1, that is to say, primal repression. Freud indicates this in *Inhibition, Symptom, Anxiety*: it is anxiety which produces repression. Anxiety is the cause of repression. Dick's lack of such anxiety is precisely what Klein notes from the outset. This is her starting point, and she articulates for us, in three points, what guides her action as therapist in this treatment. Firstly, what is at stake for her is to access the unconscious of the subject—we would rather say that there is no trace of the unconscious in him, and that she intervenes on his structure; then, to arouse the child's anxiety by attenuating its latent form, by unknotting it through interpretation; finally, to elaborate this anxiety so as to allow for the development of symbolization.

In other words, the anxiety thereby produced is necessary for repression, for the fall of the S_1 under which the subject was petrified, and correlatively alienation, namely the choice of the Other, can take place. Anxiety is strictly correlative with this advent of the subject in the Other, an operation which stages the Other as barred and produces a remainder, the object a.

Thus, faced with this child who manifests no interest for the toys she shows him, as early as the first session, Klein immediately intervenes, on the basis of ideas she already has : "I took a big train that I placed beside a smaller train and I called them 'Daddy-train' and 'Dick train.'" On the spot, he took the train I had called 'Dick,' made it roll over to the window and said 'Station.' I explained to him that 'the station is Mummy; Dick is going into Mummy.'"

From then on, everything unfolds for Dick, and as early as the end of the first session, he formulates a call. Through her speech, Klein forces the Symbolic onto him, and precisely in the form of the oedipal myth. She appends the bare core of a myth to him, that is to say, a symbolization of the Real. Through this graft of oedipal symbolization, "she literally gives names to what doubtless does indeed partake in the symbol, since it can be named immediately, but which was, up to that moment, for this subject, just reality pure and simple," says Lacan (*Seminar I*, p. 69).

Could we not see here, under this form of the Oedipus, of the oedipal myth, this nomination of the Real that Lacan designates for us as one of the Names of the Father: anxiety as supplementation, as nomination of a Real, makes a hole in the undifferentiated Real in which Dick lives, through the appending of oedipal symbolization, as primary nomination, to the ring of the Real.

Ultimately, this is the form of the four-ring knot as introduced by Lacan in R.S.I. on the 14th of January 1975 in order to show the function of the Oedipus complex for Freud as the necessary fourth for the knotting of R, S, and I.

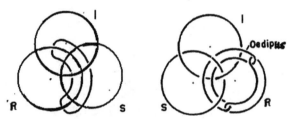

Figure 11–6.

We have seen that the symptom as supplementation can, as letter, come to complement the Symbolic on the Real side of the signifier.

Here, oedipal symbolization as fourth, as Symbolic hold on the Real, is "the one which gives us anxiety, which is the sole, definitive apprehension, and as such very real."[9] It complements the Real and introduces a degree of equivalence between R, S, and I, namely it is constituted as a mode of defense against what is unbearable of the Real. The advent of the subject in the Other is henceforth possible, and Dick can formulate a call, produce an S_2.

Klein's speech is operative; it touches the very structure of the subject, at the precise point where this subject was accessible to this intervention. The Symbolic graft amounts to a supplementation; Dick accedes to the signifying chain.

However, does this particular mode of birth of the subject to the signifier, a birth forcibly induced by Klein, carry the same consequences as the mythical time in which the subject, in the Other where "it" (*ça*) speaks of him, recognizes himself under an S_1, an insignia, a letter, and as such the repository of the function of the symptom which is then, as nomination of the Symbolic, a Name-of-the-Father in its place as fourth?

In the register of oedipal symbolization as supplementation, let us note here that, in the case of Dick, this supplementation pertains to the contingent—for him, it ceases not writing itself—and, by enabling access to the Other, it includes an effect of emptying-out, of separation from *jouissance*. In this respect, the paternal metaphor singularly resembles the delusional metaphor. This is what J.-A. Miller reminded us in 1979 at the *Journées* on psychoses.[10]

To conclude this attempt at presenting some clinical articulations on the basis of topology, and especially on the basis of the Borromean knot, I will make three remarks.

- Borromean topology—in which one can situate around the object *a* the places of mythical sexual *jouissance*, which is forbidden as such to the speaking being, of phallic *jouissance*, and of "enjoyed-sense" (*sens-joui*)—accounts for the very structure of the analytic experience as a process of emptying-out of *jouissance* and of localization of its remainder insofar as what takes place there is the condensation, the close circumscription of the object *a* as non-analyzable remainder, as left-over of *jouissance*, as letter, its isolation as the very cause of the subject.
- These examples have allowed us to perceive the extent to which Lacan's advance, which takes its bearings on Ø and relies on the topology of the knots, brings neurosis and psychosis closer to each other—at least with respect to the function of supplementation as correlative to the generalization of foreclosure as structural—while maintaining the radicality

of what separates them. It thus announces an entirely new differential clinic, and one which remains to be constructed: a clinic of supplementation indexed on the Borromean knot.

• Finally, and to finish, let us recall the terms in which Lacan formulates the fundamentally topological character of the analytic experience in *L'étourdit*: "A topology is necessitated because the real only returns to it from the discourse of analysis, which confirms this discourse, and because it is from the gap that this discourse opens by virtue of its closing upon itself beyond other discourses, that the real derives its ex-sistence."

ENDNOTES

1. Jacques Lacan, "*La question préliminaire à tout traitement possible de la psychose*," *Ecrits*, Paris: Seuil, 1966, p. 582; "On a Question Preliminary to Any Possible Treatment of Psychosis" (1957–1958), *Ecrits: A Selection*, trans. by Alan Sheridan, New York: W. W. Norton, 1977.

2. Jacques-Alain Miller, *Cours* 1985–1986, *Extimité*, unpublished.

3. Jacques Lacan, *Séminaire XXII, 1974–1975, R. S. I.*, unpublished.

4. Jacques Lacan, "*Conférences et entretiens dans des universités Nord-Américaines*," *Scilicet*, no. 6/7, Paris: Seuil, 1976, pp. 40–58.

5. Jacques Lacan, *Séminaire XXIII, 1975–1976, Le Sinthome* (May 11, 1986), unpublished.

6. Jacques Lacan, "*Joyce le symptôme I*" (June 16, 1975), *Joyce avec Lacan*, ed. by Jacques Aubert, Paris: Navarin, 1987.

7. Melanie Klein, "*L'importance de la formation du symbolique dans le développement du moi*" (1930), *Essais de Psychanalyse*, Paris: Payot, 1968; *Love, Guilt and Reparation 1921–45*, vol. I, intro. by R. E. Money-Kyrle, London: The Hogarth Press and The Institute of Psychoanalysis, 1975.

8. Jacques Lacan, "*Position de l'inconscient*," *Ecrits*, Paris: Seuil, 1966, p. 841; "Position of the Unconscious" (1964), trans by Bruce Fink, *Reading Seminar XI: Lacan's Four Fundamental Concepts of Psychoanalysis*, ed. by R. Feldstein, B. Fink, and M. Jaanus, Albany, NY: SUNY Press, 1995, pp. 259–282.

9. Jacques Lacan, *Séminaire X, 1962–1963, L'Angoisse* (July 3, 1963), unpublished.

10. Jacques-Alain Miller, "*Supplément topologique à la 'Question préliminaire,'*" *Lettres de l'Ecole*, no. 27, 1979.

12

The Square of the Subject*

JEAN-PAUL GILSON

> An "exemplary" decision of the matriarchal bourgeoisie (cf., P. Legendre) which rules the courts in Belgium, forbids me from circulating freely in Europe. We all know that the Name-of-the Father is unconscious and that its figure only takes on consistency when it is scorned; that is to say, "humiliated." I propose to you in the following, the testimony of what, like the guard, I do not surrender. He dies, one says, but does not give way. Does one not find there the law of the paternal function?

From *Seminar IV* on, some little designs [as listed below] begin to come to life in Lacan's Seminar.[1]

Some triangles, some arcs of circles, some right angles cross over each other and recross themselves in the manner of a web that weaves itself locally without our being able to grasp what it is about, neither the stakes of the affair, nor even the profession which weaves it. Some tetrades arise as well that support Lacan's discourse.

The necessity of Writing is patent; its surplus value on this simple thought is indisputable! It would be false to believe that there is any didactic worry at the origin of this topology which is in the process of being born and which links together the former intuitions of Lacan from the time of his discovery of the mirror stage.[2]

Four points of anchoring seem necessary in order that the subject become manifest. Lacan gave them the name of anchoring points as early as his Seminar on the psychoses.[3]

---

*Translated by Ellie Ragland.

Freud himself, in a little article entitled "Formulations on the Two Principles of Mental Functioning,"[4] let it be known that these two principles must in some way combine with a libidinal dyad constituting a quadrillage whose writing we have proposed in *L'Ecriture* around 20 years ago and reported in our book on Lacan's topology.[5]

Basically, let us write "to love and to work" (*lieben und arbeiten*), the two fields of human activity with which psychoanalysis concerns itself in the words of Freud. These are mixed in a series of overdetermined point-squares, waiting for a cut to restore their proper field to them, submitted as they are to the *drives of the ego and to the sexual drives*. These last are themselves intricated in the language which weaves them like a cloth. But one could equally make them depend more or less on pleasure or on reality.[6]

We could make an image of the thing as a matrix doubled between them.

It would be a question, then, of conceiving the intrication of these four vectors of which one immediately measures the elective convergences since the sexual drive and the pleasure principle are made to go together, as well as the life drive and the principle of reality. It leaps to your attention that this duality doubled twice over can form an elementary network and install the guideposts of the "four nodal points," as Freud called them. These four points meet each other on more than one occasion in the work of Lacan, beginning with the essential crossings of his graph.

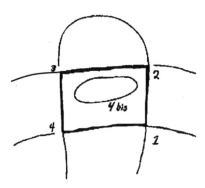

Figure 12–1.

We know that more than once Lacan explained the point to which it was necessary in order to found subjectivity on the presence of this quadripode, here identified at the meeting of the Other of language A in 1; of the dependence of the subject on demand ($ ◊ D) in 2; on the non-response of the Other, S (A) in 3; to the return that differs from the meaning; finally S(A), in 4, and made different under the curious, Imaginary form of the fantasy ($ ◊ a), in 4, repeated.

It is not unthinkable to link up this quadripode on the function of the names of the father, that is to say, to make these equal to each one of the nodal points.

It ought not to be impossible, however it is done, to admit the superimposition of the graph and of the network constituted there starting with these two principles of psychic life.[7]

Let us identify the pleasure principle with the unconscious discursive function about which one knows that Freud will never forget to link it to the primary processes of pleasure (line 3-2).

The second parallel will be the one of the Symbolic discourse thanks to which reality clothes itself (line 2-1). These two parallel curves are found hooked by the reversive buckle of the drive which makes a turn around its object without maintaining a link.

Before its possible refusal, the life drive or eros is in its ascending curve under the form of this demand made to the Other; it raises the aforementioned demand to the status of desire by which everyone can measure the link with the sexual drive.

We remain Freudian in our commentary in this sense, that Freud's text indicates that it is necessary to think of a progressive disengagement of the two drives (p. 139)—the pleasure principle and the reality principle—and even of a distinct succession of the two principles (pp. 136–137) starting at a confused time.

It seems indeed that a similar view joins the elementary production of these first moments of Lacanian topology: that of responding to the Freudian view itself which was to encircle the loss of perceptible reality as much in psychosis as in neurosis.

Let us propose, then, that in the graph, if Lacan tried to describe this problem raised by Freud by tracing a first vector which connects the ego to his ideal, it is in the buckling of the graph as such and under the terms of subjective realization that we best retrieve, in the French formulation used by Freud in the text already cited, loss "of the function of the real," and not of reality (*Realität*), and even less of *Wirklichkeit* (effectivity).

At the point that we could Write, it will be by anticipating that our point of fall will be nodal, which with its egoistic vector of satisfaction, clones a homology in the unconscious field under the form of the plane of the fantasy. We could just as well link the two together.

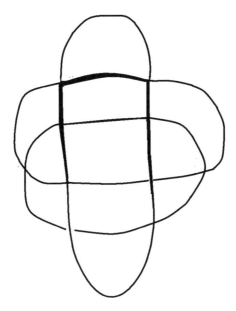

Figure 12–2.

Let us stop for an instant on this point.

It is possible even here to introduce a first reflection concerning the status of Writing since that is, indeed, the theme of our debate in this conference. The mental operation of thought which, for some years now pushes me to superimpose the Freudian text on the Lacanian text, is itself induced by the fact that these two discourses are before anything else *Ecrits*. Or, on the contrary, is it Writing their proposals that makes the structure of a Real surge forth, a temporary Real, but, however, one not perceived until then? Nor is it certain, furthermore, that the conceptual dimension of the thought is sufficient to produce a similar Writing even if it contains the germs of it. It is possible that without a resolved operation of formalization, however rudimentary it may be, we would not be able to perceive the very curious harpooning of reality by the mental. Let us agree, then, in order to silence the critics who say that the Real, for its part, will surge forth only in the margins of this encounter, precisely by structural stubbornness.

Still, we must give ourselves over to this act of Writing and not take it as being acquired in advance. This is what our friend Pierre Souris never ceased reminding us of. This fact of Writing is an act that one will act upon as he or she must.

The dimension of Writing does not limit itself to a simple representivity of verbal language or of thought. There are several different layers of Writing: indeed, differential, planary, nodal, virtual, and ternary.

One will remember that Lacan himself in "The Purloined Letter"[8] presented the effects of a Writing composed of a triple coding, thanks to which he isolated the silent sequence of a subjective pulsation, presented otherwise in the apology of the three prisoners[9] by the three temporalities of the instance (of seeing), of the time (for understanding), and of the moment (of concluding). He would just as well have been able to speak of this Writing projected by the forms of white and black disks on the backs of the alleged prisoners.

Would one, with this Writing, have been able to think they exist from this sophism?

By bringing together in the multiple writings of Lacan the underlying theses that one calls the function of the signifier, I have been able to orient a double movement of thought often hidden by the fact that the usage of the word in analysis seems to give a presence to the verbal and spoken order of the just mentioned signifier. There is nothing of that, however, since the definition of the material reconstructed and become Lacanian has permitted me to isolate an astonishing sequence and on which psychoanalysts depend very little, preferring the non-definition-boat of the "it is what represents a subject for another signifier."[10] I am going to deliver it without delaying further:

The mark of a trace erased in order to deceive the Other is regained by the subject under the form of knowledge.

Robinson [Crusoe] now and always!

The trace: These are not the steps of the savage, like those of the gazelle on the rock, still invisible to the eyes of the money changer. It is first—primordial—and makes a break into the smoothness of the wet sand from which the sea has just withdrawn, a fracture of the Written in what is washing itself. It is the unspeakable ditch which will Eroticize forever in that place the enamored gaze of the lover.

Effacing, then, in order not to give to the pirates who are disembarking on this isle which serves them as a hideout from awakening the living who are hidden there and threaten their intimacy of mysterious and secret withdrawal.

The Other suppresses by evil, as it pleased Daniel Defoe to write about it there.

It is only here that truth enters into the dance under the form of this deception which lets it be heard that a danger flies around them which their existence of living would manifest too much: what we call the enjoyment of life.

Suddenly, the subject returns to his camp and writes on the calendar that he prepares himself as a temporal reference point for the one there: Friday, let the knowledge of this trace of a mark be erased.

Ought one to think that the hysteric goes backwards on this path which leads the little man [of the phallic signifier] from the mark to knowledge, and that the hysteric deconstructs the knowledge of the master which always reigns as that of the signifier in order to recall the exquisite or traumatizing originary mark? Would that not give a meaning to the stigmata and other conversions? Is it the hysterics who gave Freud the idea of a double inscription, the one of a pure passage, and the other of the memory trace of the signifier?

Is it with the mark that we Write or with the trace of erasure, as Lacan seems to indicate by his multiple erasures?

In a certain manner, Writing seems to result from the mark which must conjure a greater danger than anything else, that of existing and that we must hide by the effacement whose cursive would be the illumination of it.

What about it, then, that Lacan's topology is a Writing?

At the very least, yes!

Mark of an erased trace, trace of the subject which fades away when the *jouissance* of the living makes a break in the heart of Symbolic repetition, as well as in the virtuality of the Imaginary, or in the inertia of the Real.

One will remember that precisely in the middle of his twisting Writings, Lacan inscribes his signature (just as Duchamp did with the Havanas he distributed at a reception in New York before elevating them to the rank of the evanescence of the readymade by asking each one there to smoke them before leaving!!!).

Lacan's knot, he said, himself of himself.

It is a little as if at the limit of a Writing, here made of knots, he placed his signature. On what? On what the trajectory, become nodal, subjectively signs of what one must hear by subjective realization of the manner of Lacan.

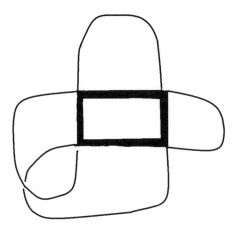

Figure 12–3.

One can read there, as much as in our preceding graphs which are traced from this third one, the central rectangle and the reversive buckle of the graph of desire.

The subjective realization is constituted by the joining together of the vectors of the first graph by this buckle which then neither closes itself nor exhausts itself in a circularity that Lacan called the circuit of the fantasy.

According to the reading that I propose, the knot proposed here by Lacan as the knot of himself, the knot of Lacan, would succeed in producing the Writing of the Freudian endeavor rewritten by Lacan.

It appears evident to me that the knot as such, by its passages over-under, but also by its well turned out nodal form, realizes as knowledge what the Writing as signifier represents for any speaking being, the mark of an effaced trace.

We could even pursue the parallel commentary by making one note how much the inhibition to Write and the tedium of reading are the results of this interdiction by which the subject starts a deception in the direction of the Other, what Lacan called, not resistance, but defense of the subject.

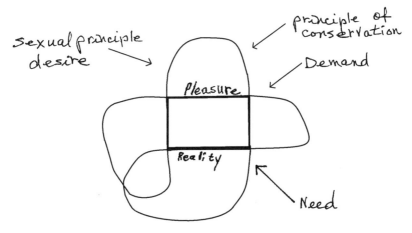

Figure 12–4. The Operation of Continuity, of the One at the Beginning of Two Signifying Pairs that the Writing Knots.

CONCLUSIONS

Here, then, are some reflections on these problems of Writings insofar as they are found condensed in this quadrature of circles knotted in a Borromean way in our design. This is a quadrature that a tetradic presentation has been able to show us differently.

From Freud to Lacan, a Writing is proposed to us just beneath the surface of the discourses which psychoanalysis carries. Certainly this Writing can appear to us as not necessary since it is outside the game of the Writings of contracts which take place with horse traders on the fields of animal fairs. A non-Written law matched by a striking of hands is worth a contract here.

It must have been the same in ancient Chinese before the piles of the shells of tortoises attest to the marks of the first contracts between humans. It is slightly probable that these Writings assured a supplementary guarantee to the status of truth that inaugurates the word in human dialogue, at least of conceiving of the Writing as a copious gift offered to the deceiving gods in order to guarantee the link of a desire and of reality. Here is a little story to illustrate this.

During the years when Lacan supervised my treatment of patients, I had the habit of taking the evening meal offered to passengers in the train returning to Brussels. This was an occasion of multiple and surprising encounters. In the course of one of them, sitting opposite the stranger who shared my table by chance, the conversation focused on the Chinese language, of which I possess some rudiments. My companion was a former ambassador of Belgium to the Far East. He made me understand both the vivacity and the extraordinary subtlety of the Chinese people.

Then he recounted to me that when a Vietnamese businessman wanted to handle a money deal in Hong Kong, it was sometimes difficult for him to furnish himself with the necessary money in local currency in order to carry out his transaction, and a certain number of political and monetary obstacles seemed to render this adventure very dangerous. He also dealt with one of the country's

banks where he had complete credit for obtaining, once the destination was known, the necessary sums and for doing his transac-
tions. In any case, it was not a question of withdrawing bills; checks
were valid there, letters of credit, and even a simple piece of newspaper torn off the daily local paper and on which an exchange agent
had written the address of his Chinese correspondent in Hong
Kong. One imagines the incredulity of our businessman who, nevertheless, could verify each time the efficacity of the system in this
matter. Because once he arrived at the place, after having held out
his piece of newspaper-receipt, he had the surprise of seeing the
employee take out of a drawer the original daily paper, torn from
the part that could now complete it.

By what mystery had this daily newspaper managed to arrive at the destination before the mandate? No one will know,
but this fact guaranteed the transaction. Thus, redoubling the
manuscript inscription that carried the receipt-piece was a sort
of rudimentary proof of the solubility of the asker; a parallel circuit existed that literally accredited the bearer of the bill, a little
like the signature of the governor of the central bank guarantee-
ing the value of a fiduciary coin or a bill of the bank. Here's the
point: it is hardly an everyday custom to tear banknotes to obtain their guarantee. This is a variation on the tessera of the Greeks
that will say the letters; good faith finds itself founded on the
single regluing together of the separated pieces of the piece initially broken in two.

This anecdote overflows widely into the economic and human
cadre for which it was told to me. There was a follow-up: Because,
wanting to know the name and address of his railroad interlocutor (that is to say, myself), my ambassador diner placed my name
and address in the guise of a visiting card, once again, Writings
on a piece of the day's newspaper, thanks to which I planned to
occupy my thoughts on the long return trip to Brussels. If our
man, like the moneychanger of Hong Kong, knows how to decipher what returns to him as a signifier, in a calculated irony, he
will certainly have recognized, slipped into the front page of a

book by Simon Leys that I had sent to him some days later so that he would know the origin of my interest in China, is the piece of the journal that he had dog-eared himself and torn off in order to write my name there. Will he know how to follow the inverse path and remount to the patronymic of the subject which was revealed in this somewhat twisted adventure? I will never know, but I wager that, decoded, this lesson is valued for him even more than a "true cheese" (even were it the one which he took for dessert) and which now demands his reading and his intelligence in following the lines.

And moreover, by *the gratuitous act* of causing him to receive the authentification of my interest, under the cover of Simon Leys, could he really modify the deal here and satisfy his suspicion, which weighed on my quality as psychoanalyst, from the fact of what my dining companion called my appearance?

WHAT DO WE HAVE TO READ THERE IN THIS LITTLE ADVENTURE?

Very simply that the function of the word does not demand in its realization that the problem treated be necessarily crucial for humankind. Because what I underlined for my interlocutor, however pastmaster in diplomatic negotiations, was a dimension of the word which goes far beyond the downstreams of the banks, as well as the sum of information that they carry. I signaled to him that whatever he thought of it, even in this world, policed and falsely disinterested in diplomacy, the word, in some exercise where it enunciates itself, always takes itself for the object of its own aiming.

And especially given that the signified of this self-reference is what incarnates itself in an act! Which incarnates Writing.

We do not always know it, but Writers present it at each detour. And it is exactly what analytic experience shows us: how in giving themselves to us as they go along that the circles of free association deploy themselves, tightening themselves around the knot of the word, toward its possible inscription. It is this tightening which is completely specific to psychoanalysis that we must Write now.

The tear in the newspaper is the "enjoying" break of a trace which makes a meeting between the coast in the unicity of the page-beach (*page-plage*) of the everyday. It is from what every letter refreshes itself in order to find its litter as Jacques Lacan first formulated it.

Thus, a finger on a cheek can break the blissful enjoyment of the living in order to introduce there the trace of the *jouissance* of the Other. What trace of effraction is aimed at by the articulated marking that my four figures of topology actualize for your eyes? Nothing other than the entrance of the Freudian discourse on the scene of human exchanges. This shattering entrance, immediately erased, owed itself to be regained in its most biting livingness (to restore the sharp plowshare of the truth) which was called a return to Freud.

Lacan proposes to us a Writing knowledge-means-of-*jouissance* from which he pulls out not only the will not to know, nor the power of the Other, but its supreme stupid and obscurantist evil. *Scilicet*, there he disguised his point. The Other in each one does not want to know anything about it; repudiation which copulates with the *Verleugnung* and topology was put there to index it.

Accept that today I shall give you a reading of another little adventure. It is that of this little magic square that I refound in the Freudian text regarding the formulation of two principles of psychic life. It would be necessary to take up once more the entire elaboration that led Freud to retain only two times two pairs of signifiers in the analysis he attempted of the libidinal word of the principles which rule it. *Zerlegung* of the pulsional states, the concept has not really created a furor, but I like this dismantling, this binary decomposition of the drives and of the principles that rule them. This Freudian effraction in the great bric-à-brac of the living erased itself as many things and Lacan returns them to the taste of the day in his graph, called the graph of desire, where he offered to refund the unicity of subjective realization without succeeding in it otherwise than under the form of the repetitive fantasy (see the graph of desire). The same magical square is readable at the heart of this graph just as it is in the elaboration of this curious knot which is perhaps given to us to read and for those, at least, who do not want at all to be on the side of the deceived others, and who seem to realize in this quadrature of the circle that the circuit of the fantasy repeats with insistence without being able to traverse itself. Is that to say that the nodal is an analyzed version of the so-called fantasy and that this object *a* can find itself in an other position from the fact of the treatment? That of re-establishing the thread of continuity of one's life, sex, and of pleasure and reality? Rewriting the nodal here, inscribing the fantasy in the knowledge to make it with the knots? The know how to do with a Writing.

This is to ask again the question regarding the extraction of the *a* with the goal of the treatment and of its re-elaboration in the Pass, as R. Lew talked about it in Brussels in an epoch when I could still make myself heard in Europe.

I recall Shi Tao:

"All the same man would not grasp the accomplishment of it . . .[a]"

Was he speaking of our topological Writing?

"Because the supreme simplicity has disassociated itself there[a]Ö"

Was he already speaking of the Freudian *Zerlegung*

"Where the rule of the unique trait of the paint brush has established itself[a]"

My thread of unicity?

"This rule of the unique trait of the paint brush once established, the infinity of the creatures is manifested. It is why it has been said: 'My way is the one of the unity which embraces the universal.'"[a]

Still must one add Shi Tao, that men are gifted by a great wisdom for accomplishing this "gift[a] of the Heavens and not to be the one which only considers the descendants while forgetting the ancestral ascendance. There you have it as to the transmission and its style."

It is man, Buffon said.[11]

ENDNOTES

1. Jacques Lacan, *Le séminaire, Livre IV (1956–1957): La relation d'objet*, ed. by Jacques-Alain Miller, Paris: Seuil, 1994.

2. Jacques Lacan, "The Mirror Stage as Formative of the Function of the I as Revealed in Psychoanalytic Experience" (1949), *Ecrits: A Selection*, trans. and ed. by Alan Sheridan, New York: W. W. Norton, 1977, pp. 1–7.

3. Jacques Lacan, *Seminar III: The psychoses (1955–1956)*, ed. by Jacques-Alain Miller, Paris: Seuil, 1981.

4. Sigmund Freud, "Formulations on the Two Principles of Mental Functioning" (1911), *SE* 12: 215–226.

5. Jean-Paul Gilson, *La Topologie de Lacan: une articulation de la cure psychanalytique*, Cap-Saint-Ignace [Québec]: Les editions Balzac, 1994, p. 52.

6. Sigmund Freud, "Three Essays on the Theory of Sexuality" (1905 [1901]), *SE* 7: 125–245.

7. ***Résultats, idées, problèmes*—I, Paris: Presses universitaires françaises.

8. Jacques Lacan, "Seminar on 'The Purloined Letter,'" (1956 [1966]), *The Purloined Poe: Lacan, Derrida & Psychoanalytic Reading*, ed. by J. Muller and W. Richardson, Baltimore, MD: The Johns Hopkins University Press, 1988, pp. 28–76.

9. Jacques Lacan, "Logical Time and the Assertion of Anticipated Certainty" (1945), trans. by Bruce Fink and Marc Silver, *Newsletter of the Freudian Field*, vol. 2, no. 2 (Fall 1988): 4–22.

10. Jacques Lacan, "The Agency of the Letter in the Unconscious or Reason since Freud" (1957), *Ecrits: A Selection*, trans. and ed. by Alan Sheridan, New York: W. W. Norton, 1977, pp. 146–178.

11. George-Louis Buffon, comte de. *Discours sur le style* (1753). Paris: Hachette, 1843.

13

The Topology of the Subject of Law: The Nullibiquity of the Fictional Fifth

VÉRONIQUE VORUZ*

> *Lacan is, without a doubt, making use of the creationist effect [of topology] to encircle the real [of the structure], to circumscribe this structure. But he also warns us against what could become a mysticism of topology, against any fascinating effect or initiatory drift associated with it—through capture by the image, the putting into play of the imaginary of the body. Is it not precisely on this point that we may recognise the reason of the tour de force accomplished by Lacan in "L'Étourdit", a text in which he articulates his topology for us with no other support than words, in which he shows us how discourse itself is topologically articulated? What Lacan formidably demonstrates in this text (. . .) is that one can do without topology on condition that one makes use of it.*
> —Pierre Skriabine[1]

> *A writing is thus an act [un faire] which provides a support for thinking. (. . .) What remains is that the signifier, in other words what is modulated in the voice, has nothing to do with writing.*
> —Jacques Lacan[2]

I. INTRODUCTION

My purpose in this chapter is twofold: I intend, firstly, to demonstrate how Lacan's Borromean topology inscribes itself in the continuity of his teaching, and secondly, to argue that this topology may be put to many practical uses with regard to defining the parameters of an intervention in a given discursive structure—my own focus here being that of law.

My epigraphs indicate from the outset the directions to follow in order to cover each limb of the proposed itinerary. Indeed,

---

*Lecturer in Law, University of Leicester, UK.

on the one hand, Skriabine's emphasis on the intimate connection that unites discourse to topology clearly signposts the way into the study of the later Lacan; and on the other, Lacan's explicit assertion of the sheer heterogeneity of speech and writing identifies the Archimedean point to lean upon in constructing the possibility for an intervention in the *symptomatic hermeneutics* playing itself out in discourse—and this, *by taking exception to the letter* or, in other words, beyond *the fictional fifth*.

Before elucidating the complex enigma ciphered in the latter statement—for it is this statement which lends its form to this paper's central claim, namely that *one can do without the Other of Love*—each of its components must be carefully situated within the framework of the argument.

It is with this purpose in mind that we may now set out on the pathways already concisely mapped out: for in effect, to combine Skriabine's statement regarding the topological structure of discourse with Lacan's assertion of the idiosyncratic status of writing will help us to delineate the importance of Borromean topology. In turn, this combination will be used to progressively trace an inroad in Lacan's complex re-articulation of subjective structure by means of the topology of knots. And the distinct understanding of subjectivity we will have acquired will expose the artificiality of the psychical construct which supports the subject's alienation to love, and thus to its addressee, one's *particular* Other.

It is this precise construct, the *fantasy*, which accounts for the eroticization of one's relation to the law and the deleterious effects which ensue—indeed, *the law is never dead enough*.[3] And if we are to take the irrational core of the social bond into account, then we must also learn how to locate the knots of signifying *jouissance* which, in the subject's discourse, both organize the structure of his repetition and resist interpretation, for it is on this basis only that it will be possible to effectively intervene in a particular subject's mode of encountering the institution and the legal order which it incarnates.

A Clinic of Fictions

But first, let me underline that Lacan's re-articulation of the subjective structure is far from being gratuitous; it is on the contrary
crucial insofar as it supports the introduction of a clinical differential that is much more appropriate to our epoch, which is that of
the well-documented pluralization of truth. Indeed, Lacan's Borromean approach announces significantly more than a change in
representational tactics; it also formalizes a novel operational distinction for the understanding of man's being in the world, and one
that no longer relies on the Other for orientation: rather, it focuses
on the subject by taking its bearings from each subject's particular
invention—or *fiction*—for the treatment of *his* Real.

Lacan's last conceptual shift ratifies his acceptance of the ir-
retrievably solipsistic nature of the subject's truth, exposed by
the contemporary reduction of oedipal meaning to *père-version*
[turning-towards-a-version-of-the-father] and the unmediated subjection to love it entails. Indeed, oedipal love, having been progressively dissociated from the *semblant* [make-belief] of universal
truth formerly associated with the father, now shows itself under
its most stagnant facet: "The law here is simply the law of love, in
other words perversion."[4]

Thus, it is with regard to the effects for the subject of the historical transformation in the patriarchal organization of social structures[5] that Borromean topology plays a central part in Lacan's
attempt to think anew the very relevance of psychoanalysis on the
basis of such changes. Indeed, the challenging task now facing
psychoanalysis no longer resides in its potential to alleviate the
weight of repression for the subject, but in that of ridding him of
the parasite of love. And it is precisely the possibility of doing away
with the Other of love that Lacan addresses with his invention of
the Borromean knot:

> The *nœud bo* does just that: it sanctions the fact that Freud
> makes everything depend on the function of the father. The
> *nœud bo* is nothing but the translation of the fact [. . .] that love,

and even more, love one could describe as eternal—is what relates back to the function of the father, addressing him in the name of this: the father is the bearer of castration. [. . .] But I am trying to give [Freud's] intuition another body, with my *nœud bo*.[6]

Some elucidation of this mysterious statement is no doubt required as a preliminary to its utilization for our purposes. Thus, Lacan's expression, "*nœud bo*," condenses several senses, for it evokes at the same time the phallus—*nœud* is a slang term for male genitals, and *nœud bo* puns *nœud beau*, thereby hinting at the imaginary phallic identification that supports the subject—Mount Nebo— which is the mountain from which Moses contemplated the Promised Land and where he died, and lastly it stands for *nœud borroméen*. Lacan's *nœud bo*, then, both deploys the mechanism of castration, which rests on the dead father of law and the *semblant* that comes in the place of the impossibility of the sexual relation—the phallus—and purports to replace it with a *writing*.

In terms of the three registers, the dead or Freudian father introduces a Symbolic hole in the Real which is then covered over by an Imaginary *semblant*. We thus see that what makes the subject consist in language stems from the introduction of a certain complex connector between the different orders. Further, we can already begin to perceive that for Lacan, such a mode of knotting RSI is undesirable—since he proposes to substitute a writing for it—and this insofar as its corollary is a deeply rooted belief in the Other of Love.[7] The Freudian mechanism of castration—that which organizes human sexuality along the lines of oedipal logic—has been mapped by Lacan on his tables of sexuation in terms of logical propositions and will be further developed in section IV, where the relation between belief in the Other of love and the oedipal organization of sexuality should become apparent.

For now, let us circumscribe what Lacan purports to gain from his topology with respect to the subject's perennial alienation to the Other of love, or in other words to the place first indexed as such by Freud with his concept of the father. Indeed, in this quote, Lacan clearly expresses his hope that the Borromean knot will come to provide a support for the subject to be able to replace the Imaginary consistency he derives from the father as "bearer of castration" with something else, of another order: *another body*, says Lacan, since it is the *Imaginary* which is in question.

Why the Imaginary, when in this Seminar Lacan talks of the Real of the symptom? Because it is the Imaginary which "solidifies" the fragmented body of the subject, divided into part-objects by the cut of the drive, and this solidification obtains through the gaze of the loving Other. The stake for psychoanalysis thus resides in the possibility of building a new Imaginary for the subject, and this on the basis of a writing, in other words through a *use of the drive that would no longer be enslaved to the fulfillment of the fantasy*.[8]

It is concerning this precise point that knot topology becomes fundamental in Lacan's elaboration, since *the knot is to be this other body* which may free the subject from his debilitating alienation to love, an alienation which keeps him incarcerated in a fictional Panopticon, the oppressive nature of which is mistaken for "reality" and "enjoyed" by means of the fantasy: in this mental construct indeed the subject is *utterly dependent on the gaze of the Other for his identity*.

The Letter Lends Its Materiality to the Body of the Knot

What is it about the knot that allows Lacan to claim it has the status of a body, though?

At the level of analytic practice, Borromean topology responds to the necessity of anchoring an emergent clinic of fictions to something which, in language, is structurally of the Real—indeed, in view of the partial failure of this *agent of universalization* that the Oedipus is, the only alternative would be to recognize the at least clinical obsolescence of psychoanalysis.

Thus, in order to ground this new orientation of analytic theory on each subject's fiction, two elements need to be combined: the

Real and language. Indeed, the fragmenting of the oedipal Other leaves us with the Real for sole anchoring point, and yet this Real needs to be located in language in order for it to be mobilizable by the intervention of the analyst.[9]

However elusive the concept of the Real may be, we know it to be characterized by inertia, for "the real is that which always comes back to the same place."[10] The next step logically ensues: What, in language, always returns to the same *physical* place, irrespective of the meaning attributed to it, if not the *letter*? This analogy explicates how Borromean knots may provide analytic theory with the support of a *real* point of fixation in *language*: by offering *the solid body of a writing to the incorporeal breath of the signifier*: "It seems to me that I have already accounted for the fact that the Borromean knot may be written, since it is a writing, *a writing which supports a real*. This in itself already points to the following: it is not only that the real can be supported by a writing, but *that there is no other tangible idea of the real*."[11] This is why writing, the letter, now comes to the fore of the Lacanian problematic of the symptom, while meaning, the Other, are demoted to the secondary status of recruits enrolled for the fictional treatment of *jouissance*.

Furthermore, Lacan's reliance on writing entails a re-invention of the Real itself, henceforth intimately associated with *the act of writing in its materiality*, and thus bound up with language: "I have invented what can be written as the real.[. . .] I have written this real in the form of the Borromean knot."[12]

The Borromean knot is a writing, then, *a writing of the real* even. And most importantly for our purposes, it is a writing the four-ring structure of which inscribes the dispensable nature of the *Other of love*, as the latter performs a function which is in fact already fulfilled by the subject's symptom: hence my *fictional fifth*, which consists in the belief that it is the Other that knots, whereas Lacan defines the symptom as the fourth ring knotting RSI.

Bearing these major developments in mind, let us backtrack a little and retrace the steps which will have brought us to the threshold of Lacan's most radical and possibly least exploited theoretical innovation.

II. FROM THE OTHER TO THE LETTER

Writing—the letter—is in the Real, and the signifier in the Symbolic.
                                           —Jacques Lacan[13]

The title of this section names the distinctive shift in emphasis Lacan introduces psychoanalytic theory to in the last part of his teaching, in which he reduces the symptom to its bare structure: that of a *letter* coupled with a *signifier*.[14] In effect, what Lacan demonstrates in his *Seminar XXIII*, dedicated to the *writings* of James Joyce, is that the traumatic kernel of the symptom is nothing other than the S_1 taken in its twofold dimension of *mark of language on the body*—the unary trait—and its *subjectification*, which takes it *from alterity to Otherness*. It is the meaning ascribed to this primary subjectification that the subject will endlessly reproduce, and it is for this purpose that he will tirelessly construct the Other he requires as partner to his symptom.[15] This conception, which exposes the Freudian unconscious as nothing other than *a ciphering of the S_1 in the service of the* jouissance *of repetition*, indubitably calls for a radical rethinking of psychoanalysis, for it can no longer aspire to lift the bar of repression but must instead devise ways of isolating the S_1 and working with it.[16]

Let us now examine the elements of response Borromean topology brings to the theoretical turmoil such a fundamental change of orientation left in its wake.

The Topological Structure of Discourse

To begin with, it may not be superfluous to underline that topology will *not* take us to any mythical beyond of language, and if we are to follow Lacan *to the letter*, nothing ever will. On the contrary, topology's fundamental attraction lies in that it provides us with a representational support with which to grasp the mechanism of language: for topological figures are visual illustrations of the fact that discourse itself is "topologically articulated," that it is produced in the *discordant assemblage of heterogeneous registers*.

There exists however an unquestionable parallelism between the evolution in Lacan's use of topology and the major conceptual shifts traversing and reorganizing his theory of discourse. Indeed, in the first two decades of his teaching, Lacan had not yet radicalized his conception of the signifier in terms of a "parasite of *jouissance*," and he was still attempting to conceive the subject as the thwarted product of a conflict with the Other, resolving itself *in a manner of speaking*: or in the precipitation of proteiform symptomatic constructs. Such was the belief informing Lacan's erstwhile use of topology: that the *xenopathic* effect of language on the subject *was to be ascribed to its originating in the Other*.

Consequently, at this point in his teaching Lacan relies on topology in order to visualize the entanglement of the subject in the Other in terms of *positions* and *relations*. This intricate intertwining is itself conceived as finding its center of gravity in a point of *alterity*, corresponding to the residual irreducibility, or *trauma*, of the subject's particularity to dimensions of sameness and difference—*the measures of the law* characteristic of the Symbolic order.

The tripartite structure of the subject's relation to Other and object can be extrapolated from Skriabine's introduction of the topology of the "a-sphere": "In order to account for the foundational entrapment of the subject in the signifier and the primal repression correlative to this emergence of the subject, we need a topology that is no longer that of the sphere, but constructed on the basis of the structuring function of the hole, in other words a topology of the *a-sphere*."[17] Surface topology is thus brought in by Lacan in order to lend Imaginary consistency to an otherwise abstract vision of the complicated, three-dimensional structure of the subject's organization in the Symbolic: hole, Other, subject. In giving an image to the dissonant coupling of two dissymmetrical registers, self and Other, in their relation to a third term—the hole in the Symbolic in its "structuring function"—Lacan acquires a compelling visual instrument to support his challenge of the traditional inside/outside dichotomy. It also allows him to define the modus operandi pertaining to the "a-sphericality" of subjective structure in terms of demand, desire, and repetition, and to identify their respective modalities: *reading* (the signifier of demand), *interpreting* (the text of the Other), *circling* (the drive-object).

Yet, for all its clarification of the contradictory tensions the subject is host to, surface topology fails to account for the solid core of the symptom[18]—already connoted by Freud with his *character*[19]—which insists beneath what appears to be a *discontinuous heterogeneity* only kept together by the forceful and repeated imposition of a name, originating in the father but by definition *indecipherable*: for the subject, although it may be a signification, cannot be reduced to a signifier.

It is this illegibility of the name which explicates why the subject should always be trying to elicit a nomination from the Other of love, desperately wanting to believe that it would only take the Other to read his name for a precipitation of his identity to ensue. And it is this relentless demand of a *Tell me who I am?* that we can hear pulsating in each statement, in a covert plea the artful masks of which are so familiar to the analyst.[20]

From Not-Wanting-to-Know Anything about It to Self-nomination[21]

Borromean topology, on the other hand, which intervenes in Lacan's teaching after the decade he spent elaborating the structure of discourse and the propositional logic that supports speech—we will later see why—reverses a number of the previous conclusions of psychoanalysis: it is thus that it represents the subject as the instance of a *heterogeneous continuity* operating on the trace of the *unary trait*, with the latter orienting the punctuation of enunciation in its progressive *making* sense of the Real. Essentially, this conception evidences that nomination is present *ab initio* in the subject, though it is latent, and that its actualization no longer rests with a hypothetical father but is of the order of the subject's own invention, involving *a form of writing* insofar as what names the subject is not of the order of the signifier but of the *act*.

Such a radical inversion in psychoanalytic theory, which takes the emphasis away from interpretation and its corollary, the analyst as subject-supposed-to-know, to place it on the *invention* of the subject favored by the *intervention* of the analyst, resonates with the concurrent mutation in institutional discourse. Indeed, in the course of the twentieth century, the very real repression of deviant desire carried out by the organs of power, patristic and secular alike, progressively gave way to other modes of social organization. It is thus that 30 years ago, the belief in the Other sustained by mythological— to use Legendre's excellent encapsulation of the function of the father in both its *mythical* and *logical* dimensions[22]—incarnations of figures of authority was still strong enough for him to uncover convincingly the repressive strategy at play in the discourse of the institution and indict its "malevolent" purpose, the recuperation of the subject's desire through an eroticization of the relation to the Law: "The sinner, suffering from his desire, is thus invited to seek substitutes; the object of replacement *par excellence*, ideal and sublime, is Law itself, transformed into an object of love."[23] Today however, Legendre's account is no longer sufficient to describe accurately the institutional picture, infinitely complicated by the ongoing dispersal of both the means and the ends of the politics organizing the socialization of the subject.

Repression and Disavowal

To begin to map the parallel transformations occurring in the institution and in the subject, a correspondence justified by the primacy of the function of exception[24] in both social and subjective organizations, let us note that if on the one hand, the former view— that of an external *imposition* of identity dispensed against the "pound of flesh" of sexual renunciation[25]—retains something of its compelling character, on the other, the increasing dissociation of the Other of love from the place of unique truth announces the prevalence of the function of disavowal in modern subjective structures, a change *named* by Lacan when his *names-of-the-father* became *père-version*.

In order to support my claim as to the current prevalence of the function of disavowal, I will make a brief theoretical detour. Indeed, recall that Freud identified three distinct psychical mechanisms at the foundation of the three classical modalities of the unconscious: primal repression (*Urverdrängung*), which institutes the neurotic unconscious, disavowal (*Verleugnung*), which characterizes perversion, and lastly, that which Lacan renamed foreclosure (*Verwerfung*), which defines the psychotic structure.[26]

I will not study these three mechanisms here but will simply note the importance of disavowal in the psychical structure of neurosis, which is oriented by the perverse trait of the fantasy. Indeed, if disavowal is a mechanism first identified by Freud in his studies on perversion and fetishism, he later identified its subsidiary function in neurotic structures.[27]

It is the psychical operation of disavowal indeed which situates subjective division in its principle: for at the same time, the subject denies castration in the Other[28]—for to accept that the Other lacks introduces the unbearable anguish associated with being reduced to the status of object for the Other[29]—and affirms this castration in order to retain the possibility of being the object of the Other's love. It is this simultaneous denial and affirmation of castration by the neurotic subject which frames the sexual relation: indeed, to be loved by the Other, the Other must be lacking so that the subject may incarnate the phallus for him, and yet the subject must avoid being the object of the Other's *jouissance*. In other words, *the subject has to disavow castration for the sexual relation not to exist in the Real in order to then affirm it so that the sexual relation may exist in the Symbolic.* Furthermore, the sexual relation may only exist in the Symbolic by way of the mediation of this Imaginary function that the phallus is. Indeed, it is on the basis of an Imaginary identification with the phallus that he/she is for the Other that the subject will find his/her place in the sexual relation (see section IV).

If this conundrum no doubt evidences the indispensable function served by denial in the constitution of the subject, the increasing importance of disavowal is also, albeit more mundanely, attested to by the fact that since these days the Other of meaning is more lacking than a sieve; only love and its amazing delusional capacity has a power sufficient to blind the all-too-willing subject to its deficiencies.

I will return to the disturbing prevalence of the mechanism of disavowal in its supplementation of repression for the subject in my section III, after having situated more precisely the potential of the Borromean knot to replace the father and thus separate the subject from his alienation in the Other.

The Borromean Knot is a Writing That Names the Subject in Place of the Father

> The lie of the ideal has hitherto been the curse on reality.
> —Friedrich Nietzsche[30]

It is with regard to the function of the Ideal that the Borromean knot may intervene in order to free the subject from his entrapment in the double-bind of disavowal, which bars all enjoyment but that obtained through the fantasy.[31] Indeed the unary trait, the mark inflicted on the subject by the Other's castration, is disguised by the subject's Ideal identification. This Ideal identification provides the substance of a *corpus juris* to the subject's nonsensical sense of malaise, thereby allowing for motivated decisions on the alternate adjudication of love and guilt in a process that fixes the sense of what of the Real manifests itself as the superego, reduced by Lacan to its core; namely, the deathly injunction to "enjoy!"[32] As to the fantasy, it clothes such an injunction with a scenario that allows the subject to "enjoy" his submission, implemented through his "forced choice" of the meaning of the Other's lack, and that results in an inscription of its text on the subject's body, turning the latter into the *very tables of the law*—they would otherwise remain *dead letter*.

There lies the relevance of the Borromean knot, for it purports to return the perverse trait to its unary core with a view to affirming the possibility of a degree of self-identity for the subject, one that would no longer depend upon the gaze of the Other or the tyranny of the Ideal for its permanence. Let us see how Lacan proposes to do so: "The Borromean knot is not a knot but a chain with a number of properties, and in the minimal form in which I have inscribed it, at least three are required."[33] How can we understand this statement? Maybe as follows: the Borromean knot is a chain insofar as its elements are tied two by two, and it is only the intervention of a fourth term which knots the three. The fourth ring is thus a *name* that ties the knot, or again a "metaphor" of how *being*; a *body*; in *language*, are knotted by a nomination.

No doubt, the fourth ring that knots the chain is usually that identified by Lacan with his concept of the Name-of-the-Father, the signifier of exception—*which can be any signifier*.[34] Indeed, the signifier Name-of-the-Father, once pluralized by Lacan, simply refers to the oedipal structure of those symptoms organized by reference to a certain modality of the function of exception. To believe in the Name-of-the-Father, however, since it is a signifier, the *meaning* of which is located in the Other by virtue of the mechanism of disavowal briefly exposed earlier, implies eternal subjection to a truth supposedly elsewhere.

This is doubtless why Lacan devises another solution:

> I consider that having articulated the real in question in the form of a writing has the value of what is generally called a traumatism. Not that it has been my aim to traumatise anybody.[. . .] Let's say that it is the forcing of a new writing which, through metaphor, has a bearing which must certainly be termed symbolic. It is a forcing of a new kind of idea which is not of the kind that blooms spontaneously simply out of what makes sense, namely the imaginary.[35]

Lacan's use of the term "metaphor" in this context affords us two precious insights: firstly, that the metaphor of his own invention also symbolizes something of the Real, not unlike the paternal metaphor.[36] Secondly, it indicates that it does so by means of a writing: Lacan's writing of the Real in the form of a knot amounts to a *symbolization* of the discrete, three-ring chain, which as such institutes a degree of identity: the function of symbolization, indeed, is traditionally to unify a certain heterogeneity under the aegis of the signifier.

However, there stops the comparison, for as Lacan says a little later in the same session, *this real is his symptom.* He then elucidates this mysterious statement as follows: by taking Freud's "degree of symbolism to the second degree" in his writing of the Real, he demonstrates that "one can do without the Name-of-the-Father on condition that one makes use of it."[37] The latter statement, combined with the expression "second degree of symbolism," can be understood to mean that one must use one's alienation in the Symbolic and the dependency on love it entails[38] in order to reach the point at which one is finally able to recognize that there is no father that names, that one's symptom is one's only name—which, in passing, also explicates Lacan's appellation for Joyce: Joyce-the-symptom. But, and this is the crucial advance accomplished in this Seminar, *one can only make use of one's symptom as a nomination through the acceptance of the inexistence of the Other and the affirmation of the Real as impossible.* It involves a writing of sorts then, since it comes with the obligation of an invention on the basis of the only mark of the Real there is: the trait of castration, which anchors language in being.

In the light of such a radical claim, the function of the father reveals itself to reside essentially in its concealment of the Real of castration: variously, the solipsistic nature of human reality, the absence of knowledge in the Real, the structural failure of sense, or again the impossibility of the sexual relation. And Borromean topology paves the way for the formalization of the analytic clinic in the era of *père-version*, characterized by a symptomatology of disavowal in lieu of that of repression.

Since the concept of the father, tightly bound up with the function of exception of which it is the favored embodiment, is central to the analogy that grounds the claim of a psychoanalytic jurisprudence to be capable of alleviating the necessity of law—"the laws of the real world," of which Lacan says "that it's a question that remains entirely open"[39]—let us try to fathom the correspondence between such a radical revision of psychoanalysis's key tenets and the evolution in the function of law.

III. LOVE, LAW AND PSYCHOANALYSIS

> The task of the lawyer (and of his present successors in the dogmatic enterprise) lies precisely in the art of inventing reassuring words, of designating the object of love where politics situates prestige, and of manipulating the fundamental threats.
>
> —Pierre Legendre[40]

The Freudian Father and the Lacanian Symptom

Lacan's drastic reduction of the symptom to its structure demonstrates that the validity of psychoanalysis is not conditional upon the perennial immutability of its concepts—quite the contrary: for the analytic discourse is a discourse the subject-matter of which is *the product of other discourses*. To be more explicit, psychoanalysis's recognition that there is no meaning in the Real—save for that introduced there by man—requires flexibility, since the analytical discourse must both be able to identify the invariant elements of man's being in language *and* accommodate historical modifications: the latter indeed revolve around *changes of discourse*.

The reduction in question therefore resonates with the contemporaneous transformation of the institutional discourse. I am referring here to the slow discredit of traditional figures of authority which, coupled with the now irrevocable ubiquity of liberalism, inaugurated a new era for what Legendre calls the "dogmatic order." In his account, the dogmatic order is *the discourse of reason in the service of universal truth*, prevalent in European nation-states which, as we know, were deeply marked by monotheism and its pyramidal hierarchy, topped by the mytho-logical father in his lawgiver outfit—*a castrated figure bearing the mask of omnipotence*.

In effect, prior to the many crises which deeply scarred the twentieth century, institutional discourse had been operating by means of an exclusive appropriation of truth, which it then redistributed in the guise of the universal Good. More recently however, it had to exchange the ostentatious trappings of an overt if benevolent repression for the considerably less alluring attire of utilitarian pragmatism which, although still dealt out in the name of love, no longer lays convincing pretense to universal truth.

We see that such changes echo with the evolution of psychoanalytic theory: for if Freud's symptom manifested itself as a message ciphering the return of the repressed desire of the subject, the unsurprising consequence of a centralized, authoritarian social order, Lacan's latest theorization denudes the symptom of its narrative garb and presents it as *a necessary fiction*, the function of which is to operate as a supplementary device [*suppléance*] to knot RSI, exposed as such in view of the lesser purchase of reason and the consequent overcompensation on the side of a demand for love.

The Imaginary Degradation of the Ideal[41]

It may be the case that today's "father" no longer operates in the name of an a-temporal truth, adapted for good or worse to the temporal exigencies of regulating life through a complicated procedure organizing the interpretation of the fictitious commandments of an eternal justice—that instituted by natural and divine laws. But let us not, for all that, be oblivious to the fact that the need for love of the subject, although it may no longer be exhaustively absorbed through sublimation by a nation, a religion, or an ideology, is nonetheless still being recuperated. But the recuperation now in question aims to fuel the consumerist dynamics of the market and animate its circuits, those of an evermore demanding surplus-enjoyment [*plus-de-jouir*], in which judges and lawyers themselves are unwittingly drawn to play a well-orchestrated part—for if they are no longer the privileged mouthpiece of Reason, they still are the preferred make-beliefs of fatherly love: their *innocence*[42] is the guarantee that they always speak in its name.

Indeed, I would even go so far as asserting that to an extent, they are by way of becoming *the respondents of a right to juridical truth*—although in our civilizations, the demand is not so much that a timeless justice be rendered but rather consists in a request for a tailored truth, providentially in endless supply in the ever-expanding prêt-à-porter collection of legal provisions.

It is in that respect that the evolution of what I choose to call the *politics of love*, which permeates our "post-industrial" institutions just as much as it did those of our ancestors, may prove even more pernicious than the more authoritarian structures of power of yore. For one could encapsulate the shift in the status of the institutional "father" as follows: *from administrator of a monopoly on truth to addressee of a universal demand for love.*

This is the shift which I understand to be designated by the expression "the Imaginary degradation" of the Ideal. It indexes a profound modification in the structure of the contemporary social bond, one which foregrounds the importance of understanding the role of the fantasy in the subject's relation to the Other, over and above the meaning ascribed to one's place in the Symbolic.

The Imaginary degradation of the Ideal in question is to be coupled with the consequent supplementation of the failure of *any signifier* to order social structures by means of a vertical identification to the empty place of the lawgiver—that of the castrated father—and thus with the growing reliance on the horizontal dimension of identification[43] in the constitution of the social bond.[44]

The shift in analytic theory introduced by Lacan with his Borromean topology thus resonates with a much deeper mutation which traverses the field of social organization. No doubt, it is against the background of the imaginarization of the Ideal, consequent upon the weakening symbolic efficacy of repression,[45] that we must heed Lacan's warning: "Our future as common markets will be balanced by an increasingly hard-line extension of the process of segregation."[46] There is no need for me to go over Lacan's well-known developments on the nefarious effects of the Imaginary, a mode of identification which locks the subject in the dialectic of recognition, the sole outcome of which is rivalry and the consequent struggle to death that it entails.[47] I will simply note the increasingly detailed taxonomy ordering the treatment of social symptoms—such as the *DSM-IV*—and recognize the relevance of Lacan's announcement of a forthcoming culture of segregation. For when repression fails to order the social by means of transference to an ideology, utilitarianism steps in to deal with the subject on the basis of an infinitesimal normativization of his particularity, with the destructive consequences that such a labeling process entails: or the silencing of the subject's inventions.

It is with regard to the identification of such crucial modifications in the structure of the social bond that the political pertinence of psychoanalytic theory lies, insofar as such perceptions support a subject-oriented vision of the social treatment of the discontents pertaining to all civilizations.

But before concluding on the law, let us briefly examine the already mentioned logic of exception insofar as it may elucidate somewhat man's obstinate *love of subjection*.

IV. THE PROPOSITIONAL LOGIC OF EXCEPTION *OR* HOW TO MAKE THE OTHER EXIST?

> The Other, in my terminology, can thus only be the Other sex.
> —Jacques Lacan[48]

There is no Other but the Other sex. This phrase encapsulates the central postulate which orients Lacan's Seminar on love, *Encore*, and which inscribes itself as the logical corollary of his concurrent reduction of the Real to the sexual non-rapport. These two propositions, taken together, elucidate why Lacan should elect to introduce the logic of sexuation as that which structures man's relation to the Other—and thus to language. Indeed, to identify the Real as the impossibility of the sexual relation situates the whole of man's symbolic organization as a construction, the sole purpose of which is to establish a substitute for the absence of the sexual rapport.

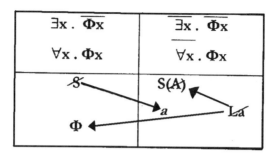

Figure 13–1. The Tables of Sexuation, Seminar XX:
March 13, 1973.

These tables show man's relation to the Other sex to be organized
by means of an Imaginary identification with the semblant of the
phallus, which modulates itself in the two auxiliary forms of *having*
and *being* under which the subject will conjugate him- or herself in
language: for *the phallus occupies in the symbolic the place of the ab-*
sent signifier of the real of the sexual non-rapport.[49]

To flesh out such a condensed account of sexuation, the terms
of its tables will now be defined during which the different facets
of the function of exception will progressively emerge.

1) *The Logic of Truth* (*top left*)

For those unfamiliar with Lacan's tables of sexuation, let me recall the classical reading of the symbols involved. Thus the first
formula

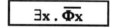

is to be read as follows: there exists one x for whom the phallic
function (Φx) is not operative, or there exists a non-castrated Other.
This is the place occupied by the Freudian father of the primal
horde, the father of unbound *jouissance.*[50]

As to the second formula,

$$\boxed{\forall \mathbf{x} \cdot \mathbf{\Phi x}}$$

it is to be read as follows: for all x the phallic function exists, namely all men are castrated. In Freudian terms, the set of "brothers" is subjected to the law of the father.

In *L'étourdit*, Lacan proposes to read the first two formulae in a much less Imaginary fashion than in the Freudian account, for indeed he sees them as formalizing respectively the *particular negative* of existence and the *universal affirmative* of truth—or to phrase it in the more familiar terms of sexuation, it is because there exists one man who is not subjected to the phallic function that all other men are subjected to it. Lacan opens his *L'étourdit* by articulating the logic which supports "male" sexuation in discourse: "That one speaks remains forgotten behind what is said in what is being heard. This statement, which appears to be an assertion since it is presented in a universal form, is in fact modal, existential as such: the subjunctive through which its subject is modulated testifies to it."[51] What Lacan accomplishes here is *the reduction of the structure of truth to the grammatical artifice that supports it*, and he does so by showing that universally affirmative propositions are conditional upon the ex-sistence of enunciation to the statement: "there is no universal proposition that does not have to contain itself by means of an existence which negates it."[52] It ensues that the place of enunciation is what will without fail give the lie to the universality of all statements, which explicates in passing why our philosophical tradition should be so attached to the pretense of "the nullibiquity" of enunciation, a nullibiquity which provides an "alibi to the discourse of the master"[53] and which is established through a process of dissimulation in the course of which the contingency of enunciation is effaced beneath the constructs of reason.

Lacan's logical reduction leads him to draw a number of illuminating consequences with regard to the functioning of discourse, which I will summarize here: firstly, since for there to be truth, it must be enunciated, truth only exists by virtue of an exception to itself, and it is this grammatical *sine qua non* which accounts for the structural indispensability of a place of exception. Secondly, the supposedly empty place of exception shows itself to be inseparable from contingent enunciation, and this exposes the semblant-value of truth. Two seemingly paradoxical observations can then be made: on the one hand, the affirmation of truth requires the willful denial of that which ex-sists to it—for the contingency of enunciation undermines truth—but on the other, without the ex-sistence of enunciation there would be no truth, since it is the particularization of the function of exception which lends Imaginary consistency to a given statement.

To clarify matters further, let us list our advances:

1) There can be no truth without ex-sistence;
2) ex-sistence cannot be effaced;
3) there can thus be no truth that does not involve a disavowal of ex-sistence; and
4) finally, and most radically, it is however this disavowed ex-sistence which affords its credibility to truth, for indeed truth needs to be libidinally cathected in order to have any substance. This though may only occur through phallicization, which is itself a *function* of the Other of love. *Belief in discursive truth, then, is a function of the phallus.*

To conclude on the logic of truth, it is worth noting that this modality of the logic of exception is an accurate description of the mechanism that attests to the *innocence of juridical enunciation* and, more generally, of all discourses deriving their legitimacy from a claim to embody the universal. Indeed the law always comes *in the name of* an Other, thereby *disavowing* the political value-choices enforced in the courts of justice, and it is this disavowal which affords law its legitimacy—that which stems from its claim to *abstract neutrality*.

2) The Logic of Speech (top right)

Again, let us begin by recalling the classical reading of the two formulae placed by Lacan on the top right of the tables. Thus the first formula postulates that there exists no x for whom the phallic function is not operative, while the second formula indicates that not-all of x is subjected to the phallic function.

In his *L'étourdit*, Lacan also recasts these formulae in terms of the logic of discourse. Indeed, the second set of formulae indicates that there exists another mode of subjective articulation in discourse, one that could be characterized as follows: "I speak, therefore it enjoys." Indeed, this is how one may read the formulae of "female" sexuation: a universal proposition in the form of a *double negative*—there is nothing that cannot be said of the phallic function[54]—and its consequence, that *not-all* of woman is exhausted by the signifier; for, if all can be said, then not-all that is said can be true. This formulation, which is not indexed on truth, does not for all that disprove the necessity of exception but designates a different modality thereof: speech indeed is a function of the exception that she *is* for the Other.

While spatial constraints prevent me from engaging further in a discussion of the logic of speech on the not-all side of sexuation, it is nonetheless worth noting that the logic of the not-all, taking its bearings as it does on the absence of truth in the Other—noted $S(\bar{A})$ on the tables—is a demonstration in action that all claims to universality can but structurally rely on a very specific exclusion: that of the particularity of the subject of enunciation. By way of consequence, it is a powerful critical tool to be used in order to reinstate the polyphony of subjective particularities.

3) The Logic of Sexuation (bottom tables)

Before all, let me recall the signification of the notations used by Lacan on the bottom half of the tables. Thus S is the barred subject, Φ refers to the phallic signifier, $S(\bar{A})$ is the signifier of the lack in the Other, the letter *a* indexes the object *a* and $\overline{La}$ represents woman as not-all subjected to the signifier.

In the previous two subsections, we studied two modalities of the function of exception, although we have seen that both are organized by means of the same element, which defines the position of the subject for the Other: the signifier of sexuation. Two different interpretations of this signifier and of the Other's castration correspond to these two modalities: the Other of truth is *incomplete*, for it lacks something which the subject *has*, and the Other of speech is *inconsistent*, for it lacks something which the subject *is*.

The second half of the tables responds to the enigma posed by Lacan's very precise formalization of the propositional logic of exception, namely: How can there be an Other sex for each sexuated position on the basis of a single signifier of sexuation? Quite simply, it implies that both sexuated positions must make a complementary use of the lack in the Other, which in turn entails a different relation to language, truth, speech, and exception for both, and thus successfully substitutes the regulated Otherness of the Other sex for the unpredictable alterity of the other.

On the "female" side, the signifier of the barred Other indexes the position "being the phallus" for the Other, or in other words that woman speaks from the position of *being* the signifier of what lacks in the Other. Then, she is "not-all" because she is not subjected to her belief in the truth of the Other; indeed, *she is the truth of the Other*. Her Other lacks on the side of the signifier so that she may *be* the phallus, and does not lack on the side of *jouissance*, so that it may not enjoy her as object. She however finds herself dependent upon an Imaginary identification with an other in the position *having the phallus* in order to also be able to *have* truth.

As to the "male" side, the Other's castration on the side of the signifier is disavowed but that on the side of *jouissance* is affirmed, which results in the subject's identifying with the position "having the phallus"; or *having the jouissance that the Other lacks*. Consequently, if man corroborates the fictional nullibiquity of enunciation, it is only insofar as to be the dupe of the signifier allows him to preserve his *having* what the Other lacks. The outcome of man's identification with the semblant of *jouissance* is the refusal of desire, for one cannot lack what one has identified with as *having*, and this leaves the "male" subject no alternative but to alleviate the solitude consequent upon such a denial through a fantasmatic relation to the Other sex on the basis of the fantasy.

We see that both sides of sexuation are equally grounded on the simultaneous disavowal and affirmation of castration which install both sexes in a similarly solitary relationship to the phallus, and that this solitude is further compounded by the correlative dependency on there being a lack in the Other.

The inevitable conclusion to be drawn from Lacan's exposition of the fictional organization of *being a body in language* by means of the phallic semblant is that it maintains both sexuated positions in an utter and absolute dependency on there being an Other that is at the same time castrated and not-castrated. And this oscillation constantly reinforces subjective division and the fragility of identity it implies, which in turn entices the subject to appeal to the "external" support offered by an identification with whichever image or signifier is prevalent of what it is to be a man or a woman.[55] Whether the Ideal identification is with an image or with a signifier will resolve itself in the prevalence of an Ideal on the side of the Imaginary or of the Symbolic, and this in passing may also cast some light on Freud's puzzled realization of the weakness of the Ideal in most women.[56]

The Importance of Sexuation for Law

It is in view of these supplementary elements that Lacan's last theoretical advances take on their full importance. Indeed, his invention of a writing of the Real amounts to a contingent nomination that *symbolizes* the sexual non-rapport for the subject, and this thereby introduces the possibility of doing without the phallus. *Sexuation* indeed is a defense against the *real of sexuality*, while on the contrary the letter is *a*-sexuated and therefore enables the subject to elaborate his *jouissance* without the mediation of the phallicized fantasy.

As to "the laws of the real world," locus par excellence of the encounter with the Other of exception, Lacan's theorization offers us the necessary support to understand that juridical enunciation can but fail for the subject, for it is taken up in the circuits of the subject's interpretation of what he or she is for the Other, and that alternative means of being with the subject of law must be devised to supplement the legal apparatus where possible; indeed, the function of the law is none other than *to keep its subjects at its door*.[57]

It is on the basis of the recognition of the subject's alienation to a phallicized fantasy, which defines him or her as the lacking term in the Other, that a number of psychoanalysts have recently engaged with the social under the aegis of an organization named CIEN.[58] Indeed, this relatively recent organization, founded in 1996, elects to take its bearings precisely on the fantasy of the subject, for it perceives the problematic nature of the institutional treatment of the social malaise: "The only way to curb *jouissance* in the particular is to operate on the fantasy on a one-by-one basis, a fantasy which resides in a relation of being-for-sex."[59] Further, this precise direction echoes with the latest and most daring inversion of psychoanalysis which will no doubt seem paradoxical to those who perceive the analytic treatment to still be aiming at restoring the subject to a less problematic sexuality;[60] for indeed, this statement also implies a recognition that being-for-sex is the seat of the subject's foremost alienation.

It is with this precious indication in mind that we can now turn to the conclusion, where I will attempt to knot the many threads of my argument into something of a useful metaphor.

V. CONCLUSION

> *The hold of the institution on the subject is assured by means of the* semblant.
> —Pierre Legendre[61]

Legendre's statement, placed as epigraph to this conclusion, is to be read against the background of the enlightening insights provided by Lacan's lucid analysis of the function of the semblant. Indeed, if Legendre's semblants are those of institutional truth, there is no doubt that they borrow their structure and draw their strength from the subject's own skewed relation to the Real and the structure of his belief in the Other.[62] One could even suggest that there exists a certain topological continuity between the structure of the institutional discourse and that of the unconscious: Are both not indexed on the function of exception?

To orient one's approach to the law on the basis of Lacan's work on the letter allows us to see through the semblants of juridical enunciation which, even when seemingly cut-to-size and however guaranteed by the procedural make-beliefs of judicial innocence, have for effect the entrapment of the subject in his belief that the truth of his being lies unread in the Other. The nefarious effect of such a blind profession of faith is remarked upon by Legendre, who states that "Law discolours the universe, from which it subtracts history; *it dispossesses any human being of the pretension of having to say something.*"[63] In other words, to insist on the desirability of "universal" solutions forecloses the subject's invention from the institutional environment.

Thus, although the weakening of repression and the prevalence of disavowal in the contemporary social bond indexes a certain decline in the symbolic efficacy of the function of exception—or sovereignty—it is not for all that that law and the institution will be able to remedy its deficiencies: "The text of law will not be able to regulate what of *jouissance* results in the indiscipline of the body, nor will it be able to deal with all that the family no longer regulates, namely the irruption of private *jouissance* in the public domain."[64] Further, beyond recognizing the inadequacy of law as universal supplementation, one must also challenge the proposed devices for the institutional containment of such irruptions, for imprisonment—or *institutionalization*—represents the reduction of the problem posed by the subject's "irruptive *jouissance*" to one of management, and as such it amounts to an utter disrespect for human particularity.[65]

Although psychoanalysis does not hold the key to the discontents of modern civilization, Lacan's last attempts at devising means to mobilize the weight of the symptom signpost a way forward which is not that of the universal. Indeed, it involves the slow exposure of the inexistence of the Other, supposed repository of truth. This path returns the difficult task of *inscribing* one's solitude in the social bond to the subject's own invention in a process that involves *taking exception to the letter*, a process which culminates in a contingent act of nomination that renders belief in the Other superfluous.

To say it otherwise, it is by reducing the fictional universality of the function of exception to its contingent core that the subject may de-eroticize his relation to the law, which could henceforth be returned to the simple truth it strives to conceal, namely, that it is an apparatus which serves a purely regulating function in the service of those in power, and that it does so with a view to perpetuating an entrenched status quo and to defusing the particular dangers potentially posed by "social deviants."

ENDNOTES

1. P. Skriabine, "Clinique et Topologie," *La Cause Freudienne* 23 (1993), pp. 117–133, at 123; or Parts I and II of *Lacan: Revue de Topologically Speaking*.

2. J. Lacan, *Le Séminaire XXIII: Le Sinthome*, May 11, 1976. It is in this Seminar that Lacan elaborates the four-ring Borromean knot and its corollary, the clinic of generalized foreclosure (on this concept, see Skriabine, *op. cit.* at 127). I would like to thank Luke Thurston for generously sharing his translation of *Le Seminaire XXIII, Le Sinthome*, which will be used in this paper, although with some modifications.

3. For an elucidation of this statement, see S. Zizek, "Beyond Discourse-analysis," in *New Reflections on the Revolution of Our Time*, E. Laclau (London: Verso, 1990).

4. J. Lacan, *Le Séminaire XXIII, loc. cit.* Lacan renames the Oedipus complex "*père-version*" to take account of the increasing importance of disavowal (traditionally associated with perversion) in the structure of modern subjectivity.

5. This patriarchal organization is exhaustively and fascinatingly mapped out and traced to its medieval roots in the very erudite work of P. Legendre, *L'amour du censeur: essai sur l'ordre dogmatique* (Paris: Seuil, collection Le champ freudien, 1974). All quotes from this book will have been translated by myself.

6. J. Lacan, *Le Séminaire XXIII, loc. cit.*

7. Note that the Other of Love is the Other of Law for the neurotic subject, for the speech of the father is that which humanizes symbolic law.

8. A possibility already hinted at by Lacan in *Seminar XI*: ". . . after the mapping of the subject in relation to the *a*, the experience of the fundamental fantasy becomes the drive." (*The Four Fundamental Concepts of Psychoanalysis*, London: Penguin, 1977, at 273).

9. I am evidently not denying the importance of the Other for the subject, quite the contrary: the analytic clinic introduced alongside Borromean topology by Lacan proposes to use the letter in order to do away with an Other whose fictional nature, if not new, is now more apparent than ever in view of its multiple failings. The main consequence of this "dereliction" of the Other is that the Other is no longer "real" enough to support an efficient treatment of the subject's *jouissance*. From the perspective of the analytic treatment, this orientation implies that the analyst will take his bearings on the subject's relation to the drive, starting from the fantasy ($ ◊ a$), rather than on the meaning of his symptom. The letter *a* in the formula on the fantasy inscribes the subject's imaginarized relation to the drive, namely the subject's relation to the drive as mediated through the locus of his fictional Other. Analysis will thus aim at the progressive reduction of this Other in a process known as the *construction of the fundamental fantasy*. J.-A. Miller, after Lacan, talks of this process as a dis-imaginarization, which he explicates as follows: "the construction of the fundamental fantasy is the same thing as its reduction to the drive" (J.-A. Miller, "The *Sinthome*, a Mixture of Symptom and Fantasy," *La Cause Freudienne* 39 (1998), 7–17, translated in *Psychoanalytical Notebooks* 5 (2001), 9–31, at 27. Information on this publication is available at: www. londonsociety.nes.org.uk).

10. J. Lacan, *Seminar XI*, *op. cit.* at 49.

11. J. Lacan, *Le Séminaire XXII: RSI*, December 14, 1974, my translation (emphasis added).

12. J. Lacan, *Le Séminaire XXIII*, *op. cit.*, April 13, 1976.

13. J. Lacan, *Le Séminaire XVIII: D'un discours qui ne serait pas du semblant*, May 12, 1971, my translation.

14. I have presented the reduction of the symptom to a letter and a signifier in a recent paper on Lacan's Seminar on Joyce, "Acephalic Litter as a Phallic Letter," in *Re-inventing the Symptom*, ed. Luke Thurston (New York & London: Other Press, 2002.)

15. In passing, this explains why the discourse of the unconscious is that of the master, with the S_1 in the position of agent.

16. See for example J.-A. Miller, "L'interprétation à l'envers," *Revue de la Cause Freudienne* 32 (1996), 9–13; translated in *Psychoanalytical Notebooks* 2 (1999), 9–16.

17. P. Skriabine, *op. cit.* at 121 French version, his italics; see pp. 73–97 in this book.

18. On the subject's mode of *jouissance* as core of his symptom, see J.-A. Miller, *L'expérience du réel dans la cure analytique*, 1999–2000.

19. S. Freud, "Some Character-Types Met With in Psychoanalytic Work" (1916), *Art and Literature* (London: Penguin Books, *PFL* vol. 14). Character, in Freud's conception, is that which insists beyond the meaning of the symptom and instinctual impulses alike (293).

20. We can think here of what J.-A. Miller has recently called the commodification of the analyst-object insofar as he has become the respondent of a right-to-sense, "Les contre-indications au traitement psychanalytique," *Mental* 5 (July 1998), 9–17, at 16; translated in *Psychoanalytical Notebooks* 4 (2000), 65–73.

21. By Lacan's own admission in the first few lines of his *Seminar XX, Encore: On Feminine Sexuality, Love and Knowledge 1972–1973*, trans. B. Fink (New York & London: Norton, 1998): "With the passage of time, I learned that I could say a little bit more about it. And then I realised that what constituted my course was a sort of 'I don't want to know anything about it,'" at 1.

22. P. Legendre, *op. cit.* at 114.

23. P. Legendre, *op. cit.* at 142.

24. I have recently dedicated an article to the function of exception and the mechanism of foreclosure with a particular focus on the case of President Schreber (D. P. Schreber, *Memoirs of My Nervous Illness,* London: Harvard University Press, 1988): "Psychosis and the Law: Legal Responsibility and Law of Symbolisation," *International Journal for the Semiotics of Law* 13–2 (2000), 133–158.

25. For a detailed historical account of the regulations of sexual pleasure, see P. Legendre, *op. cit.*, pp. 143–164.

26. See *The Seminar of Jacques Lacan, Book I, Freud's Papers on Technique 1953–1954*, trans. John Forrester, New York & London: Norton (1988). It is in this Seminar that Lacan reformulates Freud's three "founding" moments in terms of the structure of the unconscious.

27. S. Freud, "Splitting of the Ego in the Process of Defence" (1938), *Metapsychology* (London: Penguin Books, *PFL* vol. 11); *An Outline of Psychoanalysis* (1938) (London: *Standard Edition* 23), chap. VIII.

28. See S. Freud, "Fetishism" (London: Penguin Books, *PFL* vol. 7), where denial is presented as the "scotomization" of the absent maternal penis.

29. Generally on anguish, the object and the Other, see J. Lacan, Seminar X: *L'angoisse*, unpublished.

30. F. Nietzsche, *Ecce Homo*, (London: Penguin, 1992), at 4.

31. And the perverse trait, core of the fantasy, implies that the subject enjoys as if he were the Other enjoying the subject as object.

32. In his *Seminar XVIII, op. cit.*, June 16, 1971, adding that this command is "impossible to satisfy, this being at the origin of all that is being elaborated [. . .] under the term of moral conscience." J-A. Miller adds that this "Lacanian superego [. . .] is the truth of the Freudian superego," in "L'Autre qui n'existe pas et ses comités d'éthique," *op. cit.* at 14.

33. J. Lacan, *Le Séminaire XXIII, op. cit.*, April 13, 1976.

34. J. Lacan, "Joyce le symptôme," *Lacan avec Joyce*, ed. J. Aubert (Paris: Navarin, 1987), at 27.

35. *Ibid.*

36. Elaborated by Lacan in "On a Question Preliminary to Any Possible Treatment of Psychosis," *Ecrits: A Selection*, translated by Alan Sheridan (London: Routledge, 1977), 30–113.

37. J. Lacan, *Le Séminaire XXIII, op. cit.*, April 13, 1976.

38. We think here of the mechanism of transference and its reliance on love. See the conclusion of my paper on Joyce, "Acephalic Litter as a Phallic Letter," *op. cit.*

39. J. Lacan, *Le Séminaire XXIII, op. cit.*, May 11, 1976.

40. P. Legendre, *op. cit.* at 25, his emphasis.

41. I borrow this phrase, "Imaginary degradation of the Ideal," from Philip Dravers. See his article in this volume, pp. 205–246.

42. For they speak the text and not their desire. Note that this is why it is so important that the father be castrated, for there lies the only guarantee that He does not enjoy the subject but speaks for his or her good: because He loves him or her.

43. On the horizontal and vertical dimensions of identification, see S. Freud, "Group Psychology and the Analysis of the Ego" (London: Penguin Books, *PFL* 12).

44. See J.-A. Miller and E. Laurent, "L'Autre qui n'existe pas et ses comités d'éthique," *Revue de la Cause Freudienne* 35 (1997), 7–20.

45. Indexed by Lacan when he notes "the convergence of psychoanalysis with the dereliction of the antique bond through which pollution is contained in our culture," "*Lituraterre*," in *Littérature* 3 (1971), 3–10 at 3, my translation.

46. J. Lacan, "Proposition of 9 October 1967 on the Psychoanalyst of the School," in *Analysis* 6 (1995), 1–13, at 12.

47. See Lacan's reading of the Hegelian master/slave dialectics, *The Seminar of Jacques Lacan, Book II, The Ego in Freud's Theory and in the Technique of Psychoanalysis 1954–1955*, Cambridge: Cambridge University Press (1988), chapter VI.

48. *Seminar XX, op. cit.* at 39.

49. This is no doubt why in *L'étourdit*, *Scilicet* 4 (1973), pp. 5–52, Lacan calls the phallus the *ab-sense*, at 16.

50. See S. Freud, *Totem and Taboo* or *Moses and Monotheism* (London: Penguin Books, *PFL* 13).

51. "L'étourdit," *op. cit.*, at 5, my translation.

52. *Ibid.*, at 7.

53. *Ibid.*

54. *Ibid.*, at 22.

55. The frequency of such recourses to a ready-made identification can be schematically exemplified by the current proliferation of eating disorders, partially explained by the fact that the response to the question of what it is to be a woman lies in an identification with "to be thin" (as argued by analyst Geneviève Morel at the Xth Encounter of the Freudian Field in Barcelona, July 24–26, 1998).

56. Recalled by J.-A. Miller and E. Laurent in "L'Autre qui n'existe pas et ses comités d'éthique," *op. cit.*

57. In the manner of the man from the country in F. Kafka's famous parable of the door-keeper, *The Trial* (London: Penguin Modern Classics, 1984), 161ff, who spends his life waiting to be allowed into the law and dies in the process, whereupon the door-keeper closes the door, declaring that it was meant for the sole benefit of the expectant man.

58. CIEN is a Freudian Field organization with links in France, Argentina, and Brazil, and aims to introduce something of the analytic practice in the institution.

59. P. Lacadée, "Là où sont les enfants, CIEN, le social au singulier," in *CIEN, Document de travail no. 1 pour la Journée du 10 janvier 1999*, 11–15, at 13.

60. Cf., M. Foucault's take on psychoanalysis, *The Will to Knowledge, The History of Sexuality: 1*, Harmondsworth: Penguin (1998).

61. P.Legendre, *op. cit.*, at 146.

62. *Ibid.*

63. P. Legendre, *op. cit.*, at 91, emphasis added.

64. P. Lacadée, "Y mettre du sien et le bruissement du CIEN," *op. cit.*, 22–24, at 23.

65. Such containment strategies are particularly evident in the United States, where the rate of imprisonment is 645 per 100,000 heads of population, and in the UK where the rate, although considerably lower at 125 per 100,000 (Roy Walmsley: *World Prison Population List*, Home Office Research Findings no. 88) is nonetheless the second highest in the European Union and set to increase consistently alongside the privatization of carceral facilities and New Labour's emphasis on incapacitative sentencing (the *Crime [Sentences] Act 1997*, for instance, introduces mandatory life sentences for second time serious offenders as well as "three-strikes"

provisions for burglars and Class A drug traffickers, and the *Crime and Disorder Act 1998* considerably toughens the regime applicable to young offenders, notably by generalizing the possibility of incarceration for 12- to 14-year-olds by means of the introduction of Detention and Training Orders, indiscriminately applicable to 10- to 17-year-olds—the category 10–12, for now, has been reserved by Parliament).

14

Specious Aristmystic: Joycean Topology

LUKE THURSTON

The real is not of this world: Lacan's bold antiphrasis, uttered in Rome in 1974,[1] is both a provocation and a warning. *Caveat lector*, Lacan seems to say: for unlike the Imaginary and the Symbolic (although to link the categories together in a Borromean chain would radically unsettle such conceptual distinctions), *la troisième*, the third term in the triad, is not to be integrated into any semiology, made part of a psychoanalytic science of reading. The Real, in other words, cannot be *identified*, circumscribed, or written on; it is rather defined as the very mark of the impossibility of such circumscription or superscription, a pure cipher beyond any deciphering.

But in what sense, it might immediately be asked, is this introduction of an "impossible" category or non-category to psychoanalytic discourse more than a bland amphibology, its "paradoxical" character ready to evaporate in the face of rigorous philosophical scrutiny (along the lines, say, of Judith Butler's intervention[2])? An initial response to these questions can be traced out, we will argue, in Lacan's engagement with Joycean writing, where topology—or the mysterious geometry of letters and lines—is brought together with a quintessentially modernist problematic: that which is "not of this world."

*

In the final period of Lacan's work, the topological conundrums of knots and chains are consistently bound up with, thought alongside, the question of names or of name-giving, *nomination*. There is a passage in Joyce's early writing that might have provided this Lacanian interrelation with a veritable *Urszene*; it occurs in *A Portrait of the Artist as a Young Man* (P), a text which Lacan discusses in his *Seminar Le sinthome*—although there he makes no reference to the passage in question, and may have overlooked it. The passage comes early in the book, when Stephen is at school and pondering a textbook, his "geography":

> He turned to the flyleaf of the geography and read what he had written there: himself, his name and where he was.
>
> > *Stephen Dedalus*
> > *Class of Elements*
> > *Clongowes Wood College*
> > *Sallins*
> > *County Kildare*
> > *Ireland*
> > *Europe*
> > *The World*
> > *The Universe*
>
> [. . .] Then he read the flyleaf from the bottom to the top till he came to his own name. That was he: and he read down the page again. What was after the universe? Nothing. But was there anything round the universe to show where it stopped before the nothing place began? It could not be a wall; but there could be a thin thin line there all round everything. It was very big to think about everything and everywhere. Only God could do that. He tried to think what a big thought that must be; but he could only think of God. God was God's name just as his name was Stephen. *Dieu* was the French for God and that was God's

name too; and when anyone prayed to God and said *Dieu* then God knew at once that it was a French person that was praying. But, though there were different names for God in all the different languages in the world and God understood what all the people who prayed said in their different languages, still God remained always the same God and God's real name was God. [*P*, pp. 16–17]

I have quoted at length because the passage contains in embryo almost all of the ideas adumbrated in *Le sinthome*, and more besides: problems of naming and self-inscription, citation and translation, topography and "the nothing place." Joyce's stylistic brilliance allows him to use Stephen's childish syntax as a way to frame urgent "philosophical" questions. The boy's sense of being stupefied and dwarfed by the immensity of those questions is captured by the insistent verbal and logical rhythm, culminating with the final tautological loop. All of Joyce's subsequent writing will continue to grapple with the "big" thoughts which are sketched here, and which exhaust young Stephen, cause him to shrivel up. We could even define Joyce's entire oeuvre as one long attempt to be *big enough* to have such thoughts, without—and this will be the crucial factor from a psychoanalytic perspective—recourse to a tautologous, castrating father-God.

What is not of this world, what lies beyond it without not being or being simply nothing, is defined in Stephen's imagination by an act of *geometry*: "there could be a thin thin line there all round everything." Crucially, the *act* of inscribing this vast, all-inclusive line—even if it only occurs in the indeterminate realm of the possible, which will later famously preoccupy Stephen at the beginning of *Ulysses*³—is immediately disavowed, ascribed to an omnipotent Other: "Only God could do that." Only God, that is, could inscribe, in an essential tautology—a self-identical mark as untranslatable as His name—the definition of the universe, a moment of immaculate symbolic purity which Stephen's language (with its repeated "there" and "thin") can only gesture clumsily to evoke. His impotent withdrawal from the struggle to think thoughts which properly belong to God the Father—"It was better to go to bed to sleep," he decides (*P*, p. 17)—corresponds effectively to Stephen's *erasure of his own subjective agency*: he shrinks back from acknowledging the possibility that the "thin thin line" is logically the last term in his own list, with his own name inscribed at the top in the position of author.

The effect of Stephen's withdrawal to bed here is twofold. Although "it pained him [. . .] that he did not know where the universe ended" (Joyce manifestly rendering this sense of impotence as castration or de-tumescence: "he felt small and weak"), nevertheless the universe itself—as intact, integral whole—is thus salvaged, preserved as an objective given from the dim vagaries of his childish scribbling. And likewise, Stephen himself is left fantasmatically intact as subject when he steps back (the name *Step*hen including a silent echo of a decisive act of moving forward, back or beyond) from the abyss opened up by the question of who is authorized to write the last line in the encyclopedic list, the impossible line beyond "The Universe." He thus fends off the sheer megalomania of imagining himself writing a "commodius vicus" (*Finnegans Wake* [*FW*], 3.2), where the convenience of an all-encompassing philosophy would blend with the imperialist ambition of a deranged emperor. Stephen's list, nothing but a "poor trait of the artless" (*FW*, 114.32), cannot—or *not yet*, in the key temporal mode of the *Wake*[4]—return on itself, seek to complete its line by drawing its last step back to its first: in Joycean franglais, Stephen's *pas* is always still "passencore" (*FW*, 1.4–5), *pas encore*.

We should not mistake Lacan's work with knots and names in the 1970s for an attempt, like Stephen's, to write an "allincluding" list, in the kind of totalizing discourse that had been condemned as a "discourse of the master" in *Seminar XVII*. But let us dwell briefly on a moment in the seminar *Le sinthome* (*SXXIII, 1975–6*) where something emerges which seems to recall Joyce's play, through Stephen, with epistemophilia and disavowal. After the session on December 9, 1975, Lacan is asked a bold question by one of his audience:

H. Cesbron-Lavau: You also speak of the Borromean knot and
    state that it does not constitute a model. Could you clarify
    that?

Lacan: It does not constitute a model in the sense that it en-
    tails something before which the imagination is insuffi-
    cient. I mean that, properly speaking, the imagination as
    such resists imagining the knot. And the mathematical
    approach to it in topology is also not enough.[5]

The knot is not of this world, then; like the line Stephen hesi-
tates to imagine circumscribing the universe, Lacan's Borromean
chain defies the power of the human imagination, remaining radically alien to any semantic form. Is this because, in its ambition to
trace out the contours of Symbolic, Imaginary *and Real* (in other
words: to encompass somehow even what is "not of this world"),
the knot seeks to be nothing less than universal, to inscribe "a thin
thin line there all round everything"? Lacan's paradoxical response
had come two years earlier, in *L'étourdit*:

> If what I am saying necessitates not, as is said, a model, but the
> task of articulating topologically the discourse [of psychoanaly-
> sis] itself, this springs from the lack in the universe—with the
> condition that what I say does not in turn offer to make up for
> this lack.[6]

It is a *défaut dans l'univers*, the non-totality or deficiency of
the universe which dictates the necessity of this topological supplement to Lacan's discourse; but even once it is equipped with such
a resolutely non-imaginary resource, that discourse is unable to
furnish a *suppléance* that would do away with or perversely paper
over the defect or lack in the universe. This notion of an irremedi-
able gap or incompleteness in the universe—which evidently undermines the conceptual basis of the latter term, making it necessary
to write it *sous rature*, "under erasure": Lacan's notation of this being
[A̶]—is the fundamental principle of the final period of Lacan's
work. Pierre Skriabine relates it to the different moments of Lacanian
topology:

> . . . Lacan's topology in the 1960s takes the Other as its point
> of departure, to end . . . by bringing into effect the incomplete-
> ness of the Other, the structural position of lack in the Other.
> Beginning with A, it ends with [A], while the topology of the
> 1970s, that of knots is explicitly founded on [A].[7]

Before tackling the apparent paradox here—of a concept being "founded" on a point simultaneously declared to be beyond the reach of Symbolic alienation or linguistic mediation—we should pursue a little further our juxtaposition of these two unthinkable inscriptions: on one side, the universal line which in Stephen's imagination can only be thought by God; and on the other, Lacan's knot which lies beyond the habitual geometry of meaning. It is clear that in both of these inhuman topologies, meaning is radically suspended: for Stephen, the "nothing place" beyond the universe can only be delimited by a "thin thin line" that is impossible to locate or properly envisage, while the Borromean knot corresponds to—indeed, somehow encapsulates—precisely that which does not exist but *ex-sists*, in the quasi-Heideggerian expression used by Lacan to designate an irreducible remainder outside of the Symbolic and Imaginary registers.

At first glance, then, there would seem to be a stark opposition between Stephen's struggle to imagine a complete universe circumscribed by God, and Lacan's insistence on a constitutive lack in the universe, the absence of any final cause or end. Both "topologies," though, share a common preoccupation with *naming*: if, for Stephen, the turbulence generated by the impossible effort to think of "everything and everywhere" can only be rendered stable by the binding assurance that "God's real name was God," Lacan in turn centers his Borromean topology on the function of the proper name. In Lacan's view, as he puts it in the seminar of February 17, 1976, it was only through "making a name for himself"—literally, so to speak—that Joyce was able to compensate for the *carence paternelle*, the radical failure of the Name-of-the-Father, which threatened the topological coherence of his subjectivity.[8] It is *nomination* that provides the fourth term required to make the

Borromean knot hold together, as Lacan had concluded at the end of the seminar *RSI* in 1975. Thus, in the following year's Seminar, *Le sinthome*, he pursued the eminently Joycean theme of naming as a way to approach the enigmatic fourth term of the knot, without which Real, Symbolic, and Imaginary would fall apart.

Like Lacan's teaching, with its *dénouement* in an unworldly Real, its interstellar mission to *la planète Borromée*, Joyce's writing entails something radically *immonde*, something "out of this world." If Stephen's reverie about the universe and the name of God offers an *Urszene* linking naming and topology at the very edge of the human imagination, that scene is gradually refigured and displaced throughout Joyce's writing, until by *Finnegans Wake* it has gravitated to the absolute center, like a dark singularity in that text's "decentred universe" (to borrow Norris's title). Later, in *A Portrait*, with Stephen having grown into a young intellectual who wishes to devise an aesthetic theory based on "applied Aquinas," we encounter a renewed preoccupation with naming, but now figured as a paradoxical linguistic act whereby the *quidditas* or "whatness" of an object can be captured. In glossing the scholastic term *claritas*, Stephen mentions one interpretation for which such divine "radiance" would "make the esthetic image . . . outshine its proper conditions" (*P*, p. 212); and although he makes a show of rejecting such an idealist emphasis, Stephen certainly retains a notion of aesthetic transcendence in his evocation of the "mysterious instant" of artistic creation: "The artist, like the God of creation, remains within or behind or beyond or above his handiwork, invisible, refined out of existence, indifferent, paring his fingernails" (*P*, p. 215).

Whereas as a child, then, Stephen had withdrawn to bed "small and weak," overwhelmed by the magnitude of God, as a young man he is ready to identify with God's transcendence in a megalomaniac fantasy thinly cloaked with irony. If Stephen has grown into a grotesquely self-inflated narcissist, he is still—crucially—withdrawn or subtracted from the world, "refined out of existence." What this subtraction or refinement accomplishes, as earlier with the "thin thin line" drawn only by God, is to preserve intact the

fantasmatic wholeness and oneness of the Other, a perfect mirror
for the puffed-up self-image.

It is precisely this fantasy of a specular and global cosmos
governed by a single identity which, having lampooned it so effectively in his earlier writing, Joyce sets out in *Finnegans Wake* to
demolish or deconstruct. If *A Portrait* can be read as an essay on
the Imaginary or on the formations of human meaning, the last of
Joyce's texts deliberately aims to dismantle those formations and
reassemble them in unimagined—and sometimes unimaginable—
ways. The "topology" of *A Portrait*, imagined by Stephen in some
nebulous virtual zone unthinkably removed from the real world,
collapses in the *Wake* into the concrete "penstroke, paperspace"
(*FW*, 115.7) of the writing itself. Just as we juxtaposed an early
Joycean topology with the question of how Lacan's knot can be said
to exceed meaning, we should now attempt to read in parallel a
figure from Lacan's "Joycean" topology and one that appears at the
exact center of *Finnegans Wake*.

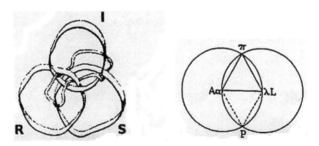

Figure 14–1: Borromean knot and Wakean figure.[9]

Let us read from the left. "The Borromean knot is a writing,"
comments Lacan in the seminar *RSI*, adding that "there is no other
perceptible idea of the Real than the one offered by . . . the trait of
writing."[10] A year later, addressing a non-psychoanalytic audience
at Yale University, he is more explicit about the ultimate aim of
his topology: "I am seeking to produce another geometry that would
be able to tackle this kind of chain. This has never, never been done

before. Such a geometry would not be imaginary, like that of tri-angles, but real, using rings of string."[11]

What immediately strikes us about Lacan's figure is the way it seems to dramatize a contrast between the knot "itself," made up of the relatively consistent or topologically stable rings R, S, and I, and a "rogue" fourth element with a more variable, elastic shape (and even perhaps a suggestion that it is mobile). This latter element appears somehow "extra," something alien to the structure of the knot, added to it in an *ad hoc* manner. Lacan names this fourth term "the symptom" in his Yale seminar (although it should be noted that the text is at the mercy of the vagaries of understanding and transcription: Lacan may well have intended this to be read *le sinthome* and thus have been invoking the title of his seminar).

The *sinthome*, of course, is Joyce's *name*, Lacan insists: no mere predicate of a subject but its constitutive mark of identification. It is undoubtedly language, but not language used in a way that would fall within the axis of the Symbolic or Imaginary—the domain of meaning; but nor is it simply reducible to a pre-linguistic scribble (which is presumably what Lacan designates by a Real that must be written outside discourse).

In Joyce, as we saw already developing with Stephen's charac-ter, a special linguistic status is ascribed to names. This status is immediately ambiguous, and becomes less stable as Joyce's writing unfolds: on the one hand, the name is what guarantees, authorizes, fixes meaning in place; while on the other—as in *Ulysses*, where we encounter "L. Boom" and Stephen's "Nother"—the name, like any signifying element, is thoroughly caught up in an ungovernable tex-tual dissemination.

Lacan's Borromean figure seems to point to a similar kind of ambiguity. The fourth term of the knot is at once the key to its co-herence—it literally constitutes the knot as such, since without it R, S, and I remain incommensurable—and simultaneously appears to be its *least* stable element. This ambiguity is related, in my view, to another "ambiguity," which in fact masks a crucial distinction: that between symptom and *sinthome*. "The Oedipus complex, as such, is a symptom," declares Lacan in the seminar of November 18, 1975, before linking this to the father's place as agent of *nomination*, as "father of the name."[12] In this sense, there is an implicit move beyond Freud in Lacan's elaboration of the knot: whereas for Freud psychoanalysis is still essentially governed by the oedipal symptom—by a *symptom*, precisely: in other words, by an instance still predominantly Symbolic, bound up with the Name-of-the-Father—Lacan for his part can no longer rely on such structural stability or consistency to orient his work. (Another way of putting this would perhaps draw on social history to oppose the "classical" Freudian symptomatology of hysteria to the new varieties of psychical disorder, principally so-called borderline conditions).

If the Oedipus complex is a symptom in the "classical" sense, and thus able to furnish a relatively stable topology of the subject, in Joycean writing Lacan found an exemplary index of how that topology had drastically mutated, was in urgent need of rethinking. Let us now attempt to read the figure from *Finnegans Wake* and its textual site in order to indicate something of how far Joyce's writing has drifted from Stephen's fearful insistence that "God's real name was God."

At first glance, Joyce's figure appears to be a complete contrast to Lacan's knot. The Wakean diagram, McHugh informs us, comes from Euclid's first proposition[13]: it might thus be inscribed—and its precise symmetrical form might be said to confirm this—at the very root of the "imaginary" geometry which Lacan claims to be seeking to outthink with his knot. In no sense, however, does this Euclidian origin of Joyce's figure correspond to some constraint upon or closure of its signification, as is clear from Rose and O'Hanlon's commentary:

> The intersecting spheres are symbolic as well as representative; they comprehend among other things a word (zoo), a map of heaven, hell and earth, a map of Dublin, a drawing of the pudendum and of buttocks, a letter, a mystic symbol of the harmony of contraries, the gyres from Yeats' *Vision*, a bicycle, an egg-beater, and so on.[14]

Joyce's figure might thus be said to *reverse* the impetus of Lacanian topology: if the latter seeks precisely to be a silent *monstration* of something irreducible to the *dit-mension* of the speaking subject, the former is merely another pretext for more textual production, for endless semantic transformation and multiplication.

Yet if we look more closely into the Joycean text, we will see that these antithetical aspects of our Wakean figure—at once more geometrical than the Borromean knot and more polysemic than it—come together at an eminently Lacanian-Joycean point: once again, that of the name. If we turn to p. 293 of *Finnegans Wake*, we see that the very first line of the page brings together the main themes of our reading: "Coss? Cossist? Your parn! You, you make what name?" McHugh refers us to the rule of Coss in algebra, from the Arabic *cosa*, meaning "unknown quantity, *x*," as well as to the Italian *che cosa?* (what?) and the German *was ist?* (what's that?), which together with "I beg your pardon?" form an interrogative cluster. The next phrase, introducing the question of naming (the pidgin for "what's you name?" doubling as a question about fabricating or inventing names), also inevitably recalls the moment in the "Circe" episode of *Ulysses* when Bloom is confronted by the fantasmatic reproaches of his father, Rudolph:

RUDOLPH

What you making down this place? Have you no soul? (*with feeble vulture talons he feels the silent face of Bloom*) Are you not my son Leopold, the grandson of Leopold? Are you not my dear son Leopold who left the house of his father and left the god of his fathers Abraham and Jacob?[15]

The algebraic enigma of the diagram, which may well make us exclaim *che cosa?* or *was ist?*, is immediately folded into the question of "making a name," the wording evoking a paternal rebuke which turns on precisely the *nom du père* and the son's errant disregard for his heritage. Further down p. 293, we find another, more dramatic collision of algebra and names, where the intertextual reference to biblical paternity is explicitly taken up:

Allow me! And, heaving alljawbreakical expressions out of old Sare Isaac's* universal of specious aristmystic unsaid, A is for

Anna like L is for liv. [. . .]
*[O, Laughing Sally, are we going to be toadhauntered by that
old Pantifox
Sir Somebody Something Burtt, for the rest of our secret stripture?

The jaw-breaking algebraical expressions are to be taken from Sir
Isaac Newton, who considered algebra to be a "universal arithmetic." The footnote is riddled with mock-erudite references to
scientists (Todhunter, editor of Euclid; Sir Edwin Arthur Burtt,
author of *The Metaphysical Foundations of Modern Physical Science*);
but by being addressed to "Laughing Sally" the note highlights a
comical pun in this Joycean name-making. "Old Sare Isaac," as well
as naming Sir Isaac Newton, also evokes old Sarah, the wife of
Abraham, who in Genesis (Chapter 12) is told by God that, at the
age of 90, she is to give birth to a child; her response is to laugh,
and thus the son is named Isaac, meaning "he laughs." So "Laughing Sally" is a version of Sarah, or rather of "old Sare Isaac": the
miraculous conjunction of an old woman and a child's laughter.

So by punning on Sir Isaac Newton's name—on the name, that
is, of one of the fathers or founders of the world of modern scientific
rationality, those who established its "metaphysical foundations" (in
Burtt's title)—Joyce enacts a multiple dissemination of patriarchal
and rationalistic authority. And the pun conjoins old Sarah and Isaac,
but *without Abraham*: there is no third position assigned to the father
as the guarantor of a triangular, normalizing structure of desire (to
recall the paradigm sketched out in Lacan's earlier work). "Old Sare
Isaac" is thus a quintessentially Joycean conjunction: it simultaneously names one archetypal father (of Western science) and deliberately omits to name another (of the Jewish people), combining
reason and the miraculous, science and laughter.

Such a *coincidentia oppositorum* takes us back to our Wakean
figure. If, by evoking or quoting Euclidian geometry and Newton,
Joyce places his text firmly in the modern world—a world shaped,
defined, circumscribed by Enlightenment reason—the re-inscription
and disfiguration of geometry as "specious aristmystic" (attrac-
tive or deceptive and mystical or mystifying arithmetic) opens the

figure up to a polysemic unveiling whose "secret stripture" far outstrips the boundaries of that world. The figure is of course an emblem, an "untitled mamafesta" (*FW*, 104.4), of the Wake's great mother Anna Livia Plurabelle, the "Bringer of Plurabilities" (*FW*, 104.2): a central triangle linking the Wakean motif of her name, ALP, is doubled by a dotted line below, as if to imply movement or reversibility, a kind of "plurability."

In conclusion, then, we can frame Joyce's Wakean figure as a perfect emblem for a post-Freudian era, a time after the governing oedipal "symptom" has collapsed. By making his arithmetic into "aristmystic"—by forcing the paternal name and its rational geometry to coalesce with a scene of pre-modern wonder and maternal laughter—Joyce deliberately installs an intractable particularity at the heart of a "universal" geometry. The ambi-valence or dubious doubling at the center of the figure is here strictly equivalent to Lacan's *sinthome*: impossible to stabilize or pin down to a single location (to *identify*, that is), it is nonetheless the central element of the entire structure, the very principle of its cohesion. It is as if Law were governed by an act of transgression, a general pattern determined by a particular instance, a universal system founded on an untranslatable *hapax*.

ENDNOTES

1. J. Lacan, "La troisième," *Lettres de l'Ecole freudienne*, 1975, no. 16, p. 184.
2. Cf., J. Butler, "Arguing with the Real," in *Bodies that Matter*, New York: Routledge, 1993, p. 207.
3. See J. Joyce, *Ulysses* (1922), London: Bodley Head, 1986, esp. pp. 31–42.
4. For an exploration of that temporal mode, see D. Attridge, "Wakean History: Not Yet," in *Joyce Effects: On Language, Theory and History*, Cambridge: Cambridge University Press, 2000, pp. 86–92.
5. J. Lacan, *Le sinthome* (*SXXIII*), A. F. I. text, p. 40 (my translation).
6. J. Lacan, "L'étourdit," *Scilicet* 4, 1973, pp. 33–34 (my translation).

7. P. Skriabine, "Clinique et topologie," *Revue de la Cause freudienne*, 1993, p. 119 (my translation).

8. J. Lacan, *Le sinthome* (*SXXIII*), A.F.I. text, p. 113.

9. *Scilicet 6/7*, p. 39; *Finnegans Wake*, p. 293.

10. J. Lacan, *RSI* (*SXXII*), 17/12/74, *Ornicar?* 2, 1975, p. 100 (my translation).

11. J. Lacan, "Conferences et entretiens dans des universités nord-américains," *Scilicet 6/7* p. 40 (my translation).

12. J. Lacan, *Le sinthome* (*SXXIII*), A. F. I. text, p. 21.

13. R. McHugh, *Annotations to Finnegans Wake*, Baltimore: Johns Hopkins University Press, 1991, p. 293.

14. D. Rose & J. O'Hanlon, *Understanding* Finnegans Wake: *A Guide to the Narrative of James Joyce's Masterpiece*, New York: Garland, 1982, p. 156.

15. J. Joyce, *Ulysses, op. cit.*, p. 357.

Making Rings: The Hole of the Sinthome in the Embedding of the Topology* of the Subject

JEAN-MICHEL VAPPEREAU

We must distinguish the topology of the subject from its projection in the instant of the fantasy, the place of its practice, in the way that we want to show it in what follows. These two different registers are often confused because of the use in the structure of the terms from graphs, surfaces and knots, borrowed from the domain of differential varieties which characterize the second register.

I. FROM THE SCHEMA OF FREUD TO KNOT STRUCTURE

Lacan has us follow an itinerary which goes from the series proposed by Freud in his Perceptions, Perception Signs; Ucs, Preconscious, Conscious schemas, to the R and L schemas. For this purpose, we will construct the F schema.

---

*Translated by Ellie Ragland and Jane Ruiz-Lamb.

1.1. Duality and Quotient of Graphs[1]

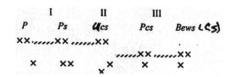

Figure 15–1.

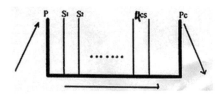

Figure 15–2.

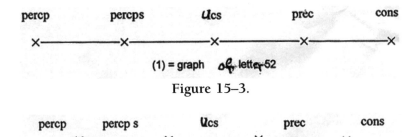

Figure 15–3.

Figure 15–4.

Folding of the line graph towards P = Cs (Quotient)

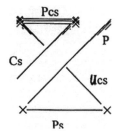

Figure 15–5.

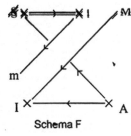

Figure 15–6.

The R and L schemas with their reciprocal articulation are presented even better at the surface of the projective plane—in this case the Möbius strip—which he transcribes to the dimension of the knot in order to impose on it, without possible detour, the ordeal [test] itself of this writing.

1.2. Three Versions of the Elements of the Structure

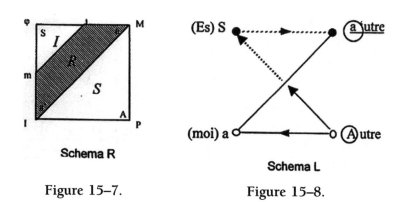

Schema R

Figure 15–7.

Schema L

Figure 15–8.

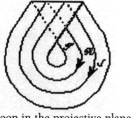

Simple loop in the projective plane R
Möbius strip in the Möbius strip

Figure 15–9.

Double loop in the projective plane
with shrunken R
Cut in the Möbius strip

Figure 15–10.

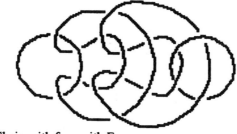

Chain with four with Σ

Figure 15–11.

Chain with three: Σ glides there

Figure 15–12.

The question of this writing is therefore posed. Lacan speaks of a signifying involution. "The copula which unites the identical with the different"[2] in regards to the articulation of these elements which try to write the structure of the subject.

1.3. Three Versions of the Signifying Involution

1. In terms of schemas

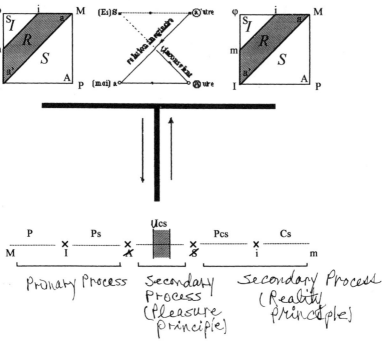

Legend of the drawings: P = Perception   Ps = Perception signs
Ucs = Unconscious   Pcs = Preconscious   Cs = Conscious

Figure 15–13.

2. In terms of surfaces

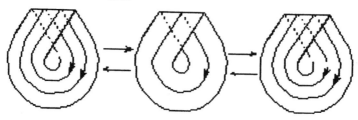

Figure 15–14.

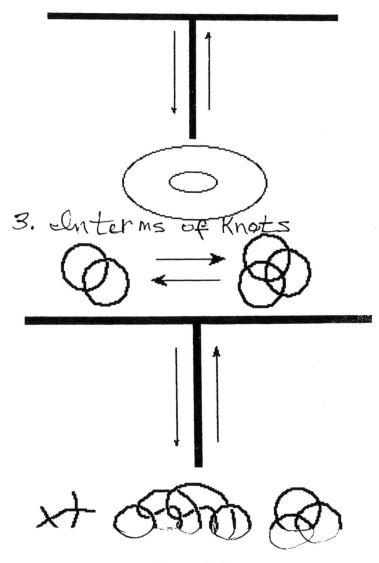

Figure 15–15.

The knot version of this involution is particularly appropriate; that which determines this movement like a writing. Indeed, it is always about accounting in writing for the psychic event at the same time as the trickling down of and ravaging by this event.

But the different versions of this topological structure depend—because it is seeking to write it—on the topological structure which is discovered in logic.

FROM THE PHALLIC FUNCTION TO CASTRATION . . .

We must deal with this structure in terms of speech (*parole*), in
other words, in terms of enunciation and of the structure of language. Contrary to the opinion of psychoanalysts and linguists, Law
of speech and Structure of language can be defined with precision
after several decades of exercise of the seminar, thanks to Tarski
for the first and thanks to Jakobson for the second. Then, we must
deal with the embedding of the structure—the place of practice
where the reader can note that this is about *drawing the graph* which
is the intersection of circles on the sphere, of *making closed cuts on
the* surface of the torus and the projective plane, of *studying the knots
and the links* finally—which are none other than embeddings of the
circles laid out in various ways in the space with three dimensions.
In a word, it is always a matter of making some loops in various
circumstances of two dimensions and three dimensions, in all conceivable manners.

We shall propose in this regard a first small exercise in logic
in terms of loops on the plane (the holed sphere) that we owe
to Spencer Brown through Louis Kauffman's essay "Knots and
Logic."[3]

Taking into account the Imaginary—the Imaginary in this
discourse is the body—incorporation, narcissism and the drive,
the projection of topology of the subject in diachrony (which is
called history), thus provides a place for the study of the different ways of making loops. We must make clear what we understand by these terms of incorporation, narcissism, and drive, in
opposition to the subject, that we want to define in what is going
to follow after having formulated the Law of speech and the Structure of language.

In his teaching Lacan worked furiously at making loops, starting in 1957. He did so for nearly 30 years, in all possible and imaginable ways, in order to put this topology to the test.

It is amusing to hear certain people, even in the family circle, those closest, some little Lacanians, come to tell us that this realization of topology matters little in Lacan's teaching, while they are all fascinated by the illusion of easy money on the occasion of the fortune accumulated by Lacan. Now we must testify that this money was earned by the last *self-made man* in the great difficulties of having to dissimulate his strategy, even from those he loved the most.

His is a *horse treatment* for a humanity who is prey to autism in matters of structure, whose thought is covered by an excrement poultice. The treatment consists of introducing the psychotic dimension into humanity's education. The exit from the current delirium can only be made by adding the knot, since by retrenching it, the discourse of the analyst is susceptible to the structure of the delirium of President Schreber. A situation attested to today.

A SMALL, SIMPLE TOPOLOGICAL INTERLUDE

In the lower part of our simplified graph which has the form of the letter T, we propose a rudimentary exercise which can serve as an entrance.

It is about considering the S figures as a small elementary geometry, presenting all the loop configurations defined by a primitive clause and two formative clauses.

(**cp. 0**) The empty space of the plane denuded of any trait is a figure X of this geometry.

(**cf. 1**) If X is a figure of this geometry, then X surrounded by a loop is a figure of this geometry.

(**cf. 2**) If X and X' are figures of this geometry, then X X' is a figure of this geometry.

Here is an example from the point of view of a figure X.

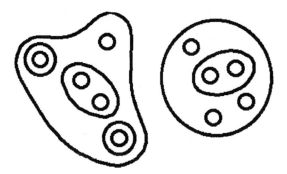

Figure 15–16.

Furthermore, secondly, we have available to us three geometrical axioms for this little geometry of the most simple kind.

(**ag. 1**) Two figures X X' can move around the plane without X' X's ever meeting, going by, or crossing each other.

(**ag. 2**) Two identical figures X X in the same zone of the plane are reduced to a single copy of this figure X.

(**ag. 3**) Two concentric loops surrounding an empty space are erased.

So, for the analysand, this is about putting to the test, for logicians who someday want to undertake an analysis and, consequently, think with this, this is about demonstrating that all the X figures of this geometry are reduced either to a loop or are purely and simply erased.

We will show this a little further on in the example used. Let the reader try his or her hand at this and undergo the counterblow of this test. The reader will perceive how very amusing it is, but also how often he or she does not even know where to begin to ask him- or herself about this rudimentary problem which requires no particular designer talent. So we advise the reader to make some loops to see if it is as easy as he or she imagines.

Meanwhile, we will again return to the thread of our proposals.

The reproach, addressed to Freud this time, consists in contesting the salient fact of *phallic function*—brought to light by his psychoanalysis. It is true that his psychoanalysis permits him to formulate an exclusive interest in the presence or absence of the organ, the phallus and castration, without lending any attention whatever to the other elements of the genital apparatus, for the male as well as for the female.

In fact, this reproach does not carry, when one knows what it is about, since this function concerns, to tell the truth, enunciation. It can in no case be addressed to Lacan since he adds in what way its cause and its effect remain a hole.

The traumatism (*troumatisme*) of the misunderstanding [*malentendu:* poor hearing] of the parents . . . . They do not understand the infant's cry. Hole which, from that point on, constitutes the *sinthome*. The *sinthome* is a hole, an infinite right angle,[4] a loop. A body, already foreign to itself, has to deal with a hole with which it does not know what to do.

So the image of the saint is appropriate, showing a body outfitted with a halo which floats above his or her head.

But also, woman is a *sinthome* for man—she does not fit him like a ring fits a finger. He does not know what to do with her. It is not worth the trouble recalling the novel by Longus, *Daphnis and Cloé*, in order to legitimize an interest now carried to the hole linked to repression because it will be established in reason by what comes next. We have something—up to and including Freud's discovery of the threat of castration, which becomes the complex of the same name—finally made clear by Lacan as an irreducible lack in the barred Other, here, Real.

We call this hole, this loop, *the Ucs.* with Freud, and *parlettre* [speaking being by the letter] with Lacan. How have we arrived at this point with such tight formulas?

In order to present in the discourse analysis, to introduce it there, if one is allowed to speak like this, we will talk about the topology of the subject and about its realization in the instant of the fantasy. We must once more point out two currents of correlated thoughts in Freud which extend out along two winding paths in the teaching of Lacan.

TWO CURRENTS OF THOUGHTS

There is, on the one hand, the construction of a psychic apparatus by Freud. It becomes structure of the subject with Lacan.

There is, on the other, a question of logic for Freud at the foundation of this construction; it becomes topology with Lacan.

At each stage of his work, Freud presents the unconscious in two ways.

Either as an instance in the construction of the psychic apparatus.

Or as a remarkable problem of logic in a polemic with the school of Professor *Wundt*, a *portemanteau* word, as are all the contemporary scholars of Locke,[5] on this occasion, the inventor of European consciousness.

For Lacan it will be a matter first of the never resolved question for Freud of the closing of the psychic apparatus, which, nevertheless, the discoverer of the unconscious had noted as necessary.

Then it will be a matter of the transformation of this apparatus into a synchronic, logical and topological structure, the structure of the subject and of his or her being embedded or precipitated into diachrony, history, the place where the loops are deployed, constituting dimensions between the narcissistic image, drives, and dual circuits of the neuronic tree structures of the signifying crystal.

FREUD'S TWO CURRENTS OF THOUGHT

3.1. The Unconscious in the Psychic Apparatus

Each time Freud presents the unconscious as an instance of the psychic apparatus whose construction he projected starting in 1895 in his "Project for a Scientific Psychology."[6]

What remains now is to read this text. It did not escape anyone that Lacan devoted the first lessons of his Seminar dealing with the ethics of psychoanalysis to this Project, because it presents the same structure as the second part of the ethics of Spinoza where his physics of bodies is constructed. So from the outset, it is a matter of the physics of neurons.

Add to that the second datum for starting out, which consists in following the consequences of the duality between branching and cyclical structures.

A Tree is a graph from which it suffices to remove any stopping point at all to render it unconnected. That's saying that trees do not present cycles.

A cycle is a path whose extremities are identical.

The neuronic structures (support of the ego in the projected apparatus) are shown as trees.

Circuits in the territory, also called extensions of the libido, are cycles, our loops.

These circuits show greater connectivity and provide the solution to the Freudian problem of the closing of the trees, characterized by the absence of a cycle, thus offering only some regressive solutions in the psychic apparatus.

But, before undertaking these works of topology, we needed to clarify what it is a matter of when we speak of the unconscious. It is the second line of argumentation, showing the logical pattern of psychoanalysis.

3.2. The Unconscious and the Psyche, Logical Law

Let us formulate the problem of logic. Freud speaks of the unconscious. Professor Wundt and his school oppose him, saying that it is incoherent. Freud takes up the argument of this school of philosophy in order to respond. Let us follow him in the manners of his response in the course of his work, on the occasion of the three stages of Freud's progression, by going to the text at each of these stages.[7]

3.2.1. *From the first, a beginning.*

The problem of the unconscious in psychology is, according to the strong words of Lipps, less a psychological problem than the problem of psychology itself. As long as psychology was content to respond by saying that "*psyche*" and "the conscious" were equivalent terms and that the expression "unconscious psychic process" was truly meaningless, it [psychology] could not imagine utilizing the observations that the doctor can make on abnormal psychic states (S. Freud, *Traumdeutung* 1900, "La signifiance des rêves," Paris: PUF, p. 519, our translation into English).

At the time, Freud's response was to shrug his shoulders.

> The doctor can only shrug his shoulders when one affirms that "consciousness is the indispensable character of the psyche." [Freud, p. 519, our translation]

The argument can seem to be weak, but he accompanies it with another reason. He evokes clinical experience and especially his practice of the interpretation of dreams.

3.2.2. *Then, during the period of crisis that he underwent, with the failure he encountered in 1915 writing about what he planned as being his metapsychology he writes:*

> We also think at present that repression and unconscious are correlative to such an extent that we have to put off the moment of deepening the essence of repression until we have learned even more about the structure of the succession of psychic instances and about the difference between conscious and unconscious. [S. Freud, "Le refoulement," in *Métapsychologie* 1915, Paris: Gallimard, p. 48, our translation]

And again a little further, regarding a careful analysis of the results of repression,

> But I can only propose to also defer this work until we ourselves have formed sure representations concerning the rela-

tionship of the conscious to the unconscious. [Freud, "Le refoulement," in *Métapsychologie*, 1915, Paris: Gallimard, p. 58, our translation]

He formulates the same problem again.

We are contested from all sides regarding the right to admit an unconscious psyche and to work scientifically with this hypothesis. [Freud, "L'inconscient," in *Métapsychologie*, 1915, Paris: Gallimard, p. 66, our translation]

And responds by stressing the characteristics of the argument against him

But it is more important, however, to realize that the objection rests on the assimilation (*Gleichstellung*) not expressed (*Nicht ausgesprochenen*), but posed at the onset (*Vorherein fixierten*) between consciousness and the psyche. [Freud, "L'inconscient," p. 68, our translation]

because it is indeed the logical status of this assimilation (*Gleichstellung*) with which we intend to deal.

Its non-expressed character (*Nicht ausgesprochenen*) is linked, according to us, to this other trait that it presents of being posed at the outset (*Vornherein fixierten*). We recognize here the question of the truth formulated by Tarski, which is the principle of Anglo-American pragmatism, but also of the *Critique of Pure Reason* by Kant insofar as it is a matter of a synthetic *a priori* (*Vornherein fixierten*) judgment (*Gleichstellung*).

If such judgments are not expressed (*Nicht ausgesprochenen*) we cannot say that the question that they pose is not expressed.

But Freud, who cites Kant for having shown how much our external perceptions are deceptive, accompanies his formulation of the problem with some remarks on this question which

. . . threaten to end up in a quarrel of words. [Freud, "L'inconscient," in *Métapsychologie*, 1915, Paris: Gallimard, p. 69, our translation]

He makes it clear that what is precious for our debate concerning the resistance to psychoanalysis is

> the obstinate refusal to accord a psychic character to latent psychic acts explained by the fact that most of the phenomena considered have not been an object of study outside psychoanalysis. [Freud, "L'inconscient," p. 69, our translation]

There is still the clinical reference, but he proposes a solution.

> We would be putting an end to all the misunderstandings if, from now on, in the description of various sorts of psychic acts, we leave aside the question of knowing whether they are conscious or unconscious. [Freud, "L'inconscient," p. 75, our translation]

And still

> One could also try to avoid the confusion in designating the psychic systems, that we have recognized, by arbitrarily chosen names which would not make the slightest allusion to the fact of being conscious. [Freud, "L'inconscient," p. 75, our translation]

One thus sees the reason emerge for the introduction of the id from his second topic but he adds that, by doing without the term "unconscious," that is not possible. So he proposes to literalize this use, as in mathematics, by writing Ucs for the unconscious, Pcs for the preconscious, and Cs for consciousness.

3.2.3. Still later, at the end of his life, Freud always returned to the same question and seemed to have adopted an attitude then that was much more infused with disillusionment due to the fact it distanced him from the text of **The Outline** *he was writing.*

> And yet, what psychoanalysis must do is here and that is what constitutes its second fundamental hypothesis. It maintains that the processes accompanying the so-called somatic

order do constitute the psyche and is not at all at first concerned about the quality of the conscious. Besides, it is not the only thing that emits this opinion. Certain thinkers, Th. Lipps, for example, have upheld the same point of view in the same terms and, as the generally admitted conception that what is psychic does not satisfy the mind, it follows that the idea of an unconscious always demanded even greater rights of the city in psychology, but in a fashion so imprecise and so vague that it could not influence science. [Freud, "Abrégé de psychanalyse," Paris: PUF, p. 19, our translation]

An editors' note follows which is going to keep us busy a long time. But let's go back to the third occurrence of our problem. We do observe that at the end of his work, Freud has not totally renounced this presentation of the problem but that he marks a hesitation, for although he formulated the problem precisely, he set it aside as if he were forever giving up on making himself heard on this point. The editors provide it in a note.

> In the posthumous papers of the author there is an other version from October 1938 and from which we reproduce certain passages here: "And here is something strange that everyone or almost everyone agrees upon in finding a common psychic characteristic to everything that is psychic, a characteristic which translates its very essence. It is the unique indescribable character—which, moreover, which does not need to be described—of the *conscious* (*Bewussheit*). Everything which is conscious is psychic and, inversely, everything which is psychic is conscious. How can one deny something so evident? [Freud, "Abrégé," p. 19, our translation]

In this context, the best defenders of Freud would be Karl Popper and John Austin with their attachment to the theory of correspondence.

They say that the predicate of truth is not superfluous and that the truth depends on the correspondence between the segments of language and the segments of facts in reality.

They thus open up the possibility of talking about the unconscious, but they too are also referring to empirical observation to do so.

NOW FREUD IS WRONG (FREUD DOES NOT HAVE A REASON)

The problem does not lie here and to show it, let us give again the argumentation of what is at issue in a few lines.

Wundt objects to Freud:

(1) "The psyche is conscious = the psyche."

Freud moves forward by saying that there is the unconscious: he uses a negative formula and marks a negation of this equivalence.

(1) "The psyche is conscious □ the psyche."

In this regard, Wundt is in agreement with the philosophers like Locke and all the others who see themselves confirmed by the semantic conception of the truth of Tarski:

(2) "The snow is white" is true = "The snow is white."

There are places in discourse where this structure of a useless marker, because it is present by principle, cannot be written.

The enemies of psychoanalysis thus have a good reason, with support from logicians, to object to Freud and his doctrine.

But then Hans, and children his age have a reason for saying:

(2) "My sister has a widdler (*un fait pipi*) = my sister."

The character in the family who is designated in this way can change; it is most often the mother. But it makes little difference; that changes nothing in the logical argument. The function of the symbolic phallus that is impossible to negativize is made clear here.

We can say with Lacan that each of them, Wundt and the philosophers, Tarski and the logicians, Hans and the children his age, et alia, are subjected to the phallic function, [that] the fetishistic attitude is not far away even if it is necessary to distinguish it firmly from this structure—never before clarified—of which it is only a consequence.[8]

Consequently, we are advancing that all scholars are subjected to the function of the symbolic phallus, all of the members of the scientific community at the four corners of the planet are hostage to a pact which consists of rejecting sexuation, an agreement which arises from the structure of the fetish, that is to say, from perversion. Elsewhere, we have called this attitude, the love of the all, tototemism (*toutaisme*) today. The irony of this story appears when claimants to the representation of psychoanalysis adopt the same position. It is certainly better that this be so rather than to not ask oneself the question about the absence or the presence. But of what, in fact? Indeed, with what sort of entities are we in fact dealing in this sort of problem? It's what is aimed at in the language of the Lacanians when one speaks of the signifier.

So it is a pity for the adversaries of Freud and even for his adepts, that one has not posed the question to oneself, by pretending to understand too quickly what elements which constitute the unconscious are about.

. . . WHERE FREUD IS RIGHT (FREUD HAS A REASON)

Lacan tells us that it is a matter of signifiers. We say with him that it is a matter on such occasions, said by Emile Benveniste to be subjectivity in language—personal pronouns, deitics, performative verbs—of elements that may avoid this kind of *synthetic a priori judgments*, but which, however, may not be isolated and especially may not be justified through empirical observation. Their reason lies elsewhere—as is the case for the truth in opposition to the true/false couple—from the order of speaking.

Because, indeed, Freud was right and had a reason in proposing to speak of the unconscious since the fact that my mother has a penis is not strictly equivalent logically to the fact that she is my mother: (1)

(3) "My mother has a penis $\square$ my mother."

As:

(1) "The psyche is conscious $\square$ the psyche"

Leaves a place for what we are going to call the Ucs.

(3) "The psyche is Ucs. = a negation of the psyche."

But what negation of the psyche? It is what we are going to construct, it is what we have constructed with the modification of classical logic into the topology of the subject.

We do see that it is necessary to return to the reason of this type of judgment that we call synthetic *a priori*; in relation to the stated judgments, it is the debate between Hume and Kant.

THE SIGNIFYING DRIVE

The structure of Oedipus which is formulated in a double question by the child to the parents is: Is it one? Is it two? is embodied through narcissism. But what is narcissism?

Narcissism is the pulsation of tension and eros between the fact of being subject to the body and of taking the body as an object, between the object and its commentary, between the language taken as an object and metalanguage, between the intrinsic and the extrinsic.

That is what must be maintained in the doctrine; the structure of the subjective division, by the construction of "the copula which unifies the identical with the different," rules the relationship that is not there between structure and history, between discourse and the clinic.

In terms of the geometry of optics, the difference between the objects of dimension two, identical with their mirror image (non-specular) and the objects of dimension three, different in the general cause of their mirror image (specular). In this case, one of the three dimensions is inverted, but we do not know which one. In a formula, the mirror does not especially invert the right and the left of an object of three dimensions; it can be the top and the bottom or the in front and the behind: it can be either, as how one is willing to consider it. To grasp this, one must return to the Program of Erlengen of Félix Klein and to the notion of a group of transformations.

In logic, this function is written in the topology of the subject as the negative particle that distinguishes the Ucs. from the Cs. In a formula: "It is false that this is Cs and it is false that this is not Cs."

That is,

$$\text{Ucs.} = \overline{Cs} = (\neg Cs. \wedge \neg \sim Cs.)$$

The only modification brought to the classical logic so dear to Quine consists in the construction of this little modified negation, that allows the formation of a supplementary[9] clause of the statements (*énoncés*).

(cfm$_4$). If P is an ebf, then ~ P is an ebf.

And from a simple supplementary axiom,[10] in order to clarify the usage.

(am$_5$). (~p $\square$ (~q/$\square$q))

Now, from here, the reason is no longer the same, the reason is transformed.

With that we can respond to the question that we have raised, despite Tarski, Wundt, Locke, Hans, and the other doctors and philosophers. We can say the place of what we are going to call Freud's Ucs. without recourse to any experimental verification (reproach of Karl Popper who cannot do it any longer).

In a formula:

(4) The psyche is Ucs./($\square$ psychic life $\square$ $\square$ ~ psychic life)

And in language:

(4') "The psyche is Ucs. is equivalent to it is false that this is psychic and it is false that this is not psychic."

Add that *what is not psychic is somatic* if you like and you have the exact formulation of the situation of Freud's psychoanalysis in spite of Galilean, Cartesian, and Newtonian Science, despite the fact that the dominant law for this does not contravene the semantic conception of the Tarskian truth transposed into the domain of scientific psychology.

(1) The psyche is conscious/the psyche resolves it by showing that it is about another, consistent and incomplete, logic. But
that is another debate which also concerns technique.

Only commitment to the discourse of analysis, in keeping both
our feet in the ditch until the end, enables us, as the result of the
discovery of the overall articulation of this type of formula, to get
back on the road without the fear of having to go back into the
ditch, then to climb out again, and to go back into it, to climb back
out, go back into, climb out, go back into . . .

THE STRUCTURE OF LANGUAGE

This is how we resolved the difficult questions raised by the structure of language; there is no metalanguage, structure and history,
Freud's biologism, what is called "his scientism," of the Freudian
knot, etc. . .

There is a lot to laugh about in reading certain authors:

> . . . (<<[my topological presentation] was doable by a pure
> literal algebra . . . >>. L'étourdit, p. 28)[11] For the knot, the tresses,
> etc., the question is completely different. Without a doubt they
> come from mathematics, but rather as curiosities (sic), the
> knot is exhausted (resic) in its untirelessly varied monstration
> (<<little fabrications>>) and does not require being integrally
> written, to legitimate its efficacity.[12]

Here, recourse is had to L'étourdit for once, but then to Seminar XX. Now the trap, set for some good reasons by Lacan, is not
the same thing . . . It closes and clarifies the end of this work.

What modesty, indeed, on Lacan's part, as Koyré remarks
about Descartes when the latter revolutionized the discourse of
science by supporting it with geometry.

But who-speaks of justification, and who are the good students
who recite the lesson by imitating the master? For us, it is a question of reason.

Allusion to my work is then made without citing me, of course; it is the habit of these people. But if they are right and have a reason to lean on Kojève in matters regarding followers, which are useless to cite, they deceive themselves regarding some precursors whom they are incapable of recognizing. The piece continues thus:

> This certainly does not forbid the mathematicians from applying themselves to mathematizing the knot. Some mathematicians have tried it with brilliance, under the attentive gaze of Lacan. Perhaps, at the moment when I am writing, it is recognized that they or others have entirely succeeded. It remains that the knot had not waited for their effort to function in discourse. [Milner, p. 162]

Whatever the display of obscurantism, there remains the difference of the knot functioning as a symptom from the fact of its rejection or functioning as resolution based on writing that provides reason, and with a new mathematics, necessitated by the epoch of the completion of metaphysics, with the knot, yeah! Now without its writing, psychoanalytic discourse is "a delirium that can be the structure of the one of Schreber." Who would rejoice at that? It is the actual situation.

And you will remark in reading other contemporary contributions that it is easy to act as if there were some other works comparable to ours. Everything looks similar at the time of the gray plague. We are in the epoch of the Circle of Vienna, where everything is relative, refutation obliges, competition of theories, everything is negotiable. No judgment, above all, no commitment, about justification, about guarantee, about juridicalism, and about catechism, no act, no names. This does not stop these people from having a lot of nerve. The garbage can followers will be judged by history.

It is true that when this author writes that, he has still not renounced his conclusion of the epoch ("**at the moment when I am writing**") as he will do afterwards. (Lacan, *l'écrit*, the image . . .)

At that time, there, he is in repentance, marked by his last admirable article where it is a question of the Real of language, but where, curiously, it is written: "The material of the forgotten."[13]

We are against the mistakenness of this formula from the best linguist of his generation. On the contrary, we hold that the structure of language, with Jakobson, has finally and only recently been formulated, for our time.

LACAN

These two types of arguments are found in the teaching of Lacan, differentiated in time throughout the *Écrits*.[14]

The construction of the psychic apparatus of Freud becomes the structure of the subject. The logical aspect develops the reason for this construction in a tension between speech and writing, between the signifier and the letter, its localized, material support.

These two currents, which come together, start with the seminar called "The Purloined Letter," where Lacan gives a little topology of the graphs.[15]

He himself explains that he turned the chronological order of the *Écrits* upside down at the moment of their publication to put this fragment of the Seminar at the head of the volume. This was done for reasons of structure which are self-explanatory.

(1) We have utilized, thanks to these explications, a transformation composed of the two elementary deformations of this topology. This transformation produces, starting with the schema of Freud from letter 52 addressed to Wilhelm Fliess, homologous to the optical schema of chapter 7 of *The Interpretation of Dreams*, the schemas constructed by Lacan and that he designates in the *Écrits* as the R. Schema[16] and the L Schema.[17] This little discovery enables their coordination on the projective plane at the following stage if we follow the indications given by Lacan in a note which accompanies the Schema R at the time *Écrits* was published (Note 18, p. 223, *Écrits: A Selection*). Separate from the three first years of his Seminar, Lacan, consequently, extends Freud's construction, in terms of graphs, by

taking up his schemas again in order to resolve the question that he, Lacan, is asking himself about their closing. He goes so far as to deal with this question in terms of surface in the I and R Schemas in his "On a Question Preliminary to Any Possible Treatment of Psychosis." He will pursue this line of construction in the '60s in his Seminar once he has introduced the theory of intrinsic topological surfaces in the year devoted to identification (1962).[18]

But we can read that it was necessary for him first to mark the occasion with regard to psychosis; the narcissistic neuroses of Freud, by accounting for the triggering of the delirum in terms of foreclosure of the signifier of the Name-of-the-Father. Indeed, it did not escape Lacan, reader of Freud, that the latter addresses a simple reproach to Jung's theory in matters of psychosis: "His theory does not merit being discussed because it does not account for the triggering of the delirium."

As of the "Rome Discourse," discourse program where Lacan offers to put the function and the field of the speech and language on his work agenda, he is going to find the articulation he is seeking to clarify and is going to mark rupture in his *Écrits* after his "Remarks on the Report of Daniel Lagache."[19] He takes advantage of the "Rome Discourse" to break with the first time period of his discourse.

It is in the year 1956 that he realizes what he is saying: the "You got to it a little late," of "The agency of the letter"[20] that he addresses to himself, marks this turning point.

The same year he comes back to the role of the circuits in the analysis of Little Hans (the object relation)[21] about which he had already spoken during the second year of the Seminar. The following year he seriously undertook to makes some loops starting out with the sphere—the most elementary of the topological surface structures—with the graph of desire ("The Formations of the Unconscious").[22]

This is how he entered the second flow of logical arguments enabling the definition of the unconscious.

We hold the "Position of the Unconscious" (1964)[23] to be the principal writing (*écrit*) on this question that Lacan presents as a necessary complement to his "Rome Discourse."[24]

During this period, which goes from 1958 to 1970, Lacan makes loops and does logic. Simple knots on the sphere, then on the torus, and the projective plane. Logic of propositions ("Logic of the Fantasy"),[25] of predicates and set theory (his sexuation formulas from *Seminar XX*).

In order to propose a way into this questioning regarding the laws and the principles of thought in the way their narcissistic and drive-related aspects are accomplished in terms of the body, of simple knots, and of territory, of circuit and of path, we have recourse to our succinct geometry of loops which translate as an interplay of parentheses already present starting with the Seminar on "The Purloined Letter."

Indeed, Spencer Brown conceived this writing in terms of parentheses and it is us, following L. Kauffman, who translate this syntax into a geometry of dimension two made of loops on the plane.

Here we will give the solution to the exercise proposed above from the point of view of the reduction of our example chosen in function of the axioms of this geometry.

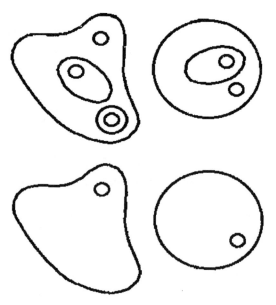

Figure 15–17.

We pass from figure S to figure S_1 in having recourse to (**ag. 2**), from figure S_1 to figure S_2 in having recourse to (**ag. 3**), from figure S_2 to figure S_f in having recourse to (**ag. 3**), in order finally to erase everything by virtue of this same geometry axiom.

The result that we announce is found well confirmed here, even if it is still not demonstrated. That is a task that we shall leave to the reader.

If this reader wants to take the adventure a little further in this n-space of the elementary loops, we propose he or she determine by virtue of what he can establish the series of theorems which correspond to the following figures.

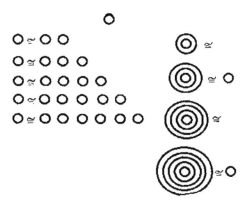

Figure 15–18.

This period ends with *"L'étourdit"* where Lacan himself resumes his path[26] before taking up again in his Seminar the set of issues posed by the knot in the years which follow.

Our little geometry of loops is the beginning of a path which ends up there by a series of stages that the reader can follow through the series of the fascicules of results.

It is towards this ultimate formulation that we have directed our studies in topology, in order to reread the entire path, starting with its end. We have succeeded in establishing a theory of the knot which has nothing to envy from works that are properly mathematical and which are only sketched out by Lacan in his style, with no intention to be the work of a mathematician. We can attest that it was sufficient for us to follow trustingly the indications—which anyone may have access to—in the various notes of the Seminar of the last ten years, in order to bring to light this topology which promises yet more very elegant works.

THE QUESTION OF THE SUBJECT

If we want to speak, with rigor, the register of reason proper to psychoanalysis and its situation in our world, the world of capital science, we are correctly led to ask ourselves the question of the subject, the subject of Galilean and Cartesian science.[27]

Lacan indeed specifies that the subject that we deal with in psychoanalysis is the subject of science. He explains a point which merits additional clarification, by advancing that psychoanalysis can only be defined as the science of the object a that he invented as the object of psychoanalysis. Psychoanalysis cannot be defined as the science of its object.

This is for a simple reason at the outset. This is because the object only presents itself to us, due to the fact of the experience that we can have of it, as already burst apart. We can only have or gather bits of it.

The object of science, for its part, remains opaque.

The question of knowing what the subject of science is is posed by the simple fact that Freud is unthinkable without Descartes, who is the witness of the coming-to-be of this subjective position.

Indeed, in science the subject is divided between the daily practice of scholars at work in science and the terms of his or her publications which require that he or she not make known his or her thoughts, calculations, or personal judgments. In a word, as an ideal worker, his or her opinion is not asked. The subject is asked to do work, and nothing will be made of the fact of the structure of this discourse.

The subject is asked to produce results so that technology can take them over to make them fail in techniques, and various arrangements proposed by ecologists and ethics committees will change nothing about this.

But how did this new subjective position that was so quickly abolished appear?

One only need read G. Canghilem[28] to seize it. He explains to us so well how for the mechanistic scholars of the seventeenth century, the world of reason in which God exists (starting with Thomistic theology replacing essence by existence) has produced this type of questioning. If the world is rational, which means mathematical, and if I am rational, how is it that I do not understand this world immediately? It is a fact that I do not immediately understand the slightest, sustained demonstration of geometry. Now, the one responsible for an error in a laboratory experiment whose protocol is well designed and must be properly followed, is the subject of the experiment, is the subject of science.[29]

It is, indeed, the same subject that Freud finds and questions, the subject of bungled acts, of lapses, the subject of dreams, the subject of the formations of the Unconscious. We retain this position of the subject to study it in place of trying to reduce it, as does the mode of communication called scientific, that is, to eliminate it as neo-Cartesian psychology does. Rejected from discourse, it returns in the Real.

THE TOPOLOGY OF KNOTS AND THE *SINTHOME*

We will leave for another occasion our explanation developed from the geometry of narcissism in mirror symmetry between intrinsic and extrinsic and our topology of the drive with the trickling of the little letters in our drawings.

These studies lead to the study of the knot which remains a proposition, made to the subject, to learn how to deal with this hole, this circle, his or her *sinthome* who, should he or she not do so, risks encountering some hindrance, even some obstacle as long as he or she does not know what to do with this hole. The subject seeks to stop it up and that fails, as is usually the case, while producing children whose education, in these terms, leaves a lot to be desired. There is the small object *a*, so favorable to supporting misrecognition, even on the distaff side—that there is no sexual rapport—but this is not a reason for not trying to anyway, in order to render reason to this very impossibility, laid bare.

Plaisance, February 24, 2001

ENDNOTES

Translators' Notes: It should be noted that the French term *rond*, loop, is also known in topology as an unknot, or trivial knot. In this paper, all square brackets refer to translation. Either the French original is provided or a meaning in English.

1. Jean-Michel Vappereau, *Étoffe*, Paris: Topologie en extension (tel:[33]01· 40·44·85·73): pp. 18 and 143–144, 1997.

2. Jacques Lacan, *Le séminaire, livre XIV* (1966–1967): *La logique du fantasme*, unpublished seminar.

3. Louis Kauffman, "Knots and Logic," *Knots and Their Application, Scientific World Collection* (Riverside, NJ: New Jersey Office) *Knots and Everything*, 1993.

4. Jacques Lacan, *Le séminaire, livre XXIII* (1975–1976). *Le sinthome*, unpublished seminar.

5. One person skilled in the genre of today claims to be challenging psychoanalysis, whereas in fact he is addressing psychoanalysts of today who are far from the issue and incapable of taking it up. But that in no way removes his responsibility for answering the question he formulates because the existence of the unconscious concerns each one of us. That's a fact, and we do not see why this person would put himself above the fray by putting a question to others without making the effort to answer it himself.

No doctrine of the unconscious can save itself the effort of questions formulated by Locke. Yes sir, that's right and it is the basis for where we begin.

It is true that the familial instances of psychoanalysis, which want to pass for official, a trap set by the will of their founder, does not give much of an impression of being able to face it in this place. Caught up as they are with other problems which *were* solved by Lacan, such as the one of the pseudo-instance of the superego whose imperative commands the subject to enjoy [*jouir*]. That titillates them to the point that they remain all excited about it in their onanism, exclusive phallic *jouissance*. A discourse that has now become generalized to the entire psychoanalytical collective of today, "bad service rendered to the organ."

6. Sigmund Freud, "Project for a Scientific Psychology" (1897–1902), *SE* 1: 283–397.

7. Sigmund Freud, "The Interpretation of Dreams" (1900); *SE* 4 & 5; "A Metapsychological Supplement to the Theory of Dreams" (1915), *SE* 14: 222–235; "The Outline of Psychoanalysis" (1938), *SE* 23: 141–207.

8. Here, it is amusing, to read Freud's remarks at the beginning of *Totem and Taboo*, addressed to Wundt, who wrote a work in which he claims to have accounted for fetishism.

9. (cfm) stands for modified formative clause

10. (am.) stands for modified axiom

11. Jacques Lacan, *"L'étourdit"* (1972), *Scilicet*, no. 4 (1973): 5–52, p. 28.

12. Jean-Claude Milner, *L'oeuvre claire*, Paris: Seuil, 1995 pp. 161–162.

13. Jean-Claude Milner, *L'usage de l'oubli*, Paris: Seuil, 1988, oeuvrage collectif, p. xxx.

14. We present these questions as a reader of the *Écrits* of Lacan. This series of texts is not interrupted in 1966 when a first volume is published by Seuil in Paris. To be able to work on a precise corpus we have brought together journal articles starting in 1966 through the time of Dr. Lacan's death in 1981, a second volume, then, of what we will call with J.-C. Milner, the Scripta of Lacan. If this reader proposes to have the Scripta and the Seminar play different roles, this agrees with our manner, even if we have it do so for other reasons. For us, the structural character leaves no doubt, but the phenomenology of the history [*histoire*: also story], the *hystoricité* cannot be neglected. So we distinguish in our sources for a reason of method. Overall, the *Écrits* (*Scripta*) present the manifest text of Lacan's teaching and the Seminars form an associative text which enable reading in the manner of Freud, that is to say, of Champolion.

15. Jacques Lacan, "Seminar on 'The Purloined Letter'" (1956), trans. by J. Mehlman. *The Purloined Poe: Lacan, Derrida, and Psychoanalytic Reading*, ed. by W. J. Richardson and J. P. Muller, Baltimore, MD: Johns Hopkins University Press, 1988.

16. Jacques Lacan, "On a Question Preliminary to Any Possible Treatment of Psychosis" (1957–1958), *Écrits: A Selection*, trans. and ed. by Alan Sheridan, New York: W. W. Norton, 1977.

17. Jacques Lacan, *The Seminar of Jacques Lacan, Book* II: *The Ego in Freud's Theory and in the Technique of Psychoanalysis* (1954–1955), ed. by Jacques-Alain Miller, trans. by S. Tomaseli, New York: W. W. Norton, 1988.

18. Jacques Lacan *Le séminaire, livre* IX (1961–1962): *L'identification*, unpublished seminar.

19. Jacques Lacan, "Remarques sur le rapport de Daniel Lagache: 'Psychanalyse et structure de la personnalité'" (1960), *Écrits*, Paris: Seuil, 1966.

20. Jacques Lacan, "The Agency of the Letter in the Unconscious or Reason since Freud" (1957), *Écrits: A Selection*, trans. and ed. by Alan Sheridan, New York: W. W. Norton, 1977.

21. Jacques Lacan, *Le séminaire, livre* IV (1956–1957): *La relation d'objet*, ed. by Jacques-Alain Miller, Paris: Seuil, 1994.

22. Jacques Lacan, *Le séminaire, livre* V (1957–1958): *Les formations de l'inconscient*, ed. by Jacques-Alain Miller, Paris: Seuil, 1998.

23. Jacques Lacan, "Position of the Unconscious," trans. by Bruce Fink, *Reading Seminar XI: Lacan's Four Fundamental Concepts of Psychoanalysis*, ed. R. Feldstein, B. Fink, and M. Jaanus. Albany, NY: SUNY Press, 1995, pp. 259–282.

24. Jacques Lacan, "The Function and Field of Speech and Language in Psychoanalysis" (1953), *Écrits: A Selection*, trans. and ed. By Alan Sheridan, New York: W. W. Norton, 1977.

25. Jacques Lacan, *Le séminaire, livre* XIV (1966–1967): *La logique du fantasme*, unpublished seminar.

26. It is curious how these texts make the reader commit an error, wishing to be as precise as J.-C. Milner when he remarks that there is no major *Écrit* in the making in the "Rome Discourse" for what Milner calls the second Lacanian classicism. He had, however, stressed in his article in *The Encyclopédie Universalis*, bearing on linguistics and psychoanalysis, that we would not know how to appreciate Lacan's *Écrits* without reading this text. He refers himself, more willingly, for this period, to the Seminar *Encore* [*Seminar XX*] which, certainly, is an admirable spoken text, once again in the majestic manner. But the fact remains that "*L'étourdit*" is a major *Écrit* for Lacanian classicism, his manifesto in the form of a theoretical testament.

27. In *L'oeuvre claire*, J.-C. Milner is obliged to make K. Popper intervene in order to deal with the strictly structural component of this question since it demonstrates—due to the distinction between the *Scripta* and the seminars—that historicism is insufficient as far as Lacan is concerned. Now here two things must be said.

Popper deals with experimental science (scientific research) in the framework of canonical deductive logic and mathematics as it stood at the time he was writing, taking the latter "as is," since he himself explains very clearly that he only wants to object to inductive logic in laboratory science. He sets aside the question of the scholar's curiosity, citing Einstein, locating the desire of the scholar in psychology. That is the first point.

Then, utilizing his discriminant, in the extensions of his major work (*Poscriptum*), he places Freud and psychoanalysis, of which he has only read *The Interpretation of Dreams* (around 1900), on the side of metaphysics as an irrefutable discipline. The reproach of verificationism is unjust since Freud tries to refute his own doctrine in the 1920s, in *Beyond the Pleasure Principle*. There is an abuse there.

Popper makes the mistake of not envisaging—because he is incapable of thinking it—that reason has moved since Freud. It must be said by way of acquittal that he is not the only one.

Psychoanalysis is indeed irrefutable but it is not a metaphysics, for metaphysics is a true discourse as science is, which is refutable. Psychoanalysis is a false and irrefutable discourse, opening onto another type of logical research. See on this subject the debate between Carvaillès, sustaining the activity, and Lautman, the object of the mathematician, in the 1930s (reproduced in Cavaillès, *Oeuvres complètes de philosophie des sciences*, Paris, Herman).

28. G. Canghilem, "Qu'est-ce que la psychologie?" in *Etudes d'histoire et de philosophie des sciences*, Vrin, 19xx, Paris.

29. What an irony when we think we know this text by Canghilem through the *Cahiers pour l'Analyse* whose first delivery published this text, no. 1/2, while the principal publisher/editor of this journal, J.-C. Milner, wrote an entire book on questioning the status of this subject without thinking for a second about finding his reference in this author whom he undoubtedly and certainly rightly considers a master in matters of the doctrinal aspects of science. Milner follows Kojève scrupulously in his book devoted to Lacan, *L'oeuvre claire*, in his cut-outs. But as too good a pupil, he does not see that if Kojève has a reason, is right, and he explains himself precisely on this, not to consider any other authors than those he cites from Tales to Hegel, thus creating an enormous gulf between Aristotle and Kant, this may be for the reason which is his, in retracing Hegel's experience to reach the end of metaphysics, another name for philosophy. If we want to handle another problem, subordinate next to this one, and which consists of dealing with the subject of science, of the appearance at the turning point of medieval philosophy in philosophy's second round at arriving at its modern phase, a finer cut-out must be made. This is the time when theology turns into anthropology with Galilean and Cartesian science. Now Milner stumbles on the sidelines, leaving the matter to his friend F. Regnault, who has merely occupied the terrain to give the

impression of handling the overall problem with his *Dieu est inconscient* [God is unconscious]. This is not good. We expected more from these young people, since one of their friends had largely lost his way in this field, through pretension undoubtedly, through mean stupidity certainly. We find those people very presumptuous, which does not seem to stop the nerve. Since, we learn from this author that he has rewritten his conclusion by abandoning Wittgenstein I and II. He could have realized this before. And the K. Popper map, when is he going to give that up in order to break with the rather cowardly style that has reigned in Paris since 1975? The style of the repentants of somewhat demanding thought for the benefit of arrangements of generalized competition.

I wonder sometimes if these people realize the responsibility they have; they are talented certainly, but what a lack of regard for the ravages they produce around themselves. A responsibility regarding which we have always held ourselves accountable in what we teach.

16

Borromean Knots, Le Sinthome, and Sense Production in Law*

DRAGAN MILOVANOVIC

INTRODUCTION

A critical perspective in law and criminology can be constructively augmented by a psychoanalytic semiotic view rooted in postmodern thought, particularly drawing inspiration from Jacques Lacan. A new direction could be defined as constitutive law and criminology.[1] This view suggests that thinking about law should be reconsidered as the coterminous discursive production by human agents of an ideology of the rule of law that sustains it as a concrete reality. Although some initial forays have appeared, a contribution to the question of agency is still in the process of development. Accordingly, this article explores the contributions of Lacanian thought, particularly his late development of topology theory, and, more specifically, the Borromean knots and *le sinthome*. This could

---

*This is a revised version of D. Milovanovic, "Borromean Knots and the Constitution of Sense in Juridico-Discursive Production," *Legal Studies Forum*, vol. 17, no. 2, 1993, pp. 171–192.

potentially lead to a macro/micro integration. The construction of
an alternative, more liberating "replacement discourse" that allows
desire fuller embodiment will be seen as implicit in this integration and will be developed somewhat in the final section.

In this chapter we want to briefly outline the constitutive approach in comparison to the various Marxist perspectives on subjectivity and sense production in law. This will be followed with a
discussion on subjectivity and psychoanalytic semiotics. We will
then turn to a short explication of the Borromean knots and *le
sinthome* in relation to sense production. In our final section, we
will illustrate how Lacanian insights on the knots and *le sinthome*
can be integrated with a constitutive approach in law, indicating
particularly how the legal subject is constituted and how discursive constructions are circumscribed in the legal arena.

MACRO-MICRO INTEGRATION:
CONSTITUTIVE PERSPECTIVE ON LAW

Approaches in the sociology of law that seek to identify law as simply an outcome of macro- or of microcontexts should be rejected.
Rather, we will argue that coproductive activity by agents both
produce and reproduce juridical-ideological phenomena. Law, in
this view, both reflects dominant social relations and constitutes
them. Driven by purposive rational constructions and reproduced
by syllogistic reasoning within relatively stabilized linguistic coordinate systems, law provides key master signifiers (S_1) that are
determinative of social relations. In other words, law has the power
to frame politics and legal processes, and hence shape political
possibilities. Dominant social relations, in turn, continuously infuse juridic constructions with energy through use, while providing, especially during crises, new material for incorporation.

In all this, we hasten to add, voices from the disenfranchised,
marginalized, oppressed, and exploited are denied their effective
contributions in semiotic production and in the stabilization
of alternative linguistic coordinate systems within which more

liberating embodiments of desire may materialize. Nor are relatively stabilized discursive subject-positions offered that provide greater opportunity for the play of spontaneity, chance, randomness, irony, and continuous variation. In this sense, subordinated, are *pas-tout(e)*, not all, not complete in the dominant Symbolic order. As we shall see below, they are more often relegated to the *discourse of the hysteric*, and hence further marginalized or, in their haste to overcome the gaps in being, resigned to suturing operations that are modal forms of the *discourse of the master* and in more refined form, the *discourse of the university*.

How can we overcome this cyclical and hegemonic reproduction of dominant reality? Let us first briefly summarize some key Marxian conceptualizations of the relationship between the "base" and "superstructure," noting some of their deficiencies, and then move on to the synthesis of constitutive theory with Lacan's idea of the Borromean knots.

MARXIST-INSPIRED VIEWS

Marxist views in the sociology of law have been the beginning points for illuminating analysis. In most cases, however, they lack a necessary component of semiotic analysis, a bona fide conception of agency, and an understanding of the intimate connection between the two.

Several Marxist views have evolved. Two broad approaches have been interpreted. First, the instrumental Marxist view in law would argue that the economic sphere is the primal causal agent behind all phenomena, be it law, crime, definitions of crime, public policy, development of consciousness, morals, ethics, and so forth (Figure 16–1a). This view was substantially criticized during the 1970s, and by the early 1980s grew into disfavor. The second approach is the structural approach that developed during the early 1980s. Here, the essential argument is that several relatively autonomous spheres exist—economic, ideological, political, juridical—and collectively contribute in a concerted manner to the development of phenomena. Thus, specifying the causal agents is an exercise in specifying the particular articulation of these relatively autonomous spheres within historical conditions. This has been referred to as an "articulation of instances." Any phenomenon, then, is overdetermined by a number of disproportionally impacting spheres.

After some polemics during the 1980s, several subcategories of the structural Marxist approach have been delineated. The commodity-exchange perspective, or the so-called capital-logic school, still places decisive weight with the economic sphere, although it does indicate that commodity-exchange in a competitive capitalist marketplace produces certain phenomenal forms such as the juridic subject, formal equality, and generally, the law of equivalence (Figure 16–1b), which then affects socioeconomic relations. A second variant of the structural version is the structural interpellation perspective rooted more in Althusser[2] and Poulantzas.[3] Here, the superstructure is the primal or decisive causal sphere. Subjects are said to be interpellated as spoken subjects by the juridical-ideological sphere (Figure 16–1c).

In all these Marxist perspectives what is lacking is a bona fide statement concerning agency and a sensitivity to nonlinear historical developments. Instrumental Marxists relegate the subject to Bentham-like utilitarian existence; commodity exchange views subjects merely acting out the logic of the movement of capital; structural interpellationists see subjects as merely "supports" of hegemonic groups. Ironically, all three, ostensibly concerned with the human condition, have been insensitive to the multidimensional nature of agency.

Constitutive theory begins with certain strengths of the structural interpellation view (Figure 16–1d), but recognizes inherent limitations within it. The necessary element in overcoming the above deficiencies is semiotic analysis and the use of nonlinear conceptions of historical change, suggested, for example, by Nietzsche, Foucault, and chaos theory. Postmodernist analysis, particularly one rooted in the insights of Lacanian psychoanalytic semiotics, offers us much potential for better conceptualizing the nature of the desiring subject in relation to discursive production. Consti-

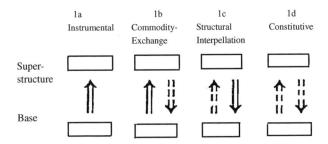

Figure 16–1. Critical Perspectives of Base-Superstructure

tutive theory, however, offers an organizing structure that applies semiotic analysis as a key element. Let us first make a distinction between the oppositional and revolutionary subject.

OPPOSITIONAL AND REVOLUTIONARY SUBJECTS

Increasingly, in a social formation, we see the tension between, on the one hand, the constituted subject (alternatively: the "interpellated," "spoken," or "good subject")[4] and, on the other, the resisting subject (i.e., ranging from the less politically aware oppositional subject to the politically articulate, revolutionary subject). Lacan's offering of four structured discourses has been instructive in these conceptualizations. Elsewhere, drawing from Lacan, we[5] have indicated that the *discourse of the master*, or its more hidden form, the *discourse of the university*, is the modal form of subjectification in hierarchical social formations, be they "capitalistic" or "socialistic" (see, also, my Chapter 9, this book). The oppositional subject (i.e., the alienated, frustrated, and revolting subject), one without a fully articulate transformative politics, can be depicted by the Lacanian *discourse of the hysteric*. The revolutionary subject, or perhaps more precisely, the cultural revolutionary, we shall show below, can be seen as constituted by the discourse of the hysteric *and* analyst[6] and is one who begins to be driven by an articulate transformative agenda.

Marxist analysis has indicated how subjects become constituted by the discourse of the master and university, but yet often revolt in the form of the discourse of the hysteric, a discourse by itself devoid of any potential for transformative politics or new visions of what could be. At best, the Marxian/Hegelian conceptualization of historical change can merely indicate that dialectical materialism will propel the disenfranchised (the "slave" in Hegel's master–slave dialectic, or the proletariat in Marx's version) to revolt, or to engage in the discourse of the hysteric. But careful examination will indicate that this is merely reactive-negative dynamics: nothing new is being offered. In fact, many of the more contemporary Marxists or postmodernists who seek help from Derrida have too quickly embraced the idea of "reversing hierarchies" as the solution. With but little reflection we can see how, without more, this merely reconstitutes forms of domination.

We hasten to disagree with both Lacan and Bracher[7] that the *discourse of the analyst*, in *itself*, offers the direction for change, for, as both indicate, this discourse can easily slip back into, and historically has slipped back into, the discourse of the master. Accordingly, in our view, a perpetual oscillation between the discourse of the hysteric and analyst, tantamount to what chaos theorists have termed a "strange attractor," is desirable and would begin to produce the cultural revolutionary. Applying the Borromean knots, below we will also provide a novel conceptualization of how new signifiers may develop with more stable structures. Some of the insights from chaos theory have also shed productive light on the milieu within which this could take place.

We now turn to a brief explication of Lacan's subject as represented by a signifier.

LACAN'S PSYCHOANALYTIC SEMIOTICS

According to Lacan, the interactive effects of three main orders lie behind phenomena: the Imaginary, Symbolic, and Real. The Imaginary order is the sphere of imagoes, of imaginary construc tions of self, others, and possible objects that offer the potential for the fulfillment of desire (*objet petit a*). These are essentially illusory, but give us hope of mastery in otherwise incomprehensible situations. The Symbolic order is the sphere of language, culture, and sociocultural prohibitions. The Other, an unconscious sphere, is the sphere within which signifying production, coordinated by the tropes of metaphor and metonymy, takes place. The Other as the "treasury of signifiers" is where signifiers "float" awaiting anchorage (*capitonnage*) to particular signifieds. And, in Lacan's enigmatic definition, a signifier is that which is the subject for another signifier.

The Lacanian desiring subject, then, is represented in discourse by signifiers who speak it. The speaking being (*l'être parlant*, or *parlêtre*) is divided, represented in Lacan's mathemes as a slashed subject or $. It exists on two levels: the level of discursive production and the level of discourse itself. At the level of discursive production, meaning "falters, slips and slides,"[8] always subject to the effects of desire seeking expression, always "insisting." Periodic punctuations provide temporary joins to particular signifiers: it is this that produces particular meaning. In Lacan's mathemes:

$$S(\emptyset) \rightarrow \$ \Diamond a \rightarrow s(O) \rightarrow \text{signifying chain, or:}$$
$$\frac{\text{S-S-S-S-S}}{\text{s}}.$$

What this means is that the inherent-lack-in-being [$S(\emptyset)$] of the *parlêtre* ($), a condition in which signifiers exist temporarily without anchorage within the Other (O), periodically leads to fantasy production ($ $\Diamond$ a), culminating in a punctuation [s(O)], a temporary and unstable knotting of a signifier to a particular signified (S/s, or *point de capiton*). S-S-S-S-S/s represents a "signifying chain," an utterance. Ultimately, of course, embodied signifiers must find expression within particular linguistic coordinate systems coordinated by the paradigm and syntagm semiotic axis to produce a narratively coherent text. It is this process that produces idiosyncratic sense.

The final Lacanian order is the sphere of the Real. It represents the phenomenal world of sense perception, beyond any accurate reflection in Symbolic constructions. It always exists in the background with effect.

In the Lacanian construct, desire is periodically mobilized due to the inherent lack-in-being of the subject, which was the cost borne by the child in its inauguration into the Symbolic order and all that it has to offer: control, mastery, understanding, and the basis for social action. Henceforth, contradictions, contrarieties, and anomalies faced mobilize desire whereby the subject $\mathcal{S}$ attempts to *suture*, or stitch over the gaps in being. This search for objects of desire (*objet petit a*) implicates the Symbolic and Imaginary orders. Existing value-laden signifiers within particular linguistic coordinate systems (legal, oppositional, pluralistic, etc.) offer linguistic forms for the embodiment of desire. The creation of sense overcomes the felt lack in being, an experience that Lacan referred to as *jouissance* (or *jouis-sense*, enjoyment in sense; in the French, the term also has connotations of an orgasm). This is essentially fantasy, or in Lacan's mathemes, $\mathcal{S} \Diamond a$. Sense production, then, entails the interplay of the Imaginary and the Symbolic orders with the Real always in the background, but nevertheless insisting.

BORROMEAN KNOTS

Lacan's late works (1972–1977) focused on topological constructions of Borromean knots. Lacan attempted to provide an alternative mapping of the psychic apparatus and sense production. These constructions are neither metaphors nor analogies to the workings of the psychic apparatus: they are offered as homologies. It is these Borromean knots that provide an explanatory mechanism of constitutive processes taking place, producing and reproducing hierarchically constituted discursive formations. The constitutive theory of law will provide a useful schema in understanding the processes of sense production in signifying practices.

In our final section, we will illuminate possible directions for reconstituting discursive regions in the form of a replacement discourse.

STRUCTURE AND FUNCTION OF BORROMEAN KNOTS

Remarkably, little in Western thought has engaged the insights generated by Lacan on the Borromean knots. From 1962 to 1972, the Möbius strip and cross-cap were key topological constructs for Lacan. From the middle of 1972 to about 1977, the Borromean knot became dominant (after 1977, Lacan's productivity and creativity were reduced dramatically due to deteriorating health). In between, beginning in 1969, the notion of the four discourses was to be a transitional step to increasingly abstract and difficult conceptualizations.

The idea of a knot, however, was already appearing in Lacan's Seminars in 1962. In short form, a Borromean knot is defined by two or more loops or rings knotted by another (each ring represents one of the Lacanian orders); cut one, and all disentangle. (Figure 16–2 below is a 2-D portrait; a 3-D portrait would more accurately indicate how the three circles are intertwined. Note, for example, that in the 3-D version there is an under-over, in-

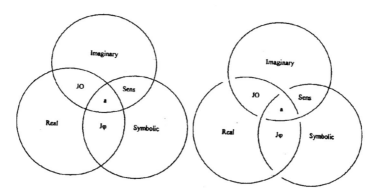

Figure 16–2 Borromean Knot, 2-D. Borromean Knot, 3-D.

terlocking form of the rings.) The Borromean knot depicts the interconnectedness of the psychic apparatus, portraying how it in fact maintains *constancy*. Here,

a = *le plus-de-jouir* (the more than enjoyment, the left out)
JO = *jouissance* of the Other; bodily *jouissance*
JΦ = phallic *jouissance*
Sens = meaning unique to the speaking being (*l'être parlant*)
R.S.I. = the three orders: Real, Symbolic, Imaginary

A ring (actually a torus), unlike a sphere, is not a container and thus something appearing within the Borromean intersections is both in and outside of it; the notion of "inside" and "outside" becomes problematic.[9] Ragland-Sullivan[10] has precisely commented on this enigma: "the space structured around the joins of these orders would be inferred into discourse as a topology of fixed positions and effects in the Other which operates language and perception, ensuring that neither discourse nor perception be purely linear, nor purely conscious." Consider, too, Marini's[11] observation that the theory of the Borromean knots implies that the subject is "mis-situated between two and three dimensions," which finds expression in Lacan with his idea of *dit-mension*.[12] In chaos theory, this would be represented by the idea of a *fractal*, depicting fractions of dimensions. Clearly, Lacan had an entirely novel conception of space, one in opposition to Newtonian physics. Unfortunately, he was not acquainted with chaos theory; some theorists inspired by him, such as Deleuze and Guattari,[13] have indeed explored some illuminating directions with this insight.

From 1972 to 1977 Lacan was to develop numerous pictures of the Borromean knots. He would construct a Borromean knot as a set of interlocking rings whereby cutting one would let loose the others. He would then construct several of these, producing a ring of such knots, a Borromean ring. For Lacan, it was a representation of the functioning of the psychic apparatus. This conceptualization was to replace his earlier idea of a signifying chain. It is within this chain that the "letter [signifier] insists."[14]

Let us relate the Borromean knots to fantasy. Fantasy production, as we have indicated, can be traced to the essential lack in being of the subject. Lack, in turn, "is iterated with specific effects in each of the Lacanian topological orders."[15] The cumulative result (symbolized by the knots) or fantasy, representing the appearing and disappearing of the subject, also becomes the basis of social action.

It should also be noted that two forms of *jouissance* appear: phallic *jouissance* ($J\Phi$) is located at the intersection of the Real and Symbolic orders—it is the upper limit of *jouissance* that exists within a given phallocentric Symbolic order. However, an *unspeakable jouissance* exists that is beyond the phallus at the intersection of the Real and Imaginary, called alternatively *supplementary*, *bodily*, or a *jouissance* of the Other (JO).[16] And here exists the potential for the development of alternative knottings, and thus, understandings.

Let us provide an example, the narrative: "Jones willfully inflicted gross bodily harm on Fred." Here, each signifier takes on value within a discursive whole; in its apparent linear construction, each completed signifier anticipates the next (the anticipatory dimension) and only with the punctuation is there a return to the beginning (Lacan's *retrograde*), providing the whole a precise sense. In Figure 16–3, we note that the divided subject now appears at the bottom left. Here the subject is represented in discourse by her or his signifiers. The discursive chain now stands for the presence of an absence, whereby the signifier is the subject for another signifier. We should add that the paradigm-syntagm level of semiotic production is only the most manifest level experienced in actual dialogical encounters within particular linguistic coordinate systems;[17] at a deeper level, however, desire begins to be embodied by the effects of condensation-displacement (discovered by Freud) and takes on additional embodiment via metaphor-metonymy (Lacan's contribution following Jakobson's work on aphasic disorders).[18]

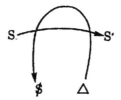

Figure 16–3. Elementary Cell of Speech Production[19]

More conscious	Paradigm	Syntagm
↑ ↓	Metaphor	Metonymy
More unconscious	Condensation	Displacement

Figure 16–4. Semiotic Grid

Each signifier embodying desire (see also Freud's idea of "figuration") finds its coordinates in the semiotic grid (see Figure 16–4). This consists of the following axes: paradigm-syntagm (at the conscious level), metaphor-metonymy (at the unconscious level), and condensation-displacement (at the most fundamental and unconscious level of the working of the unconscious). Each manifest signifier is but the loci of complex processes (i.e., the interactive effects of the three orders: Real, Symbolic, and Imaginary), which have reached an anchoring point, a knotting (*capitonnage*) that maintains degrees of constancy. Master signifiers, S_1, are the core identificatory signifiers. It is this knotting that produces an idiosyncratic sense for each speaking being (*l'être parlant*). Some of these knots, or constellation of knots, attain greater permanence within the psychic structure: these belong to the order of the symptom (*le sinthome*), and become the basis of "repetition," or as Lacan has it, the source of the periodic manifestation of the "letter insisting."[20] They become relatively stable points from which *jouissance* is experienced. In sum, Lacan's notion of structure is unique: it "is both anticipatory and retroactive; static and dynamic; prediscursive and discursive; regulatory and disruptive."[21]

The topology of the Borromean knots—its opening, closing, stasis, and transformation—in relation to the disciplining mechanisms of a political economy becomes the key in understanding change. Consider, for example, the *cuts* engendered during revolutionary upheavals, especially in contemporary Eastern Europe and the former Soviet Union, and, with it, the appearance of the good (i.e., more liberating articulations of the three orders), the bad (i.e., divisive nationalistic and ultra-right-wing movements), and the ugly (i.e., ethnic hatred and campaigns of "ethnic cleansing").

THE SYMPTOM (*LE SINTHOME*)

In late 1975, Lacan, then in his mid-70s, discovered the fourth order, that of *le sinthome*, or *le sinthome*, Σ.[22] Lacan attributed the discovery of the symptom to Karl Marx, whom he read when he was 20.[23] During his seminar of December 9th and 16th, 1975, he tells us that he had scratched his head for two months pondering the possibility of the fourth tie. He drew considerable inspiration from two friends who were mathematicians, Michel Thome and Pierre Soury. According to Ragland-Sullivan,[24] [t]he symptom may be a word, sound, event, detail, or image that acts in a way peculiar to a given subject's history . . . the enigmatic symptom belongs to the sign or the unconscious signifying chain of language because it is susceptible of being deciphered or decoded." We will briefly explain the wherewithal of the symptom, and then indicate its importance for a constitutive theory of law and for the potential of understanding the necessary dynamics of a replacement discourse.

The function of the fourth term is to repair, mend, correct, or restore a fault in the knot R.S.I.[25] is a form of "suture" that Lacan had developed in his earlier seminars. Put in another way, absent a knot, the three orders experience no constancy: they are, in Lacan's formulation, $S(\emptyset)$. In other words, an inherent lack (-1) exists in the Other. It is with the fourth term that "naming" ("*donner-nom*") takes place, a response to the lack in the Other, to the failures and breakdowns in the Other.[26] This naming operation, depicted by "doubling," is what provides relative constancy for the psychic apparatus.

Speech production, for example, constitutes itself in the doubling of the symbolic with the symptom (*le sinthome*).[27] Put in another way, these three relatively autonomous spheres must be knotted in order that consistency and a sense of permanency prevails. In the Freudian construct, the Oedipus complex performs this function. Absent this, psychosis awaits. In the Lacanian schema, it is the Name-of-the-Father that acts as the stabilizing structure. The Name-of-the-Father functions to overcome the failures in the Other by realizing the knot, R.S.I.[28] Of course it follows that a number of other candidates exist that may function in the capacity of "repairing" the knot as, for example, postmodemist feminists have pointed out. In a phallic Symbolic order, all is tainted with the phallus. The upper limit of *jouissance* is phallic ($J\Phi$), and therefore women are left out, *pas-toute*.[29]

More generally, ongoing hierarchically organized political economies need to provide "fillers" in order to overcome this inherent lack-in-being. Absent this, crises tendencies (legal, economic, political, ideological) may tend toward radical upheavals. Thus, for example, we have Imaginary constructions of agency such as the "reasonable man" in law, the rational man/woman in economic planning, and the notion of the private citizen bound within the logic of the rule of law. The advertisement industry, too, provides a plethora of discursive subject positions with which to identify.

Topologically speaking, the fourth term can be continuously deformed, producing numerous "repairings"; it can always stir elsewhere[30] with specific effects. Thus *le sinthome* can "double" the Symbolic, Real, or the Imaginary.[31]

We can see in Figure 16–5, under the doubling of the Symbolic, that the ring representing the Symbolic order is replaced by a binary, $S + \Sigma$, producing a new form of the Symbolic, S''.[32] In fact, "this binary corresponds to two slopes of the Symbolic: the signifier able to couple itself with another in order to make a chain, and the letter [that 'insists']."[33] Hence, these two are complementary functions, one acting to represent in a chain of signifiers, the other

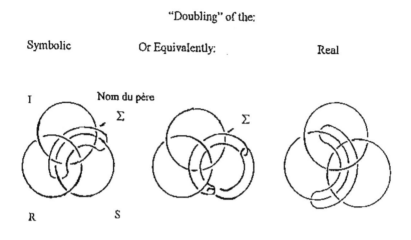

"Doubling" of the:

Symbolic   Or Equivalently: Real

Imaginary

Figure 16–5. Le Sinthome and Doubling

remaining embedded in the symptom and acting as the support. It is this that anchors the discursive chain and provides meaning (*sens*); that is, it reflects the speaking subject's truth even though s/he does not know what it is. It is also this dynamic that produces the *objet petit* (*a*) and provides a sense of plenitude, an overcoming of –1, experienced as a *jouis-sens*.[34]

Let's consider the *discourse of the master:*

$$\frac{S_1}{\text{\$}} \rightarrow \frac{S_2}{a}$$

According to Lacan, "the subject in this state can only represent itself by the signifier indicated as S_1, while the signifier indicated as S_2 represents itself . . . by the duplicity of the symbolic and the symptom."[35] The receiver of the message enacts the S_1, producing his or her symptom, and at the most manifest level, a body of knowledge, S_2. Lacan goes on to say, "S_2 there, is the author [*artisan*], in so much by the conjunction of the two signifiers he is capable of producing the *objet* (*a*). . . ."[36] Thus, in the discourse of the master, S_2, knowledge, divides itself into the Symbolic and the symptom (*le sinthome*). The symptom remains the support of S_2, knowledge. The sender's S_1 activates, or elicits S_2, which nevertheless "insists" in producing the *a*, *le-plus-de-jouir* in the unconscious. Here, something is left out, is not embodied in signifiers. This excess has only potentiality in being given form. The subject is represented by a signifier. For Lacan, the signifier is that which represents the subject for another signifier in a signifying/Borromean chain. Knowledge, therefore, is always supported by an underlying *le sinthome*, is always a function of a fractal space at work. This is why Lacan refers to the "said" as the *dit-mension*.

On the other hand, in the *discourse of the analyst*, $\frac{a}{S_2} \rightarrow \frac{\$}{S_1}$, the receiving subject (hysteric) divides itself, producing new S_1s as a response to the information that the sender (analyst) is reflecting about her or him (see also my Chapter 9, this book). These are new master signifiers that become the basis of an alternative symptom and, consequently, become a basis of an alternative *jouissance*. Put in another way, this has everything to do with the process of knot-breaking and "repairing." And if we were then to take the discourse of the hysteric and analyst together, we could see the basis for the revolutionary subject insomuch as s/he continuously reconstitutes her or his truth by giving form to alternative master signifiers and body of knowledge. Put in yet another way, a new configuration of Borromean knots now anchors being. This could be mapped as the *strange attractor* that chaos theory offers. Of course, this could only operate in a supportive milieu. Thus, again, borrowing from chaos theory, *far-from-equilibrium* conditions would seem the desirable form of a social formation.[37]

For Freud, the doubling of the Real produced the "psychic reality" of each subject; for James Joyce, whose writings Lacan analyzed extensively, the doubling of the Symbolic order produced "Joyce the Symptom"; and the doubling of the Imaginary order may produce perversion.[38] Let us be more concrete. The doubling of the Real can be seen historically as represented, in a more active mode, by "doers," such as Hobbsbaun's "primitive rebel,"[39] who are without a sophisticated political ideology but nevertheless in touch with the prevailing deprivations. In a more passive mode, we could also include here many repressed and exploited subjects who find inadequate linguistic coordinate systems within which to embody desire and to construct narratives that more accurately define their plight. Surely, the discourse of the master and university will impose its understanding. The doubling of the Symbolic produces a subject who lives his symptom in the form of being totally embedded in discourse itself;[40] on the one hand, the poet is exemplary, on the other, so too the committed (seduced) lawyer who is convinced of the liberating potentials of the rule of law ideology. For the doubling of the Imaginary, a grossly distorted view of self and others manifests itself; perhaps totally self-engrossed dreamers tend toward this pole.

In each case a temporary join is produced that is a source of *jouissance*. These joins, however, can break, or, alternatively, the fourth term may manifest itself elsewhere with entirely different effects. This is precisely what Jurgen Habermas[41] was getting at when he spoke of steering mechanisms undergoing change, and the "life-world" being coordinated by purposive rational action in advanced forms of capitalistic modes of production. It becomes the basis of new centers of articulation and thereby of sense, producing, in the end, *jouissance*. This essential instability is both the source for manipulative powers and the basis for a potentially new articulation that better embodies human desires.

LITERARY EXAMPLE OF REPAIRING THE KNOT:
JOYCE THE *SYNTHOME*

An exemplar of the functioning of the *symptom* can be offered from the literary sphere. Skriabine[42] and Ragland-Sullivan,[43] following Lacan's extensive analysis of Joyce's prose,[44] suggest that the fault in R.S.I. had to do with the Imaginary order's not being knotted with the Real and Symbolic, which are knotted (Figure 16–6a).

Localizing the *moi* (Lacan's Imaginary ego) at the fault (*faute*) can correct this deficiency and thereby connect all three Orders (Figure 16–6b). The Imaginary ego is the component of Lacan's quadrilaterally constructed subject that provides illusory but necessary perceptions of unity in order that the subject can function at all. Here, therefore, the ego is *le sinthome*.[45] It is also this resolution that gives peculiarity to Joyce's prose: "Joyce, the symptom," as Lacan would say. "This ego as a symptom [*sinthome*], as a supplement, restores two links between the Symbolic and the Real, and make the Imaginary hold."[46] Otherwise, of course, the Imaginary would continue to glide without anchorage. An initial trace of the original fault, however, remains, and with the Real and Symbolic remaining continuously enlaced, produces the different enigmatic epiphanies in Joyce's work,[47] and reproduces his uniquely constituted truth (*savoir*). As Ragland-Sullivan[48] aptly puts it: "The prose

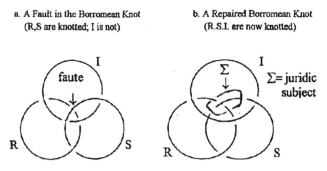

Figures 16–6a,b. *Le Sinthome* and Repairing the Knot
(James Joyce).

of *Finnegans Wake* becomes the fantasy of language, knotting together images, words, and traumas to (re)constitute knots into which signifying associative chains from the Real, Symbolic, and Imaginary can hook themselves."

CONSTITUTIVE THEORY

Let's return to constitutive theory in law. What Lacan's work on the Borromean knots offers are mechanisms by which agency in relationship to social structures could be understood. Legal ideology is transmitted by dominant linguistic coordinate systems, most importantly, the juridic form. This represents the discourse of the master, often dressed as the discourse of the university. What the dominant political economic order offers are "fillers" that provide, on the one hand, illusory conceptions for fulfillment, mastery, understanding, and, on the other, objects of desire [*objet petit (a)*], by which illusory perceptions of the unitary self can be built.

Whether it is the construction and stabilization of the juridic subject, the reasonable man or woman in law (and other forces of rationalization), or the development of new *steering mechanisms* celebrating *purposive rational action* at the expense of Symbolic action and communicatively established shared understanding, or the insidious development of ubiquitous and pervasive forms of control such as in Foucault's *disciplinary mechanisms*, or, finally, whether it is the offerings by a manipulative advertising industry providing seductive discursive subject-positions and objects of desire with which to identify—what are being provided are modal forms of knotting of the three orders. In each instance a pathway is provided for producing *le sinthome*, which is the support of *jouissance*, a safeguard against the fall into an abyss, or alternatively, a way of plugging up the hole-in-being from which all sorts of fragmentary psychic material gushes, threatening to overwhelm the subject.

In the constitutive view, subjects both constitute order out of the framing material provided by dominant discourse, and reconstitute the framing material itself. This is most apparent in law where key master signifiers such as due process and formal equality, and juridically constituted joins (*capitonnage*) of signifiers to signifieds—for example, the legal definition of "person," "insanity," "duress," "willingly," "maliciously," "negligently," and so forth—become key material from which hegemonically supported knots are constructed by litigants before the court. Oppositional groups, too, insomuch as they frame their politics within the dominant linguistic coordinate system, will reproduce, be it inadvertently, dominant conceptions and understandings of reality.

Transpraxis, which follows from the combined discourses of the hysteric and analyst, produces the revolutionary subject, one more in line with the views expressed by Nietzsche rather than Hegel. Here, the subject must self-divide, the S_1 from the S_2, and reconstitute new forms of master signifiers and produce a new knotting in the Borromean chain. This can only begin and continue to be, however, in *far-from-equilibrium* conditions. The strange attractor (one wing representing the discourse of the hysteric, the other, the discourse of the analyst) may be a modal form of being; here, self- and societal-transformation will be continuous. The task before us is not only to strive to develop alternative materialistic conditions of existence but also to engage in the development of a cultural criticism in tune with it. And here we are in agreement with Bracher[49] that the vacuous nature of the latter will certainly be counterproductive to any initiative in the former. Accordingly, the nature of desire, fantasy, objects of desire, and forms of *jouissance* must be examined. A replacement discourse to the contemporary phallocentric Symbolic order must develop in which the embodiment of desire finds fuller expression (on this point, see my Chapter 9, this book).

CONCLUSION

This chapter concerned possible integrations of Lacan's complex work on the Borromean knots and *le sinthome* with constitutive theorizing in law. It indicated that the notion of the subject and discursive production is circumscribed in political economy. The subject of desire finds constancy of her or his psychic apparatus as a legal subject in law. The so-called "reasonable man in law," a relatively recent historical construction, can be analyzed in terms of how the *sinthome* operates to fix a particular configuration of the Symbolic, Imaginary, and Real orders. Thus, it is political economy which operates the breaking and repairing of the knot. It is equally compelling for social activists to develop alternative discourses, replacement discourses, and new bases of *le sinthome* so that desire may find fuller embodiment.

ENDNOTES

1. S. Henry and D. Milovanovic, *Constitutive Criminology*, London: Sage Publications, 1996.

2. L. Althusser, *Lenin and Philosophy*, New York, *Monthly Review Press*, 1971.

3. N. Poulantzas, *Political Power and Social Class*, Atlantic Fields, NY: Humanities Press, 1973.

4. For the *interpellated subject*, see L. Althusser, *op. cit.*; for the *spoken subject* in cinema theory, see K. Silverman, *The Subject of Semiotics*, New York: Oxford University Press, 1982; for the *good subject*, see M. Pecheux, *Language, Semantics and Ideology*, New York: St. Martin's Press, 1982.

5. D. Milovanovic, "Lacan's Four Discourses, Chaos and Cultural Criticism in Law," *Studies in Psychoanalytic Theory*, vol. 2, no. 1, 1993.

6. D. Milovanovic, "Lacan, Chaos and Practical Discourse in Law," in R. Kevelson (ed.), *Flux, Complexity, Illusion in Law*, New York: Praeger, 1993.

7. M. Bracher, *Lacan, Discourse and Social Change*, Ithaca, NY: Cornell University Press, 1993. In my Chapter 9, this book, it is argued that Paulo Freire's work, *Pedagogy of the Oppressed* (New York: Herder and Herder, 1972) can be usefully integrated with Lacan's discourses of the analyst and hysteric in devising the basis of a revolutionary subject.

8. J. Lacan, *Écrits*, New York: Norton, 1977.

9. M. Sarup, *Post-Structuralism and Postmodernism*, Athens, GA: University of Georgia Press, 1989.

10. E. Ragland-Sullivan, "Counting from 0 to 6: Lacan, Suture, and the Imaginary Order," in P. Hogan and L. Pandit (eds.), *Criticism and Lacan*, London: University of Georgia Press, 1990, p. 58.

11. M. Marini, *Jacques Lacan*, New Brunswick, NJ: Rutgers University Press, 1992, p. 242.

12. J. Lacan, *The Ethics of Psychoanalysis* (1959–1960), New York: W. W. Norton, 1997, p. 242; see also his *Seminar to the North American Community of December 1, 1975*, p. 42.

13. G. Deleuze and F. Guattari, *A Thousand Plateaus*, Minneapolis, MN: University of Minnesota Press, 1987.

14. Lacan, *Écrits*, *op. cit.*, pp. 146–178.

15. H. Rapaport, "Effi Briest and Law Chose Freudienne," in P. Hogan and L. Pandit, eds., *Criticism and Lacan*, London: University of Georgia Press, 1990, p. 243.

16. J. Lacan, *Feminine Sexuality*, New York: W. W. Norton, 1985, pp. 142–144; A. Juranville, *Lacan et Philosophie*, Paris: Presses Universitaires de France, 1984, p. 335.

17. Here we are at one with Bernard Jackson's narrative coherence model, *Law, Fact, and Narrative Coherence*, Merseyside, UK: Deborah Charles Publications, 1988.

18. R. Jakobson, "Two Aspects of Language and Types of Aphasic Disorders," In R. Jakobson and M. Halle, *Fundamentals of Language*, Paris: Mouton, 1971.

19. Lacan, *Écrits*, *op. cit.*, p. 303.

20. *Ibid.*, pp. 146–178.

21. Ragland-Sullivan, *op. cit.*, 1990, p. 58.

22. J. Lacan, Seminar delivered on *Le sinthome*, December 16, 1975.

23. J. Lacan, *RSI*, February 18, 1975: 106.

24. Ragland-Sullivan, "Lacan's Seminar on James Joyce: Writing as Symptom and 'Singular Solution,'" in R. Feldstein and H. Sussman (eds.), *Psychoanalysis and . . .* , New York: Routledge, 1990, p. 73.

25. J. Lacan, *Le Sinthome*, December 16, 1975; J. Granon-Lafont, *Topologie Lacanienne et Clinique Analytique*, Paris: Point Hors Ligne, 1990, p. 141.

26. J. Lacan, *Seminar 22*, March 11, and May 13, 1975; P. Skriabine, "Clinique et Topologie," unpublished manuscript, 1989, p. 21.

27. Granon-Lafont, *op. cit.*, 1990, p. 147.

28. Skriabine, *op. cit.*, 1989, p. 24.

29. Lacan, *op. cit.*, 1985.

30. Granon-Lafont, *op. cit.*, 1990, pp. 141–142.

31. *Ibid.*

32. Skriabine, *op. cit.*, 1989, p. 24; Granon-Lafont, *op. cit.*, 1990, pp. 143–161; J. Lacan, "Conferences et Entretiens dans les Universités Nord-Américaines," *Scilicet*, 1976, vol. 6/7, pp. 5–63; 58; J. Lacan, "Joyce le Symtome 2," In J. Aubert (ed.) *Joyce avec Lacan*, Paris, Navarin, 1987, pp. 46–48.

33. Skriabine, *op. cit.*, 1989, p. 24 (my translation).

34. Lacan, *op. cit.*, 1987, p. 47.

35. *Ibid.* (my translation).

36. *Ibid.* (my translation).

37. D. Milovanovic, *Postmodern Law and Disorder: Psychoanalytic Semiotics, Chaos, and Juridic Exegeses*, Liverpool, UK: Deborah Charles Publications, 1992, pp. 236–256; Henry and Milovanovic, *op. cit.*, 1996, pp. 235–241.

38. Juranville, *op. cit.*, 1984, pp. 423–424.

39. D. Milovanovic and J. Thomas, "Overcoming the Absurd: Legal Struggle as Primitive Rebellions," *Social Problems*, vol. 36, no. 1, 1989, pp. 48–60.

40. Ragland-Sullivan, *op. cit.*, 1990, p. 72.

41. J. Habermas, *The Theory of Communicative Action*, Vol. 1., Boston: Beacon Press, 1984.

42. Skriabine, *op. cit.*, 1989.

43. Ragland-Sullivan, *op. cit.*, 1990.

44. Lacan, *op. cit.*, 1987.

45. Skriabine, *op. cit.*, 1989, p. 25: Ragland-Sullivan, *op. cit.*, 1990, p. 70.

46. Skriabine, *op. cit.*, 1990, p. 25; (my translation).

47. *Ibid.*

48. Ragland-Sullivan, *op. cit.*, 1990, p. 77.

49. Bracher, *op. cit.*, 1993, p. 192.

Index